More
ONE-STORY HOMES

 HOME PLANNERS

Published by Home Planners, LLC
Wholly owned by Hanley-Wood, LLC
Editorial and Corporate Offices:
3275 West Ina Road, Suite 110
Tucson, Arizona 85741

Distribution Center:
29333 Lorie Lane
Wixom, Michigan 48393

Rickard D. Bailey, CEO and Publisher
Cindy Coatsworth Lewis, Director of Publishing
Jan Prideaux, Senior Editor
Marian E. Haggard, Editor
Jay C. Walsh, Graphic Designer

Design/Photography Credits

Front Cover: Design 2559 by Home Planners
                 Photo by Bob Greenspan
             Design 3433 by Home Planners
                 Photo by Bob Greenspan
Back Cover: Design U112 by Ahmann Design
                 Photo provided by Ahmann Design

First Printing, August 1998

10 9 8 7 6 5 4 3 2

Printed in the United States of America

Library of Congress Catalog Card Number: 98-072349

ISBN softcover: 1-881955-48-6

Table of Contents

Color-Full Portfolio: *Our bestselling one-story homes in color* 5

Petite And Sweet: *One-story homes of 1,700 square feet and under* 17

On The Level With Luxury: *One-story homes of 2,800 square feet and up* 73

Countryside Classics: *One-story homes with a country flavor* 115

Traditional Americana: *One-story homes found in your neighborhood* 183

European Inspiration: *One-story homes with Old-World influence* 263

Look To The Future: *One-story contemporary homes* 327

Sun-Country Vistas: *One-story homes designed for sunny climes* 377

Garages-Plus: *More than just a convenient parking space* 423

Ordering Blueprints 432

Additional Plans Books 446

Editor's Note

A long-standing favorite, the one-story home remains a popular choice because of its low-slung, ground-hugging profile, and its easy adaptability and livability. For empty-nesters, the elderly or those who have physical limitations that make it impossible to climb stairs, the one-story is the clear-cut choice. Accessibility to all areas of the house and the freely adaptable floor plan mean that few if any special accommodations need to be made for living comfortably.

For a great investment and a provident addition to the simple one-story house, there is the basement. Full or partial basements are ideal for developing recreational space, hobby areas, laundries and storage facilities. Such inexpensive space can make a one-story house significantly more livable, incorporating economy and effective use of area.

The one-story home also enjoys an advantage over multi-storied houses in providing for today's indoor/outdoor lifestyle. The one-story allows all zones—from living and sleeping areas to work spaces—direct access to patios, terraces and gardens without the expense of second floor decks and balconies.

In *More One-Story Homes*, you'll find loads of ideas and be impressed with the wide variety and range of sizes offered. From Contemporary to Traditional, Sun-Country to Old-Country European and more—you're sure to find a favorite in this magnificent new collection!

About The Designers

Design Basics, Inc.
For nearly a decade, Design Basics, a nationally recognized home design service located in Omaha, has been developing plans for custom home builders. Since 1987, the firm has consistently appeared in *Builder* magazine, the official magazine of the National Association of Home Builders, as one of the top-selling designers.

Design Traditions
Design Traditions was established by Stephen S. Fuller with the tenets of innovation, quality, originality and uncompromising architectural techniques in traditional and European homes. Especially popular throughout the Southeast, Design Traditions' plans are known for their extensive detail and thoughtful design.

Alan Mascord Design Associates, Inc.
Founded in 1983 as a local supplier to the building community, Mascord Design Associates of Portland, Oregon began to successfully publish plans nationally in 1985. The company's trademark is creating floor plans that work well and exhibit excellent traffic patterns.

Larry E. Belk Designs
Through the years, Larry E. Belk has worked with individuals and builders alike to provide a quality product. Flowing, open spaces and interesting angles define his interiors. Great emphasis is placed on providing views that showcase the natural environment.

Larry W. Garnett & Associates, Inc.
Starting as a designer of homes for Houston-area residents, Garnett & Associates has been marketing designs nationally for the past ten years. A well-respected design firm, the company has regularly supplied plans to *House Beautiful*, *Country Living*, *Home* and *Professional Builder*.

Home Planners
Headquartered in Tucson, Arizona, with additional offices in Detroit, Home Planners is one of the longest-running and most successful home design firms in the United States. With over 2,500 designs in its portfolio, the company provides a wide range of styles, sizes and types of homes for the residential builder.

Donald A. Gardner Architects, Inc.
The South Carolina firm of Donald A. Gardner was established in response to a growing demand for residential designs that reflect constantly changing lifestyles. The company's specialty is providing homes with refined, custom-style details and unique features such as passive-solar designs and open floor plans.

The Sater Design Collection
The Sater Design Collection has a long established tradition of providing South Florida's most diverse and extraordinary custom designed homes. This is exemplified by over 50 national design awards, numerous magazine features and, most important, satisfied clients.

Frank Betz Associates, Inc.
Frank Betz Associates, Inc. located in Smyrna, Georgia, is one of the nation's leaders in the design of stock plans. FBA, Inc. has provided builders and developers with home plans since 1977.

Living Concepts Home Planning
With more than twenty years of design experience, Living Concepts Home Planning has built an outstanding reputation by creating many award-winning residential designs. Based in Charlotte, North Carolina, the company was founded by partners Frank Snodgrass, Chris Boush, Kim Bunting and Derik Boush. Because of its affinity for glass, and designs that take full advantage of outside views, Living Concepts specializes in homes for golf and lakefront communities.

Mark Stewart and Associates, Inc.
Founded in 1988, Mark Stewart and Associates was conceived as a perfect format to capitalize on Stewart's strengths and offer the home building industry innovative, practical and popular home designs with timeless character.

Fillmore Design Group
Fillmore Design Group was formed in 1960 in Oklahoma City by Robert L. Fillmore, president and founder. "Our designs are often characterized by their European influence, by massive brick gables and by high-flowing, graceful rooflines," comments Fillmore.

James Fahy Design
Under the direction of architectural engineer, James R. Fahy, P.E., President, and Douglas R. Bennett, Senior Designer, James Fahy Design has established itself as a leader in residential design, both regionally and nationally. The Fahy design philosophy of developing plans with a diversity of styles and sizes allows the company to better serve the needs of clients.

Greg Marquis and Associates
The designs of Greg Marquis have proven to be popular not only across the United States, but internationally as well. He is a native of New Orleans, and many of his designs incorporate various features of the architectural style of South Louisiana.

Chatham Home Planning, Inc.
Chatham Home Planning, Inc., founded over 15 years ago, is a professional member of the AIBD and the National Association of Home Builders. The company specializes in designs that have a strong historical look: Early American Southern cottages, Georgian classics, French Colonials, Southern Louisiana design and traditionals.

The Housing Associates
Rodney L. Pfotenhauer opened the doors of The Housing Associates in 1987 as a design consultant and illustrator for the manufactured housing industry. Almost from the beginning, his efforts caught the attention of the public. Pfotenhauer's designs are characterized by carefully composed traditional exteriors with up-to-date interiors.

Design Profile, Inc.
With more than twenty years in the design and construction industry, Steve Butcher directs operations for clients in the United States and abroad. The firm specializes in traditional and Southwest home designs with open, flexible floor plans and innovative exteriors.

Homes For Living
Samuel Paul and David J. Paul, a father and son team of architects, have established an outstanding reputation in the design of single family homes. Homes For Living, Inc. was founded in the early 1950s and David Paul joined the company in 1963. The firm has received professional awards for outstanding design.

Archival Designs, Inc.
David Marc Loftus of Archival Designs, Inc. has celebrated fifteen years in the residential design business. His firm has been growing at an accelerated rate because his designs reflect the collective wisdom of the past. His award-winning style is called "Classic Traditional."

United Design Associates, Inc.
United Design offers award-winning Ideal Home Plans to builders and consumers worldwide. "At United Design, we know you've got a lot more to think about than plans, so we make it simple. First and foremost, we design beautiful, intelligent homes that appeal to clients of all interests."

Kathi Burns
TAG Architects was established by Kathi Burns, a licensed architect and working mother. All of their plans are computer generated by architects who provide the highest technical standards. Merging technical ability with a creative approach to home design has allowed TAG Architects to provide the most sought after home designs available today.

Ahmann Design, Inc.
Ahmann Design is a residential design firm specializing in custom residential, stock plan sales, and color rendering. Recognized several times as a finalist in *Professional Builder Magazine's* "Best of American Living" contest, Ahmann Design, Inc. continues to grow as a leader in the residential design market.

Color-Full Portfolio

This home, as shown in the photograph, may differ from the actual blueprints.
For more detailed information, please check the floor plans carefully.

Photo by Oscar Thompson

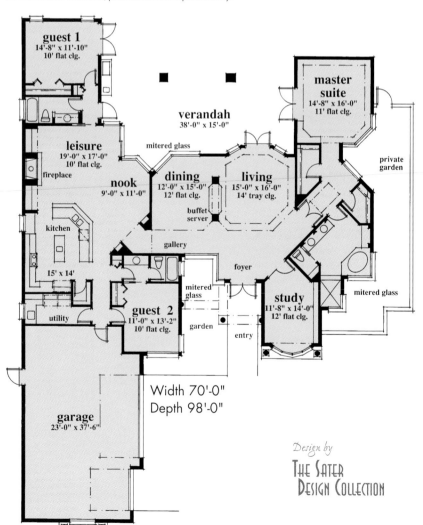

guest 1
14'-8" x 11'-10"
10' flat clg.

verandah
38'-0" x 15'-0"

master suite
14'-8" x 16'-0"
11' flat clg.

private garden

mitered glass

leisure
19'-0" x 17'-0"
10' flat clg.

fireplace

nook
9'-0" x 11'-0"

dining
12'-0" x 15'-0"
12' flat clg.

living
15'-0" x 16'-0"
14' tray clg.

buffet server

kitchen

15' x 14'

gallery

foyer

mitered glass

guest 2
11'-0" x 13'-2"
10' flat clg.

garden

entry

study
11'-8" x 14'-0"
12' flat clg.

mitered glass

utility

Width 70'-0"
Depth 98'-0"

garage
23'-0" x 37'-6"

Design by
THE SATER
DESIGN COLLECTION

Design 6602
Square Footage: 2,794

■ Classic columns, circle-head windows and a bay-windowed study give this stucco home a wonderful street presence. The foyer leads into the formal living and dining areas. An arched buffet server separates these rooms and contributes an open feeling. The kitchen, nook and leisure room are grouped for informal living. A desk/message center in the island kitchen, art niches in the nook and a fireplace with an entertainment center and shelves add custom touches. Two additional suites have private baths and offer full privacy from the master wing—the most gracious guest accommodations. The master suite hosts a private garden area, while the master bath features a walk-in shower that overlooks the garden, and a water closet room with space for books or a television. Large His and Hers walk-in closets complete these private quarters.

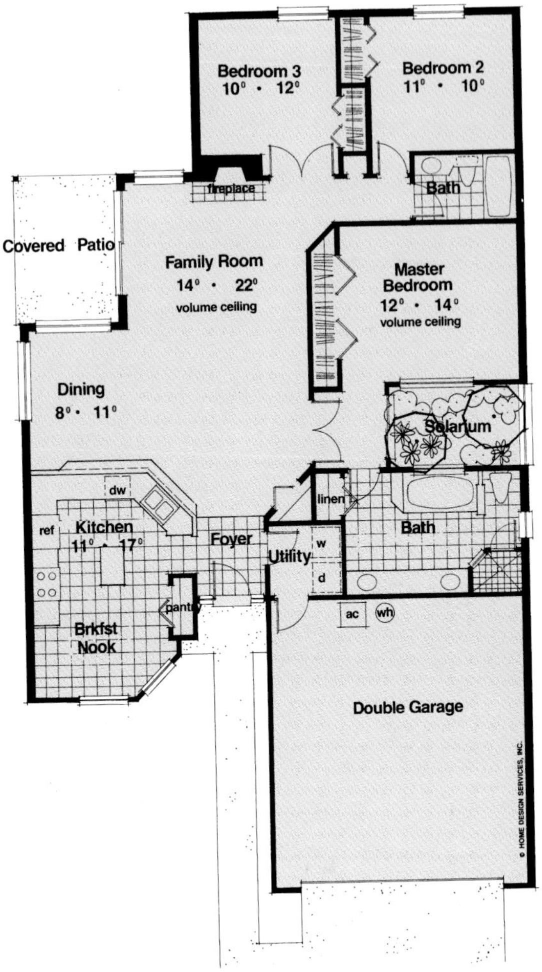

Design 8612
Square Footage: 1,576

Width 40'-0"
Depth 67'-8"

Design by
HOME DESIGN SERVICES

■ Though modest in size, this home boasts an interior courtyard with a solarium. The master suite surrounds the solarium and opens with double doors to the large open family room. The dining room shares a volume ceiling with this space and connects via a serving bar to the kitchen. Besides the fireplace in the family room, there is also a sliding glass door to a covered patio. Family bedrooms are to the rear of the plan. They share a full bath. Note the utility area just off the foyer and breakfast nook with bright multi-pane windows. Plans include three different elevation choices!

This home, as shown in the photograph, may differ from the actual blueprints. For more detailed information, please check the floor plans carefully.

Floor plan labels:
- Bedroom 3 10⁰ · 12⁰
- Bedroom 2 11⁰ · 10⁰
- fireplace
- Bath
- Covered Patio
- Family Room 14⁰ · 22⁰ volume ceiling
- Master Bedroom 12⁰ · 14⁰ volume ceiling
- Dining 8⁰ · 11⁰
- Solarium
- Kitchen 11⁰ · 17⁰
- ref / dw
- Foyer
- linen
- Bath
- Utility w / d
- ac wh
- pantry
- Brkfst Nook
- Double Garage

Photo by Home Design Services

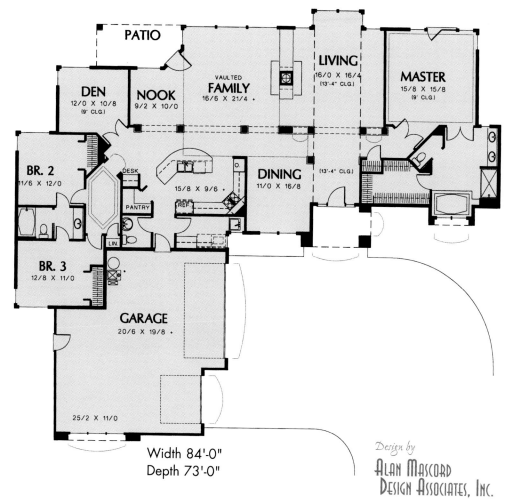

PATIO

DEN
12/0 X 10/8
(9' CLG.)

NOOK
9/2 X 10/0

VAULTED
FAMILY
16/6 X 21/4 +

LIVING
16/0 X 16/4
(13'-4" CLG.)

MASTER
15/8 X 15/8
(9' CLG.)

BR. 2
11/6 X 12/0

DESK

PANTRY

DINING
11/0 X 16/8

(13'-4" CLG.)

15/8 X 9/6 +

REF.

LIN

BR. 3
12/8 X 11/0

GARAGE
20/6 X 19/8 +

25/2 X 11/0

Width 84'-0"
Depth 73'-0"

Design by
ALAN MASCORD
DESIGN ASSOCIATES, INC.

Design 7411

Square Footage: 2,755

■ Squared columns flank an appealing entrance to this three-bedroom home. Columns continue on the interior, helping to define the formal dining room and formal living room, and separating the family room/nook area from the kitchen. The gourmet of the family will be ecstatic when presented with this amenity-filled kitchen. A fireplace is shared between the living room and the vaulted family room. A cozy den opens through double doors just off the nook area. To the left of the plan, two family bedrooms share a full bath between them. Located at the opposite end of the home, the master bedroom suite is sure to please with a double-door entry, a walk-in closet, a sumptuous bath and private access to the rear yard.

Photo by Oscar Thompson

Design 6639
Square Footage: 3,944

■ Innovative design and attention to detail create true luxury living. This clean contemporary style features a raised, columned entry with an interesting stucco relief archway. The foyer opens into the formal living room which overlooks the lanai and waterfall through walls of glass. The formal dining room has a curved wall of windows and a built-in buffet table. Two guest suites each have a walk-in closet and private bath. The owners' wing features a foyer with views of a fountain and a sunny sitting area which opens to the lanai. The bath has a soaking tub, a round shower and a large wardrobe area.

Design by
THE SATER
DESIGN COLLECTION

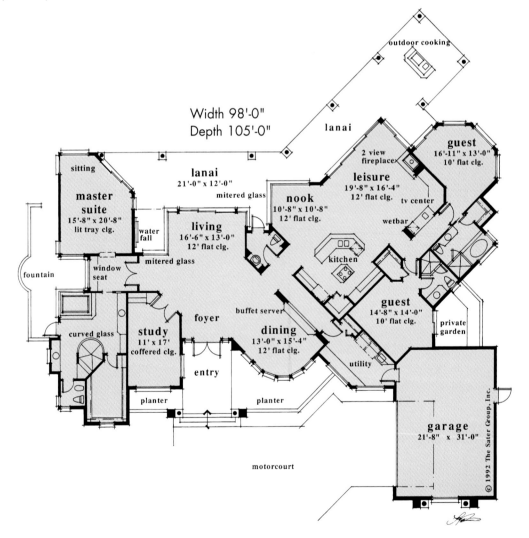

Width 98'-0"
Depth 105'-0"

outdoor cooking

lanai

sitting

master suite
15'-8" x 20'-8"
lit tray clg.

lanai
21'-0" x 12'-0"
mitered glass

living
16'-6" x 13'-0"
12' flat clg.

nook
10'-8" x 10'-8"
12' flat clg.

2 view fireplace

leisure
19'-8" x 16'-4"
12' flat clg.

guest
16'-11" x 13'-0"
10' flat clg.

tv center

wetbar

water fall

mitered glass

kitchen

window seat

fountain

curved glass

foyer

buffet server

study
11' x 17'
coffered clg.

dining
13'-0" x 15'-4"
12' flat clg.

guest
14'-8" x 14'-0"
10' flat clg.

private garden

entry

utility

planter

planter

garage
21'-8" x 31'-0"

motorcourt

© 1992 The Sater Group, Inc.

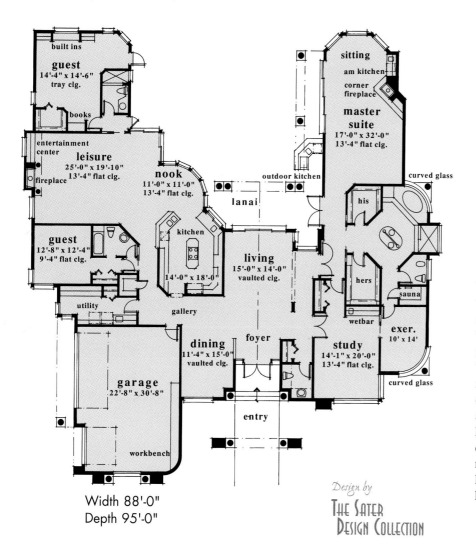

built ins

guest
14'-4" x 14'-6"
tray clg.

books

entertainment center

leisure
25'-0" x 19'-10"
13'-4" flat clg.

fireplace

nook
11'-0" x 11'-0"
13'-4" flat clg.

lanai

outdoor kitchen

sitting

am kitchen

corner fireplace

master suite
17'-0" x 32'-0"
13'-4" flat clg.

curved glass

his

kitchen

guest
12'-8" x 12'-4"
9'-4" flat clg.

living
15'-0" x 14'-0"
vaulted clg.

14'-0" x 18'-0"

hers

sauna

utility

gallery

wetbar

exer.
10' x 14'

garage
22'-8" x 30'-8"

dining
11'-4" x 15'-0"
vaulted clg.

foyer

study
14'-1" x 20'-0"
13'-4" flat clg.

curved glass

entry

workbench

Width 88'-0"
Depth 95'-0"

Design by
THE SATER
DESIGN COLLECTION

Design 6636

Square Footage: 4,565

■ A free-standing entryway is the focal point of this luxurious residence. It has an arch motif that is carried through to the rear using a gable roof and a vaulted ceiling from the foyer out to the lanai. High ceilings are found throughout the home, creating a spacious atmosphere. The kitchen that features a cooktop island and plenty of counter space, opens to the leisure area with a handy snack bar. Two guest suites with private baths are just off this casual living area. The master wing is truly pampering, stretching the entire length of the home. The suite has a large sitting area, a corner fireplace and a morning kitchen. The bath features an island vanity, a raised tub with a curved glass wall overlooking a private garden, a sauna and separate closets. An exercise room has a curved glass wall and a pocket door to the study, where a wet bar is ready to serve up refreshment. Outdoor living will be welcome, thanks to a lovely rear lanai and an outdoor kitchen.

This home, as shown in the photograph, may differ from the actual blueprints. For more detailed information, please check the floor plans carefully.

Photo by Oscar Thompson

SPIRIT OF THE SOUTHWEST

Design 3433

Square Footage: 2,350

L

■ Santa Fe styling creates interesting angles in this one-story home. A grand entrance leads through a courtyard into the foyer with a circular skylight, closet space, niches and a convenient powder room. Fireplaces in the living room, dining room and on the covered porch create a warming heart of the home. Make note of the island range in the kitchen and the cozy breakfast room adjacent.

The master suite has a privacy wall on the covered porch, a deluxe bath and a study close at hand. Two more family bedrooms are placed quietly in the far wing of the house near a segmented family room. Indoor/outdoor relationships are wonderful, with every room having access to the outdoors. The three-car garage offers extra storage.

QUOTE ONE®

Cost to build? See page 434
to order complete cost estimate
to build this house in your area!

This home, as shown in the photograph, may differ from the actual blueprints. For more detailed information, please check the floor plans carefully.

Photo by Bob Greenspan

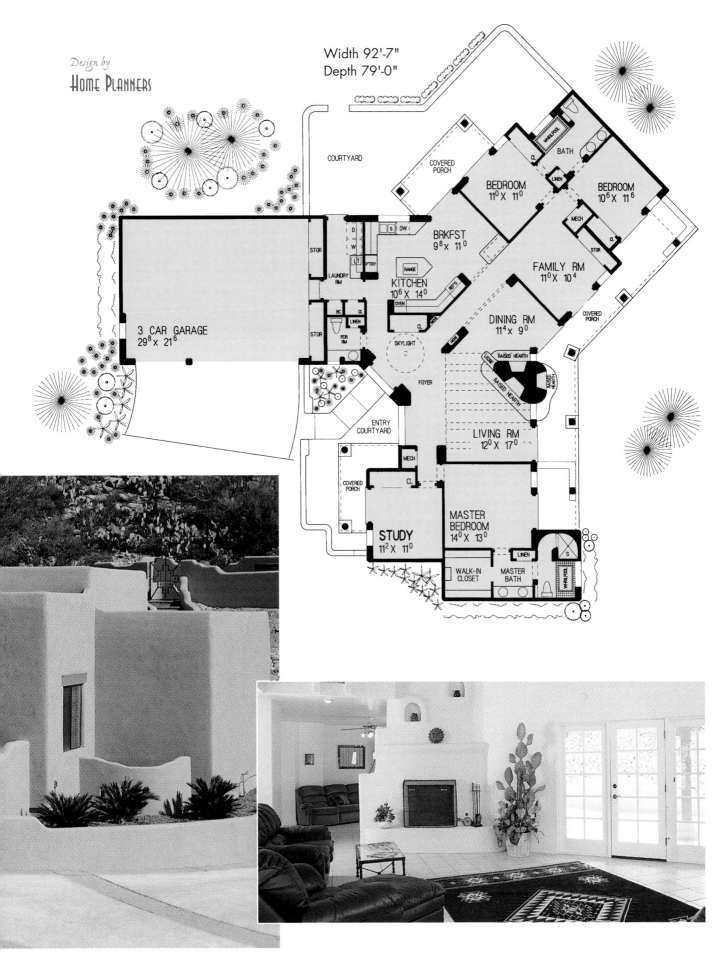

Design by
HOME PLANNERS

Width 92'-7"
Depth 79'-0"

COURTYARD

COVERED PORCH

WHIRLPOOL

BATH

CL

BEDROOM
11⁰ X 11⁰

LINEN

BEDROOM
10⁶ X 11⁶

STOR

D

W

LT

P'TRY

DW

S

BRKFST
9⁸ x 11⁰

MECH

CL

STOR

LAUNDRY RM

RANGE

KITCHEN
10⁶ X 14⁰

REF'S

FAMILY RM
11⁰ X 10⁴

3 CAR GARAGE
29⁸ X 21⁶

STOR

BC

CL

LINEN

OVEN

CL

REF'S

DINING RM
11⁴ x 9⁰

COVERED PORCH

PDR RM

SKYLIGHT

LEDGE

RAISED HEARTH

RAISED HEARTH

RAISED HEARTH

FOYER

ENTRY COURTYARD

MECH

CL

LIVING RM
12⁰ X 17⁰

COVERED PORCH

STUDY
11² X 11⁰

MASTER BEDROOM
14⁰ X 13⁰

LINEN

S

WHIRLPOOL

WALK-IN CLOSET

MASTER BATH

11

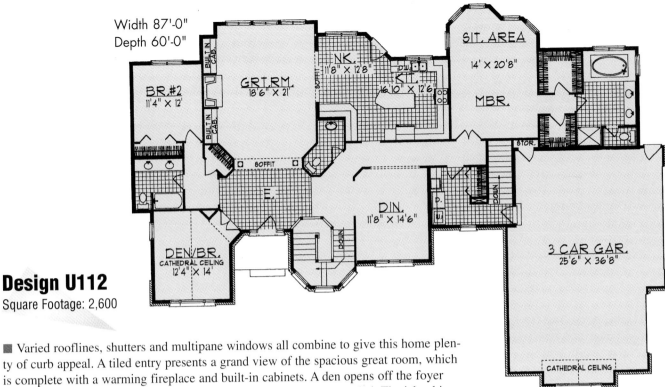

Width 87'-0"
Depth 60'-0"

Design U112

Square Footage: 2,600

■ Varied rooflines, shutters and multipane windows all combine to give this home plenty of curb appeal. A tiled entry presents a grand view of the spacious great room, which is complete with a warming fireplace and built-in cabinets. A den opens off the foyer through double doors and can be used as a guest bedroom when needed. The island in the kitchen provides plenty of work space to an already well-equipped area. With direct access to both the formal dining room as well as the sunny nook, the kitchen is sure to please. A sumptuous master bedroom suite is located off to the right, and features a bayed sitting area, two walk-in closets and a lavish bath. The three-car garage will efficiently shelter the family fleet.

Design by
Ahmann Design, Inc.

This home, as shown in the photograph, may differ from the actual blueprints. For more detailed information, please check the floor plans carefully.

Photo provided by Ahmann Design

This home, as shown in the photograph, may differ from the actual blueprints. For more detailed information, please check the floor plans carefully.

Photo by Bob Greenspan

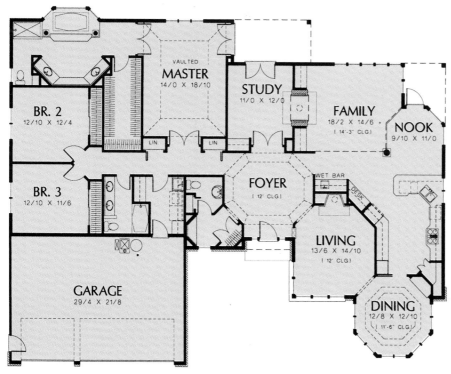

Width 74'-0"
Depth 59'-0"

Design 9454

Square Footage: 2,775

■ A quaint dining gazebo adds a delightful touch to the facade of this lovely home. It complements the formal living room with a fireplace found just to the right of the entry foyer (be sure to notice the elegant guest bath to the left). Family living takes place at the rear of the plan in a large family room with a vaulted ceiling and through-fireplace to the study. A breakfast nook enhances the well-appointed kitchen. The master suite has a vaulted ceiling as well and boasts a huge walk-in closet and pampering bath. Two family bedrooms share a full bath.

Design by
Alan Mascord
Design Associates, Inc.

13

Design 7307

Square Footage: 1,622

■ Volume ceilings add a distinctive touch to this efficient plan that's perfect for young families and empty-nesters alike. The large tiled entry leads right into the expansive great room, complete with a fireplace framed by two built-in entertainment centers crowned with windows. The step-saving kitchen has a snack bar and is joined with the breakfast room to form a comfortable family area. The master suite has a detailed ceiling, walk-in closet and a spa-style bath. The front den can be converted to a third bedroom, depending on family needs.

Rear Elevation

Design by
Design Basics, Inc.

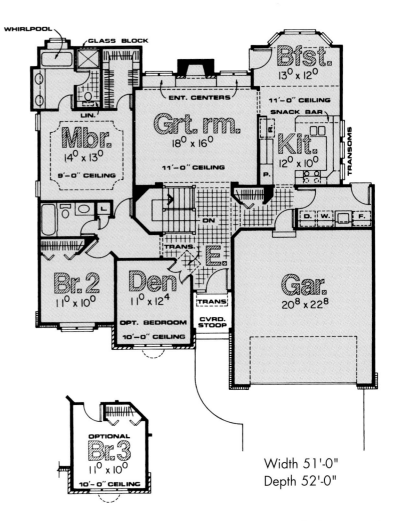

Width 51'-0"
Depth 52'-0"

This home, as shown in the photograph, may differ from the actual blueprints. For more detailed information, please check the floor plans carefully.

Photo by Design Basics, Inc.

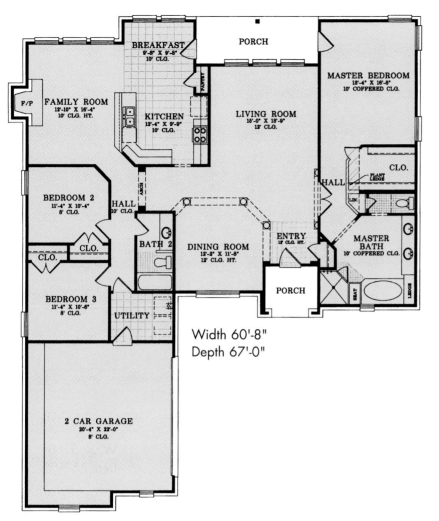

Floor plan labels:
- PORCH
- BREAKFAST 9'-8" X 9'-8" 10' CLG.
- MASTER BEDROOM 13'-4" X 16'-8" 10' COFFERED CLG.
- FAMILY ROOM 12'-10" X 16'-4" 10' CLG. HT.
- F/P
- KITCHEN 12'-4" X 9'-9" 10' CLG.
- LIVING ROOM 15'-0" X 18'-9" 12' CLG.
- CLO.
- HALL
- PLANT LEDGE
- LIN.
- BEDROOM 2 11'-4" X 10'-4" 8' CLG.
- HALL 10' CLG.
- BATH 2
- DINING ROOM 12'-8" X 11'-8" 12' CLG. HT.
- ENTRY 12' CLG. HT.
- MASTER BATH 10' COFFERED CLG.
- CLO.
- CLO.
- SEAT
- BEDROOM 3 11'-4" X 10'-6" 8' CLG.
- UTILITY
- PORCH

Width 60'-8"
Depth 67'-0"

2 CAR GARAGE 20'-4" X 22'-0" 8' CLG.

Design 8113
Square Footage: 2,279

■ Spacious rooms and a gracious division of formal and casual living areas makes this three-bedroom home perfect for the active family. Entertaining will be a pleasure in the elegant dining room that's open to the living room through a series of columns. The cozy family room and kitchen are designed for easy living thanks to an oversized fireplace, snack bar and breakfast nook. Two family bedrooms and a large hall bath are split from the master bedroom for privacy. A spa-style bath and a walk-in closet make the master suite a true owner's retreat. Please specify crawlspace or slab foundation when ordering.

Design by
LARRY E. BELK DESIGNS

This home, as shown in the photograph, may differ from the actual blueprints. For more detailed information, please check the floor plans carefully.

Photo by Karen Stuthard

This home, as shown in the photograph, may differ from the actual blueprints. For more detailed information, please check the floor plans carefully.

Photo by Andrew D. Lautman

■ Split-log siding and a rustic balustrade create country charm with this farmhouse-style retreat. An open living area features a natural stone fireplace and a cathedral ceiling with exposed rough-sawn beam and brackets. A generous kitchen and dining area complement the living room and share the warmth of its fireplace. A master bedroom with complete bath, and a nearby family bedroom with hall bath complete the main floor. Upstairs, a spacious loft affords extra sleeping space—or provides a hobby/recreation area—and offers a full bath.

Width 50'-7"
Depth 38'-0"

DINING

KITCHEN

DW

RANGE

REFG

LAUNDRY

W D

BATH

LINEN

LINEN

MASTER BATH

VANITY

SHWR

LIVING RM
20^2 x 18^2
VOL CLG

BEDRM
10^{10} x 11^8

UP

MASTER BEDRM
12^0 x 18^4

COVERED PORCH

RAILING

Design by
HOME PLANNERS

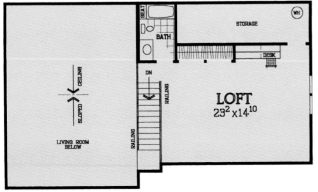

SEAT

BATH

STORAGE

WH

DESK

DN

RAILING

RAILING

SLOPED CEILING

LOFT
23^2 x 14^{10}

LIVING ROOM BELOW

QUOTE ONE®

Cost to build? See page 434 to order complete cost estimate to build this house in your area!

Design 3699

Square Footage: 1,356
Loft: 490 square feet

L D

Petite And Sweet:
One-story homes 1,700 square feet and under

Design 8246
Square Footage: 1,170

Design by
LARRY E. BELK DESIGNS

GARAGE

COPYRIGHT LARRY E BELK

STORAGE

MSTR BDRM
11-0x13-8
10 FT CLG

SLOPE CLG

FP

SLOPE CLG

LIVING
13-0x17-8
10 FT CLG

DESK

DINING
11-0x
9-2

MSTR BATH

KITCH
11-6x
8-0

BATH 2

LIN

STOR

BDRM 3
10-10x11-6

FOYER

BDRM 2
10-4x10-2

COVERED PORCH

Width 51'-10"
Depth 53'-6"

■ This charming country home gives a nod to the past but speaks to the future as well, with an interior designed for family living. A sloped ceiling lends a sense of spaciousness to the living room, which also features a corner hearth and a door to the outside. The U-shaped kitchen serves a convenient dining area, well lit by a bay window. A hall bath serves two family bedrooms, while a generous master suite has a private bath with a compartmented vanity and a walk-in closet. The two-car garage provides additional storage space and a service entrance that leads to the kitchen. Please specify crawlspace or slab foundation when ordering.

Width 53'-0"
Depth 52'-0"

MBR.
CATHEDRAL CEILING
12'8" X 15'8"

GRT. RM.
10'-1 1/8" CEILING
14'8" X 18'6"

NK.
10'6" X 10'0"

BR.#3
13'4" X 12'0"

KIT.
10'6" X 10'0"

BR.#2
10'0" X 11'4"

F.
10'-1 1/8" CEILING

DOWN

DIN.
11'0" X 11'4"

2 CAR GAR.
20'4" X 22'0"

Design by
AHMANN DESIGN, INC.

Design U266
Square Footage: 1,633

■ A volume roof line brings special appeal to this classically styled one-story plan. Horizontal wood siding and a quaint covered porch add delightful exterior touches. The main entry opens to a tiled foyer with volume ceiling. To the right is a formal dining room and straight back is the great room with fireplace and volume ceiling. Prepare meals in the well-appointed kitchen, which serves both the formal dining room and the tiled breakfast nook. Sliding glass doors in the nook open to the rear yard, handy for outdoor dining. Family bedrooms are split from the master suite and located on the right side of the plan. The master bedroom features a cathedral ceiling, a walk-in closet and luxurious bath with whirlpool tub, separate shower and twin lavatories. A two-car garage connects to the main house through a laundry area.

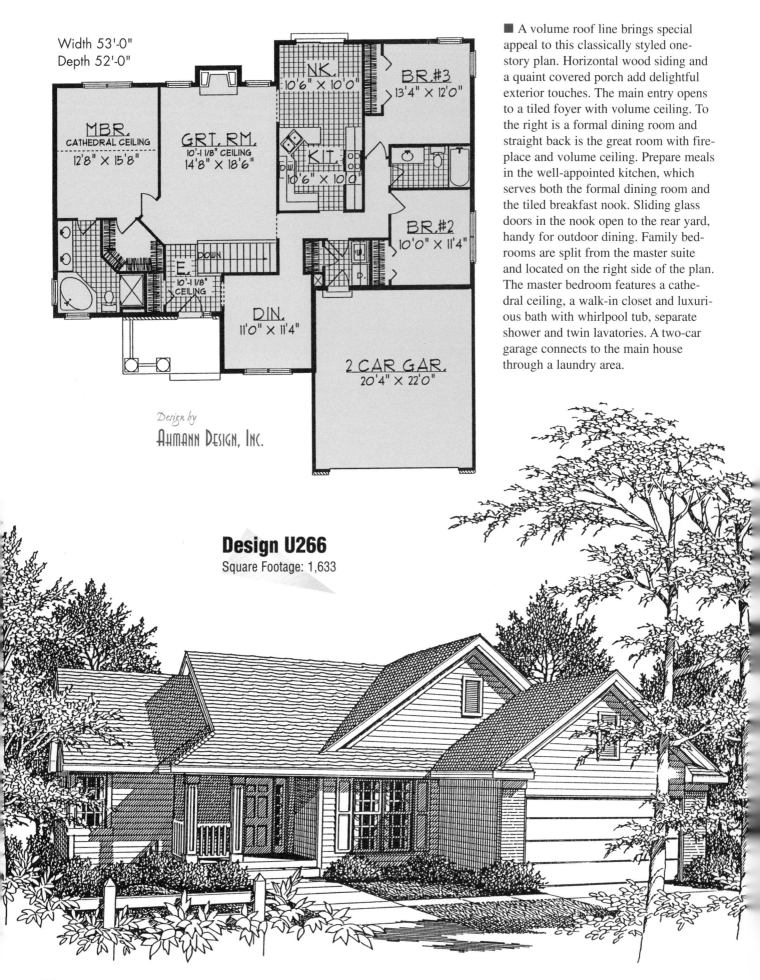

Design 9508

Square Footage: 1,523

■ The repeated roof treatments and varying exterior materials add interest to this winsome home. Inside, the great room commands attention with its fireplace, high ceiling and overall spaciousness. Double doors lead to a den where built-ins enhance a room—perfect for quiet getaways. A built-in desk adds to the inviting character of the kitchen and breakfast nook. The great room could easily support a formal dining area serviced by the angular kitchen passageway. The sleeping quarters consist of a master suite with a private bath and a walk-in closet, and a secondary bedroom for family or guests. A utility area ties the house and garage together well.

Design by

ALAN MASCORD DESIGN ASSOCIATES, INC.

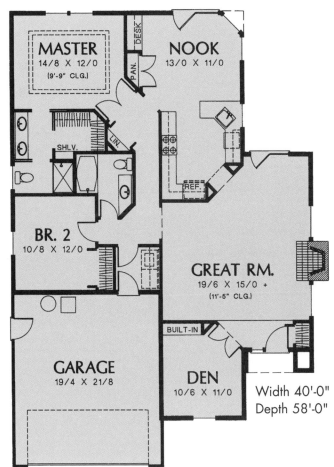

MASTER
14/8 X 12/0
(9'-9" CLG.)

NOOK
13/0 X 11/0

DESK

PAN.

SHLV.

LIN.

REF.

BR. 2
10/8 X 12/0

GREAT RM.
19/6 X 15/0 +
(11'-5" CLG.)

BUILT-IN

GARAGE
19/4 X 21/8

DEN
10/6 X 11/0

Width 40'-0"
Depth 58'-0"

Design B133

Square Footage: 1,304

■ This compact single-story plan is an excellent choice as a starter home or for an empty-nester. Details such as bay windows and a vaulted ceiling add elegance and comfort. The family room's large window is nestled to the left of the stoop, which is topped by double gables. A vaulted ceiling covers the large U-shaped kitchen and casual dining area, which are accessed either from the garage or front entry. Adjoining the dining area is the spacious family room with fireplace and 10-foot ceiling, sure to be a favorite gathering place. The master suite is tucked to the rear of the plan and features two windows in the bedroom that look onto the backyard and two more in the master bath. Either of the two secondary bedrooms, which share a hall bath, might also be used as an office or guest quarters.

Design by
GREG MARQUIS
& ASSOCIATES

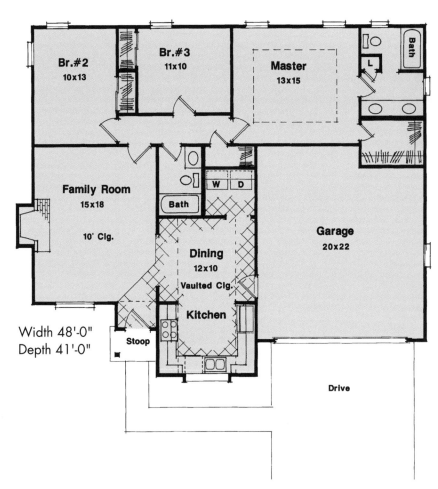

Br.#2
10x13

Br.#3
11x10

Master
13x15

Bath

L

Family Room
15x18

10' Clg.

W D

Bath

Dining
12x10

Vaulted Clg.

Kitchen

Garage
20x22

Width 48'-0"
Depth 41'-0"

Stoop

Drive

Design 9665

Square Footage: 1,345

Design by
Donald A. Gardner
Architects, Inc.

■ A dormer above the great room and a round-top window add special features to this cozy traditional plan. The great room also contains a fireplace and a sloped ceiling. Elegant round columns define the dining and kitchen areas while creating an openness with the great room. Ceilings in the dining room, kitchen and great room all slope up to a ridge above the columns. A bedroom adjacent to the foyer can double as a study. The master bedroom has a fine bath which includes a double bowl vanity, shower and whirlpool tub. The garage is connected to the house with a breezeway for flexibility. The plan is available with a crawlspace foundation.

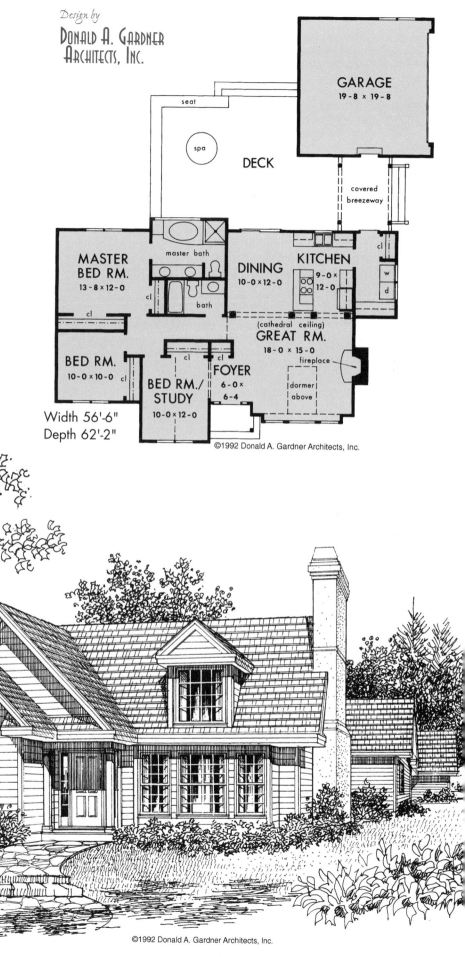

GARAGE
19-8 x 19-8

seat

spa

DECK

covered breezeway

MASTER BED RM.
13-8 x 12-0

master bath

cl

bath

cl

DINING
10-0 x 12-0

KITCHEN

9-0 x 12-0

cl

w

d

(cathedral ceiling)
GREAT RM.
18-0 x 15-0

fireplace

dormer above

BED RM.
10-0 x 10-0

cl

cl

cl

BED RM./ STUDY
10-0 x 12-0

FOYER
6-0 x 6-4

Width 56'-6"
Depth 62'-2"

©1992 Donald A. Gardner Architects, Inc.

B. NATHAN.

©1992 Donald A. Gardner Architects, Inc.

21

Design P235

Square Footage: 1,070

■ Here is a plan that packs a lot of house into just over 1,000 square feet. The front door, protected by a covered porch, opens directly into the vaulted family room with its enticing corner fireplace and sliding glass doors to the rear property. A coat closet and hall bath are near the entrance for the convenience of guests. A folding door hides the washer and dryer from the galley kitchen, which enjoys the natural light from a sunny breakfast area. The master suite boasts many of the amenities found in much larger homes—such as a vaulted bath with an oval tub and a large walk-in closet. Two family bedrooms have good closet space and front-facing windows. Please specify basement, crawlspace or slab foundation when ordering.

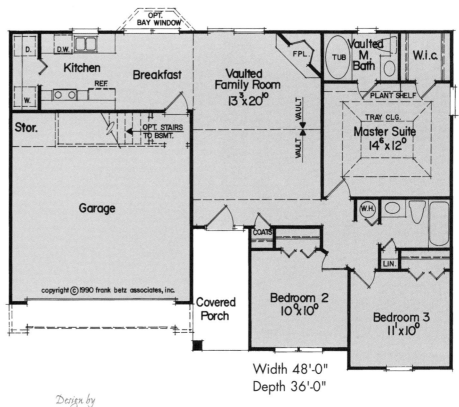

Design by
Frank Betz
Associates, Inc.

Width 48'-0"
Depth 36'-0"

■ Twin dormers perch above a welcoming covered front porch in this three-bedroom home. Inside, a formal dining room on the right is defined by pillars, while the spacious great room lies directly ahead. This room is enhanced by a fireplace, plenty of windows, access to the rear yard and a 42" ledge looking into the angular kitchen. Nearby, a bayed breakfast room awaits casual mealtimes. The sleeping zone consists of two family bedrooms sharing a full hall bath and a luxurious master bedroom suite with a huge walk-in closet and a sumptuous private bath. Please specify crawlspace or slab foundation when ordering.

Design 8239
Square Footage: 1,654

Design by
Larry E. Belk Designs

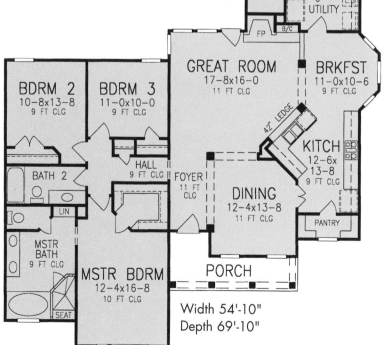

GARAGE

STORAGE

UTILITY

FP   B/C

GREAT ROOM
17–8x16–0
11 FT CLG

BRKFST
11–0x10–6
9 FT CLG

BDRM 2
10–8x13–8
9 FT CLG

BDRM 3
11–0x10–0
9 FT CLG

42" LEDGE

KITCH
12–6x
13–8
9 FT CLG

HALL
9 FT CLG

BATH 2

FOYER
11 FT
CLG

DINING
12–4x13–8
11 FT CLG

LIN

PANTRY

MSTR
BATH
9 FT CLG

MSTR BDRM
12–4x16–8
10 FT CLG

SEAT

PORCH

Width 54'-10"
Depth 69'-10"

Design 9793

Square Footage: 1,109
Optional Bedroom: 169 square feet

■ A roomy cathedral ceiling expands the feel of this compact plan filled with popular features. Open to each other for increased spaciousness, the living areas feature a fireplace in the great room and an island to increase work space in the kitchen. A deck off the kitchen amplifies living and entertaining space. The master bedroom is accentuated by a double window with a circle top for extra volume and light. The private bath opens up with a skylight and includes a relaxing garden tub and double-bowl vanity. The second bedroom is located near a skylit full bath, linen closet and utility room. An optional bedroom is available if additional space is needed.

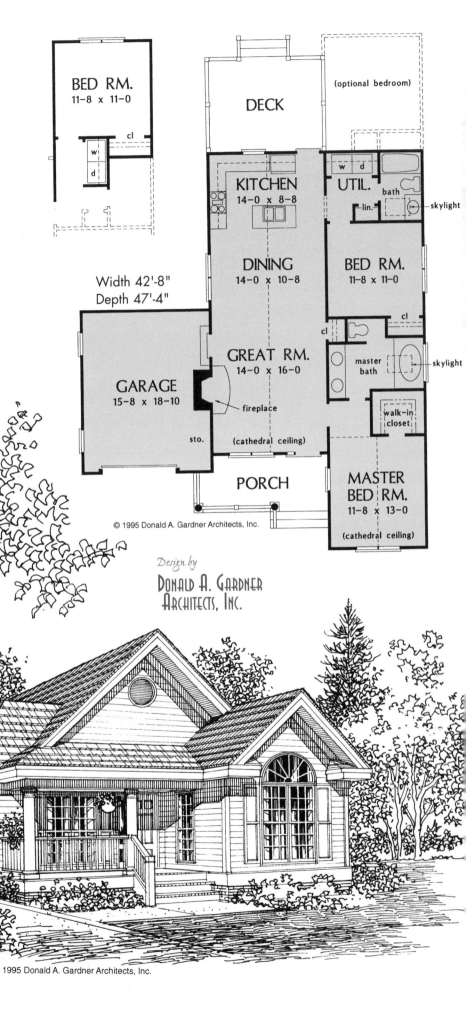

Width 42'-8"
Depth 47'-4"

© 1995 Donald A. Gardner Architects, Inc.

Design by
Donald A. Gardner
Architects, Inc.

© 1995 Donald A. Gardner Architects, Inc.

B. NATHAN

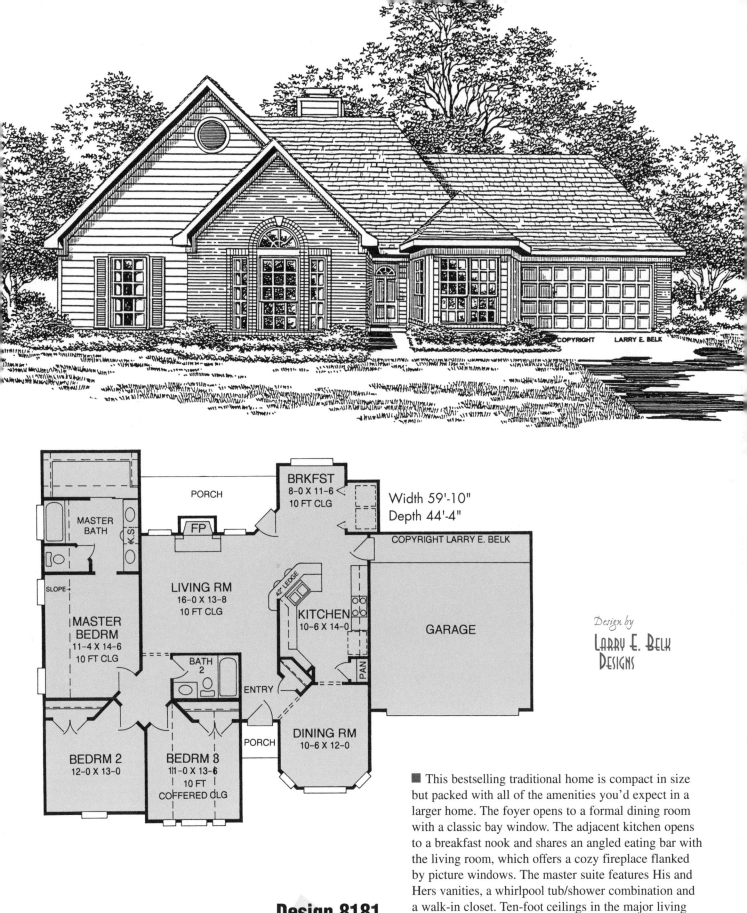

PORCH

BRKFST
8-0 X 11-6
10 FT CLG

Width 59'-10"
Depth 44'-4"

COPYRIGHT LARRY E. BELK

MASTER
BATH

K.S.

FP

LIVING RM
16-0 X 13-8
10 FT CLG

42" LEDGE

KITCHEN
10-6 X 14-0

GARAGE

PAN

Design by
Larry E. Belk
Designs

SLOPE

MASTER
BEDRM
11-4 X 14-6
10 FT CLG

BATH
2

ENTRY

BEDRM 2
12-0 X 13-0

BEDRM 8
11-0 X 13-6
10 FT
COFFERED CLG

PORCH

DINING RM
10-6 X 12-0

Design 8181
Square Footage: 1,500

■ This bestselling traditional home is compact in size but packed with all of the amenities you'd expect in a larger home. The foyer opens to a formal dining room with a classic bay window. The adjacent kitchen opens to a breakfast nook and shares an angled eating bar with the living room, which offers a cozy fireplace flanked by picture windows. The master suite features His and Hers vanities, a whirlpool tub/shower combination and a walk-in closet. Ten-foot ceilings in the major living areas as well as in two of the bedrooms contribute an aura of spaciousness to this plan. Please specify crawl-space or slab foundation when ordering.

25

Design 9637

Square Footage: 1,608

GARAGE
20-4 × 23-4

covered breezeway

spa

Width 45'-0"
Depth 83'-8"

BRKFST.
7-4 × 11-8

cl

master bath

PORCH

DINING
14-8 × 12-8

KIT.
8-4 × 12-4

MASTER BED RM.
12-0 × 13-8

w | d   linen

UTIL.

bath

walk-in closet

cl

GREAT RM.
14-0 × 19-0

fireplace

FOYER
5-0 ×
9-4

BED RM.
12-0 × 10-0

PORCH

cl

BED RM./
STUDY
11-4 × 13-0

walk-in closet

©1991 Donald A. Gardner Architects, Inc.

■ This narrow three-bedroom plan with arched windows and a wraparound porch displays a sense of comfort uncommon to a plan of this size. The great room, dining room and master bedroom all boast tray ceilings, while the front bedroom features a vaulted ceiling to accentuate the arched window. An open kitchen design conveniently services the breakfast area, dining room and deck. The master suite has a private covered porch, a large walk-in closet and a master bath with a whirlpool tub.

Design by
DONALD A. GARDNER
ARCHITECTS, INC.

©1991 Donald A. Gardner Architects, Inc.

Design A101

Square Footage: 1,383

■ Starter homebuyers and retirees alike will take pleasure in this modest-yet-handsome one-story, which can be constructed in brick or frame. A vaulted ceiling in the great room and high glass windows on the rear wall combine to create an open, spacious feel. Off the great room is an open dining room. The ample kitchen layout features a built-in pantry. A generous walk-in closet is found in the master suite. Please specify basement, slab or crawlspace foundation when ordering.

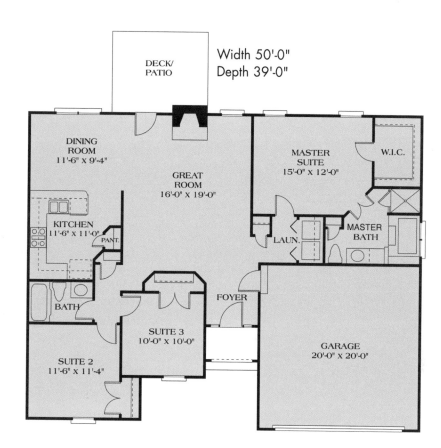

Width 50'-0"
Depth 39'-0"

DECK/ PATIO

DINING ROOM
11'-6" x 9'-4"

GREAT ROOM
16'-0" x 19'-0"

MASTER SUITE
15'-0" x 12'-0"

W.I.C.

KITCHEN
11'-6" x 11'-0"

PANT.

LAUN.

MASTER BATH

BATH

FOYER

SUITE 3
10'-0" x 10'-0"

GARAGE
20'-0" x 20'-0"

SUITE 2
11'-6" x 11'-4"

Design by
LIVING CONCEPTS

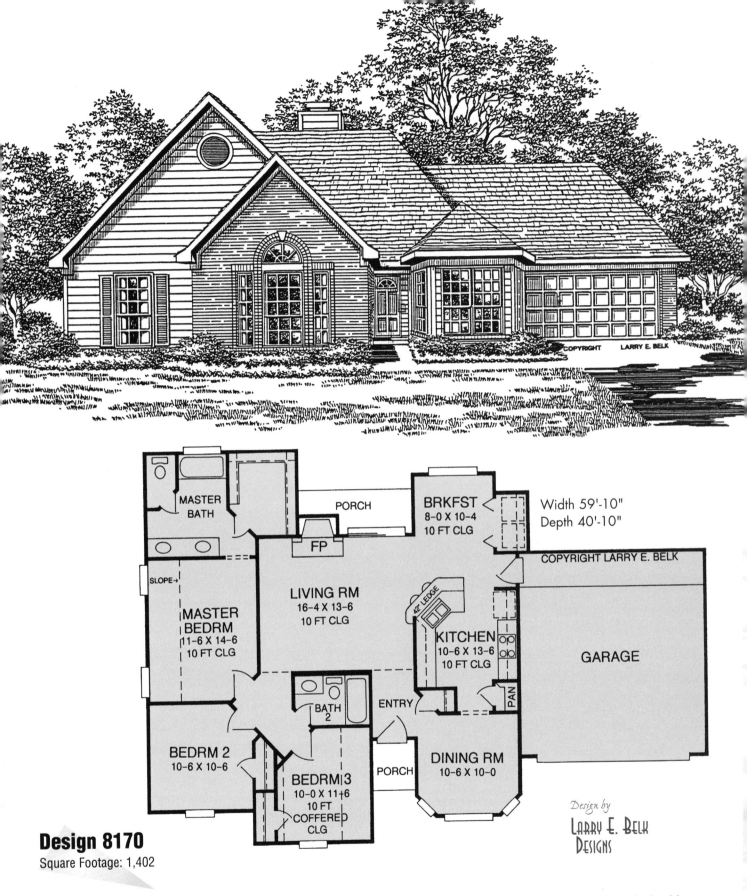

Design 8170

Square Footage: 1,402

Width 59'-10"
Depth 40'-10"

COPYRIGHT LARRY E. BELK

Design by
Larry E. Belk
Designs

■ Fine detailing and multiple roof lines give this home plenty of curb appeal. A large living room with a ten-foot ceiling and a fireplace is the focal point for this lovely small home. The dining room, with an attractive bay window, and a sunny breakfast room provide complementary eating areas. The master bedroom features a large walk-in closet, a bath with His and Hers vanities and a combination whirlpool tub and shower. Bedrooms 2 and 3 and Bath 2 complete this very livable plan. Please specify crawlspace or slab foundation when ordering.

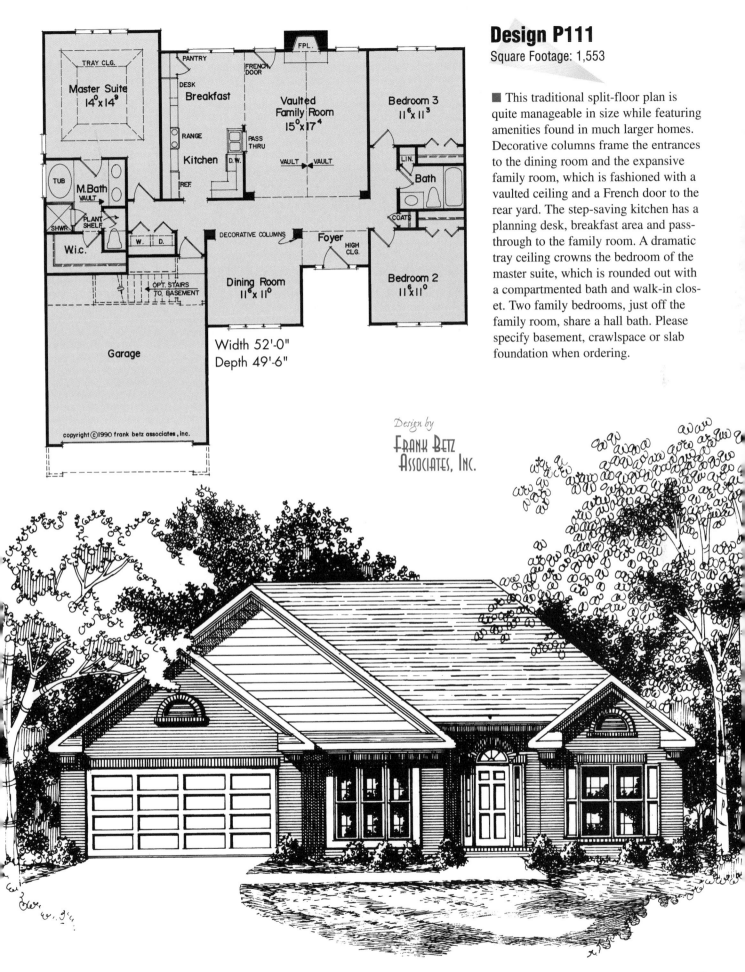

Design P111
Square Footage: 1,553

■ This traditional split-floor plan is quite manageable in size while featuring amenities found in much larger homes. Decorative columns frame the entrances to the dining room and the expansive family room, which is fashioned with a vaulted ceiling and a French door to the rear yard. The step-saving kitchen has a planning desk, breakfast area and pass-through to the family room. A dramatic tray ceiling crowns the bedroom of the master suite, which is rounded out with a compartmented bath and walk-in closet. Two family bedrooms, just off the family room, share a hall bath. Please specify basement, crawlspace or slab foundation when ordering.

Master Suite 14⁰x14⁹

Breakfast

Vaulted Family Room 15⁰x17⁴

Bedroom 3 11⁶x11³

Kitchen

Bath

M.Bath

W.i.c.

Foyer

Bedroom 2 11⁶x11⁰

Dining Room 11⁶x11⁰

Garage

Width 52'-0"
Depth 49'-6"

copyright ©1990 frank betz associates, inc.

Design by
FRANK BETZ
ASSOCIATES, INC.

Design P189

Square Footage: 1,502

■ This ambitious plan masterfully combines stylish architectural elements in a smaller square footage. Elegant ceiling details, decorative columns and fancy window treatment prevail throughout this split-bedroom design. The great room is fashioned with a fireplace and has an open view into the breakfast room and serving bar. The modified galley kitchen has a convenient rear entry to the formal dining room and a service entrance through the two-car garage. Two family bedrooms and a full bath are neatly tucked behind the breakfast nook. The master suite is truly an owner's retreat with a cozy sitting room that's accented with a vaulted ceiling and sunny windows. The compartmented bath has a twin vanity and a walk-in closet. Please specify slab or basement foundation when ordering.

Design by
FRANK BETZ
ASSOCIATES, INC.

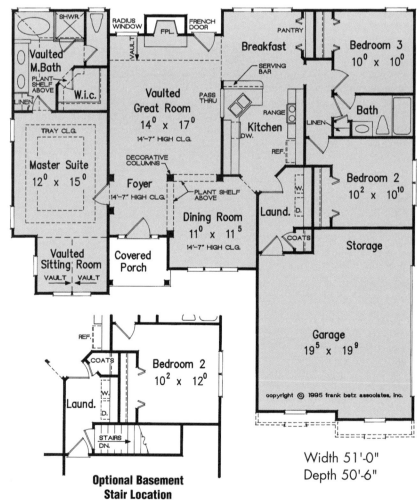

**Optional Basement
Stair Location**

Width 51'-0"
Depth 50'-6"

30

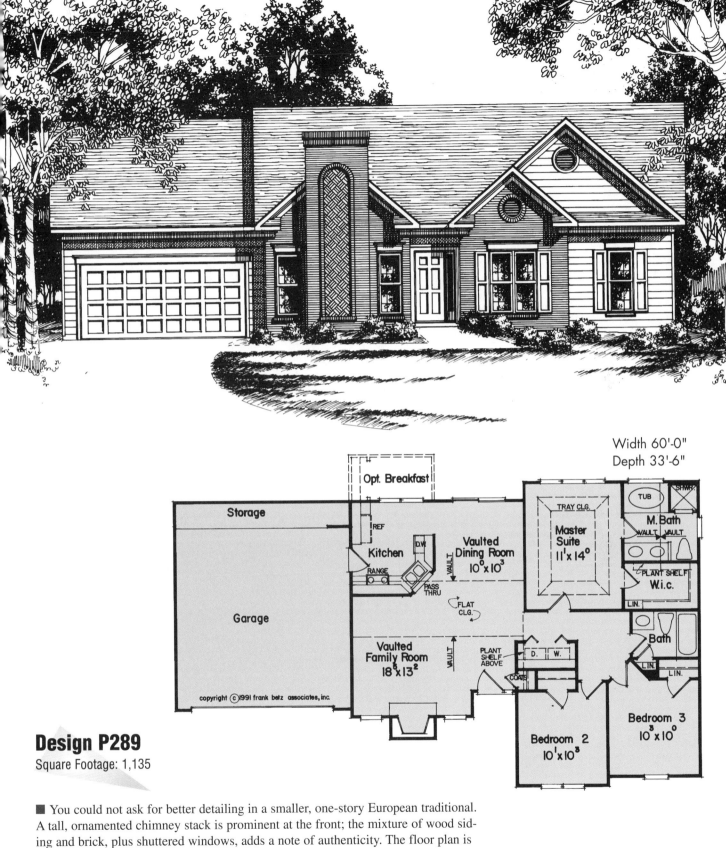

Width 60'-0"
Depth 33'-6"

Storage

Opt. Breakfast

REF

Garage

Kitchen

D.W.

RANGE

PASS THRU

Vaulted
Dining Room
10⁰ x 10³

Master
Suite
11' x 14⁰

TRAY CLG.

TUB

SHWR

M. Bath

VAULT VAULT

PLANT SHELF

W.i.c.

LIN.

FLAT
CLG.

Vaulted
Family Room
18⁸ x 13²

PLANT
SHELF
ABOVE

D. W.

COATS

Bath

LIN.

LIN.

copyright © 1991 frank betz associates, inc.

Bedroom 2
10¹ x 10³

Bedroom 3
10³ x 10⁰

Design P289

Square Footage: 1,135

■ You could not ask for better detailing in a smaller, one-story European traditional. A tall, ornamented chimney stack is prominent at the front; the mixture of wood siding and brick, plus shuttered windows, adds a note of authenticity. The floor plan is well designed and makes optimal use of space. Vaulted ceilings in both the dining room and family room create spaciousness in an already open plan. The kitchen may be complemented by an optional breakfast area if you choose. High ceilings in the master bedroom and bath—configured in a tray pattern in the bedroom—add spaciousness here as well. The bath contains both a soaking tub and a shower, plus a compartmented toilet. Family bedrooms sit to the front of the plan and share a full bath with linen closet.

Design by
FRANK BETZ
ASSOCIATES, INC.

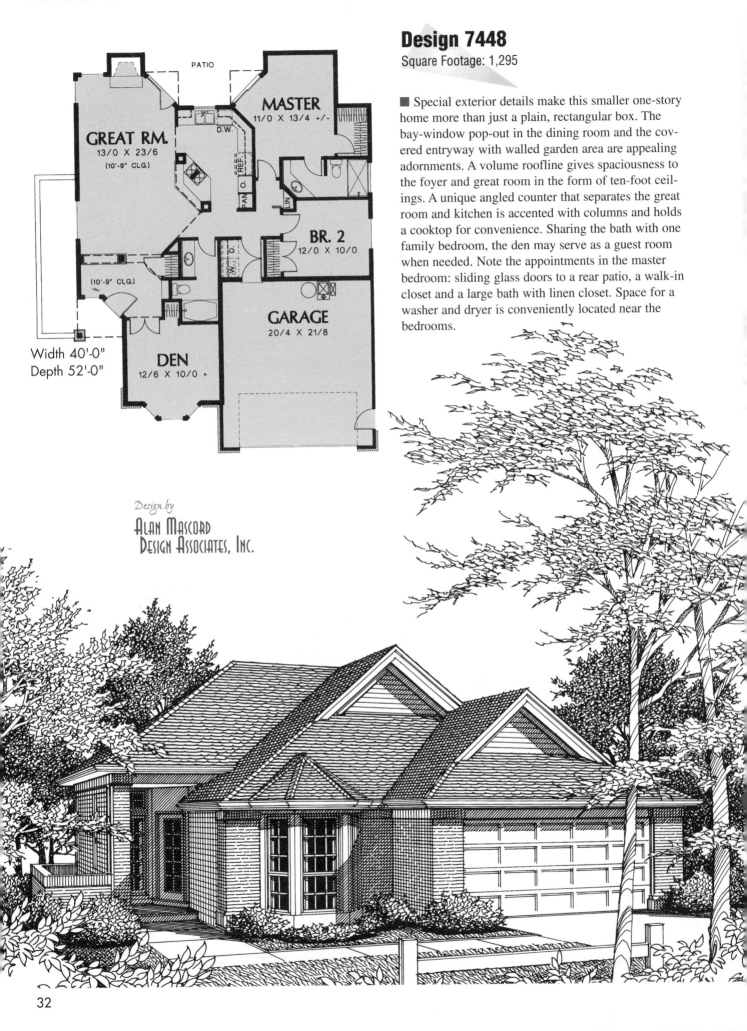

Design 7448
Square Footage: 1,295

■ Special exterior details make this smaller one-story home more than just a plain, rectangular box. The bay-window pop-out in the dining room and the covered entryway with walled garden area are appealing adornments. A volume roofline gives spaciousness to the foyer and great room in the form of ten-foot ceilings. A unique angled counter that separates the great room and kitchen is accented with columns and holds a cooktop for convenience. Sharing the bath with one family bedroom, the den may serve as a guest room when needed. Note the appointments in the master bedroom: sliding glass doors to a rear patio, a walk-in closet and a large bath with linen closet. Space for a washer and dryer is conveniently located near the bedrooms.

PATIO

GREAT RM.
13/0 X 23/6
(10'-9" CLG.)

MASTER
11/0 X 13/4 +/-

D.W.

BR. 2
12/0 X 10/0

(10'-9" CLG.)

GARAGE
20/4 X 21/8

Width 40'-0"
Depth 52'-0"

DEN
12/6 X 10/0 +

Design by
ALAN MASCORD
DESIGN ASSOCIATES, INC.

Design by
James Fahy Design

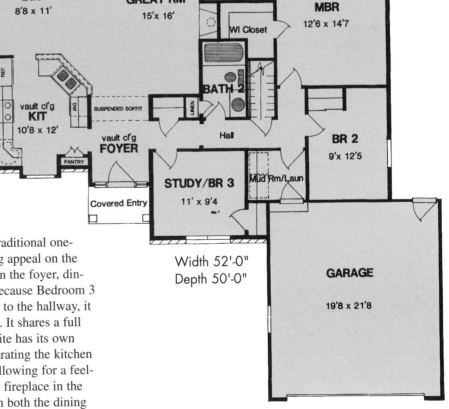

vault cl'g
DIN
8'8 x 11'

vault cl'g
GREAT RM
15' x 16'

MBATH

WI Closet

MBR
12'6 x 14'7

REF

vault cl'g
KIT
10'8 x 12'

SUSPENDED SOFFIT

DW

BATH 2

LINEN

BR 2
9'x 12'5

vault cl'g
FOYER

PANTRY

Hall

STUDY/BR 3
11' x 9'4

Mud Rm/Laun

Covered Entry

Design C153

Square Footage: 1,286

Width 52'-0"
Depth 50'-0"

GARAGE
19'8 x 21'8

■ Brick paves the way to a solidly traditional one-story home. A volume ceiling, adding appeal on the exterior, allows for vaulted ceilings in the foyer, dining room, kitchen and great room. Because Bedroom 3 opens directly to the foyer as well as to the hallway, it may easily be used as a study or den. It shares a full bath with Bedroom 2. The master suite has its own bath and a large walk-in closet. Separating the kitchen from living spaces is a peninsula—allowing for a feeling of even more openness. Note the fireplace in the great room and rear yard access from both the dining room and great room. The mud room and laundry area acts as a service entrance to the two-car garage.

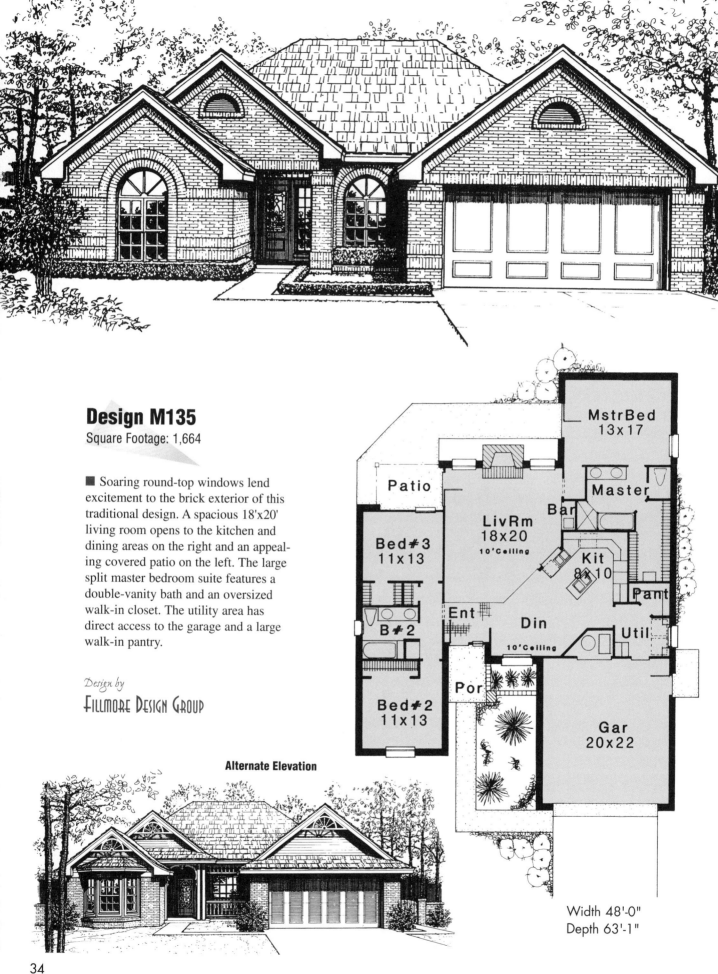

Design M135

Square Footage: 1,664

■ Soaring round-top windows lend excitement to the brick exterior of this traditional design. A spacious 18'x20' living room opens to the kitchen and dining areas on the right and an appealing covered patio on the left. The large split master bedroom suite features a double-vanity bath and an oversized walk-in closet. The utility area has direct access to the garage and a large walk-in pantry.

Design by
FILLMORE DESIGN GROUP

Alternate Elevation

Patio

MstrBed
13x17

Master

Bar

LivRm
18x20
10'Ceiling

Bed#3
11x13

Kit
8x10

Pant

B#2

Ent

Din
10'Ceiling

Util

Bed#2
11x13

Por

Gar
20x22

Width 48'-0"
Depth 63'-1"

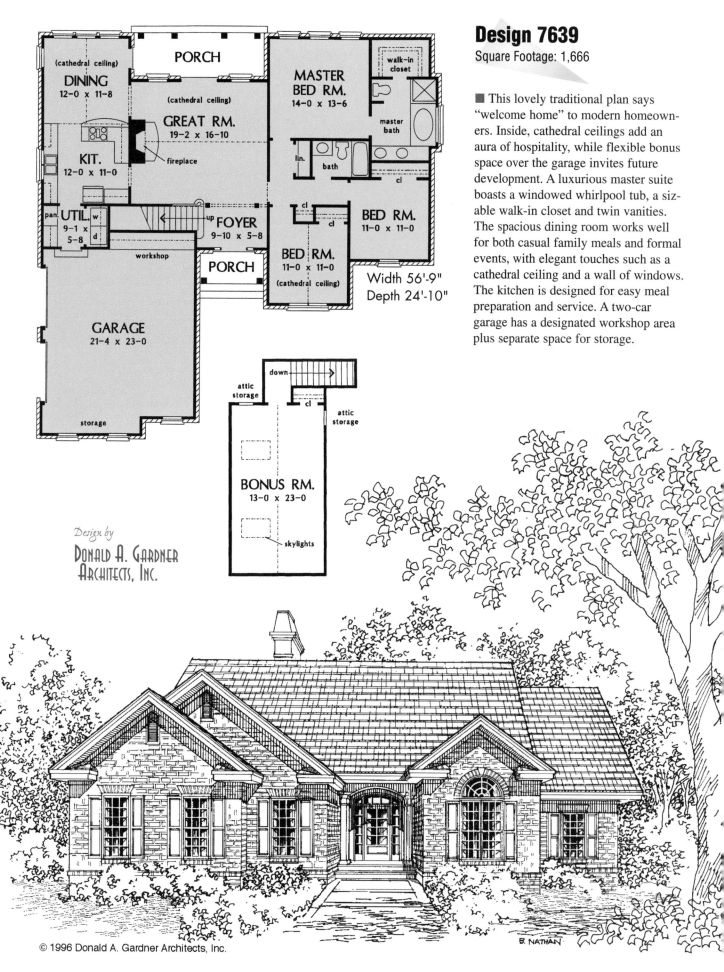

DINING
12-0 x 11-8
(cathedral ceiling)

PORCH

MASTER BED RM.
14-0 x 13-6

walk-in closet

master bath

GREAT RM.
19-2 x 16-10
(cathedral ceiling)

fireplace

KIT.
12-0 x 11-0

lin.

bath

cl

UTIL.
9-1 x 5-8

pan.

w
d

workshop

up **FOYER**
9-10 x 5-8

cl

BED RM.
11-0 x 11-0

PORCH

BED RM.
11-0 x 11-0
(cathedral ceiling)

cl

Width 56'-9"
Depth 24'-10"

GARAGE
21-4 x 23-0

storage

down

attic storage

cl

attic storage

BONUS RM.
13-0 x 23-0

skylights

Design by

Donald A. Gardner
Architects, Inc.

Design 7639

Square Footage: 1,666

■ This lovely traditional plan says "welcome home" to modern homeowners. Inside, cathedral ceilings add an aura of hospitality, while flexible bonus space over the garage invites future development. A luxurious master suite boasts a windowed whirlpool tub, a sizable walk-in closet and twin vanities. The spacious dining room works well for both casual family meals and formal events, with elegant touches such as a cathedral ceiling and a wall of windows. The kitchen is designed for easy meal preparation and service. A two-car garage has a designated workshop area plus separate space for storage.

B. NATHAN

35

Design 3451

Square Footage: 1,560

L

Design by
Home Planners

■ This eye-catching two-bedroom home is designed to make the most of the elegant brick exterior. The floor plan offers convenience combined with one-story livability. Overlooking the front yard is a comfortable second bedroom which may also function as a study. It features a bay window, sloped ceiling, built-in shelves, and direct access to a full bath. A fireplace flanked by two windows provides the focal point for the gathering room. The well-planned kitchen includes a pantry, built-in oven and cook top, snack bar and planning desk. When more formal dining is called for, there is a separate dining room with projecting bay window. The master suite is truly impressive. Take special note of the double entry capability to the bath and the duplicate niches, as well as separate wardrobe closets.

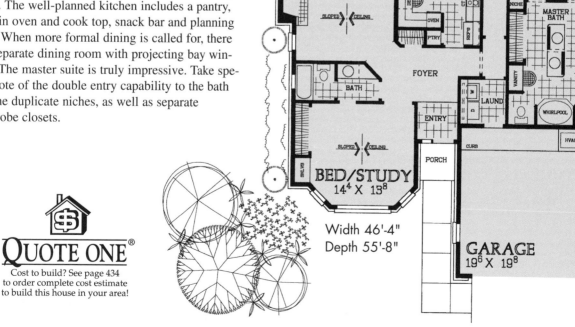

Width 46'-4"
Depth 55'-8"

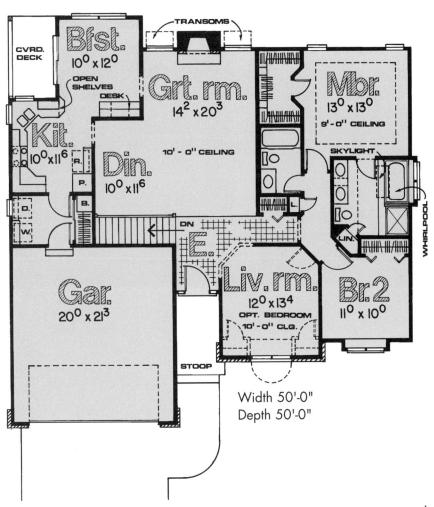

Design 9263

Square Footage: 1,561

■ Clean lines and tasteful window detailing are combined on the elevation of this sophisticated ranch home. The volume entry with transom windows offers expansive views of the great room. Just off the entry, the formal living room serves as an optional third bedroom. Flexibility is also designed into the dining room and great room which share a ten-foot ceiling. A thoughtfully designed kitchen with pantry, Lazy Susan and corner sink serves the sunny breakfast area with access to a covered deck. Don't miss the master suite which includes a volume ceiling and a master bath with whirlpool tub and skylight.

Width 50'-0"
Depth 50'-0"

Design by
Design Basics, Inc.

Design 7304

Square Footage: 1,341

■ For great livability, this one-story home places its living areas to the back of the plan. The foyer leads directly to the great room and its focal-point fireplace. Extras include a built-in entertainment center and bookcase in the great room and a snack bar separating the sunny breakfast room from the U-shaped kitchen. The master suite includes a large walk-in closet and a pampering bath with a whirlpool tub, separate shower and dual-bowl vanity. Two front-facing family bedrooms share a full hall bath.

Design by
DESIGN BASICS, INC.

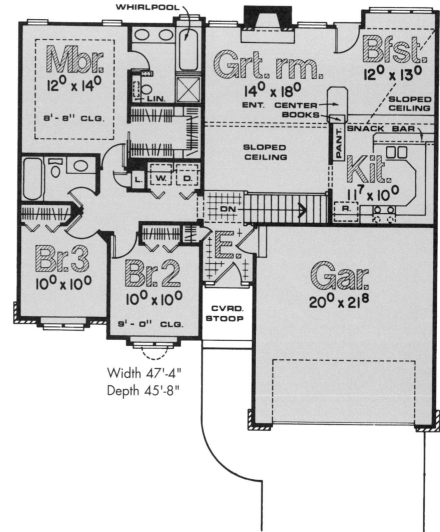

WHIRLPOOL

Mbr.
12⁰ x 14⁰
8'-8" CLG.

LIN.

Grt. rm.
14⁰ x 18⁰
ENT. CENTER
BOOKS
SLOPED CEILING

Bfst.
12⁰ x 13⁰
SLOPED CEILING

SNACK BAR

PANT.

Kit.
11⁷ x 10⁰
R.

L W. D.

DN

Br.3
10⁰ x 10⁰

Br.2
10⁰ x 10⁰
9'-0" CLG.

CVRD. STOOP

Gar.
20⁰ x 21⁸

Width 47'-4"
Depth 45'-8"

Design 7006

Square Footage: 1,660

■ A recessed entry, multi-paned windows and side-entry garage make a charming statement in exterior appeal of this tidy one-story home. The entry leads to a grand, open living space dominated by a great room with fireplace, but also containing a dedicated area for formal dining. The nearby breakfast room is warmed by a bay-window bump-out and served by an island kitchen with pantry and corner sink. It connects to a large laundry area with washer/dryer space, a utility sink and broom closet. Bedrooms are found to the left of the plan. The master bedroom features closet space almost large enough to be a room of its own. Bedroom 3 would make a superb den if needed. Both family bedrooms share a full bath. A linen closet in the hallway serves both the family bath and the master bath.

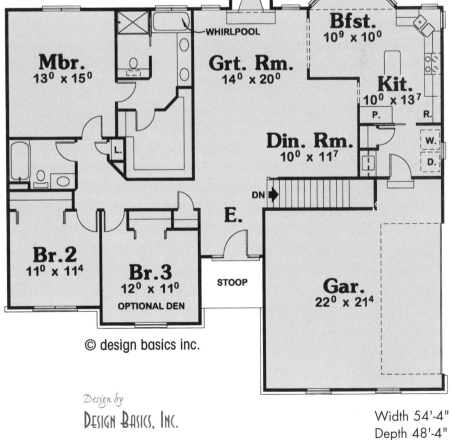

WHIRLPOOL

Mbr.
13⁰ x 15⁰

Grt. Rm.
14⁰ x 20⁰

Bfst.
10⁹ x 10⁰

Kit.
10⁰ x 13⁷

Din. Rm.
10⁰ x 11⁷

P.

R.

W.

D.

DN

E.

Br.2
11⁰ x 11⁴

Br.3
12⁰ x 11⁰
OPTIONAL DEN

STOOP

Gar.
22⁰ x 21⁴

© design basics inc.

Design by
DESIGN BASICS, INC.

Width 54'-4"
Depth 48'-4"

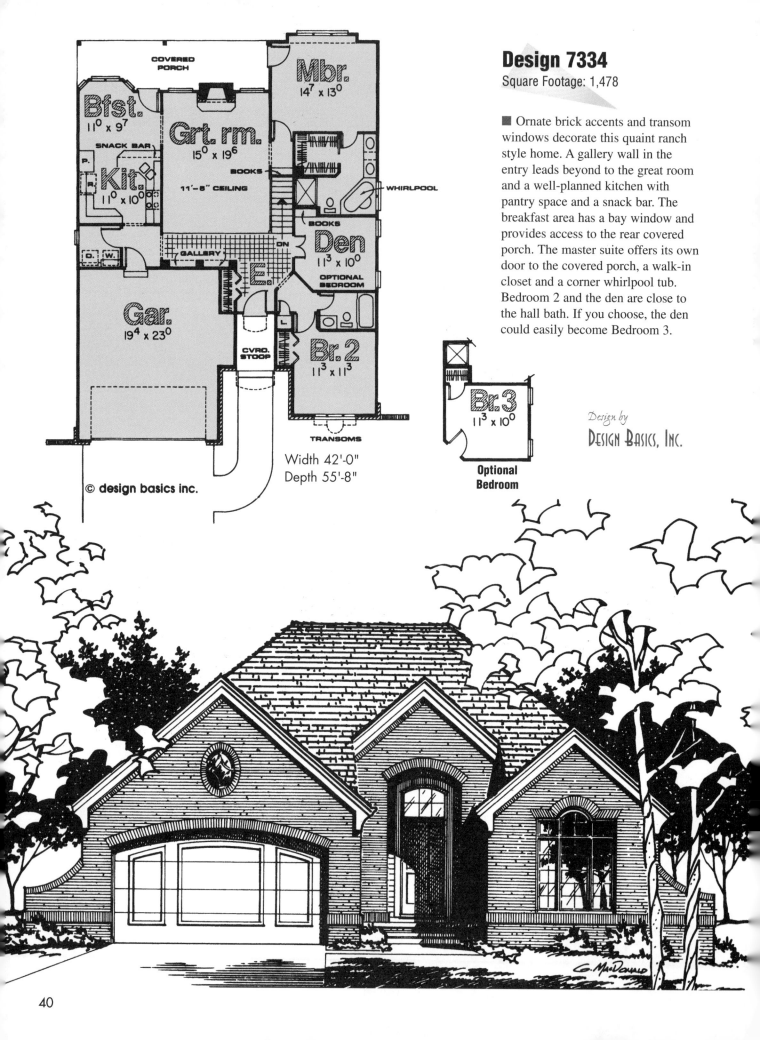

COVERED PORCH

Bfst.
11⁰ x 9⁷

SNACK BAR

Kit.
11⁰ x 10⁰

Grt. rm.
15⁰ x 19⁶

11'-8" CEILING

BOOKS

Mbr.
14⁷ x 13⁰

WHIRLPOOL

BOOKS

Den
11³ x 10⁰

OPTIONAL BEDROOM

GALLERY

DN

Gar.
19⁴ x 23⁰

CVRD. STOOP

Br. 2
11³ x 11³

TRANSOMS

Width 42'-0"
Depth 55'-8"

© design basics inc.

Design 7334

Square Footage: 1,478

■ Ornate brick accents and transom windows decorate this quaint ranch style home. A gallery wall in the entry leads beyond to the great room and a well-planned kitchen with pantry space and a snack bar. The breakfast area has a bay window and provides access to the rear covered porch. The master suite offers its own door to the covered porch, a walk-in closet and a corner whirlpool tub. Bedroom 2 and the den are close to the hall bath. If you choose, the den could easily become Bedroom 3.

Br. 3
11³ x 10⁰

Design by
DESIGN BASICS, INC.

Optional Bedroom

G. MacDonald

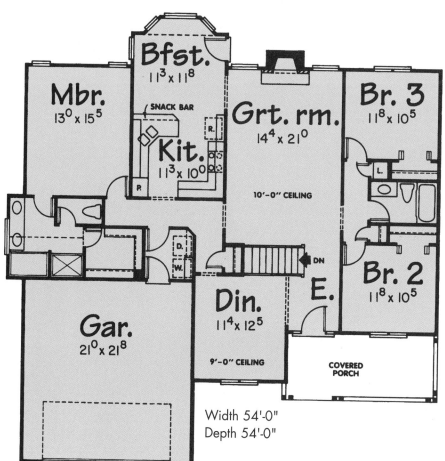

Bfst.
11^3 x 11^8

Mbr.
13^0 x 15^5

SNACK BAR

Grt. rm.
14^4 x 21^0

Br. 3
11^8 x 10^5

Kit.
11^3 x 10^0

10'-0" CEILING

L.

R.

D.
W.

Gar.
21^0 x 21^8

Din.
11^4 x 12^5

9'-0" CEILING

DN

E.

Br. 2
11^8 x 10^5

COVERED
PORCH

Width 54'-0"
Depth 54'-0"

Design 7350

Square Footage: 1,691

■ Simplicity and livability—these are the hallmarks of this one-story plan. A covered front porch leads to an entry with a formal dining room on the left and a great room straight ahead. Family bedrooms are found to the right of the great room. They share a full bath. The master suite is separated from the main body of the house by the kitchen and breakfast room. Note the snack bar in the kitchen and the bay window in the breakfast room. A two-car garage connects to the house through the utility area.

Design by
Design Basics, Inc.

Design B106

Square Footage: 1,631

■ Steep sloping roofs and a columned front porch make for a strong but simple front exterior for this lovely home. A turned stair with open railing adds a nice architectural touch to the family room which is warmed by a fireplace. The kitchen with an angled bar opens into the roomy dining area, which overlooks the expansive deck. The large laundry room is an added bonus to this fine home. Two large family bedrooms share a full hall bath, while the master suite pampers with a deluxe bath, a tray ceiling and a walk-in closet. The two-car drive-under garage easily accommodates the family vehicles.

Design by
GREG MARQUIS & ASSOCIATES

Deck

Dining
12x12

Kitchen

Master
14x15

Bath

Utility

Dn.

Drive Under

Bath

Family Room
15x18

B.R.#3
10x12

Foyer

B.R#2
11x12

Porch

Width 48'-0"
Depth 44'-0"

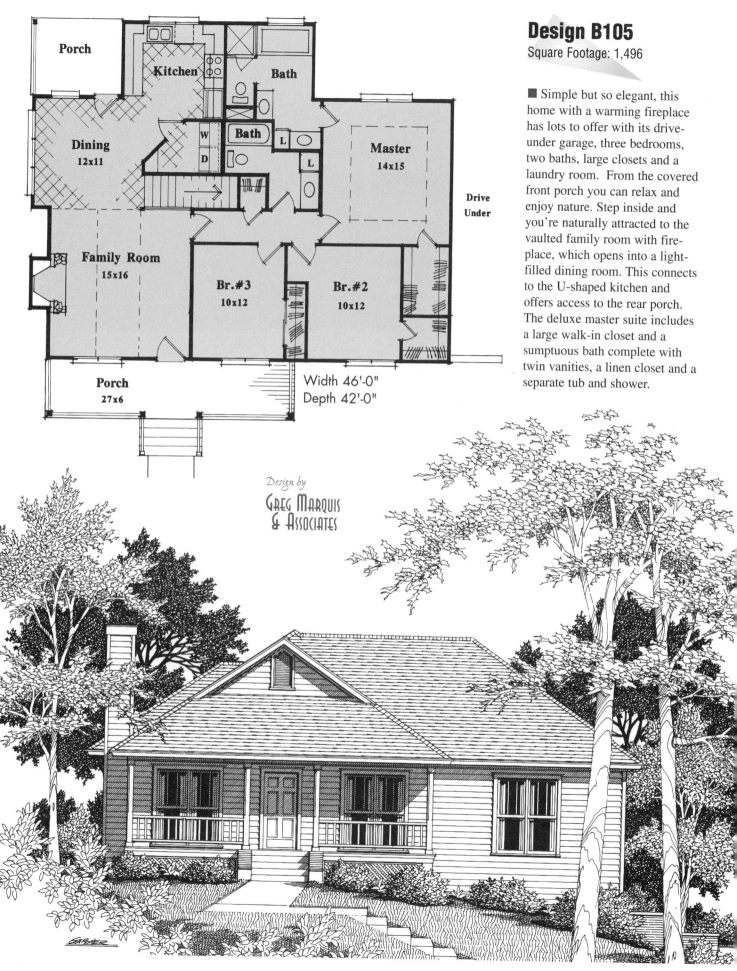

Porch

Kitchen

Bath

Dining
12x11

Bath

W
D

L

L

L

Master
14x15

Drive
Under

Family Room
15x16

Br.#3
10x12

Br.#2
10x12

Porch
27x6

Width 46'-0"
Depth 42'-0"

Design by
Greg Marquis
& Associates

Design B105

Square Footage: 1,496

■ Simple but so elegant, this home with a warming fireplace has lots to offer with its drive-under garage, three bedrooms, two baths, large closets and a laundry room. From the covered front porch you can relax and enjoy nature. Step inside and you're naturally attracted to the vaulted family room with fire-place, which opens into a light-filled dining room. This connects to the U-shaped kitchen and offers access to the rear porch. The deluxe master suite includes a large walk-in closet and a sumptuous bath complete with twin vanities, a linen closet and a separate tub and shower.

Design P110

Square Footage: 1,429

■ This home's gracious exterior is indicative of the elegant, yet extremely livable, floor plan inside. Volume ceilings that crown the family living areas combine with an open floor plan to give the modest square footage a more spacious feel. The formal dining room is set off from the foyer and vaulted family room with stately columns. The spacious family room has a corner fireplace, rear yard access and serving bar from the open galley kitchen. A bay windowed breakfast nook flanks the kitchen on one end while a laundry center and wet-bar/serving pantry lead to the dining room on the other. The split-bedroom plan allows the amenity-rich master suite maximum privacy. A pocket door off the family room leads to the hall housing the two family bedrooms and a full bath. Please specify basement, crawlspace or slab foundation when ordering.

Design by
Frank Betz Associates, Inc.

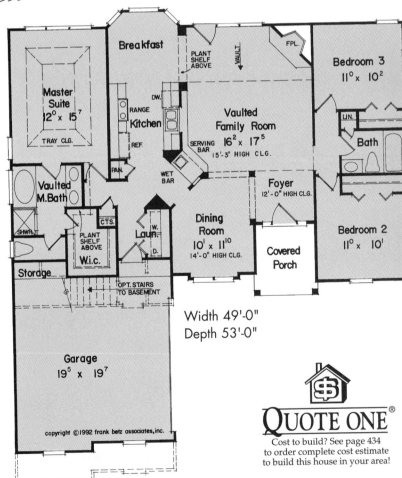

Width 49'-0"
Depth 53'-0"

Quote One®
Cost to build? See page 434 to order complete cost estimate to build this house in your area!

44

Design P128
Square Footage: 1,575

Vaulted Sitting Room

Master Suite
13⁰ x 15⁰

TRAY CLG.

Vaulted M. Bath

SHWR

W.i.c.

PLANT SHELF ABOVE

LIN.

Bath

Foyer

LIN.

COATS

Bedroom 3
11⁰ x 11⁰

Bedroom 2
11² x 11⁰

RADIUS WDW.

OPT. FRENCH DR.

FPL.

Vaulted Breakfast

FRENCH DOOR

PLANT SHELF ABOVE

REF.

Great Room
17⁰ x 15¹⁰
16'-0" HIGH CLG.

RANGE

SERVING BAR

Kitchen

PLANT SHELF ABOVE

D.W.

WET BAR

PAN.

Laun.

D. W.

Dining Room
11³ x 10⁷

Storage

Garage
19⁵ x 19⁸

Design by

Frank Betz Associates, Inc.

Width: 50'-0"
Depth: 52'-6"

copyright © 1992 frank betz associates, inc.

GARAGE LOCATION W/ BASEMENT

GARAGE LOCATION W/ BASEMENT

■ This impressive home will be the envy of the neighborhood during holiday parties. The massive great room, with its fireplace flanked by windowed views to the rear yard, will become entertainment central. A serving bar connects it to the amenity-filled kitchen, which flows into the formal dining room or into the vaulted breakfast nook. The sleeping wing is on the left side of the plan and features a luxurious master suite with a tray ceiling, a separate sitting room (big enough for an office) and a vaulted master bath with dual sinks and a walk-in closet. Two family bedrooms and a full hall bath complete this stunning plan. Please specify basement or crawlspace foundation when ordering.

QUOTE ONE®
Cost to build? See page 434 to order complete cost estimate to build this house in your area!

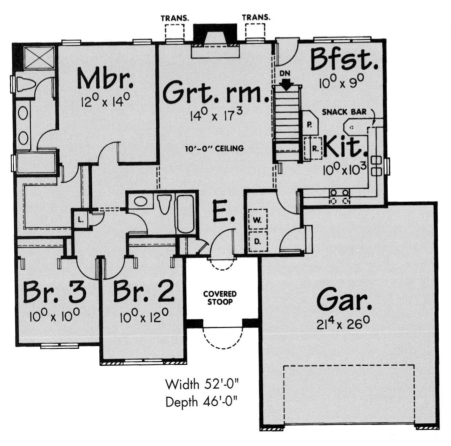

TRANS. TRANS.

Mbr.
12⁰ x 14⁰

Grt. rm.
14⁰ x 17³

10'-0" CEILING

Bfst.
10⁰ x 9⁰

DN

SNACK BAR

P.

R.

Kit.
10⁰ x 10³

L.

E.

W.

D.

Br. 3
10⁰ x 10⁰

Br. 2
10⁰ x 12⁰

COVERED
STOOP

Gar.
21⁴ x 26⁰

Width 52'-0"
Depth 46'-0"

Design 7374

Square Footage: 1,360

■ Brick and siding work well together, especially on a delightful facade such as this. A curved, recessed entry opens to a short foyer and then leads on to an expansive great room. Highlights here include a central fireplace flanked by transom windows, and a ten-foot ceiling. Enter the kitchen/breakfast area from the hallway, or through a doorway on the right side of the great room. Either way, you'll love the snack-bar counter defining the areas and the large window area in the breakfast room. Bedrooms are to the left of the plan. The master suite has a capacious walk-in closet and a full bath with spa tub, separate shower and dual sinks. Family bedrooms share a full hall bath. Note the extra space in the two-car garage for a workshop or storage.

Design by
DESIGN BASICS, INC.

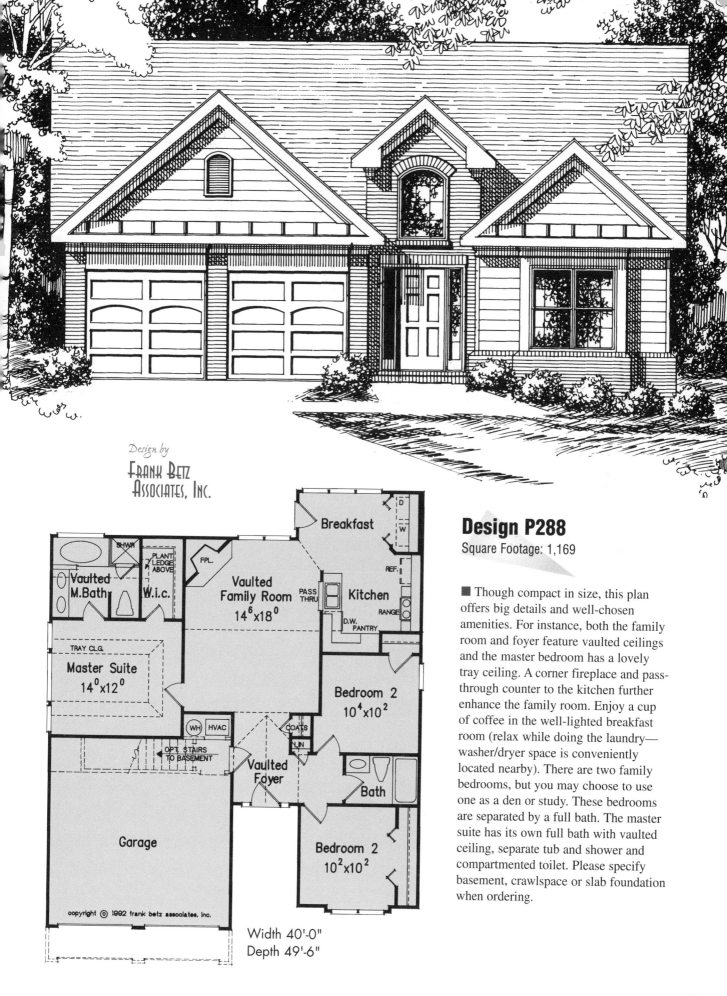

Design by

FRANK BETZ
ASSOCIATES, INC.

Breakfast

Vaulted
M.Bath

W.i.c.

PLANT
LEDGE
ABOVE

SHWR

FPL.

Vaulted
Family Room
14⁶x18⁰

PASS
THRU

Kitchen

REF.

RANGE

D.W.
PANTRY

TRAY CLG.

Master Suite
14⁰x12⁰

WH   HVAC

COATS

LIN

Bedroom 2
10⁴x10²

OPT. STAIRS
TO BASEMENT

Vaulted
Foyer

Bath

Garage

Bedroom 2
10²x10²

copyright © 1992 frank betz associates, inc.

Width 40'-0"
Depth 49'-6"

Design P288

Square Footage: 1,169

■ Though compact in size, this plan offers big details and well-chosen amenities. For instance, both the family room and foyer feature vaulted ceilings and the master bedroom has a lovely tray ceiling. A corner fireplace and pass-through counter to the kitchen further enhance the family room. Enjoy a cup of coffee in the well-lighted breakfast room (relax while doing the laundry—washer/dryer space is conveniently located nearby). There are two family bedrooms, but you may choose to use one as a den or study. These bedrooms are separated by a full bath. The master suite has its own full bath with vaulted ceiling, separate tub and shower and compartmented toilet. Please specify basement, crawlspace or slab foundation when ordering.

Design 7371

Square Footage: 1,579

■ Simple and sound, this fine one-story choice gives you many options. Build Bedroom 2 as an optional den with double-door access if you choose and you will also gain an additional linen closet. The remainder of the floor plan is eminently livable. The great room and dining room feature ten-foot ceilings. They attach directly to the breakfast room/kitchen area. Besides great work space, this area offers sunlit casual dining and access through a pocket door to the laundry room. The master bedroom suite has fine appointments, including a walk-in closet and a bath with a separate tub and shower, dual sinks and compartmented toilet. The two-car garage resides to the front to help shield the main house from noise.

Design by
DESIGN BASICS, INC.

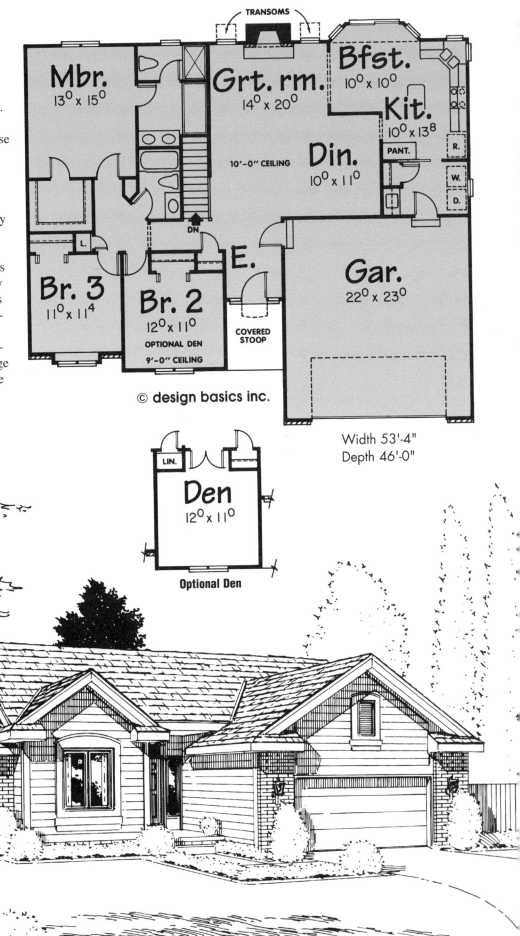

TRANSOMS

Mbr.
13⁰ x 15⁰

Grt. rm.
14⁰ x 20⁰

10'-0" CEILING

DN

E.

Bfst.
10⁰ x 10⁰

Kit.
10⁰ x 13⁸

Din.
10⁰ x 11⁰

PANT.

R.

W.

D.

Gar.
22⁰ x 23⁰

Br. 3
11⁰ x 11⁴

Br. 2
12⁰ x 11⁰
OPTIONAL DEN
9'-0" CEILING

COVERED
STOOP

© design basics inc.

Width 53'-4"
Depth 46'-0"

LIN.

Den
12⁰ x 11⁰

Optional Den

Design 7349
Square Footage: 1,392

■ With an unusually narrow footprint, this one-story will fit on most slender lots and still provide a great floor plan. The entry is graced with a handy coat closet and leads back to the spacious great room (note the ten-foot ceiling here) and to the right to two family bedrooms and a full bath. Stairs to the basement level are also found, just beyond the entry hall. The breakfast room and kitchen dominate the left side of the plan. Separating them is a snack-bar counter for quick meals-on-the-go. To the rear on the right is the master suite. Pampered amenities include a walk-in closet, windowed corner whirlpool tub, dual sinks and separate shower. A service entrance through the kitchen to the garage leads to a convenient laundry area and broom closet.

Design by
Design Basics, Inc.

Mbr.
14⁸ x 13⁰

Bfst.
12⁰ x 10⁰

SNACK BAR

Grt. rm.
14⁰ x 20⁰

Kit.
12⁰ x 11²

R.

LIN.

10'-0" CEILING

W.

D.

DN

Br. 3
11³ x 10⁰

P.

Gar.
19⁴ x 22³

E.

L.

COVERED STOOP

Br. 2
11³ x 10⁰

Width 42'-0"
Depth 54'-0"

49

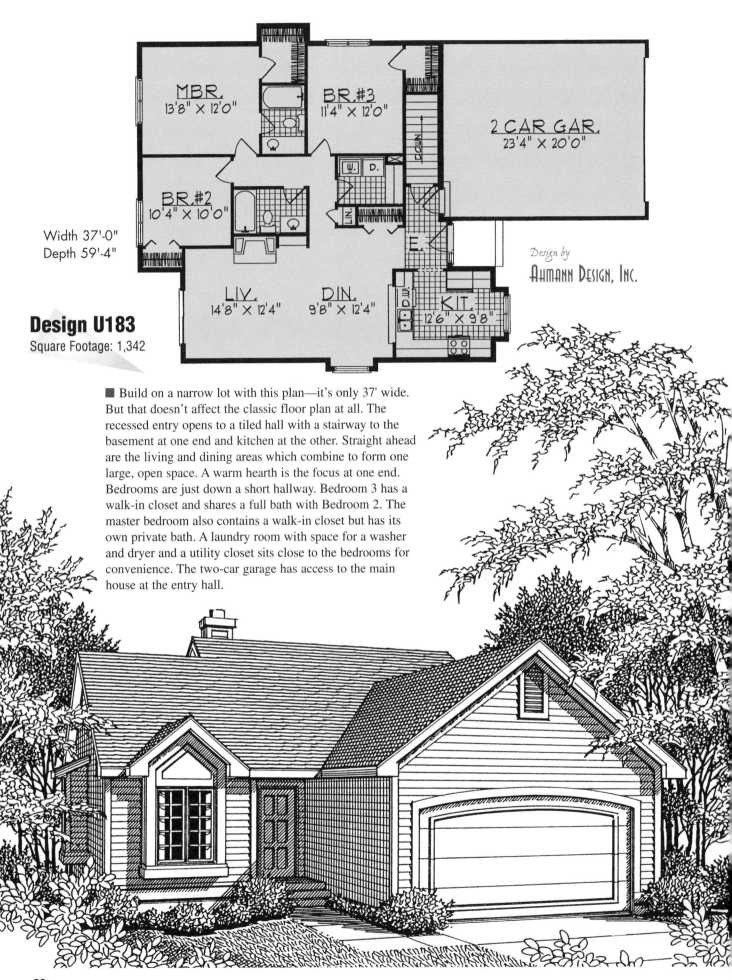

MBR.
13'8" X 12'0"

BR.#3
11'4" X 12'0"

2 CAR GAR.
23'4" X 20'0"

DOWN

W. D.

LIN.

BR.#2
10'4" X 10'0"

Width 37'-0"
Depth 59'-4"

Design by
Ahmann Design, Inc.

LIV.
14'8" X 12'4"

DIN.
9'8" X 12'4"

KIT.
12'6" X 9'8"

Design U183
Square Footage: 1,342

■ Build on a narrow lot with this plan—it's only 37' wide. But that doesn't affect the classic floor plan at all. The recessed entry opens to a tiled hall with a stairway to the basement at one end and kitchen at the other. Straight ahead are the living and dining areas which combine to form one large, open space. A warm hearth is the focus at one end. Bedrooms are just down a short hallway. Bedroom 3 has a walk-in closet and shares a full bath with Bedroom 2. The master bedroom also contains a walk-in closet but has its own private bath. A laundry room with space for a washer and dryer and a utility closet sits close to the bedrooms for convenience. The two-car garage has access to the main house at the entry hall.

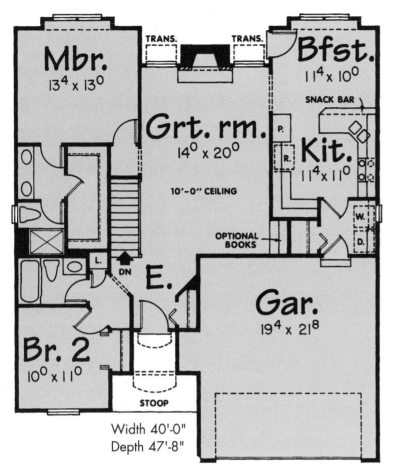

Mbr.
13⁴ x 13⁰

TRANS.   TRANS.

Bfst.
11⁴ x 10⁰

SNACK BAR

Grt. rm.
14⁰ x 20⁰

10'-0" CEILING

P.

R.

Kit.
11⁴ x 11⁰

W.

D.

OPTIONAL
BOOKS

DN

E.

Gar.
19⁴ x 21⁸

L.

Br. 2
10⁰ x 11⁰

STOOP

Width 40'-0"
Depth 47'-8"

Design 7375

Square Footage: 1,212

■ Attractive and uncomplicated, this two-bedroom home is perfect for first-time or empty-nest builders. Living, eating and cooking areas are designated as the center of activity in an open and unrestricted space. The master bedroom offers plenty of closet space and a private bath. Other features include a front coat closet for guests, a linen closet for hanging clothes in the laundry room and a warming fireplace in the great room, flanked by transom windows. A two-car garage easily shelters the family fleet.

Design by
DESIGN BASICS, INC.

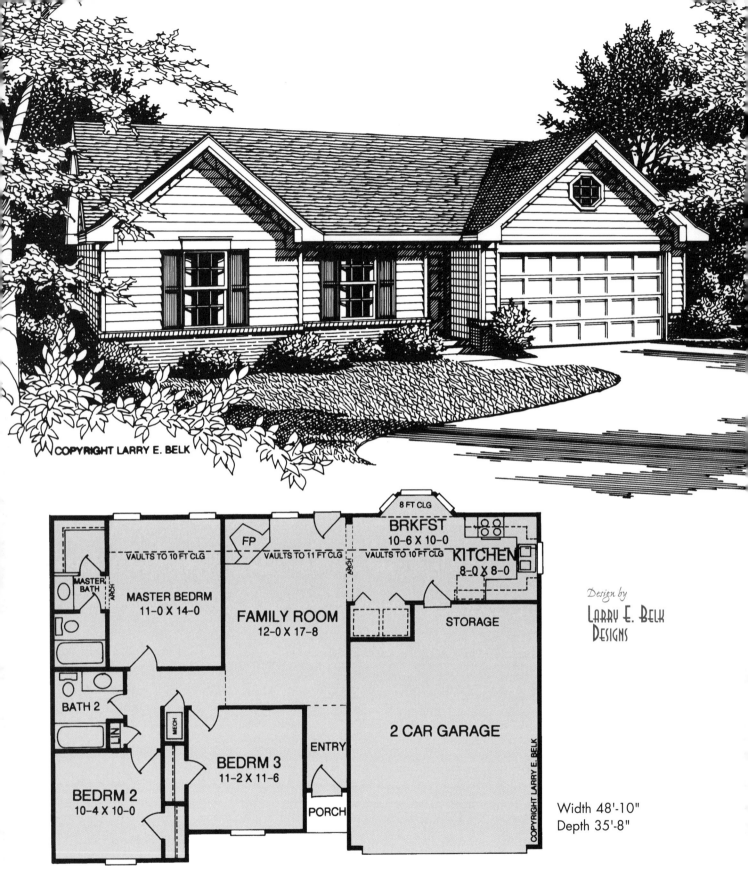

COPYRIGHT LARRY E. BELK

8 FT CLG

BRKFST
10-6 X 10-0

KITCHEN
8-0 X 8-0

VAULTS TO 10 FT CLG

FP

VAULTS TO 11 FT CLG

VAULTS TO 10 FT CLG

Design by
LARRY E. BELK
DESIGNS

MASTER BATH

MASTER BEDRM
11-0 X 14-0

FAMILY ROOM
12-0 X 17-8

STORAGE

BATH 2

MECH

2 CAR GARAGE

ENTRY

BEDRM 3
11-2 X 11-6

LIN

BEDRM 2
10-4 X 10-0

PORCH

COPYRIGHT LARRY E. BELK

Width 48'-10"
Depth 35'-8"

Design 8199
Square Footage: 1,142

■ This one-story cottage plan caters to family living. The two-car garage with ample storage space leads to an efficient kitchen and a bay windowed breakfast nook with a vaulted ceiling and space for a washer and dryer. The central family room provides plenty of space for entertaining and is complemented by a corner fireplace. Two family bedrooms share a full bath while the master bedroom features a private bath with a walk-in closet. This is a design you will be proud to call home. Please specify slab or crawlspace when ordering.

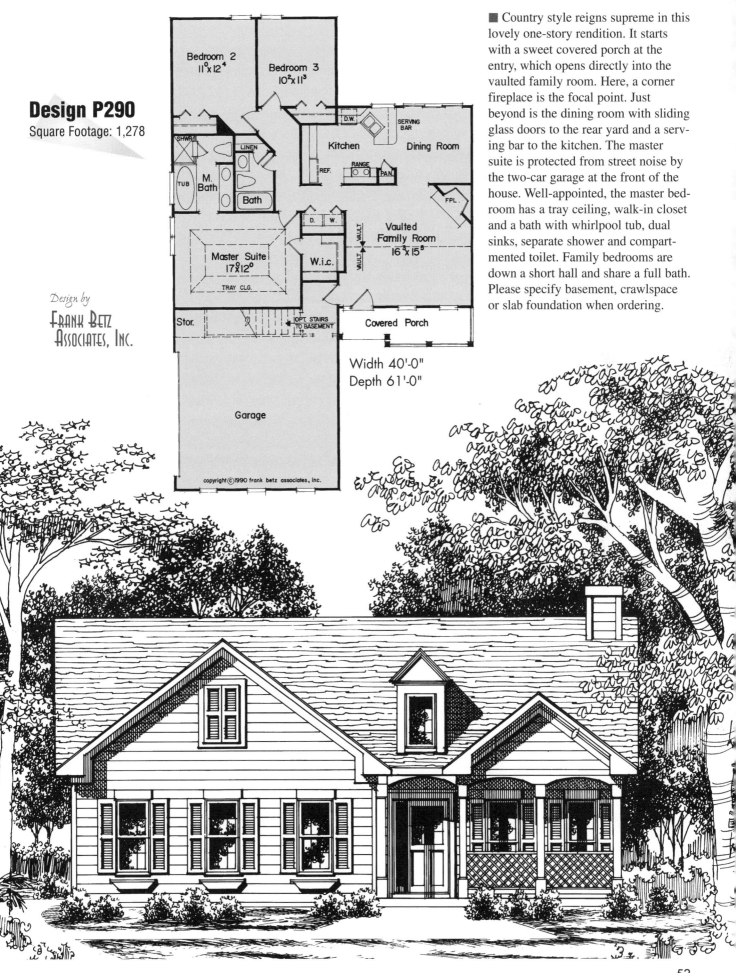

Design P290
Square Footage: 1,278

Design by

Frank Betz
Associates, Inc.

Bedroom 2
11⁰ x 12⁴

Bedroom 3
10² x 11³

D.W.

SERVING
BAR

Kitchen

Dining Room

SHWR.

LINEN

TUB

M. Bath

Bath

REF.

RANGE

PAN.

FPL.

D. W.

VAULT VAULT

Master Suite
17⁰ x 12⁰

W.i.c.

Vaulted
Family Room
16³ x 15⁵

TRAY CLG.

Stor.

OPT. STAIRS
TO BASEMENT

Covered Porch

Garage

Width 40'-0"
Depth 61'-0"

copyright © 1990 frank betz associates, inc.

■ Country style reigns supreme in this lovely one-story rendition. It starts with a sweet covered porch at the entry, which opens directly into the vaulted family room. Here, a corner fireplace is the focal point. Just beyond is the dining room with sliding glass doors to the rear yard and a serving bar to the kitchen. The master suite is protected from street noise by the two-car garage at the front of the house. Well-appointed, the master bedroom has a tray ceiling, walk-in closet and a bath with whirlpool tub, dual sinks, separate shower and compartmented toilet. Family bedrooms are down a short hall and share a full bath. Please specify basement, crawlspace or slab foundation when ordering.

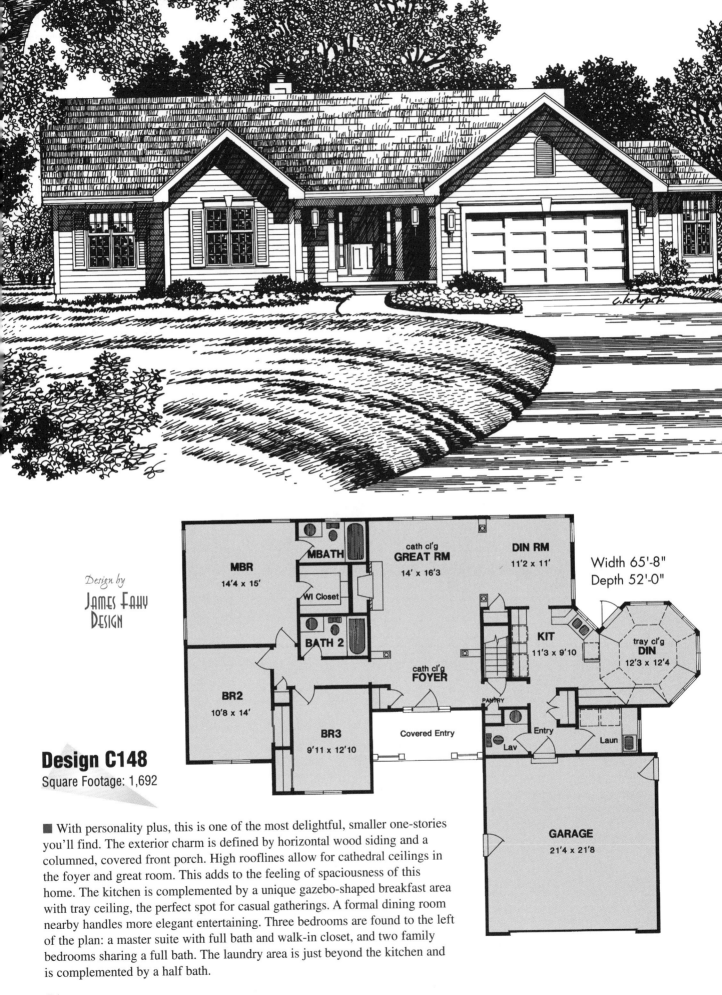

Design by
James Fahy
Design

MBR
14'4 x 15'

MBATH

WI Closet

BATH 2

BR2
10'8 x 14'

BR3
9'11 x 12'10

cath cl'g
GREAT RM
14' x 16'3

cath cl'g
FOYER

Covered Entry

DIN RM
11'2 x 11'

Width 65'-8"
Depth 52'-0"

KIT
11'3 x 9'10

tray cl'g
DIN
12'3 x 12'4

PANTRY

Lav   Entry   Laun

GARAGE
21'4 x 21'8

Design C148
Square Footage: 1,692

■ With personality plus, this is one of the most delightful, smaller one-stories you'll find. The exterior charm is defined by horizontal wood siding and a columned, covered front porch. High rooflines allow for cathedral ceilings in the foyer and great room. This adds to the feeling of spaciousness of this home. The kitchen is complemented by a unique gazebo-shaped breakfast area with tray ceiling, the perfect spot for casual gatherings. A formal dining room nearby handles more elegant entertaining. Three bedrooms are found to the left of the plan: a master suite with full bath and walk-in closet, and two family bedrooms sharing a full bath. The laundry area is just beyond the kitchen and is complemented by a half bath.

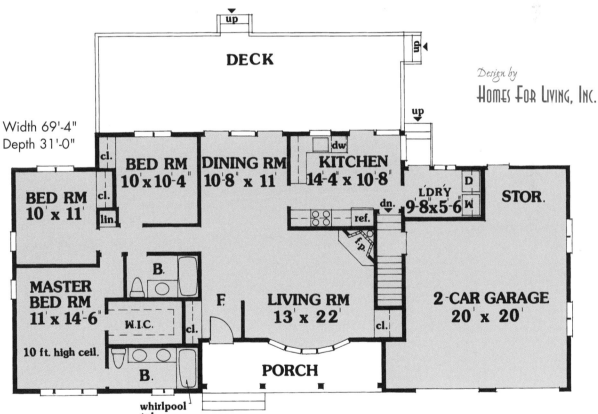

DECK

Design by
HOMES FOR LIVING, INC.

Width 69'-4"
Depth 31'-0"

BED RM
10'x10'-4"

DINING RM
10'-8" x 11'

KITCHEN
14'-4" x 10'-8"

LDRY
9'-8"x5'-6"

STOR.

BED RM
10' x 11'

ref.

f.p.

MASTER
BED RM
11' x 14'-6"

W.I.C.

LIVING RM
13' x 22'

2-CAR GARAGE
20' x 20'

10 ft. high ceil.

F.

B.

B.

PORCH

whirlpool
tub

Design N107
Square Footage: 1,387

■ Entering from a gracious front porch, the main activity spaces of this traditional, one-story farmhouse are grouped to the right of the foyer. The large living room has a corner fireplace and front-facing bow window. The dining room and kitchen have French doors leading to an outside deck. In the sleeping area, the master bedroom has a vaulted ceiling and a spacious walk-in closet. The master bath has a whirlpool tub and two sinks. Two bedrooms off the hall share a bathroom.

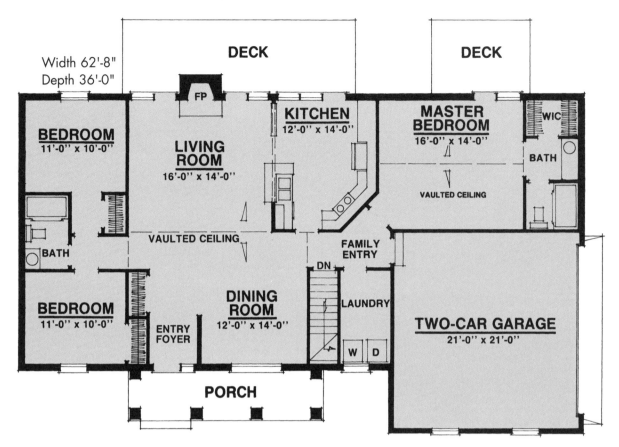

Width 62'-8"
Depth 36'-0"

DECK

DECK

FP

KITCHEN
12'-0'' x 14'-0''

**MASTER
BEDROOM**
16'-0'' x 14'-0''

WIC

BEDROOM
11'-0'' x 10'-0''

**LIVING
ROOM**
16'-0'' x 14'-0''

BATH

VAULTED CEILING

BATH

VAULTED CEILING

FAMILY
ENTRY

DN

LAUNDRY

BEDROOM
11'-0'' x 10'-0''

**DINING
ROOM**
12'-0'' x 14'-0''

ENTRY
FOYER

TWO-CAR GARAGE
21'-0'' x 21'-0''

W D

PORCH

■ A handsome porch dressed up with Greek Revival details greets visitors warmly into this one-story Early American home. From the entry, one is struck by the volume of space provided by the vaulted ceiling in the dining room, the living room, and the kitchen with eating space. The secluded master bedroom also sports a vaulted ceiling and is graced with a dressing area, a pri-vate bath and a walk-in closet. Two decks located at the rear of the plan are conveniently accessed by the master bedroom, kitchen and living room. A full bath serves the two family bedrooms and is readily accessible by guests. Adjacent to the two-car garage is a laundry room that handily accom-modates all family members.

Design F117
Square Footage: 1,550

Design by
R.L. Pfotenhauer

Design by
Homes For Living, Inc.

■ The exterior of this warm farmhouse style reflects this country's rich design heritage and has a plan firmly grounded in today's lifestyles. The sheltering entrance porch opens to a central foyer which leads to the main living space. Filling the large central area is a high-ceilinged living room with natural light flowing in through the skylight and the tall windows on either side of the fireplace. To the right of the foyer is a comfortable dining room with a bow window facing the front porch. Adjacent to the formal dining room is a large kitchen and convenient dinette area. The master bedroom suite contains a five-fixture bath and a large walk-in closet. Two additional bedrooms share a bath. An extra "flex" room near the entrance can be used as a den which opens directly into the living room, or closed, as a private fourth bedroom or home office with optional exterior door. Please specify basement or slab foundation when ordering.

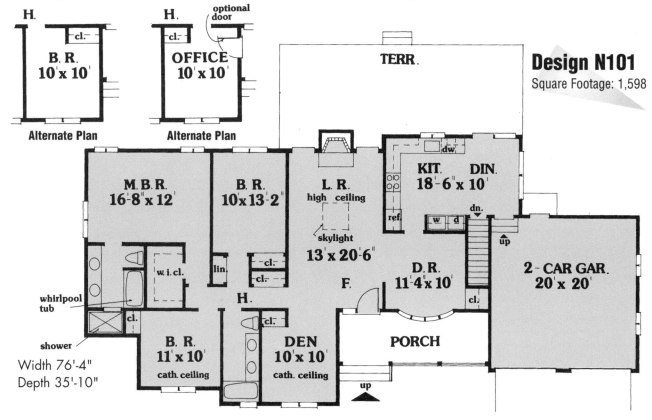

Design N101
Square Footage: 1,598

H.
B. R.
10' x 10'
cl.
Alternate Plan

H.
optional door
OFFICE
10' x 10'
cl.
Alternate Plan

TERR.

M. B. R.
16'-8" x 12'
whirlpool tub
shower
w. i. cl.
cl.

B. R.
10 x 13'-2"
lin
cl.
cl.

L. R.
high ceiling
skylight
13' x 20'-6"

KIT.
DIN.
18'-6" x 10'
dw
ref
w d
dn.
up

2 - CAR GAR.
20' x 20'

H.
B. R.
11' x 10'
cath. ceiling

DEN
10' x 10'
cath. ceiling
cl.

F.
D. R.
11'-4" x 10'
cl.

PORCH
up

Width 76'-4"
Depth 35'-10"

57

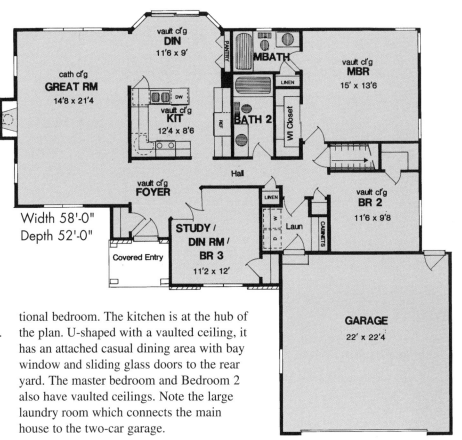

Design by
James Fahy Design

Design C154
Square Footage: 1,443

Width 58'-0"
Depth 52'-0"

■ An interesting floor plan is the key to great livability in this cozy one-story home. Enter the plan through the off-set, covered entry and you'll find a vaulted foyer that leads to the roomy great room with fireplace or down a hallway to the bedrooms. A study, or formal dining room, opens through double doors just at the entry. If needed, this room could serve as an additional bedroom. The kitchen is at the hub of the plan. U-shaped with a vaulted ceiling, it has an attached casual dining area with bay window and sliding glass doors to the rear yard. The master bedroom and Bedroom 2 also have vaulted ceilings. Note the large laundry room which connects the main house to the two-car garage.

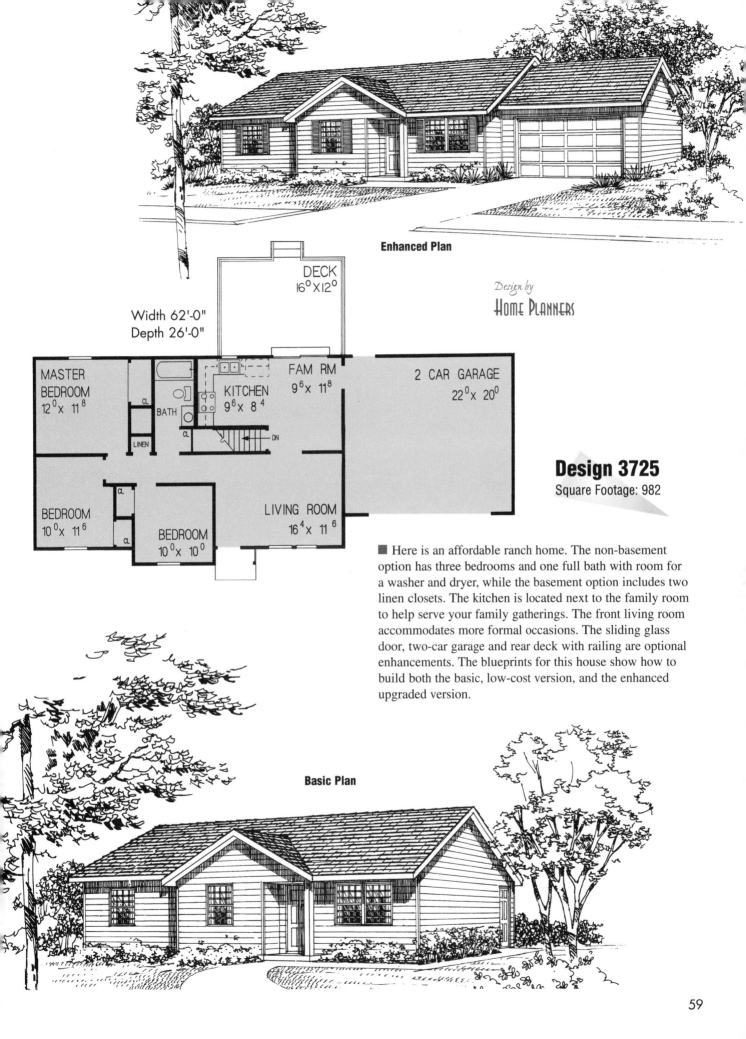

Enhanced Plan

Design by
Home Planners

DECK
16⁰ X 12⁰

Width 62'-0"
Depth 26'-0"

MASTER
BEDROOM
12⁰ x 11⁸

CL

BATH

LINEN

KITCHEN
9⁶ x 8⁴

FAM RM
9⁶ x 11⁸

2 CAR GARAGE
22⁰ x 20⁰

DN

BEDROOM
10⁰ x 11⁶

CL

BEDROOM
10⁰ x 10⁰

CL

LIVING ROOM
16⁴ x 11⁶

Design 3725
Square Footage: 982

■ Here is an affordable ranch home. The non-basement option has three bedrooms and one full bath with room for a washer and dryer, while the basement option includes two linen closets. The kitchen is located next to the family room to help serve your family gatherings. The front living room accommodates more formal occasions. The sliding glass door, two-car garage and rear deck with railing are optional enhancements. The blueprints for this house show how to build both the basic, low-cost version, and the enhanced upgraded version.

Basic Plan

COPYRIGHT LARRY E. BELK

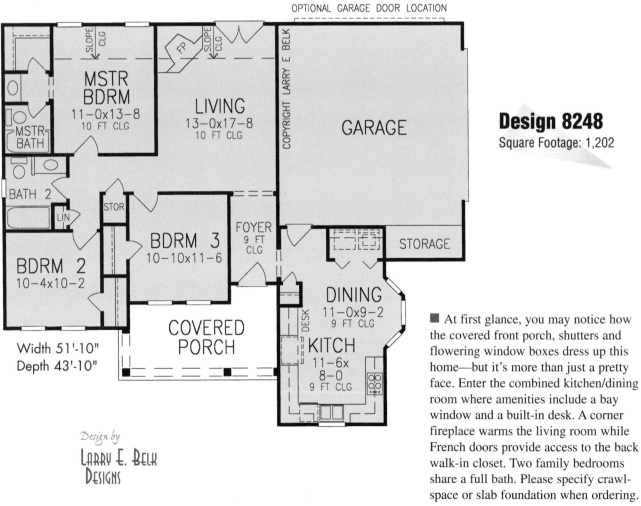

OPTIONAL GARAGE DOOR LOCATION

COPYRIGHT LARRY E BELK

MSTR BDRM
11-0x13-8
10 FT CLG

LIVING
13-0x17-8
10 FT CLG

GARAGE

MSTR BATH

BATH 2

STOR

BDRM 3
10-10x11-6

FOYER
9 FT CLG

STORAGE

BDRM 2
10-4x10-2

Width 51'-10"
Depth 43'-10"

COVERED PORCH

DESK

DINING
11-0x9-2
9 FT CLG

KITCH
11-6x
8-0
9 FT CLG

Design by
Larry E. Belk
Designs

Design 8248
Square Footage: 1,202

■ At first glance, you may notice how the covered front porch, shutters and flowering window boxes dress up this home—but it's more than just a pretty face. Enter the combined kitchen/dining room where amenities include a bay window and a built-in desk. A corner fireplace warms the living room while French doors provide access to the back walk-in closet. Two family bedrooms share a full bath. Please specify crawl-space or slab foundation when ordering.

Design C127

Square Footage: 1,586

Design by
James Fahy
Design

■ An unusual L-shaped covered entry porch leads to an angled foyer within this single-story, two-bedroom cottage. On the left is a study with cathedral ceiling and built-in bookshelves. Ahead and to the right of the entry foyer is a large open area defined by columns to create a great room with bay window and a formal dining room, both with cathedral ceilings. Under vaulted ceilings, the kitchen is open to a cheerful dinette bordered by windows and also has easy access to the dining room. The sleeping wing features a cathedral ceiling in the master bedroom and your choice of layouts for the master bath.

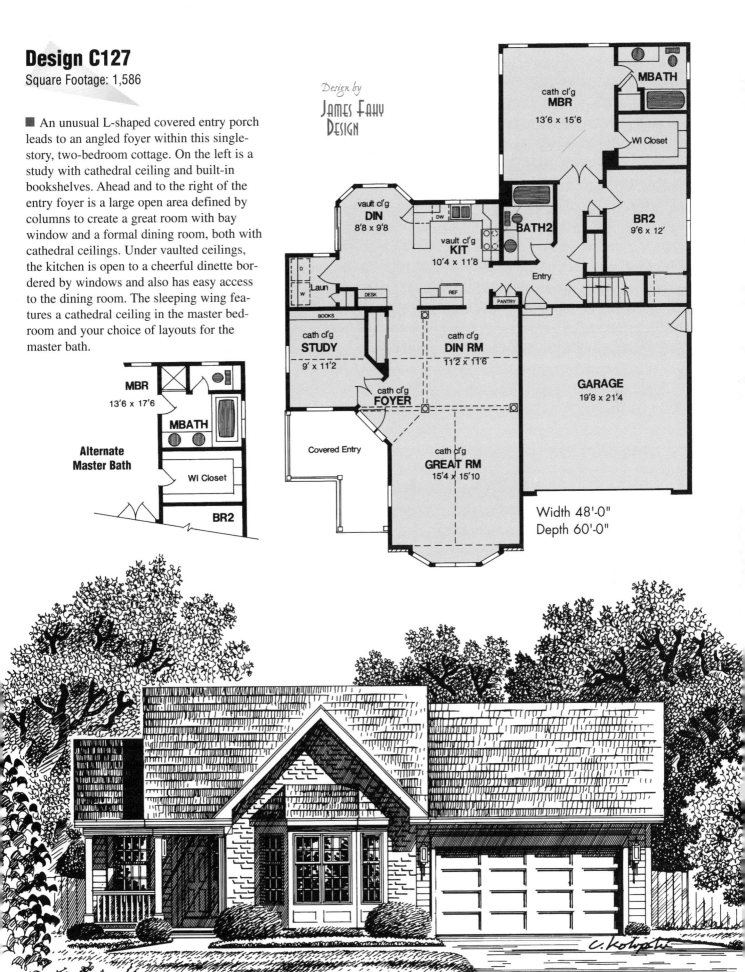

Alternate Master Bath

MBR 13'6 x 17'6

MBATH

WI Closet

BR2

MBATH

cath cl'g
MBR
13'6 x 15'6

WI Closet

BR2
9'6 x 12'

vault cl'g
DIN
8'8 x 9'8

DW

vault cl'g
KIT
10'4 x 11'8

BATH2

Entry

D

W

Laun

DESK

REF

PANTRY

BOOKS

cath cl'g
STUDY
9' x 11'2

cath cl'g
DIN RM
11'2 x 11'6

GARAGE
19'8 x 21'4

cath cl'g
FOYER

Covered Entry

cath cl'g
GREAT RM
15'4 x 15'10

Width 48'-0"
Depth 60'-0"

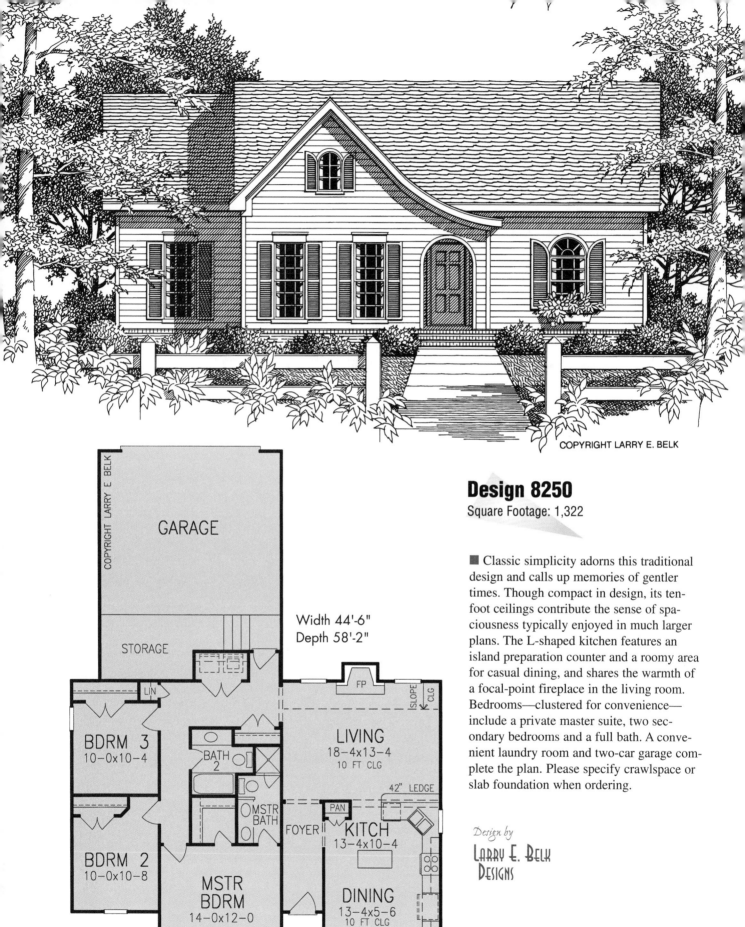

COPYRIGHT LARRY E. BELK

COPYRIGHT LARRY E BELK

GARAGE

STORAGE

LIN

BDRM 3
10-0x10-4

BATH
2

MSTR
BATH

LIVING
18-4x13-4
10 FT CLG

FP

slope

CLG

42" LEDGE

PAN

FOYER

KITCH
13-4x10-4

BDRM 2
10-0x10-8

MSTR
BDRM
14-0x12-0

DINING
13-4x5-6
10 FT CLG

PORCH

Width 44'-6"
Depth 58'-2"

Design 8250

Square Footage: 1,322

■ Classic simplicity adorns this traditional design and calls up memories of gentler times. Though compact in design, its ten-foot ceilings contribute the sense of spaciousness typically enjoyed in much larger plans. The L-shaped kitchen features an island preparation counter and a roomy area for casual dining, and shares the warmth of a focal-point fireplace in the living room. Bedrooms—clustered for convenience— include a private master suite, two secondary bedrooms and a full bath. A convenient laundry room and two-car garage complete the plan. Please specify crawlspace or slab foundation when ordering.

Design by
LARRY E. BELK
DESIGNS

COPYRIGHT LARRY E. BELK

Design 8249
Square Footage: 1,322

■ This traditional-style homestead is a delight, with clapboard siding, classic shutters and a box-paneled door. A columned covered porch leads the way through a gallery foyer to wide open living space with a centered fireplace flanked by windows. The gourmet kitchen boasts wrapping counters, a walk-in pantry, a work island and casual dining space with interior vistas to the living room and fireplace. Clustered sleeping quarters offer a master suite with a walk-in closet and twin vanities. Two family bedrooms share a full bath and include plenty of closet space. A utility area, set off by double doors, offers room for a full-size washer and dryer, while a service entrance leads to additional storage space in the garage. Please specify crawlspace or slab foundation when ordering.

Design by
Larry E. Belk
Designs

GARAGE

STORAGE

LIN

BDRM 3
10-0x10-4

BATH
2

BDRM 2
10-0x10-8

MSTR BDRM
14-0x12-0

PORCH

FOYER

MSTR
BATH

FP

SLOPE
CLG

LIVING
18-4x13-4
10 FT CLG

PAN

DINING
9-2x7-8
10 FT CLG

KITCH
13-6x7-6
10 FT CLG

Width 44'-6"
Depth 58'-2"

Design J155

Square Footage: 1,610

■ Two covered porches, plus a private master-suite terrace go above and beyond in offering outdoor options for this plan. You'll also have options inside: Choose a three-bedroom layout, or turn the third bedroom into a cozy den with double doors. The living room/dining room combination to the left of the plan is countered by a large family room with fireplace and porch access. The central kitchen is designed for convenience. The circular flow of the floor plan makes it very livable and allows for private spaces as well as open living areas. Because all of this is offered in just over 1600 square feet, this plan is a perfect choice for a starter home, empty nester home or retirement home.

Design by
Mark Stewart & Associates

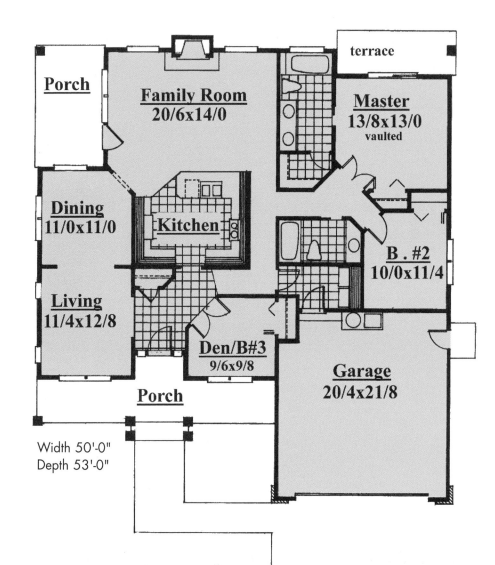

Porch

Family Room
20/6x14/0

terrace

Master
13/8x13/0
vaulted

Dining
11/0x11/0

Kitchen

B . #2
10/0x11/4

Living
11/4x12/8

Den/B#3
9/6x9/8

Garage
20/4x21/8

Porch

Width 50'-0"
Depth 53'-0"

Covered Patio

Family Room
14⁰ • 12⁰
volume ceiling

Bedroom 2
13⁰ • 9⁰
volume ceiling

Breakfast

Kitchen
14⁰ • 9⁰

Dining
11⁰ • 12⁰

Bath

Bedroom 3
10⁰ • 9⁰
volume ceiling

w d

Bath

Foyer

Double Garage

Master Bedroom
13⁰ • 12⁰
volume ceiling

Width 40'-0"
Depth 48'-0"

Design by
HOME DESIGN SERVICES

Design 8610
Square Footage: 1,280

■ This plan is ideal for the young family looking for a house that's small but smart. As in larger plans, this home boasts a private master's retreat with lots of closet space, dual vanities and a shower. The living area embraces the outdoor living space. The family eat-in kitchen design allows for efficient food preparation. Note the interior laundry closet included in the home. This plan comes with three options for Bedroom 2 and one option for the master bath. It also includes blueprints for three elevation choices!

■ This rustic retreat is updated with contemporary angles and packs a lot of living into a small space. Indoor/outdoor relationships are well developed and help to create a comfortable home. Start off with the covered front porch, which leads to a welcoming foyer. The beamed-ceiling great room opens directly ahead and features a fireplace, a wall of windows, access to the screened porch (with its own fireplace!) and is adjacent to the angled dining area. A highly efficient island kitchen is sure to please with a cathedral ceiling, access to the rear deck and tons of counter and cabinet space. Two family bedrooms, sharing a full bath, are located on one end of the plan while the master suite is secluded for complete privacy at the other end. The master suite includes a walk-in closet and a pampering bath.

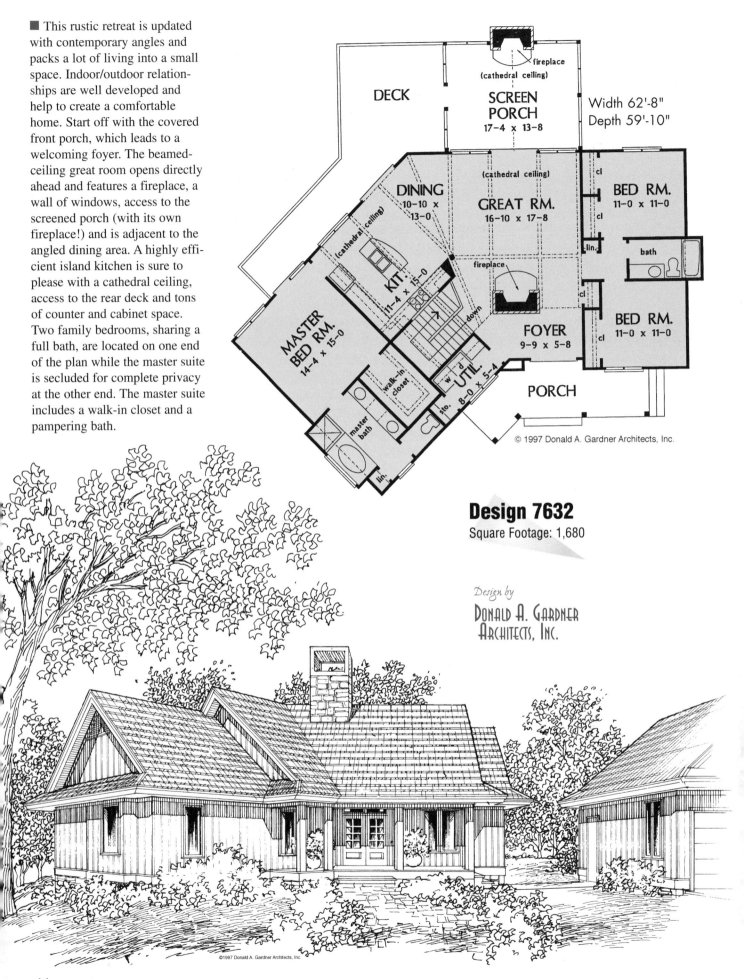

DECK

SCREEN PORCH
17-4 x 13-8

fireplace
(cathedral ceiling)

Width 62'-8"
Depth 59'-10"

(cathedral ceiling)

DINING
10-10 x 13-0

GREAT RM.
16-10 x 17-8

BED RM.
11-0 x 11-0

cl
cl
lin.

(cathedral ceiling)

KIT.
11-4 x 15-0

bath

fireplace

down

MASTER BED RM.
14-4 x 15-0

FOYER
9-9 x 5-8

BED RM.
11-0 x 11-0

cl
cl

walk-in closet

UTIL.
8-0 x 5-4

sto.

master bath

PORCH

lin.

© 1997 Donald A. Gardner Architects, Inc.

Design 7632
Square Footage: 1,680

Design by
Donald A. Gardner
Architects, Inc.

©1997 Donald A. Gardner Architects, Inc.

66

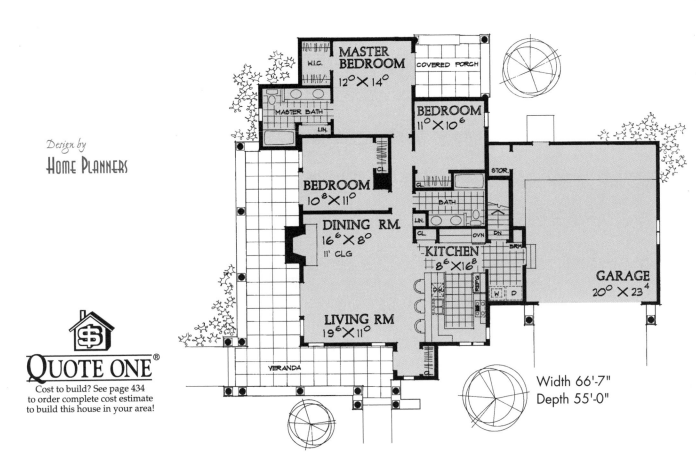

MASTER BEDROOM 12⁰ X 14⁰

COVERED PORCH

W.I.C.

MASTER BATH

LIN.

BEDROOM 11⁰ X 10⁶

STOR.

BEDROOM 10⁸ X 11⁰

CL.

BATH

LIN.

CL.

OVN

DN

DINING RM. 16⁶ X 8⁰

11' CLG

KITCHEN 8⁶ X 16⁸

BRM.

REF.

W D

GARAGE 20⁰ X 23⁴

LIVING RM 19⁶ X 11⁰

VERANDA

Width 66'-7"
Depth 55'-0"

Design by
HOME PLANNERS

QUOTE ONE®
Cost to build? See page 434
to order complete cost estimate
to build this house in your area!

Design 3465
Square Footage: 1,410
L

■ An L-shaped veranda employs tapered columns to support a standing seam metal roof. Horizontal siding with brick accents and multi-pane windows all enhance the exterior of this home. Most notable, however, is the metal roof with its various planes. Complementing this is a massive stucco chimney that captures the ambience of the West. A hard-working interior will delight those building within a modest budget. The spacious front room provides plenty of space for both living and family dining activities. A fireplace makes a delightful focal point. The kitchen, set aside, has a handy snack bar and passageway to the garage. To one side is the laundry area, to the other, the stairs to the basement. The centrally located main bath has twin sinks and a nearby linen closet. One of the two secondary bedrooms has direct access to the veranda. The master bedroom is flanked by the master bath and its own private covered porch.

B. NATHAN.

© 1996 Donald A. Gardner Architects, Inc.

Design 7635

Square Footage: 1,417

■ Three box-bay windows dress up a
hip roof on this stunning stucco exterior.
A contemporary floor plan offers an
open, airy feel with a cathedral ceiling
and a colonnaded opening in the great
room. A fireplace warms this common
area, designed for family gatherings as
well as planned events. The master suite
boasts a U-shaped walk-in closet, a
dressing area and a sensational private
bath with a whirlpool tub and a skylight. A hall bath serves two family bedrooms, one with its own walk-in closet.
The side-entry garage offers a service
entrance to the kitchen and additional
storage space.

Design by

DONALD A. GARDNER
ARCHITECTS, INC.

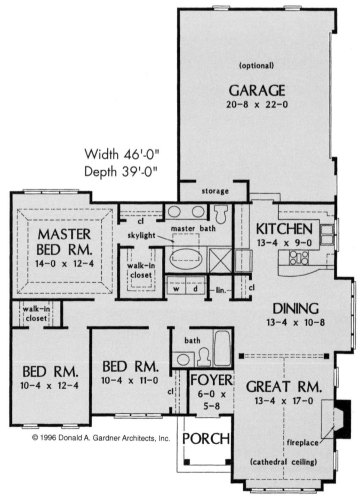

Width 46'-0"
Depth 39'-0"

© 1996 Donald A. Gardner Architects, Inc.

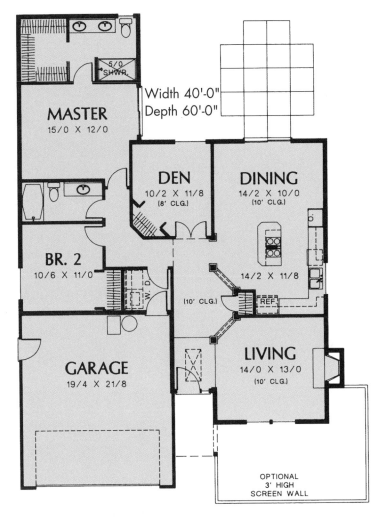

MASTER
15/0 X 12/0

Width 40'-0"
Depth 60'-0"

DEN
10/2 X 11/8
(8' CLG.)

DINING
14/2 X 10/0
(10' CLG.)

BR. 2
10/6 X 11/0

14/2 X 11/8
(10' CLG.)

REF.

GARAGE
19/4 X 21/8

LIVING
14/0 X 13/0
(10' CLG.)

OPTIONAL
3' HIGH
SCREEN WALL

Design 9507
Square Footage: 1,401

■ Vertical siding succeeds in moving the eye up in this compact one-story plan. For added interest, an optional three-foot-high screen wall encloses the area just outside the living room window. The foyer unfolds with a skylight and a ten-foot ceiling. Columns lend an air of formality to the living and dining rooms and the kitchen. A den is found straight ahead from the foyer and offers privacy for studies or the occasional out-of-town guest. The kitchen showcases an island cooktop and ample counter space. The dining room, with its ten-foot ceiling, has sliding glass doors that lead to a back terrace. The master bedroom also features sliding glass doors to this outdoor area.

Design by
ALAN MASCORD
DESIGN ASSOCIATES, INC.

Design G300

Square Footage: 324

■ Start small with this elegant, 324 square-foot, free-standing garden room. Use the space as a garden retreat for reading or music, or as an arts-and-crafts studio. Two tall, arched windows topped with fan-lights grace three sides. A window and entry door flanked by narrow mock shutters are found in the front. The vented cupola and weathervane centered on the cedar shake roof add an air of rustic charm. To expand the living area an additional 664 square feet, extend the floor plan to each side. Add an entry foyer and full bath to one side of the existing structure and a breakfast nook with its own door to the garden on the other. Existing windows become doorways and, in one case, a window is replaced by an interior wall. To complete this outstanding expansion, add an 11' x 15' bedroom with generous closets off the foyer, and an 11' x 10'-10" kitchen with pass-through window off the breakfast nook. Behind the kitchen is space for more storage or a mini-workshop.

GARDEN RM
17⁰ x 17⁰

Width 18'-0"
Depth 18'-0"

E. REINKE

70

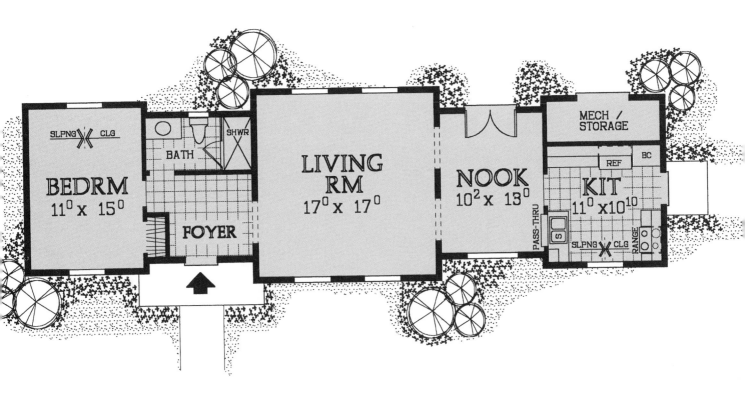

BEDRM
11⁰ x 15⁰

SLPNG CLG

BATH

SHWR

FOYER

LIVING RM
17⁰ x 17⁰

NOOK
10² x 13⁰

PASS-THRU

MECH / STORAGE

REF

BC

KIT
11⁰ x10¹⁰

SLPNG CLG

RANGE

S

Design by
HOME PLANNERS

Expanded Version
Width 62'-0"
Depth 18'-0"

E. REINE

Design 3728

Square Footage: 1,533

■ Here is a ranch home that offers a floor plan of convenience and simplicity. The master bedroom features a walk-in closet and a private bath. Two secondary bedrooms share a full bath. The dining room is open to the great room and connects to an L-shaped kitchen that offers a breakfast nook. Options for enhanced livability include a rear deck with a railing and a fireplace in the great room. A two-car garage easily shelters the family fleet.

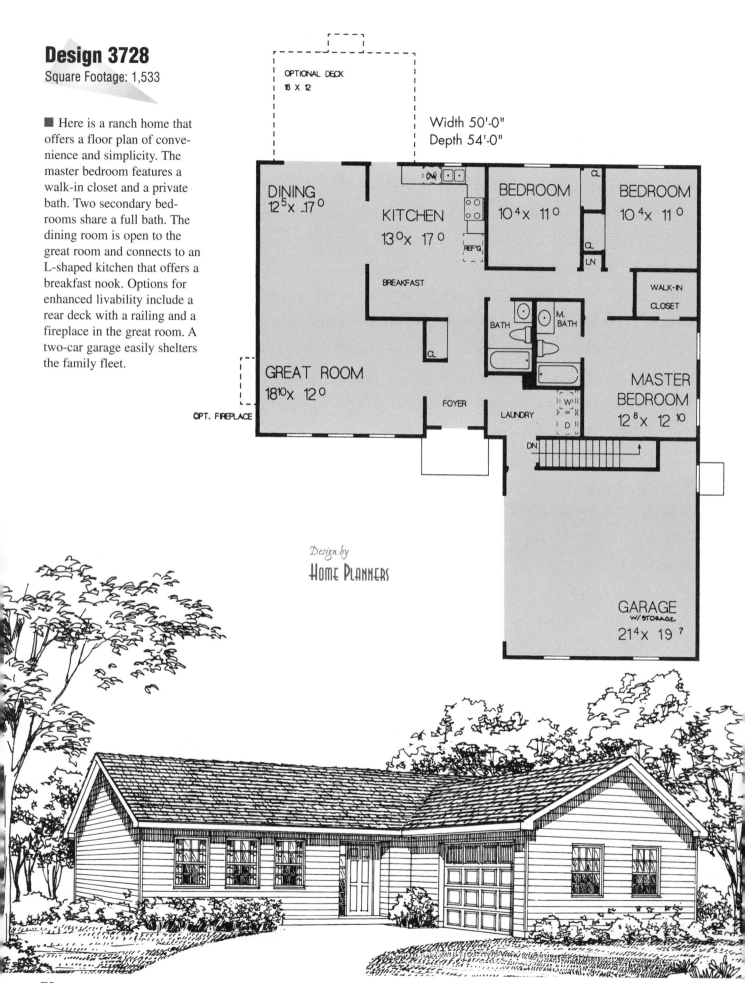

OPTIONAL DECK
18 X 12

Width 50'-0"
Depth 54'-0"

DINING
12^5x 17^0

KITCHEN
13^0x 17^0

BEDROOM
10^4x 11^0

BEDROOM
10^4x 11^0

CL

LN

REF'G

BREAKFAST

WALK-IN
CLOSET

BATH

M.
BATH

GREAT ROOM
18^{10}x 12^0

CL

MASTER
BEDROOM
12^8x 12^{10}

OPT. FIREPLACE

FOYER

LAUNDRY

W
D

DN

Design by
Home Planners

GARAGE
W/ STORAGE
21^4x 19^7

On The Level With Luxury:
One-story homes from 2,800 square feet and up

Design M150
Square Footage: 4,615

■ The hip-roof French country exterior and porte cochere entrance are just the beginning of this unique, and impressive, design. An unusual pullman ceiling graces the foyer as it leads to the formal dining room on the right, to the study with a fireplace on the left and straight ahead to the formal living room with its covered patio access. A gallery directs you to the island kitchen with its abundant counter space and adjacent sun-filled breakfast bay. On the left side of the home, a spectacular master suite will become your favorite haven and the envy of your guests. The master bedroom includes a coffered ceiling, a bayed sitting area and patio access. The master bath features a large doorless shower, a separate exercise room and a huge walk-in closet with built-in chests. All of the family bedrooms offer private baths and walk-in closets.

Width 109'-10"
Depth 89'-4"

Design by
FILLMORE DESIGN GROUP

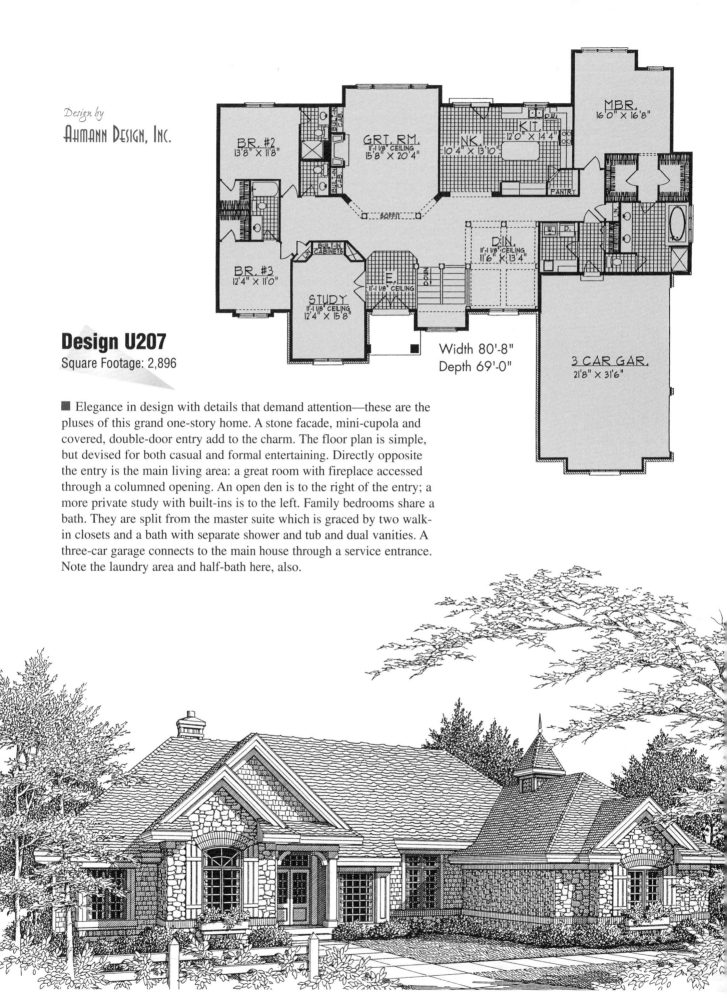

Design by
AHMANN DESIGN, INC.

BR. #2
13'8" X 11'8"

GRT. RM.
11'-1⅛" CEILING
15'8" X 20'4"

NK.
10'4" X 13'10"

KIT.
12'0" X 14'4"

MBR.
16'0" X 16'8"

PANTRY

BUILT-IN CABINETS

BR. #3
12'4" X 11'0"

STUDY
11'-1⅛" CEILING
12'4" X 15'8"

E.
11'-1⅛" CEILING

DIN.
11'-1⅛" CEILING
11'6" X 13'4"

DOWN

SOFFIT

Design U207

Square Footage: 2,896

Width 80'-8"
Depth 69'-0"

3 CAR GAR.
21'8" X 31'6"

■ Elegance in design with details that demand attention—these are the pluses of this grand one-story home. A stone facade, mini-cupola and covered, double-door entry add to the charm. The floor plan is simple, but devised for both casual and formal entertaining. Directly opposite the entry is the main living area: a great room with fireplace accessed through a columned opening. An open den is to the right of the entry; a more private study with built-ins is to the left. Family bedrooms share a bath. They are split from the master suite which is graced by two walk-in closets and a bath with separate shower and tub and dual vanities. A three-car garage connects to the main house through a service entrance. Note the laundry area and half-bath here, also.

Design M103

Square Footage: 2,985

Design by
FILLMORE DESIGN GROUP

Alternate Elevation

Width 80'-0"
Depth 68'-0"

■ Varying rooflines, a stately brick exterior and classic window treatment accentuates the beauty of this traditional one-story home. Inside, formal living areas flank the entry—living room to the left and dining room to the right—presenting a fine introduction. Double French doors provide an elegant entrance to the centrally-located study. To the right you will find the casual living areas: a U-shaped kitchen, a dinette and a large family room with a cathedral ceiling. Three secondary bedrooms and two full baths complete this side of the plan. Tucked behind the living room is the master suite. Amenities enhancing this private getaway include a sitting area with built-in space for a TV, a huge walk in closet, and a master bath with a whirlpool tub and a separate shower.

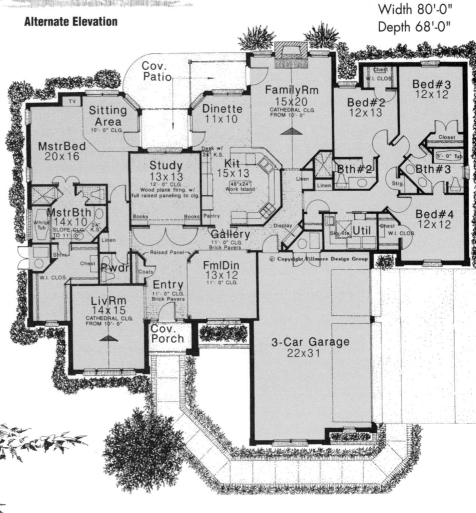

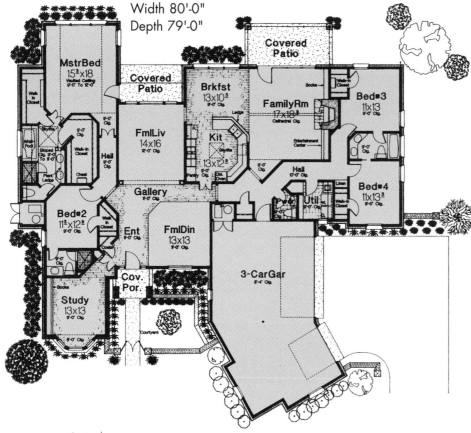

Width 80'-0"
Depth 79'-0"

Design M156

Square Footage: 3,056

■ Depending on European and French influences for its exterior beauty, this regal one-story belies the theory that a single-story has no character. A volume roofline helps make the difference, both inside and out, allowing for vaulted ceilings in many of the interior spaces. There are more than enough living areas in this plan: formal living and dining rooms, a huge family room with fireplace and a study with bay window. The kitchen has an attached, light-filled breakfast area and is open to the family room. Four bedrooms include three family bedrooms; two on the right side of the plan and one on the left. The master suite has a private covered patio, a vaulted ceiling, two walk-in closets and a bath fit for a king. A three-car garage contains ample space for cars and recreational vehicles.

Design by
FILLMORE DESIGN GROUP

Design M158

Square Footage: 3,352

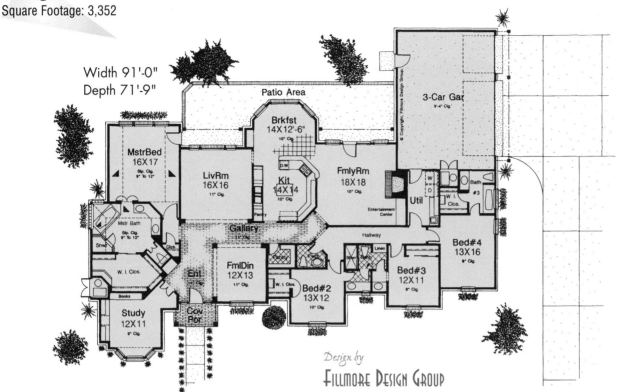

Width 91'-0"
Depth 71'-9"

Patio Area

Brkfst 14X12'-6"

MstrBed 16X17

LivRm 16X16

Kit 14X14

FmlyRm 18X18

3-Car Gar

Mstr Bath

Shwr

W. I. Clos.

Books

Gallery

FmlDin 12X13

Ent

Study 12X11

Cov Por

Bed#2 13X12

Bed#3 12X11

Bed#4 13X16

Util

Bath #3

W. I. Clos.

Entertainment Center

Hallway

Linen

W. I. Clos.

Pantry

Design by
FILLMORE DESIGN GROUP

■ This home combines the rustic charm of shutters and a random stonework wall with the elegance of molded cornices and arched multi-pane windows to create a look all its own. From the nicely detailed covered porch, enter upon the formal dining room to the right and living room to the rear. The arched gallery leads past the kitchen with island and bar to the family room with fireplace and built-in entertainment center. Adjoining the kitchen and family room is the bay-windowed breakfast nook which looks out onto the rear patio. Three family bedrooms are located to the front. Bedroom 4 offers a private full bath, while Bedrooms 2 and 3 each has its own private vanity in the shared full bath. The left side of the plan is comprised of the master suite and the double-doored, bay-windowed study with built-ins. The master bedroom offers a triple window overlooking the rear property, a private door to the patio, sloped ceiling, walk-in closet, corner garden tub and compartmented toilet.

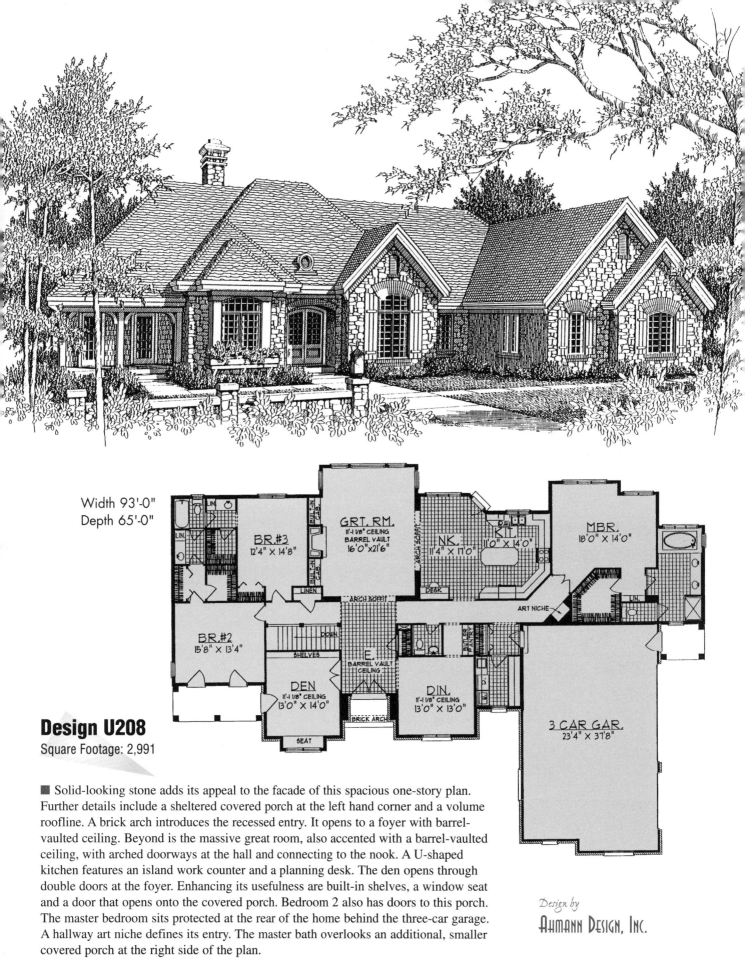

Width 93'-0"
Depth 65'-0"

BR.#3
12'4" X 14'8"

GRT. RM.
11'-1 1/8" CEILING
BARREL VAULT
16'0" X 21'6"

NK.
11'4" X 17'0"

KIT.
11'0" X 14'0"

MBR.
18'0" X 14'0"

ARCH SOFFIT

LIN.

BUILT-IN CAB.

LINEN

ARCH SOFFIT

DESK

ART NICHE

LIN.

BR.#2
15'8" X 13'4"

SHELVES

DOWN

E.
BARREL VAULT
CEILING

DEN
11'-1 1/8" CEILING
13'0" X 14'0"

DIN.
11'-1 1/8" CEILING
13'0" X 13'0"

BUTLER PANTRY

3 CAR GAR.
23'4" X 37'8"

BRICK ARCH

SEAT

Design U208
Square Footage: 2,991

■ Solid-looking stone adds its appeal to the facade of this spacious one-story plan.
Further details include a sheltered covered porch at the left hand corner and a volume
roofline. A brick arch introduces the recessed entry. It opens to a foyer with barrel-
vaulted ceiling. Beyond is the massive great room, also accented with a barrel-vaulted
ceiling, with arched doorways at the hall and connecting to the nook. A U-shaped
kitchen features an island work counter and a planning desk. The den opens through
double doors at the foyer. Enhancing its usefulness are built-in shelves, a window seat
and a door that opens onto the covered porch. Bedroom 2 also has doors to this porch.
The master bedroom sits protected at the rear of the home behind the three-car garage.
A hallway art niche defines its entry. The master bath overlooks an additional, smaller
covered porch at the right side of the plan.

Design by
Ahmann Design, Inc.

Design M157

Square Footage: 3,268

■ Brick, with accents of stone, define the stately facade of this home. It gives some hint of the grand floor plan inside. The entry hall is centrally located to provide convenient access to the study (or make it a bedroom), the formal dining room, the formal living room and the kitchen. Living spaces to the rear include a breakfast nook with snack bar and the angled family room with great views to the rear yard. Across the back and connecting to the formal living room, casual dining area and family room, is a covered porch/patio area. Three family bedrooms dominate the right side of the plan—one has a private bath. The master suite is on the left side and has access to the rear patio and an amenity-filled bath with two walk-in closets, whirlpool tub, shower and double sinks.

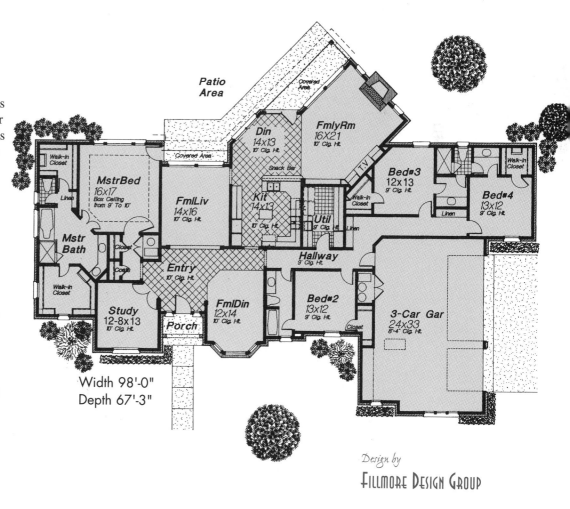

Width 98'-0"
Depth 67'-3"

Design by
FILLMORE DESIGN GROUP

Design 9179

Square Footage: 2,528

■ This grand brick home offers a lovely European facade with a luxurious floor plan that is filled with amenities that accommodate a variety of needs and desires suited to your lifestyle. The entry foyer is raised and leads in several directions. To the right is a formal dining room connecting to the kitchen. To the left is the living room with fireplace and built-ins and a columned gallery leading to the study, library and master suite. A glass-enclosed breakfast room allows for sunny casual dining and complements the island kitchen. The master suite features a bright sitting room, huge walk-in closet and well-appointed bath. Three additional bedrooms also have walk-in closets. Bedroom 4 has a private bath; Bedrooms 2 and 3 share a full bath.

Design by
Larry W. Garnett
& Associates

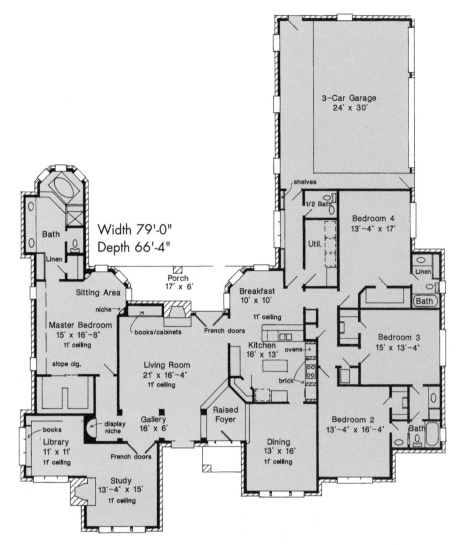

Width 79'-0"
Depth 66'-4"

Bath

Linen

Sitting Area

niche

Master Bedroom
15' x 16'-8"
11' ceiling

books/cabinets

slope clg.

books

Library
11' x 11'
11' ceiling

display niche

French doors

Gallery
16' x 6'

Living Room
21' x 16'-4"
11' ceiling

Study
13'-4" x 15'
11' ceiling

Porch
17' x 6'

French doors

Raised Foyer

Dining
13' x 16'
11' ceiling

Breakfast
10' x 10'

11' ceiling

Kitchen
16' x 13'

ovens

brick

shelves

1/2 Bath

Util.

3-Car Garage
24' x 30'

Bedroom 4
13'-4" x 17'

Linen

Bath

Bedroom 3
15' x 13'-4"

Bedroom 2
13'-4" x 16'-4"

Bath

■ Hipped rooflines, fine brick detailing and twin sets of square columns flanking the entrance all combine to give this home a touch of grandeur. Inside, the octagonal foyer leads to the formal living and dining rooms as well as to a noise-free study and two family bedrooms. The large island kitchen easily services the bayed breakfast room and the spacious family room, which is enhanced by a warming fireplace. A lavish master suite has two walk-in closets, a bay window and a whirlpool tub.

Patio/Garden View

Width 90'-11"
Depth 81'-3"

Design by
Design Basics, Inc.

Design 7388
Square Footage: 3,312

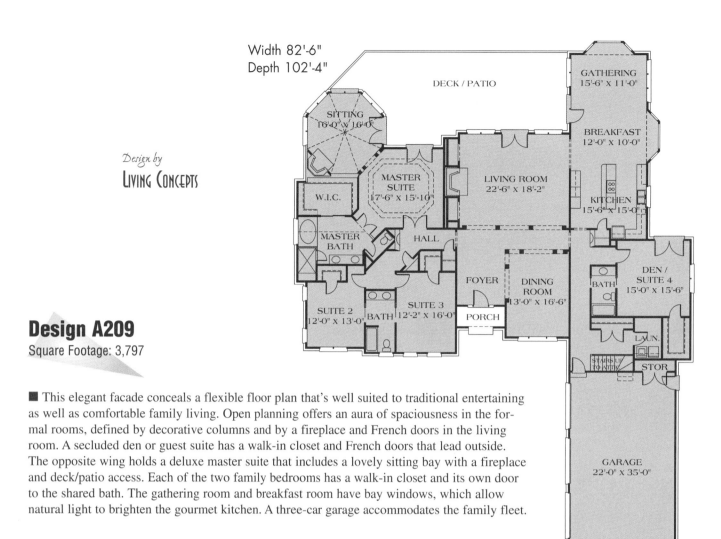

Width 82'-6"
Depth 102'-4"

DECK / PATIO

GATHERING
15'-6" x 11'-0"

SITTING
16'-0" x 16'-0"

BREAKFAST
12'-0" x 10'-0"

Design by
LIVING CONCEPTS

MASTER
SUITE
17'-6" x 15'-10"

LIVING ROOM
22'-6" x 18'-2"

W.I.C.

KITCHEN
15'-6" x 15'-0"

MASTER
BATH

HALL

DEN /
SUITE 4
15'-0" x 15'-6"

BATH

Design A209
Square Footage: 3,797

FOYER

DINING
ROOM
13'-0" x 16'-6"

SUITE 2
12'-0" x 13'-0"

BATH

SUITE 3
12'-2" x 16'-0"

PORCH

LAUN.

STAIRS UP
TO ATTIC

STOR.

■ This elegant facade conceals a flexible floor plan that's well suited to traditional entertaining as well as comfortable family living. Open planning offers an aura of spaciousness in the formal rooms, defined by decorative columns and by a fireplace and French doors in the living room. A secluded den or guest suite has a walk-in closet and French doors that lead outside. The opposite wing holds a deluxe master suite that includes a lovely sitting bay with a fireplace and deck/patio access. Each of the two family bedrooms has a walk-in closet and its own door to the shared bath. The gathering room and breakfast room have bay windows, which allow natural light to brighten the gourmet kitchen. A three-car garage accommodates the family fleet.

GARAGE
22'-0" x 35'-0"

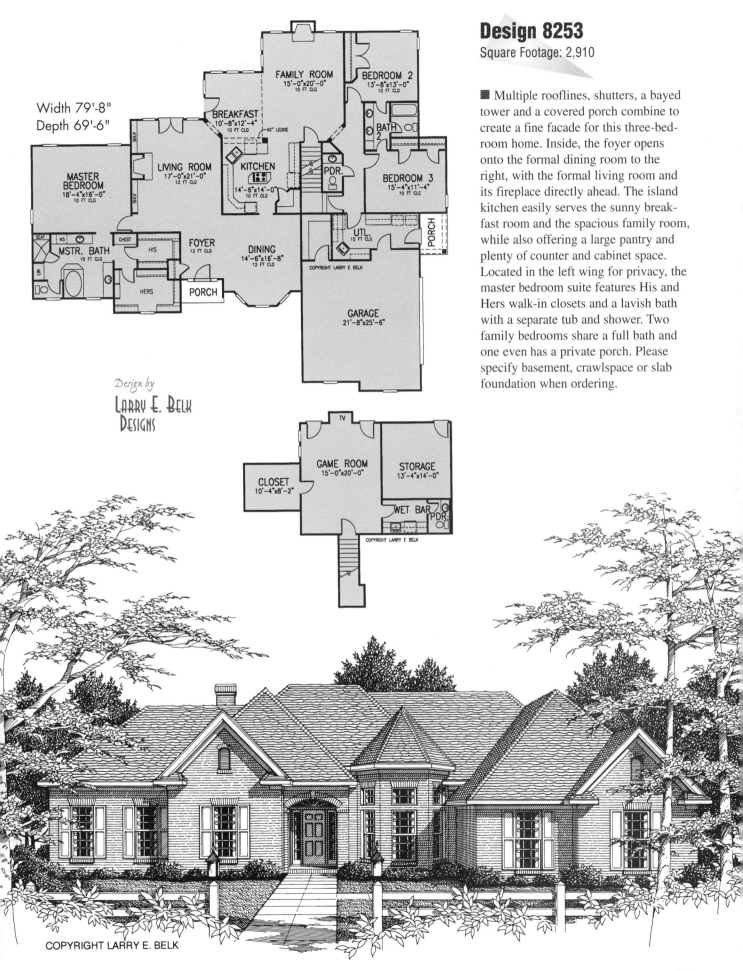

Width 79'-8"
Depth 69'-6"

MASTER BEDROOM
18'-4"x16'-0"
10 FT CLG

MSTR. BATH
10 FT CLG

SEAT
KS
CHEST
HIS
HERS

FOYER
12 FT CLG

PORCH

LIVING ROOM
17'-0"x21'-0"
12 FT CLG

KITCHEN
14'-6"x14'-0"
10 FT CLG

BREAKFAST
10'-8"x12'-4"
10 FT CLG

FAMILY ROOM
15'-0"x20'-0"
10 FT CLG

42" LEDGE

BEDROOM 2
13'-8"x13'-0"
10 FT CLG

BATH 2

PDR.

BEDROOM 3
15'-4"x11'-4"
10 FT CLG

DINING
14'-6"x16'-8"
12 FT CLG

UTL.
10 FT CLG

PORCH

COPYRIGHT LARRY E BELK

GARAGE
21'-8"x25'-6"

Design by
LARRY E. BELK
DESIGNS

CLOSET
10'-4"x8'-2"

GAME ROOM
15'-0"x20'-0"

STORAGE
13'-4"x14'-0"

TV

WET BAR
PDR.

COPYRIGHT LARRY E BELK

COPYRIGHT LARRY E. BELK

Design 8253
Square Footage: 2,910

■ Multiple rooflines, shutters, a bayed tower and a covered porch combine to create a fine facade for this three-bedroom home. Inside, the foyer opens onto the formal dining room to the right, with the formal living room and its fireplace directly ahead. The island kitchen easily serves the sunny breakfast room and the spacious family room, while also offering a large pantry and plenty of counter and cabinet space. Located in the left wing for privacy, the master bedroom suite features His and Hers walk-in closets and a lavish bath with a separate tub and shower. Two family bedrooms share a full bath and one even has a private porch. Please specify basement, crawlspace or slab foundation when ordering.

Rear Elevation

Design 9156
Square Footage: 2,885

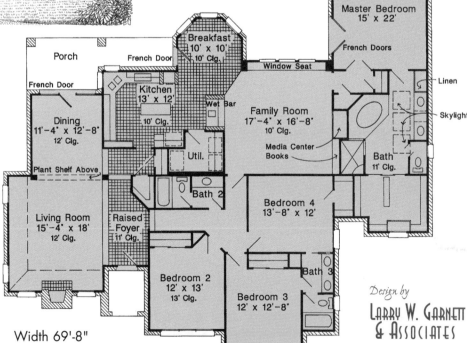

Sitting Area
10' x 10'

Gazebo Clg.

Master Bedroom
15' x 22'

French Doors

Linen

Breakfast
10' x 10'
10' Clg.

Porch

French Door

Window Seat

Skylights

Kitchen
13' x 12'

Wet Bar

Family Room
17'-4" x 16'-8"
10' Clg.

Bath
11' Clg.

French Door

Dining
11'-4" x 12'-8"
12' Clg.

10' Clg.

Media Center
Books

Plant Shelf Above

Util.

Bath 2

Bedroom 4
13'-8" x 12'

Living Room
15'-4" x 18'
12' Clg.

Raised
Foyer
11' Clg.

Bath 3

Bedroom 2
12' x 13'
13' Clg.

Bedroom 3
12' x 12'-8"

Design by
Larry W. Garnett & Associates

■ The entire floor plan of this house is dedicated to making the owners feel at home. The master bedroom includes an octagonal sitting area with gazebo ceiling and French doors to the rear yard. Three sky-lights illuminate a lavish master bath with tub, shower, and dual vanities, as well as abundant closet space. Three family bedrooms and two full baths complete the sleeping areas. A large family room features a wet bar, a built-in media center and book-shelves. A breakfast bay is adjacent to the island kitchen. To the left of the home, formal areas include the dining room with French door and the living room with a fireplace and plant shelf.

Width 69'-8"
Depth 68'-4"

Design A107

Square Footage: 3,377

■ Traditional in nature, this home is designed with classic embellishments. An arched entry, circle-top windows, corner quoins and a bay window all lend their appeal to the facade. The floor plan is classic in nature, as well. Centered around the family room, additional rooms include a formal living room, formal dining room, home office (or study) and fully windowed breakfast room. The kitchen has an island cooktop and loads of counterspace. You'll love the special appointments in the master suite: tray ceiling, two walk-in closets, nearby study or fourth bedroom and corner whirlpool tub. The two-car garage has extra storage space. Note the covered porch to the rear, with doors leading from the family room and the office to the outside.

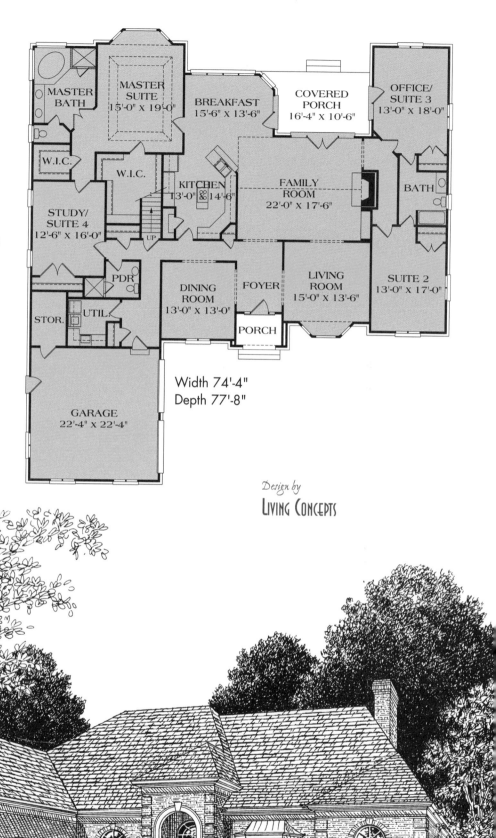

MASTER BATH

MASTER SUITE
15'-0" x 19'-0"

BREAKFAST
15'-6" x 13'-6"

COVERED PORCH
16'-4" x 10'-6"

OFFICE/ SUITE 3
13'-0" x 18'-0"

W.I.C.

W.I.C.

KITCHEN
13'-0" x 14'-6"

FAMILY ROOM
22'-0" x 17'-6"

BATH

STUDY/ SUITE 4
12'-6" x 16'-0"

UP

SUITE 2
13'-0" x 17'-0"

PDR

DINING ROOM
13'-0" x 13'-0"

FOYER

LIVING ROOM
15'-0" x 13'-6"

STOR.

UTIL.

PORCH

GARAGE
22'-4" x 22'-4"

Width 74'-4"
Depth 77'-8"

Design by
LIVING CONCEPTS

Design T238

Square Footage: 2,814

■ Space to move and room to live well—that's the promise of this elegant one-story design. From the columned entry, the plan opens to a foyer with tray ceiling and extends along a central hallway. The formal dining room, with nearby wet bar, opposes the private study at the other side of the foyer. Both also open to the hallway for easy access. The great room is designed for super gatherings. It is introduced by columns at the hallway entry, has two double-door accesses to the rear covered porch and sports a focal-point fireplace. The breakfast room also accesses the porch and connects to the kitchen (note the island work counter here). Two bedrooms sharing a full bath are on the right side of the plan. The master suite is on the left side. Look for all the best features: walk-in closet, huge shower, whirlpool tub, double sinks and compartmented toilet.

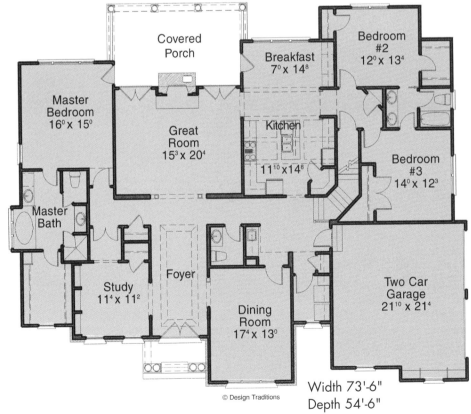

Covered Porch

Master Bedroom
16⁰ x 15⁰

Great Room
15³ x 20⁴

Breakfast
7⁰ x 14⁸

Kitchen
11¹⁰ x 14⁸

Bedroom #2
12⁰ x 13⁴

Bedroom #3
14⁰ x 12³

Master Bath

Study
11⁴ x 11²

Foyer

Dining Room
17⁴ x 13⁰

Two Car Garage
21¹⁰ x 21⁴

© Design Traditions

Width 73'-6"
Depth 54'-6"

Design by
Design Traditions

86

Keeping Room
16⁴ x 11²

Breakfast
14⁶ x 13⁸

Covered Porch

Master Bedroom
18⁰ x 15⁴

Kitchen

Dining Room
17⁴ x 12⁵

Great Room
17⁴ x 15³

Master Bath

One Car Garage
17⁴ x 12⁵

17⁴ x 12⁵

Width 75'-0"
Depth 70'-0"

Bedroom #2
14⁰ x 11⁴

Two Car Garage
21⁴ x 21⁴

Bedroom #3
12⁸ x 13⁸

Bath

© Design Traditions

Design by
DESIGN TRADITIONS

Design T240

Square Footage: 2,973

■ This home has a rather unique floor plan—and for those who like to entertain in style, it works well. Enter through double doors and find a bedroom or study immediately to the right. Through columns, straight ahead, is a large, open area defined by more columns, that holds the formal dining room and the great room (a fireplace and built-in bookshelves are amenities here). Views here are stunning, past the covered porch and on to the backyard. The kitchen separates this area from the breakfast nook and keeping room—perfect for more casual pursuits. Each bedroom has a private bath and walk-in closet. The master suite has porch access and a lovely tray ceiling. Notice the two separate garages—one a two-car garage and the other a one-car garage.

Design 9455

Square Footage: 2,835

■ Besides all the great living on the main level of this house, there's additional space under the right side. It will complement first-floor living areas: formal living and dining rooms, private den, family room and breakfast nook. The kitchen has an island work area and overlooks the wooden deck reached from the nook.

Fireplaces warm both the family and living rooms. Three bedrooms include a master suite with a tray-vaulted ceiling. There are bay windows in the master bedroom and one of the two family bedrooms that complete the sleeping quarters. Please specify basement or crawl-space foundation when ordering

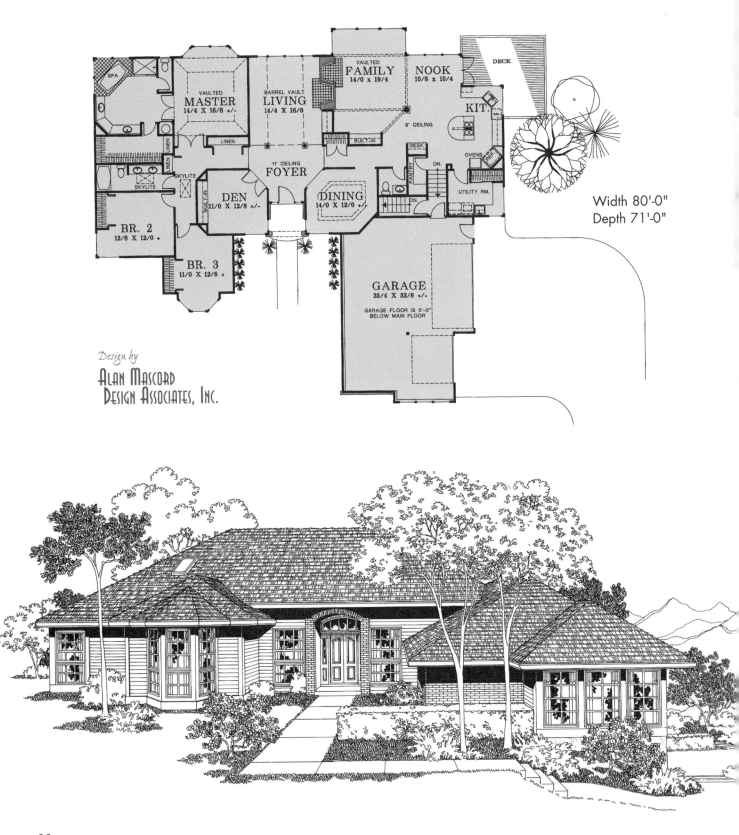

Width 80'-0"
Depth 71'-0"

Design by
Alan Mascord
Design Associates, Inc.

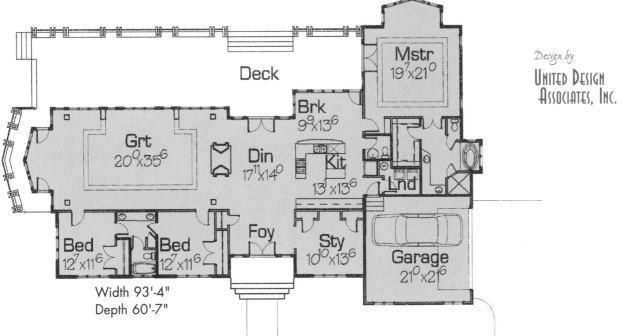

Deck

Mstr
19⁷x21⁰

Design by
United Design
Associates, Inc.

Brk
9⁹x13⁶

Grt
20⁰x35⁶

Din
17¹¹x14⁰

Kit
13⁰x13⁶

Lnd

Bed
12⁷x11⁶

Bed
12⁷x11⁶

Foy

Sty
10⁰x13⁶

Garage
21⁰x21⁰

Width 93'-4"
Depth 60'-7"

Design V004

Square Footage: 2,927

■ This is truly a light-filled design—with full and transom windows in many of the interior spaces to give a feeling of connectedness to the outdoors. Double doors open directly to the foyer. At the right is a study with double closets. Ahead is the formal dining area, separated from the great room by a through-fireplace. The island kitchen has an attached nook and nearby powder room. The full-width deck to the rear of the plan can be reached from the dining area, the great room and the master bedroom. Family bedrooms share a full bath with dual sinks. The master bedroom boasts a private bath with garden tub and walk-in closet. A congenial sitting area works well for a chaise or other comfy reading chair.

Design S132

Square Footage: 3,823
Unfinished Bonus Space:
 1,018 square feet

■ This Neo-Classical home has plenty to offer! The elegant entrance is flanked by a formal dining room on the left and a beam-ceilinged study—complete with a fireplace—on the right. An angled kitchen is sure to please with a work island, plenty of counter and cabinet space and a snack counter which it shares with the sunny breakfast room. A family room with a second fireplace is nearby. The lavish master bedroom suite features many amenities, including a huge walk-in closet, a three-sided fireplace and a lavish bath. Two secondary bedrooms each have private baths. A three-car garage easily shelters the family fleet.

Design by
ARCHIVAL DESIGNS

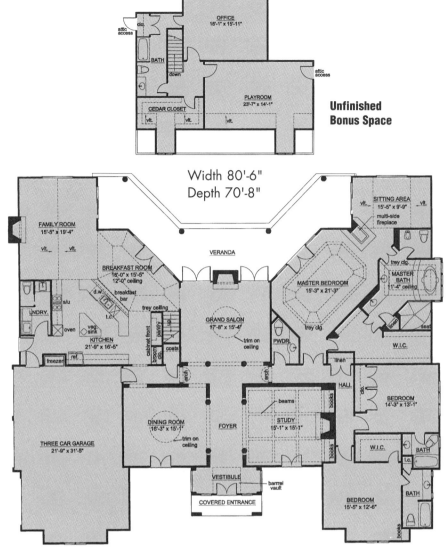

Unfinished Bonus Space

Width 80'-6"
Depth 70'-8"

Design A221

Square Footage: 4,405
Bonus Room: 539 square feet

■ Whoever says luxury can't be found on one level hasn't seen this attractive stucco home. From the high class exterior to the very accommodating interior, this design is sure to please. If entertaining is your forte, this plan is the one for you. Note the way the formal dining room and spacious grand room flow into each other—making formal dinner parties a breeze. If a casual get-together is more your style, take a look at the kitchen/ bayed breakfast area/sun room space. The master retreat is aptly named and includes amenities such as a bayed sitting area, a two-sided fireplace, two closets (one a walk-in), His and Hers bathrooms and direct access to the rear deck. The three secondary bedrooms are complete with their own full baths, providing plenty of room for family and friends.

Design by
LIVING CONCEPTS

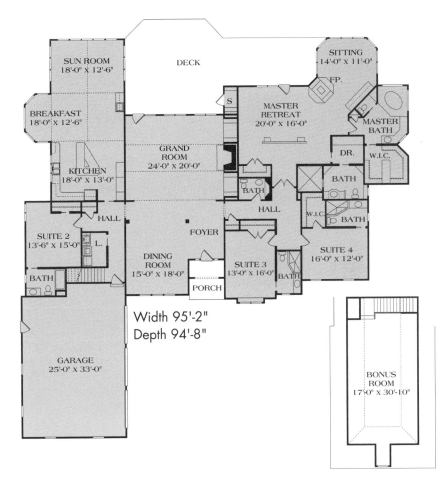

Width 95'-2"
Depth 94'-8"

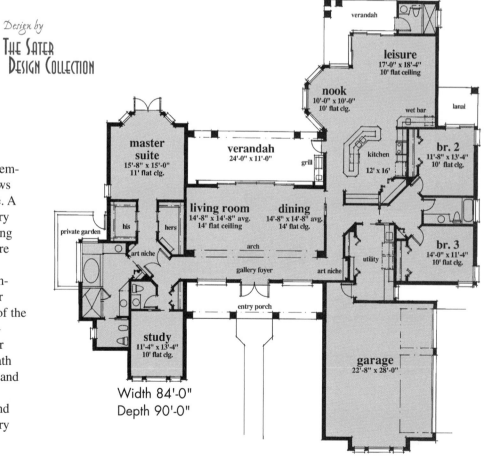

Design by
THE SATER
DESIGN COLLECTION

Design 6604

Square Footage: 2,978

■ This Neo-Classic split design exemplifies elegance. Circlehead windows grace the front from the streetscape. A large covered entry leads to a gallery foyer that overlooks the formal living and dining rooms. Informal areas are located in a private wing. A large kitchen, nook and leisure room complete with wet bar overlook the rear veranda and enjoy fantastic views of the backyard. Also on this side are secondary bedrooms. The gallery foyer also leads to the master suite. Its bath features large His and Hers closets and vanities, a garden tub and a glass-enclosed shower. A private study and large utility room round out this very special home.

verandah

leisure
17'-0" x 18'-4"
10' flat ceiling

nook
10'-0" x 10'-0"
10' flat clg.

wet bar

lanai

br. 2
11'-8" x 13'-4"
10' flat clg.

master
suite
15'-8" x 15'-0"
11' flat clg.

verandah
24'-0" x 11'-0"

grill

kitchen
12' x 16'

living room
14'-8" x 14'-8" avg.
14' flat ceiling

dining
14'-8" x 14'-8" avg.
14' flat clg.

private garden

his

hers

art niche

arch

gallery foyer

art niche

utility

br. 3
14'-0" x 11'-4"
10' flat clg.

entry porch

study
11'-4" x 13'-4"
10' flat clg.

garage
22'-8" x 28'-0"

Width 84'-0"
Depth 90'-0"

■ Classic columns, a tiled roof and beautiful arched windows herald a gracious interior for this fine home. Arched windows also mark the entrance into the vaulted living room with a tiled fireplace. The dining room opens off the foyer with vaulted ceiling. Filled with light from a wall of sliding glass doors, the family room leads to the covered patio (note the wet bar and range that enhance outdoor living). The kitchen features a vaulted ceiling and unfolds into the roomy nook which boasts French doors onto the patio. The master bedroom also has patio access and shares a dual fireplace with the master bath. A solarium lights this space. A vaulted study/bedroom sits between two additional bedrooms—all share a full bath.

Design 8624
Square Footage: 2,987

Width 74'-4"
Depth 82'-4"

Design by
HOME DESIGN SERVICES

This home, as shown in the photograph, may differ from the actual blueprints. For more detailed information, please check the floor plans carefully.

Photo by Peter A. Burg

Design by
HOME PLANNERS

QUOTE ONE®
Cost to build? See page 434
to order complete cost estimate
to build this house in your area!

Width 77'-4"
Depth 74'-8"

COVERED MASTER SUITE TERRACE

COVERED ENTERTAINMENT TERRACE

SITTING

MASTER SUITE
15⁰ x 19⁶
SLOPED CEILING

PLANT SHELF ABV

WALK-IN CLOSET

MASTER BATH

TUB

SHWR

PDR

WET BAR

W.I.C.

DEN/STUDY
11⁸ x 13¹⁰
SLOPED CEILING

PLANTER WALL

PRIVACY PATIO

GARDEN AREA

PRIVACY PATIO WALL

HVAC

MECH

LINEN

NICHE

FOYER
9'-0" CLG

LIVING RM
22⁰ x 14⁰
SUNKEN
14'-0" CLG

RAISED HEARTH

PLANT SHELF ABV

KIT
13⁰ x 15²
9'-0" CLG

OWN PANTRY

BREAKFAST BAR

NOOK
9⁶ x 12⁰
11'-0" CLG

11'-0" CLG
9'-0" CLG

FAMILY RM
14⁰ x 19⁴

CABANA

SHWR

BATH

BEDRM
11⁴ x 12⁰
9'-0" CLG

STORAGE

LINEN

WH

HVAC

DINING RM
13⁰ x 11⁰
13'-0" CLG

PLANT SHELF ABV

LAUNDRY

LT

BEDRM
12⁸ x 11⁶
9'-0" CLG

PATIO WALL

COVERED PORCH

GARDEN AREA

PLANTER WALL

GARAGE
21⁴ x 21⁰

Design 3475
Square Footage: 3,286

L

■ The colorful, tiled hip roof with varying roof planes and wide overhangs sets off this Spanish design. Meanwhile, the sheltered front entrance is both dramatic and inviting with double doors opening to the central foyer. In the sunken living room, a curved, raised-hearth fireplace acts as a focal point. Double glass doors lead to a covered terrace. The U-shaped kitchen is efficient with its island work surface, breakfast bar, pantry and broom closet. An informal nook delights with its projecting bay and high ceiling. This generous, open area extends to include the family room, catering to many of the family's informal living activities. A major floor-planning feature of this design is found in the sleeping arrangements; notice the complete separation of the parents' and children's bedroom facilities.

© **The Sater Group, Inc.**

lanai
58'-0" x 10'-0" avg.

leisure
20'-0" x 19'-0"
10' clg.

nook
10' x 11'
10' clg.

living
15'-2" x 12'-0"
13' clg.

master
14'-0" x 18'-2"
13' tray clg.

master garden

atrium

fountain

entertainment center

arch

arch

art niche

gallery

high glass

guest patio

desk

kitchen
13' 15'

arch

dining
15'-0" x 12'-8"
13' clg.

arch

foyer

books

study
13'-8" x 13'-10"
13' clg.

guest
14'-6" x 15'-0"
10' clg.

gallery

art niche

entry

guest
13'-0" x 14'-4"
10' clg.

garden

util.

garage
22'-0" x 32'-0"

© The Sater Group, Inc.

Width 90'-0"
Depth 105'-0"

Design by
**The Sater
Design Collection**

Design 6657
Square Footage: 3,244

■ A high, hip roof and contemporary fanlight windows set the tone for this elegant master plan. The grand foyer opens to the formal dining and living rooms that are set apart with arches, highlighted with art niches and framed with walls of windows. Discreetly removed from the entertaining area is the leisure room, where casual living takes precedence. Featuring a gourmet kitchen, breakfast nook and leisure room with built-in entertainment center, this area has full view and access to the lanai. Secondary bedrooms are privately situated through a gallery hall and both have private baths and walk-in closets. The master wing is preceded with a gallery hall and houses a full study and master suite with a private garden. An oversized closet and spa-style bath complete this luxurious retreat.

Design 6641

Square Footage: 3,896

■ This elegant exterior blends a classical look with a contemporary feel. Corner quoins and round columns highlight the front elevation. The formal living room, complete with a fireplace and a wet bar, and the formal dining room access the lanai through three pairs of French doors. The well-appointed kitchen features an island prep sink, walk-in pantry and a desk. The secondary bedrooms are full guest suites, located away from the private owner's wing. The master suite has enormous His and Hers closets, built-ins, a wet bar and three-sided fireplace that separates the sitting room and the bedroom. The luxurious bath features a stunning, rounded glass-block shower and a whirlpool tub.

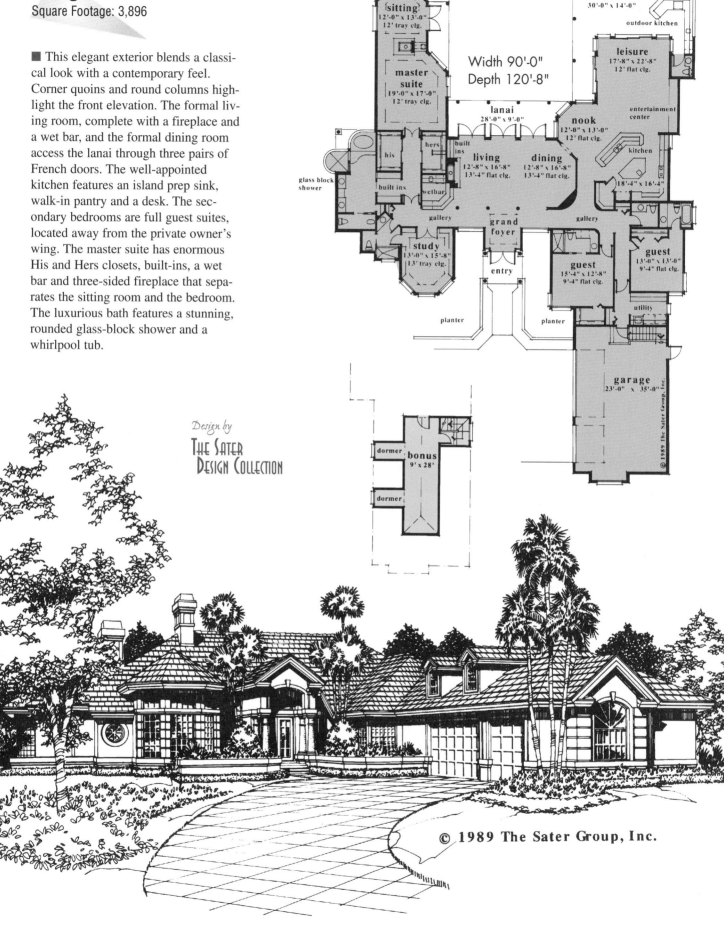

Design by
THE SATER
DESIGN COLLECTION

© 1989 The Sater Group, Inc.

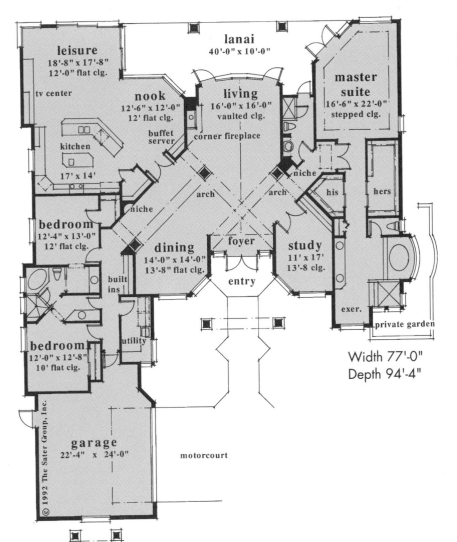

leisure
18'-8" x 17'-8"
12'-0" flat clg.

tv center

lanai
40'-0" x 10'-0"

master suite
16'-6" x 22'-0"
stepped clg.

nook
12'-6" x 12'-0"
12' flat clg.

living
16'-0" x 16'-0"
vaulted clg.

buffet server

corner fireplace

kitchen
17' x 14'

niche

his

hers

arch

arch

niche

bedroom
12'-4" x 13'-0"
12' flat clg.

dining
14'-0" x 14'-0"
13'-8" flat clg.

foyer

study
11' x 17'
13'-8 clg.

built ins

entry

bedroom
12'-0" x 12'-8"
10' flat clg.

utility

exer.

private garden

© 1992 The Sater Group, Inc.

garage
22'-4" x 24'-0"

motorcourt

Design 6642
Square Footage: 3,743

■ An exciting elevation makes the exterior of this home as special as the interior details. A custom grill archway and keystone columns add to the style. The gable roof detail at the entry is carried through to the rear of the house. Columns and archways grace the formal areas of the home. A bow window at the living room overlooks the lanai. A large nook, complete with a buffet server, highlights the family area. The master bedroom has a stepped ceiling and overlooks the lanai. The bath features His and Hers closets, a garden tub and an area for exercise equipment.

Width 77'-0"
Depth 94'-4"

Design by
The Sater
Design Collection

Design 6609

Square Footage: 3,324

■ If spacious, contemporary living sounds like your style, this home may be just the ticket. With gardens on either side, the barrel-ceilinged entry sets the tone for a grand interior. Raised ceilings in the open living and dining rooms—as well as in the study—lend light and air. Through an archway to the right, the gourmet kitchen opens up with an island cook-top and an abundance of storage space. A leisure room here features a tray ceiling and access to a veranda. Nearby, two bedrooms share a full bath with dual lavatories. An arch-way on the left side of the plan leads to the master bedroom suite where elegance is the byword. His and Hers closets and a lavish bath overlooking a private garden define this room. A study with plenty of built-ins and a full bath with outside access complete the plan.

Design by
THE SATER
DESIGN COLLECTION

Width 74'-0"
Depth 89'-8"

leisure
20'-0" x 24'-0"
tray clg.

verandah
40'-0" x 11'-0"

grill

kitchen
15' x 18'

master
suite
16'-2" x 22'-0"
tray clg.

living
17'-2" x 14'-6"
12' clg.

guest
13'-0" x 13'-6"
10' clg.

hers

his

arch

desk

arch

gallery

built ins

foyer
barrel clg.

dining
12'-8" x 17'-8"
12' clg.

utility

guest
13'-0" x 13'-2"
10' clg.

study
11'-8" x 12'-0"
12' clg.

entry
barrel clg.

private garden

garden

garden

© 1991 The Sater Group, Inc.

garage
22'-0" x 28'-0"

This home, as shown in the photograph, may differ from the actual blueprints. For more detailed information, please check the floor plans carefully.

Photo by Oscar Thompson

98

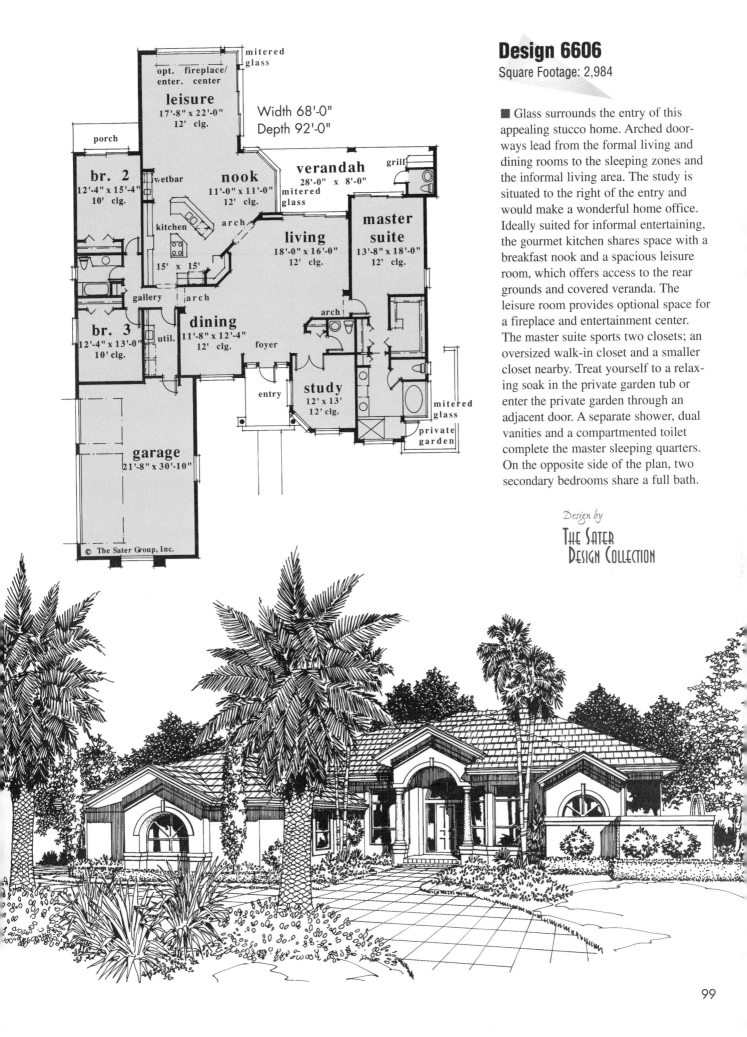

leisure
17'-8" x 22'-0"
12' clg.

opt. fireplace/
enter. center

mitered glass

porch

br. 2
12'-4" x 15'-4"
10' clg.

wetbar

nook
11'-0" x 11'-0"
12' clg.

verandah
28'-0" x 8'-0"
mitered glass

grill

kitchen

arch

living
18'-0" x 16'-0"
12' clg.

master suite
13'-8" x 18'-0"
12' clg.

15' x 15'

gallery

arch

br. 3
12'-4" x 13'-0"
10' clg.

util.

dining
11'-8" x 12'-4"
12' clg.

foyer

arch

entry

study
12' x 13'
12' clg.

mitered glass

private garden

garage
21'-8" x 30'-10"

© The Sater Group, Inc.

Design 6606

Square Footage: 2,984

Width 68'-0"
Depth 92'-0"

■ Glass surrounds the entry of this appealing stucco home. Arched door-ways lead from the formal living and dining rooms to the sleeping zones and the informal living area. The study is situated to the right of the entry and would make a wonderful home office. Ideally suited for informal entertaining, the gourmet kitchen shares space with a breakfast nook and a spacious leisure room, which offers access to the rear grounds and covered veranda. The leisure room provides optional space for a fireplace and entertainment center. The master suite sports two closets; an oversized walk-in closet and a smaller closet nearby. Treat yourself to a relaxing soak in the private garden tub or enter the private garden through an adjacent door. A separate shower, dual vanities and a compartmented toilet complete the master sleeping quarters. On the opposite side of the plan, two secondary bedrooms share a full bath.

Design by
**The Sater
Design Collection**

Design 6643

Square Footage: 4,028

■ An interesting roofline and custom details add to the charm of this home. The raised entry has a stepped column and arch detail that can be seen throughout the design. The foyer and dining room feature stepped arches and ceiling treatments. Secondary bedrooms provide full guest suites. An arched entryway leads into the master suite highlighted by a bayed sitting area. The bath has a bayed whirlpool tub and a walk-in shower.

Design by
THE SATER DESIGN COLLECTION

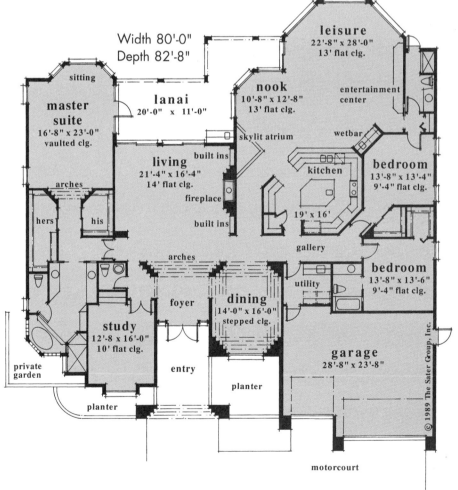

Width 80'-0"
Depth 82'-8"

leisure
22'-8" x 28'-0"
13' flat clg.

nook
10'-8" x 12'-8"
13' flat clg.

entertainment center

sitting

master suite
16'-8" x 23'-0"
vaulted clg.

lanai
20'-0" x 11'-0"

skylit atrium

wetbar

living
21'-4" x 16'-4"
14' flat clg.

built ins

bedroom
13'-8" x 13'-4"
9'-4" flat clg.

kitchen
19' x 16'

arches

hers   his

fireplace

built ins

gallery

bedroom
13'-8" x 13'-6"
9'-4" flat clg.

arches

utility

foyer

dining
14'-0" x 16'-0"
stepped clg.

study
12'-8" x 16'-0"
10' flat clg.

private garden

entry

planter

garage
28'-8" x 23'-8"

planter

© 1989 The Sater Group, Inc.

planter

motorcourt

100

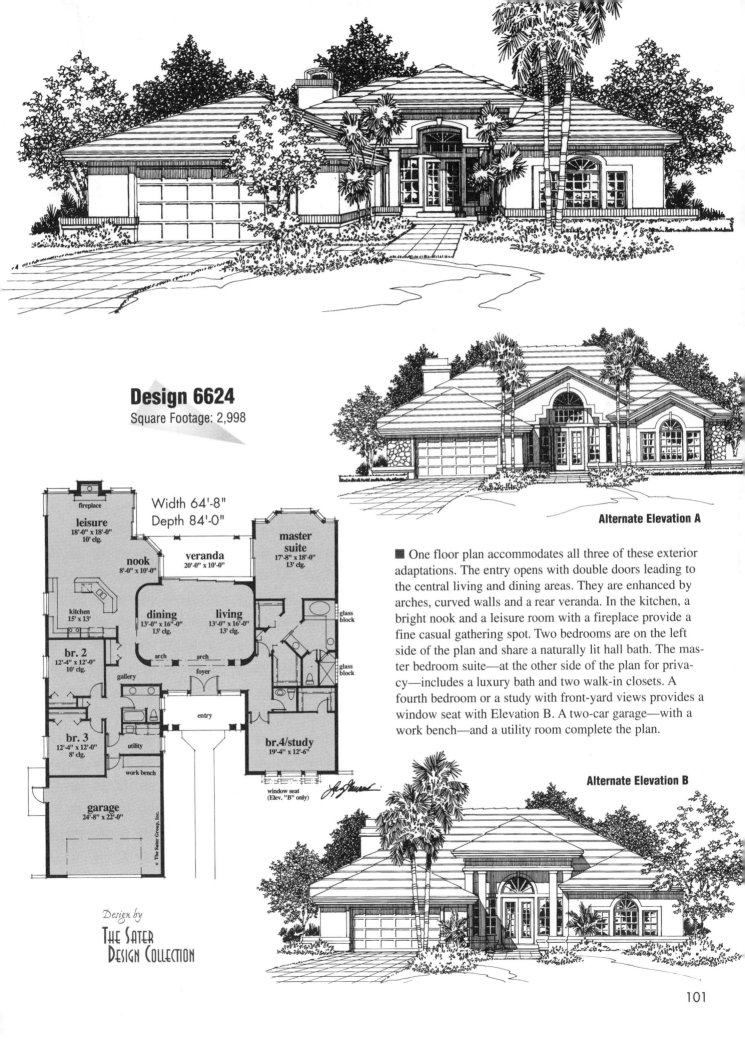

Design 6624
Square Footage: 2,998

Width 64'-8"
Depth 84'-0"

Alternate Elevation A

■ One floor plan accommodates all three of these exterior adaptations. The entry opens with double doors leading to the central living and dining areas. They are enhanced by arches, curved walls and a rear veranda. In the kitchen, a bright nook and a leisure room with a fireplace provide a fine casual gathering spot. Two bedrooms are on the left side of the plan and share a naturally lit hall bath. The master bedroom suite—at the other side of the plan for privacy—includes a luxury bath and two walk-in closets. A fourth bedroom or a study with front-yard views provides a window seat with Elevation B. A two-car garage—with a work bench—and a utility room complete the plan.

Alternate Elevation B

Design by
THE SATER
DESIGN COLLECTION

101

Design 8087

Square Footage: 5,183
Loft: 238 square feet

■ Contemporary styling coupled with traditional finishes of brick and stucco make this home a stand-out that caters to the discriminating few. The entry, with a two-story ceiling, steps down into an enormous great room with a see-through fireplace. A formal living room is open from the entry and begins one wing of the home. The bedroom wing provides three bedrooms, each with a large amenity-filled bath, as well as a study area and a recreation room. The opposite wing houses the dining room, kitchen, breakfast room and two more bedrooms. The kitchen offers a curved window overlooking the side yard and a cooktop island with a vegetable sink. A stair leads to a loft overlooking the great room and entry.

Design by
Larry E. Belk Designs

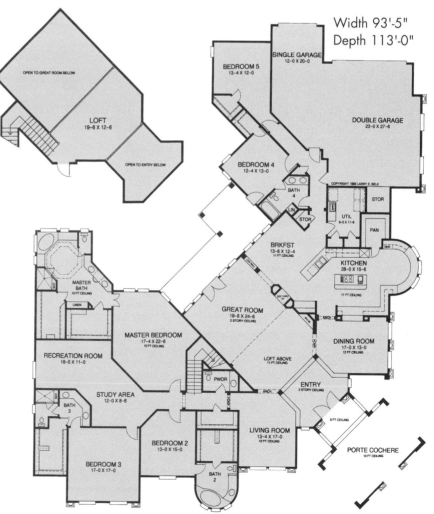

Width 93'-5"
Depth 113'-0"

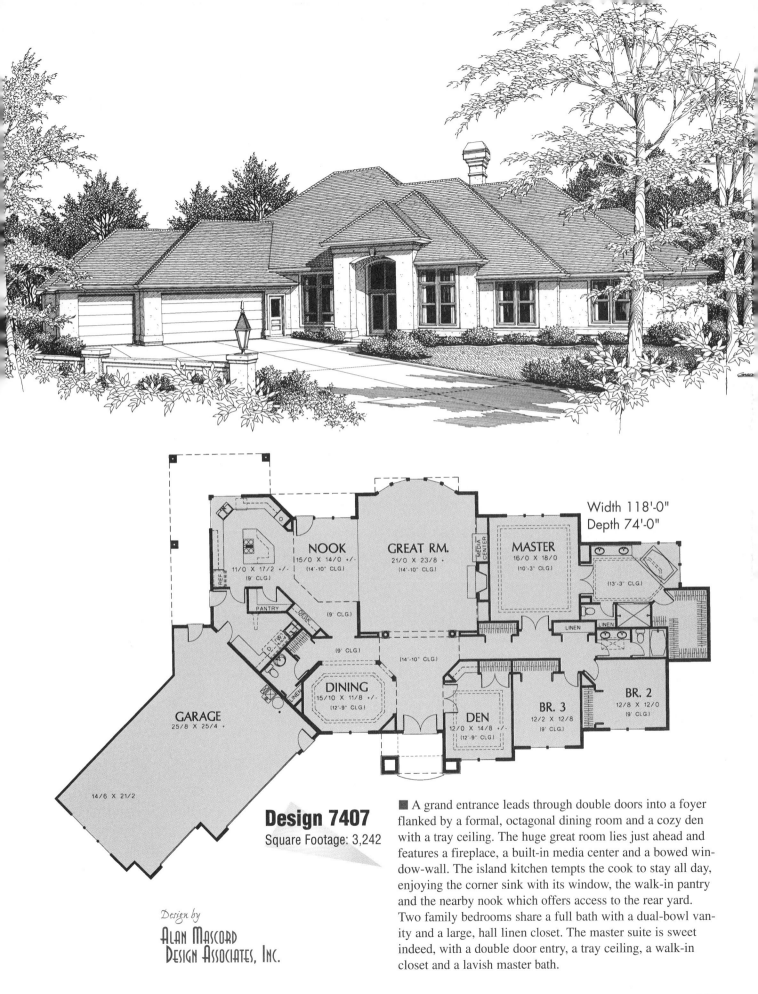

Width 118'-0"
Depth 74'-0"

NOOK
15/0 X 14/0 +/-
(14'-10" CLG.)

GREAT RM.
21/0 X 23/8
(14'-10" CLG.)

MASTER
16/0 X 18/0
(10'-3" CLG.)

MEDIA CENTER

(9' CLG.)

REF

PANTRY

DESK

(9' CLG.)

(13'-3" CLG.)

LINEN

LINEN   LINEN

(9' CLG.)

(14'-10" CLG.)

DINING
15/10 X 11/8 +/-
(12'-9" CLG.)

GARAGE
25/8 X 25/4 +/-

DEN
12/0 X 14/8
(12'-9" CLG.)

BR. 3
12/2 X 12/8
(9' CLG.)

BR. 2
12/8 X 12/0
(9' CLG.)

14/6 X 21/2

Design 7407
Square Footage: 3,242

Design by
**ALAN MASCORD
DESIGN ASSOCIATES, INC.**

■ A grand entrance leads through double doors into a foyer flanked by a formal, octagonal dining room and a cozy den with a tray ceiling. The huge great room lies just ahead and features a fireplace, a built-in media center and a bowed window-wall. The island kitchen tempts the cook to stay all day, enjoying the corner sink with its window, the walk-in pantry and the nearby nook which offers access to the rear yard. Two family bedrooms share a full bath with a dual-bowl vanity and a large, hall linen closet. The master suite is sweet indeed, with a double door entry, a tray ceiling, a walk-in closet and a lavish master bath.

Design 8665

Square Footage: 2,799

■ An impressive exterior leads to a grand interior. The living areas are highlighted by volume ceilings and double doors. A walk-in closet and nearby full bath add to the utility of the den. The central kitchen with island is convenient to the living, dining, breakfast and family rooms. The family room features a fireplace and access to the covered porch. Double doors lead to the segregated master bedroom with dual walk-in closets and a spacious bath with two vanities, whirlpool tub, separate shower and an attached solarium. Three family bedrooms and a full bath are to the right of the plan.

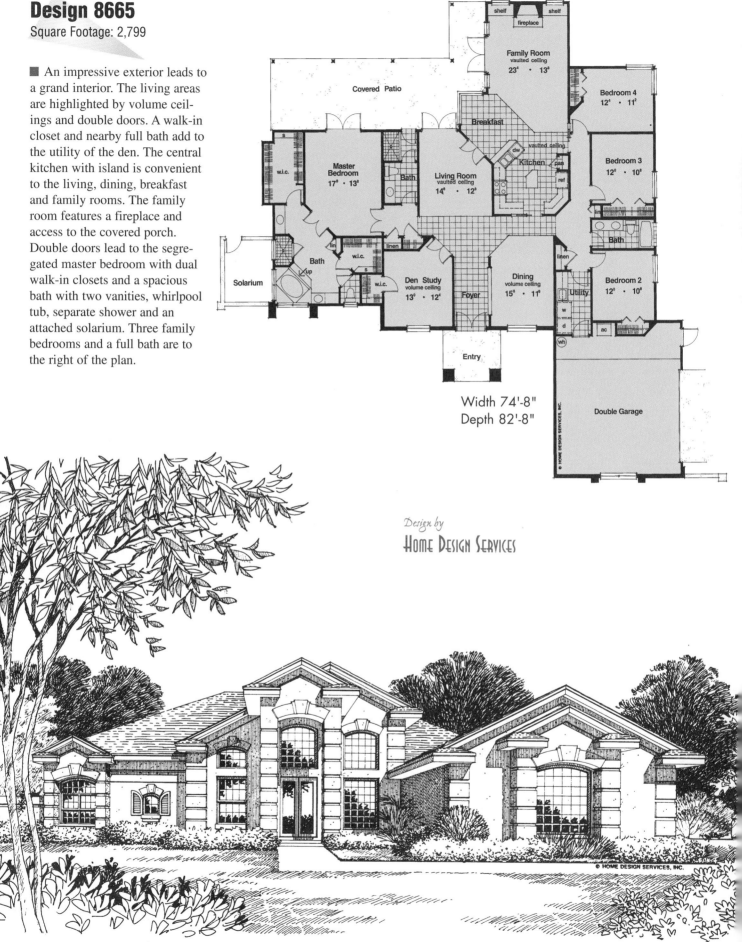

Width 74'-8"
Depth 82'-8"

Design by
HOME DESIGN SERVICES

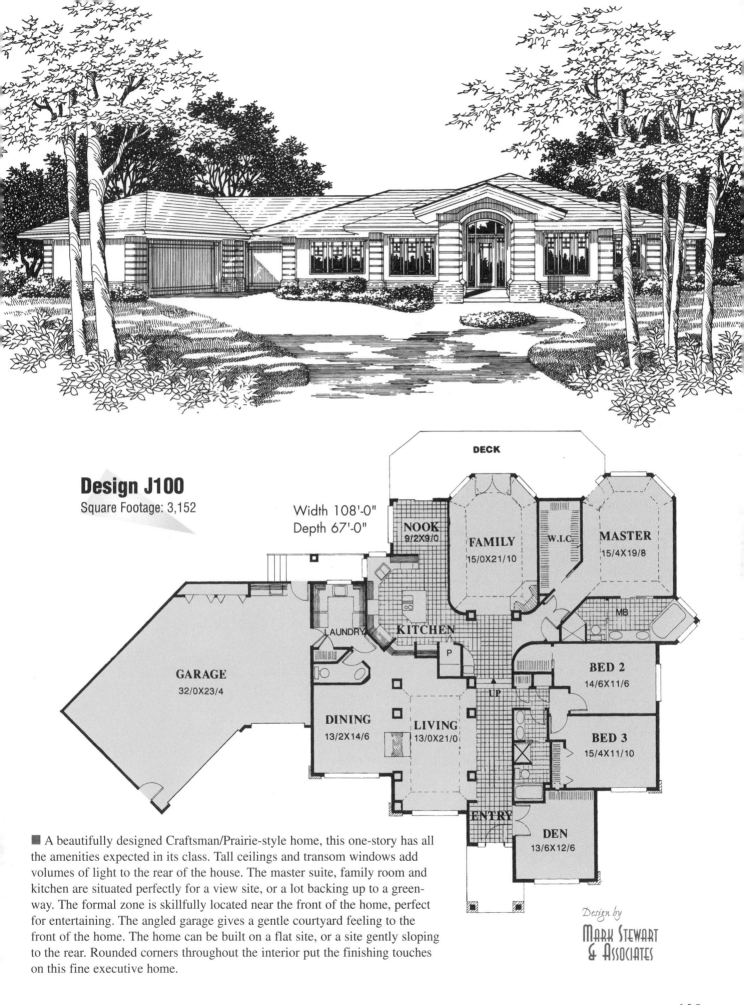

Design J100

Square Footage: 3,152

Width 108'-0"
Depth 67'-0"

DECK

NOOK
9/2X9/0

FAMILY
15/0X21/10

W.I.C

MASTER
15/4X19/8

KITCHEN

MB

LAUNDRY

P

GARAGE
32/0X23/4

BED 2
14/6X11/6

DINING
13/2X14/6

LIVING
13/0X21/0

UP

BED 3
15/4X11/10

ENTRY

DEN
13/6X12/6

■ A beautifully designed Craftsman/Prairie-style home, this one-story has all the amenities expected in its class. Tall ceilings and transom windows add volumes of light to the rear of the house. The master suite, family room and kitchen are situated perfectly for a view site, or a lot backing up to a greenway. The formal zone is skillfully located near the front of the home, perfect for entertaining. The angled garage gives a gentle courtyard feeling to the front of the home. The home can be built on a flat site, or a site gently sloping to the rear. Rounded corners throughout the interior put the finishing touches on this fine executive home.

Design by
Mark Stewart & Associates

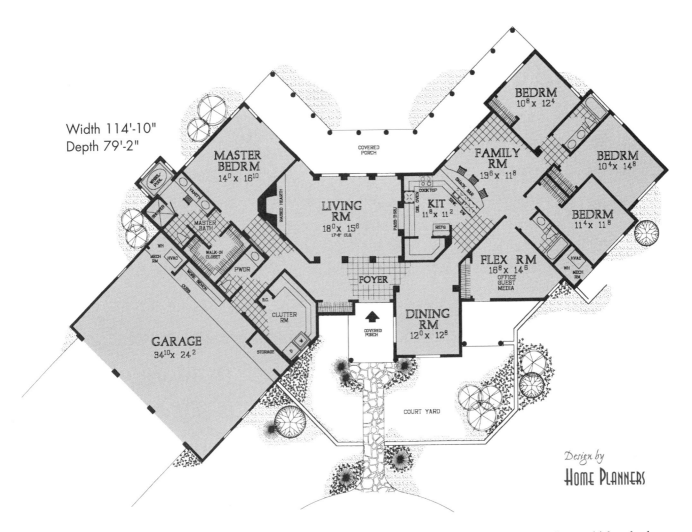

Width 114'-10"
Depth 79'-2"

MASTER BEDRM 14⁰ x 16¹⁰

LIVING RM 18⁰ x 15⁶ 17'-6" CLG.

FAMILY RM 13⁶ x 11⁸

BEDRM 10⁸ x 12⁴

BEDRM 10⁴ x 14⁸

KIT 11⁸ x 11²

BEDRM 11⁴ x 11⁸

FLEX RM 16⁸ x 14⁶ OFFICE GUEST MEDIA

FOYER

GARAGE 34¹⁰ x 24²

CLUTTER RM

DINING RM 12⁰ x 12⁸

COVERED PORCH

COURT YARD

Design by
HOME PLANNERS

Design 3629
Square Footage: 2,966
L

■ The dramatic entrance of this grand sun-country home gives way to interesting angles and optimum livability inside. Columns frame the formal living room which provides views of the rear grounds from the foyer. The private master bedroom is contained on the left portion of the plan. Here, a relaxing master bath provides an abundance of amenities that include a walk-in closet, a bumped-out whirlpool tub, a separate shower and a double-bowl vanity. A clutter room and powder room complete this wing. Centrally located for efficiency, the kitchen easily serves the living room—via a pass-through—as well as the formal dining room, family room and flex room. Three secondary bedrooms share two full baths.

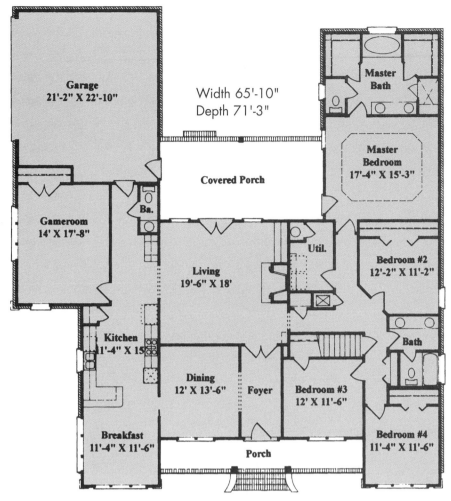

Garage
21'-2" X 22'-10"

Width 65'-10"
Depth 71'-3"

Master Bath

Covered Porch

Master Bedroom
17'-4" X 15'-3"

Ba.

Gameroom
14' X 17'-8"

Living
19'-6" X 18'

Util.

Bedroom #2
12'-2" X 11'-2"

Kitchen
11'-4" X 15'

Bath

Dining
12' X 13'-6"

Foyer

Bedroom #3
12' X 11'-6"

Breakfast
11'-4" X 11'-6"

Porch

Bedroom #4
11'-4" X 11'-6"

Design E104

Square Footage: 2,832

■ Elegant dormers and arch-topped windows offer a stately facade with this traditional design, which combines a low-maintenance exterior with an easy-living interior. Comfort and convenience abound with four bedrooms—including a spacious master suite with a raised ceiling, a whirlpool tub and separate walk-in closets—positioned for privacy just off the living area. Flaunting an inviting fireplace, built-in bookcase and French doors to the rear covered porch, the living room offers enjoyment to guests and family alike. The breakfast area allows plenty of natural light to brighten the adjoining kitchen, rich with amenities, including a built-in desk. Please specify crawlspace or slab foundation when ordering.

Design by
CHATHAM HOME
PLANNING, INC.

© Design Traditions

Design T157

Square Footage: 2,987

■ Reaching back through the centuries for its inspiration, this home reflects the grandeur that was ancient Rome...as it looked to newly independent Americans in the 1700s. The entry portico provides a classic twist: the balustrade that would have marched across the roof line of a typical Revival home trims to form the balcony outside the French doors of the study. Inside, the foyer opens on the left to a quiet study, on the right to the formal dining room, and straight ahead to a welcoming great room warmed by a fireplace. The left wing is given over to a private master suite with a master bath that offers the ultimate in luxury and a large walk-in closet. On the right side of the house, two additional bedrooms share a full bath. Separating the sleeping wings is the kitchen, with its nearby keeping room/family room. This home is designed with a basement foundation.

Deck

Master Bedroom 15⁰x17⁶

Great Room 15⁰x16⁰

Keeping/ Family Room 18³x14³

Kitchen 14⁹x12⁶

Bedroom No. 2 14⁰x12⁰

Bedroom No. 3 14⁰x12³

Dn

Study 12³x11³

Foyer

Dining Room 12⁹x16³

Two Car Garage 21⁶x21⁹

Width 74'-0"
Depth 62'-0"

Porch

Design by
DESIGN TRADITIONS

108

Porch

Master
Bedroom
14⁰x21³

Great Room
15⁹x18⁶

Breakfast
14⁹x10⁹

Bedroom
No. 2
12⁹x12⁶

Kitchen

Bedroom
No. 3
13⁹x12⁰

12⁹x16⁶

Up

Dn

Gallery

Study
12⁹x14⁰

Foyer

Dining
Room
14⁰x15⁶

Two Car
Garage
21³x23⁰

Width 72'-9"
Depth 65'-0"

Design T159
Square Footage: 2,914

■ A pedimented entry borrows from the past to lend 18th-Century charm to this Colonial adaptation, but a well-planned interior carries this design into the 21st Century. The foyer opens to a secluded study with a spider-beam ceiling and an extended-hearth fireplace set off by classic columns. A gallery hall announces the spacious great room, which offers its own fireplace and French doors to the covered porch. A tray ceiling and private door to the rear porch highlight the master suite, which also boasts a sumptuous bath with an oversized walk-in closet, a whirlpool spa-style tub and twin vanities. Family bedrooms share a full bath on the opposite side of the plan, and one has private access to the outdoors. This home is designed with a basement foundation.

Design by
DESIGN TRADITIONS

© Design Traditions

Design T156

Square Footage: 2,998

■ This Colonial adaptation enjoys classic details—like a Palladian window with an arch-top set off by a keystone—but insists on a distinctly contemporary interior. At the heart of this sophisticated floor plan lies a light-hearted spirit, with French doors in the great room to bring in the outdoors. The secluded master suite offers a private bath with twin lavatories and a walk-in closet with its own window. Each of the two family bedrooms offers a private door to a shared full bath. This home is designed with a basement foundation.

Design by
DESIGN TRADITIONS

Deck

Master Bedroom 16⁰x19³

Great Room 17³x16⁰

Breakfast 14⁰x16⁰

Bedroom No. 2 12⁰x14³

Bedroom No. 3 12⁶x14⁰

Dn

Kitchen 14⁰x15³

Living Room 12⁹x14⁰

Foyer

Dining Room 13⁹x15⁶

Two Car Garage 21³x23⁶

Porch

Width 75'-6"
Depth 57'-0"

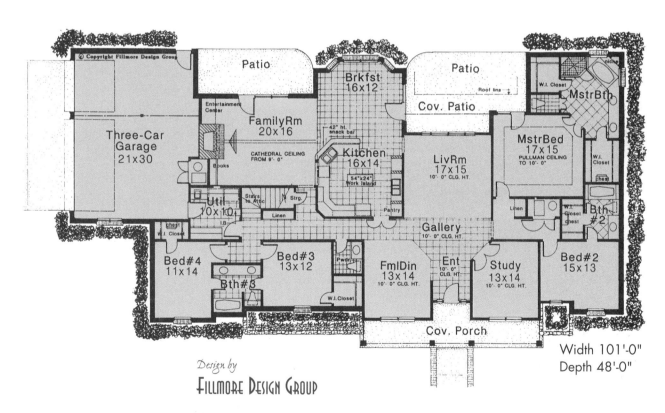

Design by

FILLMORE DESIGN GROUP

Width 101'-0"
Depth 48'-0"

Design M139
Square Footage: 3,270

■ A distinctive exterior, complete with siding, stone and brick, presents a welcoming facade on this four-bedroom home. A cathedral ceiling in the large family room, which includes a fireplace and built-ins, makes this country-style home a great choice. The island kitchen has plenty of work space and direct access to a sunny, bay-windowed breakfast room. A study and formal dining room flank the tiled entryway which leads straight into a formal living room. Three family bedrooms are ranged across the front of the house. The master suite offers plenty of seclusion as well as two walk-in closets, a lavish bath and direct access to the rear patio. A stairway leads to a future upstairs area.

Design T165

Square Footage: 3,066

Design by
DESIGN TRADITIONS

■ Descended from the architecture that developed in America's Tidewater country, this updated adaptation retains the insouciant charm of a coastal cottage. At the same time, it offers an elegance that is appropriate for any setting in any climate today. Inside, the family living area is concentrated in the center of the house. Central to the social flow in the house, the great room opens to the kitchen, the breakfast room and to the rear porch that runs across the back. The left wing contains a private master suite that includes twin walk-in closets leading into a lavish master bath. Two additional bedrooms share a bath, while Bedroom 4 (located on the right side of the house) enjoys a high level of privacy that makes it an ideal guest room. This home is designed with a basement foundation.

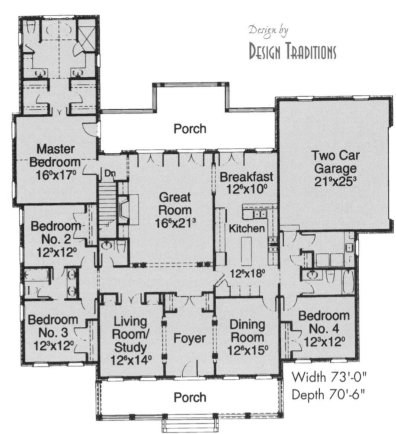

Porch

Bedroom
#2
12⁹ x 12⁶

Breakfast
14⁶ x 10⁹

Master
Bedroom
14⁰ x 21³

Great
Room
15⁹ x 18⁶

Kitchen

Up

Bedroom
#3
13⁹ x 12⁰

12⁹ x 16⁶

Dn

Study
12⁹ x 15⁶

Foyer

Dining
Room
14⁰ x 15⁶

Two Car
Garage
21³ x 23⁰

Width 72'-0"
Depth 64'-0"

Design by
DESIGN TRADITIONS

Design T239
Square Footage: 2,810

■ Four elegant columns define the front porch of this three-bedroom home. Inside, the foyer is flanked by a cozy study to the left—complete with a fireplace—and a formal dining room to the right. Directly ahead is a spacious great room which features a second fireplace and French doors out to the rear deck. An L-shaped kitchen is complete with a work island and a large pantry and offers easy access to both the formal dining room and the sunny breakfast room. Two family bedrooms each have a walk-in closet and share a full bath. Located on the opposite side of the house for privacy, the master bedroom suite offers many relaxing amenities, including a huge walk-in closet, a lavish bath and access to the rear deck.

Design M111

Square Footage: 2,539
Bonus Room: 639 square feet

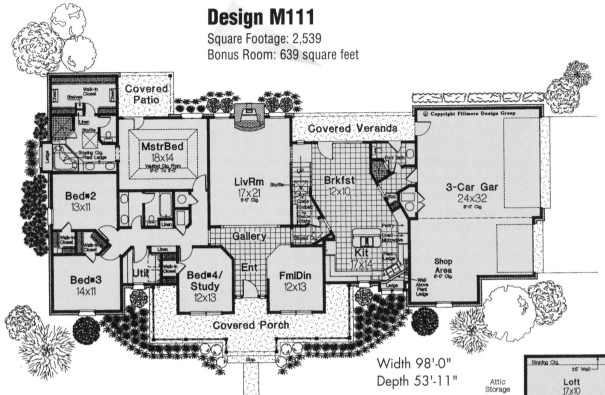

Width 98'-0"
Depth 53'-11"

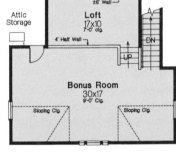

■ Classic country character complements this one-story home complete with rustic stone corners, a covered front porch and interesting gables. The entry opens onto formal living areas that include a large dining room to the right, and straight ahead to a spacious living room warmed by a fireplace. A gallery leads the way into the efficient kitchen enhanced with a snack bar and large pantry. Casual meals can be enjoyed overlooking the covered veranda and rear grounds from the connecting breakfast room. The other side of the gallery accesses the luxurious master suite and three second bedrooms—all with walk-in closets. A pool bath and a shop area in the three-car garage are welcome amenities to the first floor. For playing, studying, quiet contemplation or relaxing, the second floor contains a loft and an optional bonus room to be developed as needed.

Design by
FILLMORE DESIGN GROUP

Country-Side Classics:

One-story homes with the flavor of country

Design 7641

Square Footage: 2,027

■ This relaxed country home has all the extras, including front and rear covered porches, a dual-sided fireplace and a deluxe master suite. The great room, bright with natural light that streams in through two clerestory dormers, shares a fireplace with the breakfast bay. The formal dining room and front bedroom/study are dressed up with tray ceilings, while the master bedroom features a vaulted ceiling as well as access to the rear porch. Skylit bonus space over the garage provides the extra room today's families need.

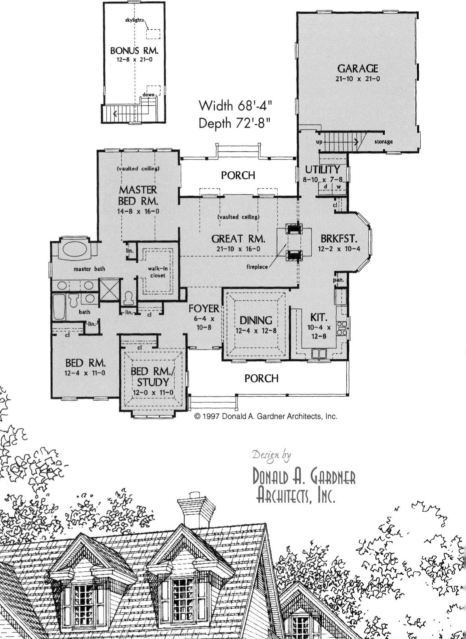

Width 68'-4"
Depth 72'-8"

BONUS RM.
12-8 x 21-0

GARAGE
21-10 x 21-0

PORCH

UTILITY
8-10 x 7-8

MASTER BED RM.
14-8 x 16-0

GREAT RM.
21-10 x 16-0

BRKFST.
12-2 x 10-4

master bath

walk-in closet

bath

FOYER
6-4 x 10-8

DINING
12-4 x 12-8

KIT.
10-4 x 12-8

BED RM.
12-4 x 11-0

BED RM./ STUDY
12-0 x 11-0

PORCH

© 1997 Donald A. Gardner Architects, Inc.

Design by
Donald A. Gardner Architects, Inc.

B. NATHAN

© 1997 Donald A. Gardner Architects, Inc.

115

B. NATHAN

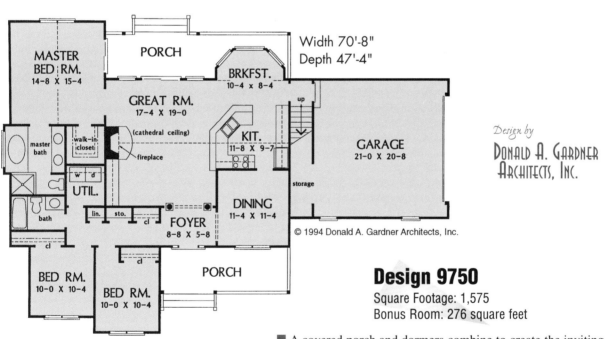

Width 70'-8"
Depth 47'-4"

MASTER BED RM.
14-8 X 15-4

PORCH

BRKFST.
10-4 x 8-4

GREAT RM.
17-4 X 19-0

(cathedral ceiling)

KIT.
11-8 X 9-7

GARAGE
21-0 X 20-8

up

master bath

walk-in closet

fireplace

w / d

UTIL.

bath

lin. sto. cl

FOYER
8-8 X 5-8

DINING
11-4 X 11-4

storage

cl

cl

BED RM.
10-0 X 10-4

BED RM.
10-0 X 10-4

PORCH

Design by
DONALD A. GARDNER
ARCHITECTS, INC.

skylights

BONUS RM.
24-8 X 11-8

down

Design 9750

Square Footage: 1,575
Bonus Room: 276 square feet

■ A covered porch and dormers combine to create the inviting exterior on this three-bedroom country home. The foyer leads through columns to an expansive great room with a cozy fireplace, built-in bookshelves and access to the rear covered porch. To the right, an open kitchen is conveniently situated to easily serve the bay-windowed breakfast area and the formal dining room. Sleeping quarters are located on the left, where the master suite enjoys access to the covered porch, a walk-in closet and a relaxing master bath complete with double-bowl vanities, a whirlpool tub and a separate shower. A utility room, two secondary bedrooms and a full bath complete the plan. A bonus room over the garage provides room for future growth.

Design W012

Square Footage: 1,736
Bonus Room: 890 square feet

Width 64'-0"
Depth 57'-0"

Great Room below

Bonus Rm.
21'-2" x 13'-3"

Bonus Rm.
22'-2" x 13'-3"

Screened Porch
21'-0" x 13'-6"
(cathedral clg.)

Porch
41'-2" x 8'-0"

Kitchen
21'-6" x 13'-0"

Great Room
19'-6" x 15'-5"
(cathedral clg.)

Master Bedroom
12'-6" x 15'-5"

Pantry

Utility

Balcony above

Foyer
8'-6" x 6'-0"

Bedroom
11'-9" x 12'-1"

Bedroom
13'-0" x 12'-1"

Garage
21'-2" x 23'-4"

Design by
Kathi Burns

■ This is a delightful little design, with a low-slung profile, yet sporting a volume roofline. It is this volume roof that gives shape to the cathedral ceiling in the great room, opening it and providing a sense of spaciousness. The covered porch beyond the great room is connected to a screened porch just off the island kitchen—alfresco dining in any weather! The master suite, with walk-in closet, is complemented by two family bedrooms sharing a full bath. Make one bedroom a den or home office, if you choose. A stairway, just at the entry, leads to a second floor, ready for completion at a future date. The two-car garage connects to the main house via the utility room.

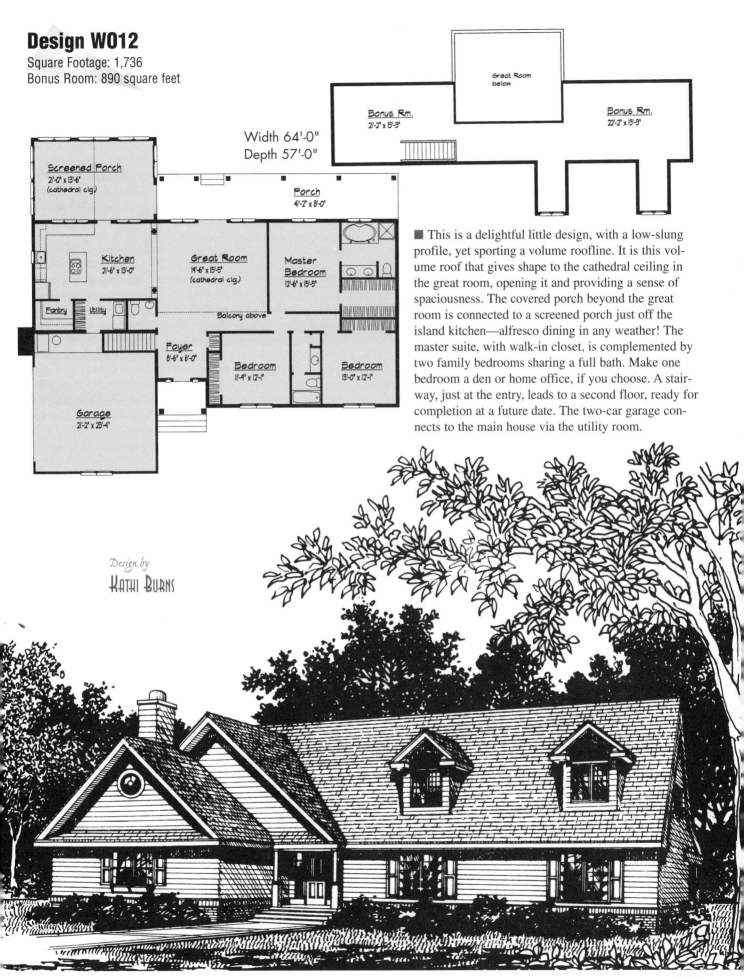

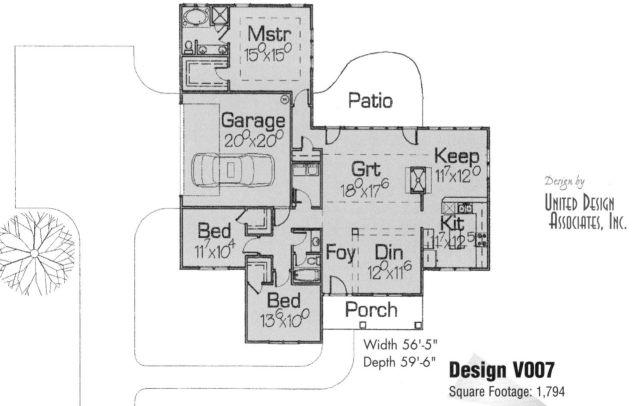

Mstr
15⁰×15⁰

Patio

Garage
20⁰×20⁰

Keep
11⁷×12⁰

Grt
18⁰×17⁶

Kit
11⁷×12⁵

Bed
11⁰×10⁴

Foy

Din
12⁰×11⁶

Bed
13⁶×10⁰

Porch

Width 56'-5"
Depth 59'-6"

Design by
UNITED DESIGN
ASSOCIATES, INC.

Design V007
Square Footage: 1,794

■ This traditional home greets you with an elegantly proportioned exterior and classic front porch. The vaulted great room, foyer, dining room, designer kitchen and large keeping room combine to create an open core of living areas. Full windows in the keeping room make this the perfect spot for enjoying morning coffee while watching the sunrise. The great room overlooks and accesses a large patio area to the rear. Featuring a tray ceiling, the master suite also contains a walk-in closet and bath with whirlpool or garden tub and separate shower. The side-entry garage is designed thoughtfully so as not to disturb the front elevation. A large kitchen includes both a bar and workspace island. Two family bedrooms share a full bath and are split from the master suite for privacy.

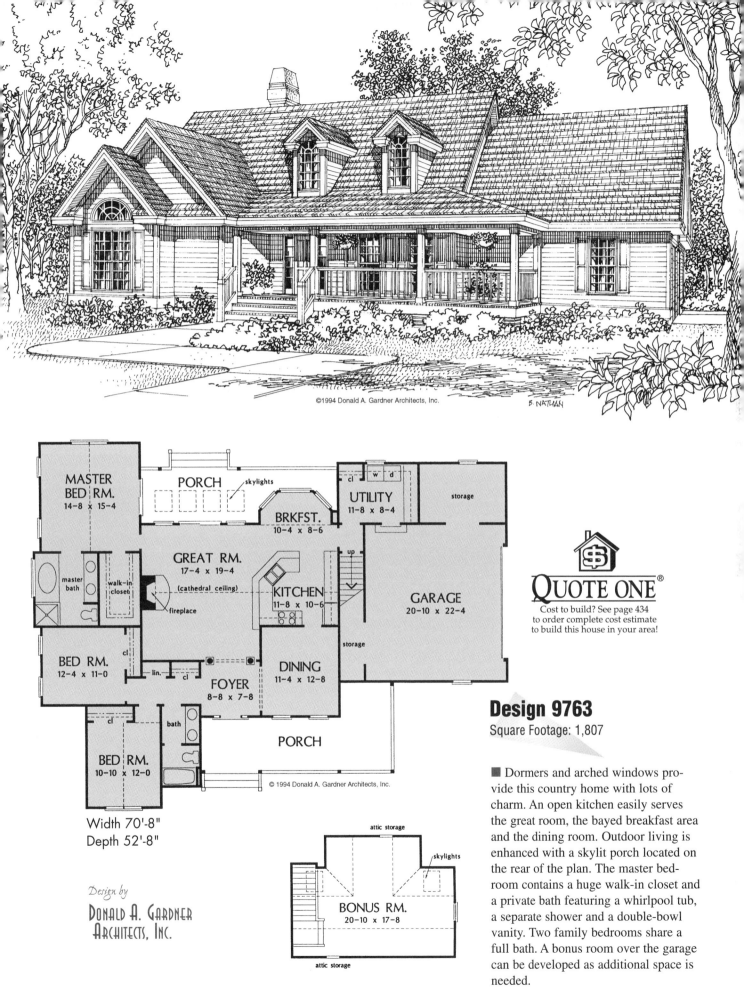

©1994 Donald A. Gardner Architects, Inc.

B. NATHAN

MASTER BED RM.
14-8 x 15-4

PORCH

skylights

UTILITY
11-8 x 8-4

storage

cl   w   d

BRKFST.
10-4 x 8-6

master bath

walk-in closet

GREAT RM.
17-4 x 19-4

(cathedral ceiling)

fireplace

KITCHEN
11-8 x 10-6

up

GARAGE
20-10 x 22-4

BED RM.
12-4 x 11-0

cl

lin.   cl

storage

DINING
11-4 x 12-8

FOYER
8-8 x 7-8

cl   bath

PORCH

BED RM.
10-10 x 12-0

© 1994 Donald A. Gardner Architects, Inc.

Width 70'-8"
Depth 52'-8"

Design by
DONALD A. GARDNER ARCHITECTS, INC.

attic storage

skylights

BONUS RM.
20-10 x 17-8

attic storage

QUOTE ONE®

Cost to build? See page 434
to order complete cost estimate
to build this house in your area!

Design 9763
Square Footage: 1,807

■ Dormers and arched windows provide this country home with lots of charm. An open kitchen easily serves the great room, the bayed breakfast area and the dining room. Outdoor living is enhanced with a skylit porch located on the rear of the plan. The master bedroom contains a huge walk-in closet and a private bath featuring a whirlpool tub, a separate shower and a double-bowl vanity. Two family bedrooms share a full bath. A bonus room over the garage can be developed as additional space is needed.

119

Design T154

Square Footage: 2,796

Porch

Keeping Room
10⁹x12⁰

Breakfast
10⁰x10⁹

Kitchen
18⁶x10⁰

Great Room
18⁹x21⁹

Master Bedroom
17⁶x16⁰

Bedroom No. 2
12⁰x13⁰

Dining Room
13³x13⁹

Foyer

Dn

Two Car Garage
21³x21³

Porch

Bedroom No. 3
12⁰x13³

■ Country details brighten the exterior of this one-story design and grace it with a warmth and charm that says "home." The floor plan includes a formal dining room and an all-purpose great room that opens to the kitchen and the keeping room. A bayed breakfast room is completely enclosed in glass. A master bedroom suite is found to the rear of the plan for privacy. It holds access to the rear covered porch and sports an extra large walk-in closet and detailed bath. The family bedrooms share a full bath but each has its own lavatory. A two-car, side-load garage has extra room for storage. This home is designed with a basement foundation.

Width 70'-9"
Depth 66'-6"

Design by
Design Traditions

© Design Traditions

Design 9684

Square Footage: 1,528
Lower Level: 394 square feet

■ Loaded with charm, this compact country plan has plenty of livability within its walls. The main floor contains a great room, formal dining room, island kitchen with attached breakfast nook, a grand master suite and one family bedroom. On the optional basement garage level is a wealth of storage in addition to a bedroom with a full bath. A rear deck adds great outdoor livability. Please specify basement or crawlspace foundation when ordering.

DECK

arched window above door

GREAT RM.
15-4 x 20-0

BRKFST.
8-0 x 10-0

fireplace

MASTER BED RM.
13-4 x 13-4

(cathedral ceiling)

KIT.
13-4 x 7-4

walk-in closet

walk-in closet

down

DINING
13-4 x 10-4

master bath

cl

FOYER
10-0 x 9-4

BED RM.
13-4 x 13-4

bath

PORCH
24-0 x 6-0

Width 45'-8"
Depth 55'-1"

Design by
Donald A. Gardner Architects, Inc.

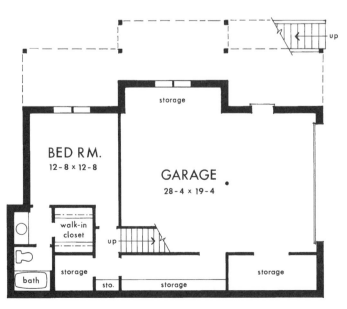

up

storage

BED RM.
12-8 x 12-8

GARAGE
28-4 x 19-4

walk-in closet

up

bath

storage

sto.

storage

storage

SCREENED PORCH
12-6 × 11-0
10 FT CLG

GREAT ROOM
17-4 × 17-6
12 FT CLG

FP

BUILT IN

SITTING
11-2 × 13-6
10 FT CLG

MASTER BEDROOM
15-2 × 15-2
10 FT CLG

K.S.

LEDGE

MASTER BATH
10 FT CLG

LIN

CHEST

BRKFST RM
12-6 × 11-0
10 FT CLG

ARCH

PWDR

BUILT IN

ARCH

FOYER
10 FT CLG

ARCH

LIN

BATH 2

42" LEDGE

KITCHEN
15-4 × 13-6

10 FT CLG

ARCH

DINING ROOM
15-4 × 13-4
10 FT CLG

ARCH

BEDROOM 3
12-4 × 12-0
10 FT CLG

BEDROOM 2
12-6 × 12-6
10 FT CLG

Width 81'-2"
Depth 67'-10"

PAN

UTIL

RAISED PLANTER

GARAGE

Design 8224

Square Footage: 2,439

Design by
LARRY E. BELK DESIGNS

■ Graceful arches and columns are a delicate complement to the brick facade of this country house. An extended foyer introduces an exciting interior plan—ten-foot ceilings throughout give a spacious feeling. A cozy fireplace will be appreciated in the great room, as will the nearby screen porch. An efficient kitchen, with cooktop island counter and an angled sink, serves both the breakfast room and the formal dining room. The master suite, located at the rear of the plan for privacy, offers many amenities. Two family bedrooms are clustered nearby and share a full bath. Please specify crawlspace or slab foundation when ordering.

Design 9602

Square Footage: 1,899

■ Dormers, a covered porch and two bumped-out windows with shed roofs at the dining room and study provide a warm country reception for the front exterior to this home. The great room has built-in cabinets and bookshelves, a warming fireplace, and has direct access to the sun room through two sliding glass doors. The convenient kitchen features a center island cooktop and provides service to both the formal dining room and the breakfast area. It is connected to the great room by a pass-through. Overlooking the private rear deck is the sumptuous master suite with a double-bowl vanity, a shower and a garden tub. Two other bedrooms are located at the other end of the house for privacy (the front bedroom could double as a study).

Design by

DONALD A. GARDNER
ARCHITECTS, INC.

Rear Elevation

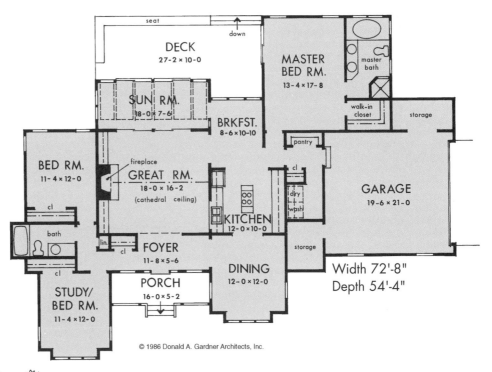

DECK
27-2 × 10-0

SUN RM.
18-0 × 7-6

BRKFST.
8-6 × 10-10

MASTER
BED RM.
13-4 × 17-8

master bath

walk-in closet

storage

pantry

BED RM.
11-4 × 12-0

fireplace

GREAT RM.
18-0 × 16-2
(cathedral ceiling)

cl

dry
wash

GARAGE
19-6 × 21-0

KITCHEN
12-0 × 10-0

bath

lin.

cl

FOYER
11-8 × 5-6

storage

STUDY/
BED RM.
11-4 × 12-0

PORCH
16-0 × 5-2

DINING
12-0 × 12-0

Width 72'-8"
Depth 54'-4"

B·NATHAN·

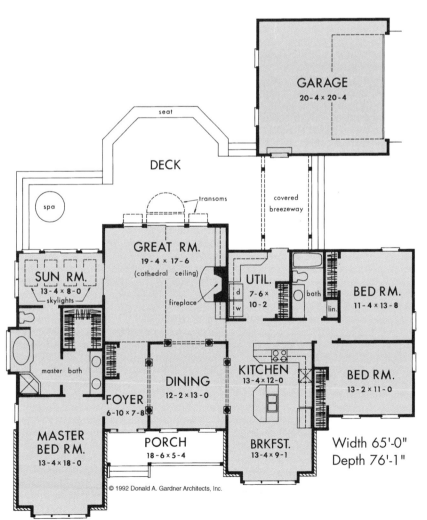

GARAGE
20-4 × 20-4

seat

DECK

spa

covered breezeway

transoms

GREAT RM.
19-4 × 17-6
(cathedral ceiling)

fireplace

SUN RM.
13-4 × 8-0
skylights

UTIL.
7-6 × 10-2

bath

lin.

BED RM.
11-4 × 13-8

master bath

DINING
12-2 × 13-0

FOYER
6-10 × 7-8

KITCHEN
13-4 × 12-0

BED RM.
13-2 × 11-0

MASTER BED RM.
13-4 × 18-0

PORCH
18-6 × 5-4

BRKFST.
13-4 × 9-1

Design 9689

Square Footage: 2,112

■ Indoor/outdoor relationships are given close attention in this plan. Windows on all sides, including dormers in the front and transoms in the great room, let in the view, while sliding glass doors in the sun room and great room provide access to a spacious deck. Bay windows enliven the master bedroom and breakfast area. Other highlights include columns setting off the dining room, and a fireplace and cathedral ceiling in the great room. Two family bedrooms share a full bath.

Width 65'-0"
Depth 76'-1"

Design by
DONALD A. GARDNER
ARCHITECTS, INC.

124

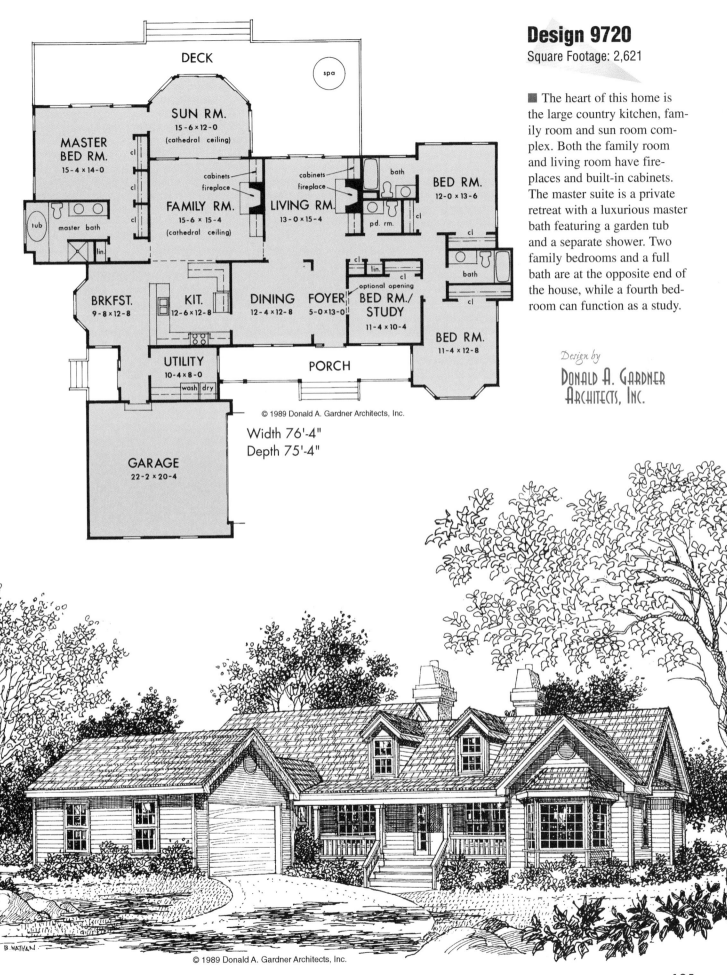

DECK

spa

SUN RM.
15-6 × 12-0
(cathedral ceiling)

MASTER BED RM.
15-4 × 14-0

cl

cl

cabinets fireplace

cabinets fireplace

bath

BED RM.
12-0 × 13-6

tub

master bath

lin.

FAMILY RM.
15-6 × 15-4
(cathedral ceiling)

LIVING RM.
13-0 × 15-4

pd. rm.

cl

cl

bath

cl

BRKFST.
9-8 × 12-8

KIT.
12-6 × 12-8

DINING
12-4 × 12-8

FOYER
5-0 × 13-0

cl

lin.

optional opening

BED RM./STUDY
11-4 × 10-4

cl

UTILITY
10-4 × 8-0

wash dry

PORCH

BED RM.
11-4 × 12-8

© 1989 Donald A. Gardner Architects, Inc.

Width 76'-4"
Depth 75'-4"

GARAGE
22-2 × 20-4

Design 9720

Square Footage: 2,621

■ The heart of this home is the large country kitchen, family room and sun room complex. Both the family room and living room have fireplaces and built-in cabinets. The master suite is a private retreat with a luxurious master bath featuring a garden tub and a separate shower. Two family bedrooms and a full bath are at the opposite end of the house, while a fourth bedroom can function as a study.

Design by
DONALD A. GARDNER
ARCHITECTS, INC.

B. NATHAN

© 1989 Donald A. Gardner Architects, Inc.

125

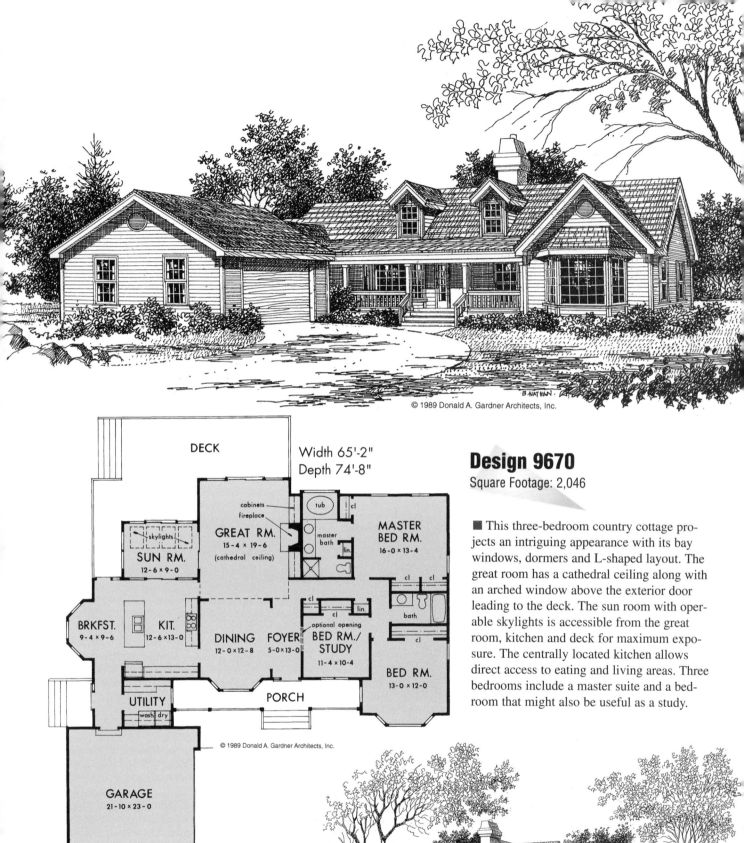

© 1989 Donald A. Gardner Architects, Inc.

DECK

Width 65'-2"
Depth 74'-8"

skylights

SUN RM.
12-6 × 9-0

cabinets
fireplace

GREAT RM.
15-4 × 19-6
(cathedral ceiling)

tub

cl

master
bath

lin.

MASTER
BED RM.
16-0 × 13-4

cl   cl

bath

cl

BRKFST.
9-4 × 9-6

KIT.
12-6 × 13-0

DINING
12-0 × 12-8

FOYER
5-0 × 13-0

cl

cl   lin

optional opening

BED RM./
STUDY
11-4 × 10-4

BED RM.
13-0 × 12-0

UTILITY

wash dry

PORCH

© 1989 Donald A. Gardner Architects, Inc.

GARAGE
21-10 × 23-0

Design by
DONALD A. GARDNER
ARCHITECTS, INC.

Design 9670
Square Footage: 2,046

■ This three-bedroom country cottage projects an intriguing appearance with its bay windows, dormers and L-shaped layout. The great room has a cathedral ceiling along with an arched window above the exterior door leading to the deck. The sun room with operable skylights is accessible from the great room, kitchen and deck for maximum exposure. The centrally located kitchen allows direct access to eating and living areas. Three bedrooms include a master suite and a bedroom that might also be useful as a study.

Rear Elevation

126

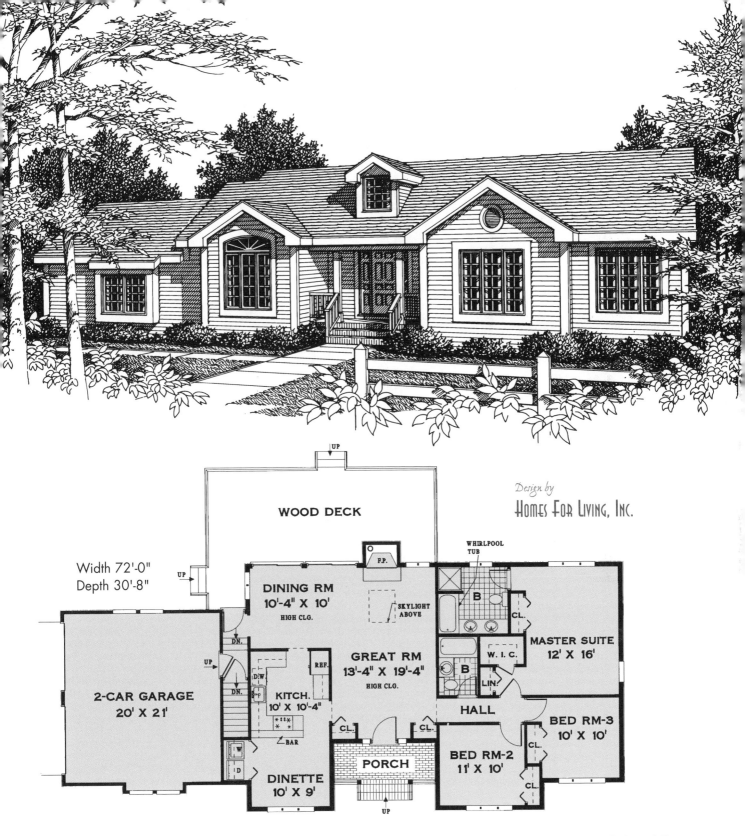

WOOD DECK

Design by
HOMES FOR LIVING, INC.

Width 72'-0"
Depth 30'-8"

UP

WHIRLPOOL
TUB

DINING RM
10'-4" X 10'
HIGH CLG.

F.P.

SKYLIGHT
ABOVE

B

CL.

MASTER SUITE
12' X 16'

2-CAR GARAGE
20' X 21'

DN.

UP

DN.

D/W

KITCH.
10' X 10'-4"

REF.

GREAT RM
13'-4" X 19'-4"
HIGH CLG.

B

W. I. C.

LIN.

HALL

BED RM-3
10' X 10'

CL.

BAR

CL.

CL.

BED RM-2
11' X 10'

CL.

W

DINETTE
10' X 9'

PORCH

UP

D

CL.

Design N145
Square Footage: 1,412

■ If traditional exteriors are what you like, this design delivers all the best features: horizontal wood siding, multi-pane windows, a centered dormer and a recessed, raised entry. The great room is the focal point of the plan. It has a fireplace and skylight and overlooks a rear wood deck. The formal dining room is open to the great room and has sliding glass doors to the deck.

Casual dining takes place in a windowed dinette on the opposite side of the U-shaped kitchen. Two family bedrooms have large front-facing windows and share the use of a full bath. The master bedroom features its own bath with whirlpool tub, separate shower and double sinks. A two-car garage is to the left of the plan. Please specify basement or slab foundation when ordering.

Design 9718

Square Footage: 1,998

■ This country cottage gets all dressed up with multi-pane windows, dormers, shed windows and a covered porch. Inside, skylights, a paddle fan and a wet bar make the sun room something to talk about. You'll also find a deck off this room; it leads to the covered breezeway connecting the garage to the house. In the great room, exposed beams, built-in shelves and a dramatic fireplace set off this wonderfully warm room. The country kitchen with its island cooktop features a pass-through counter to the great room. The generous master suite is privately located and luxuriously appointed with a whirlpool tub, a separate shower and dual lavatories. Two family bedrooms find peace and quiet at the other end of the house and share a full hall bath with a compartmented vanity.

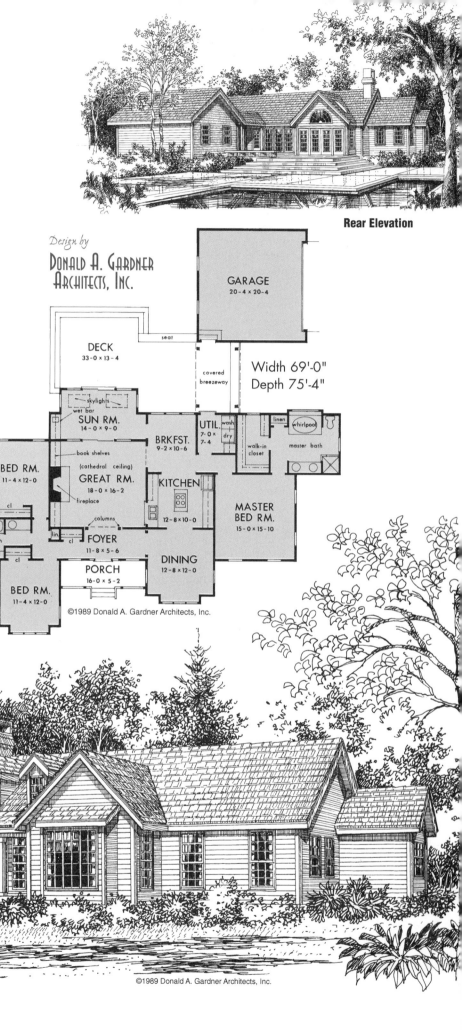

Rear Elevation

Design by

DONALD A. GARDNER ARCHITECTS, INC.

Width 69'-0"
Depth 75'-4"

GARAGE
20-4 x 20-4

DECK
33-0 x 13-4

covered breezeway

seat

SUN RM.
14-0 x 9-0
skylights
wet bar

BRKFST.
9-2 x 10-6

UTIL.
7-0 x 7-4
wash dry

linen whirlpool
walk-in closet
master bath

book shelves
(cathedral ceiling)

GREAT RM.
18-0 x 16-2
fireplace

BED RM.
11-4 x 12-0

KITCHEN
12-8 x 10-0

MASTER BED RM.
15-0 x 15-10

bath
cl
lin. cl
columns

FOYER
11-8 x 5-6

DINING
12-8 x 12-0

PORCH
16-0 x 5-2

BED RM.
11-4 x 12-0

NATHAN INC.

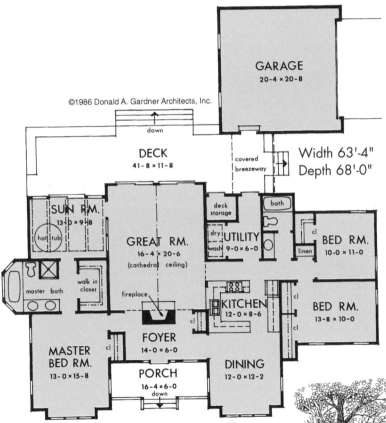

GARAGE
20-4 × 20-8

DECK
41-8 × 11-8

down

covered breezeway

Width 63'-4"
Depth 68'-0"

SUN RM.
13-0 × 9-8

hot tub

GREAT RM.
16-4 × 20-6
(cathedral ceiling)

deck storage

UTILITY
9-0 × 6-0

dry
wash

bath

cl

linen

BED RM.
10-0 × 11-0

master bath

walk in closet

fireplace

KITCHEN
12-0 × 8-6

cl

cl

BED RM.
13-8 × 10-0

MASTER BED RM.
13-0 × 15-8

cl

FOYER
14-0 × 6-0

PORCH
16-4 × 6-0
down

DINING
12-0 × 12-2

Design by
Donald A. Gardner
Architects, Inc.

Design 9682

Square Footage: 1,826

■ Multi-pane windows, dormers, a covered porch, round gable vents and two projected windows at the dining area add to the flavor of this country-style home. A sun room with hot tub sits adjacent to a deck that is accessed from the great room and master bath. The great room has a fireplace, cathedral ceiling and sliding glass doors with arched windows above to allow for natural light. The kitchen is centrally located between the dining area and the great room for maximum flexibility in layout. A generous master bedroom has a walk-in closet and spacious master bath with double-bowl vanity, shower and garden tub. Two additional bedrooms are located at the other end of the house for privacy.

Rear Elevation

129

Design 7637

Square Footage: 1,959

■ Square columns with chamfered corners set off classic clapboard siding and complement a country-style dormer and twin pediments. The vaulted great room has a focal-point fireplace and access to the rear deck. The well-appointed kitchen opens to a bright breakfast area and enjoys its natural light. The dining room, front bedroom/study and master bedroom feature tray ceilings. The private master suite also includes a skylit bath. Please specify basement or crawlspace foundation when ordering.

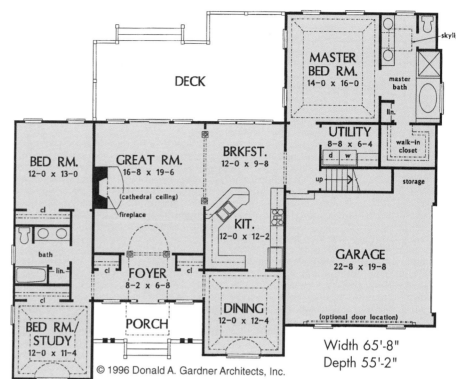

DECK

MASTER BED RM.
14-0 x 16-0

skylight

master bath

lin.

BED RM.
12-0 x 13-0

GREAT RM.
16-8 x 19-6

(cathedral ceiling)

fireplace

cl

bath

lin.

BRKFST.
12-0 x 9-8

UTILITY
8-8 x 6-4

d w

up

walk-in closet

storage

KIT.
12-0 x 12-2

GARAGE
22-8 x 19-8

cl

FOYER
8-2 x 6-8

cl

BED RM./
STUDY
12-0 x 11-4

PORCH

DINING
12-0 x 12-4

(optional door location)

Width 65'-8"
Depth 55'-2"

© 1996 Donald A. Gardner Architects, Inc.

Design by

DONALD A. GARDNER
ARCHITECTS, INC.

B. NATHAN

© 1996 Donald A. Gardner Architects, Inc.

Design 9657

Square Footage: 2,165

■ Step into the sun room from the master suite, family room or deck in this sunny, three-bedroom country home—dressed up with dormers, shutters and bay windows. Along with formal living and dining rooms, this home also has a family room flooded with light from a sliding glass door with an arched window above. The kitchen includes an island and an adjacent breakfast area. The ample master suite includes a walk-in closet and a luxurious master bath with dual lavatories, a shower and a whirlpool tub. A separate garage is reached via a covered breezeway across the deck.

Rear Elevation

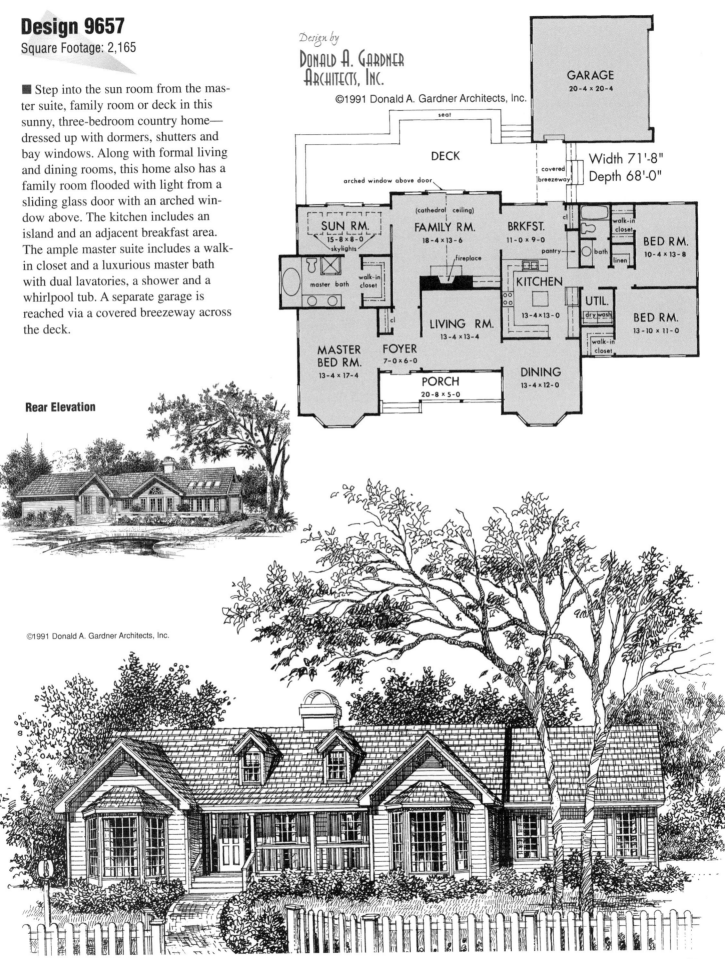

Design by

DONALD A. GARDNER
ARCHITECTS, INC.

©1991 Donald A. Gardner Architects, Inc.

GARAGE
20-4 × 20-4

DECK

seat

covered breezeway

Width 71'-8"
Depth 68'-0"

arched window above door

SUN RM.
15-8 × 8-0

skylights

FAMILY RM.
18-4 × 13-6

(cathedral ceiling)

BRKFST.
11-0 × 9-0

cl

walk-in closet

BED RM.
10-4 × 13-8

bath

pantry

linen

master bath

walk-in closet

fireplace

KITCHEN
13-4 × 13-0

UTIL.

dry wash

BED RM.
13-10 × 11-0

LIVING RM.
13-4 × 13-4

cl

walk-in closet

MASTER BED RM.
13-4 × 17-4

FOYER
7-0 × 6-0

PORCH
20-8 × 5-0

DINING
13-4 × 12-0

131

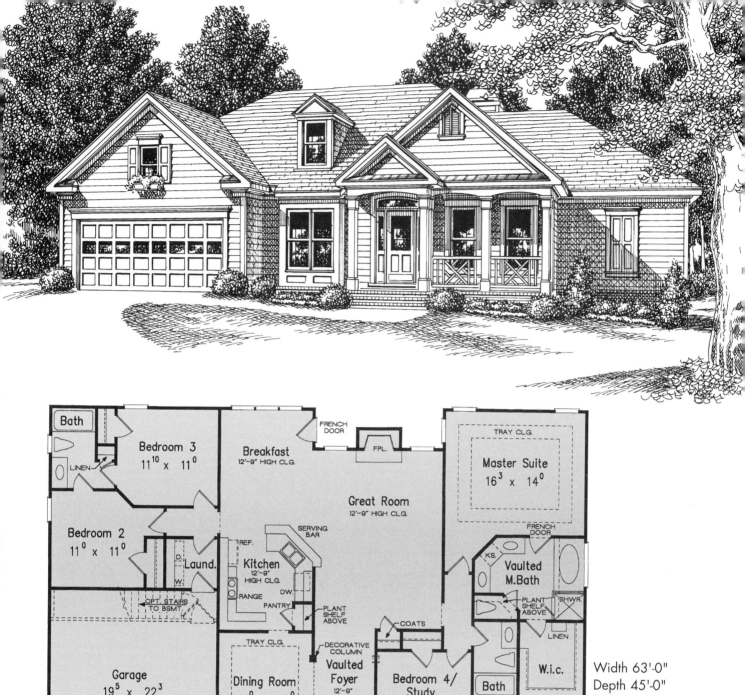

Bath

Bedroom 3
11¹⁰ x 11⁰

LINEN

Bedroom 2
11⁰ x 11⁰

D.
W.
Laund.

OPT. STAIRS
TO BSMT.

Garage
19⁵ x 22³

copyright © 1997 frank betz associates, inc.

GARAGE LOCATION WITH BASEMENT

Breakfast
12'-9" HIGH CLG.

FRENCH DOOR

FPL.

Great Room
12'-9" HIGH CLG.

SERVING BAR

REF.

Kitchen
12'-9" HIGH CLG.

RANGE

DW.

PANTRY

PLANT SHELF ABOVE

TRAY CLG.

Dining Room
11⁰ x 13⁰

DECORATIVE COLUMN

Vaulted Foyer
12'-9" HIGH CLG.

COATS

Bedroom 4/ Study
11⁰ x 10⁰

COLUMN FOR OPT. STUDY

TRAY CLG.

Master Suite
16³ x 14⁰

FRENCH DOOR

KS.

Vaulted M.Bath

PLANT SHELF ABOVE

SHWR.

LINEN

W.i.c.

Bath

Width 63'-0"
Depth 45'-0"

Design by

FRANK BETZ
ASSOCIATES, INC.

Covered Porch

Design P296
Square Footage: 1,932

■ Special architectural aspects turn this quaint home into much more than just another one-story ranch design. It is enhanced by a covered, columned front porch, large window areas, a dormer and horizontal wood siding. The floor plan is equally thoughtful in design. A central great room acts as the hub of the plan and is graced by a fireplace flanked on either side by windows. It is separated from the kitchen by a convenient serving bar. Formal dining is accomplished to the front of the plan in a room with a tray ceiling. Casual dining takes place in the breakfast room with its full wall of glass. Two bedrooms are to the left and share a full bath. The master suite and one additional bedroom are to the right. Bedroom 4 would make the perfect study, with the option of a doorway opening directly to the foyer.

Design 7396

Square Footage: 1,653

■ A front porch reminiscent of the 1920s sets the tone on this charming one-story home. The covered front porch leads to an entry foyer with twin coat closets. The dining room is just beyond, and then the superb great room with a fireplace. The den can be converted to a bedroom and offers a full bath and a bayed window overlooking the front porch. A designer kitchen has an attached breakfast room with another bay window for gracious casual meals. Plenty of extra space in the master bath leaves room for a corner make-up vanity and His and Hers sinks. The two-car garage features workbench space for the family handyman. Note the tray ceilings in both the master bedroom and the dining room.

Design by
Design Basics, Inc.

Width 48'-8"
Depth 54'-0"

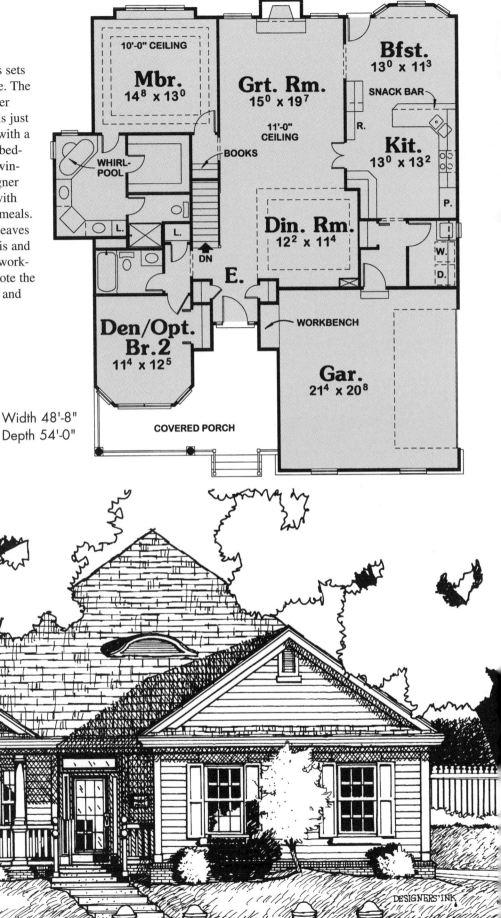

133

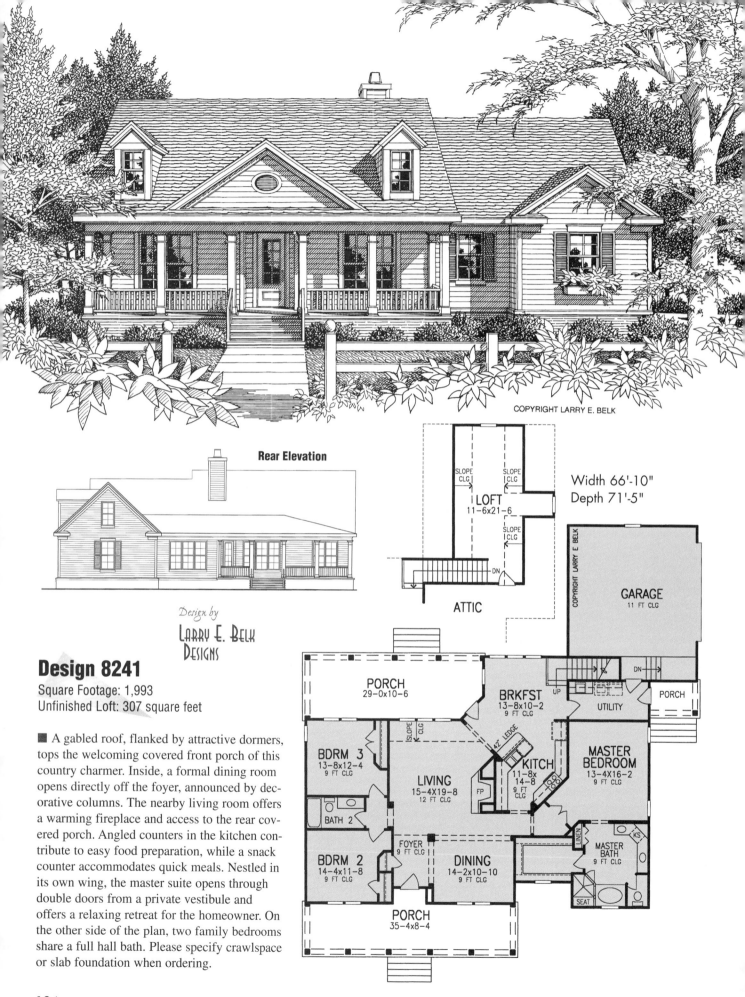

COPYRIGHT LARRY E. BELK

Rear Elevation

Design by

LARRY E. BELK DESIGNS

Width 66'-10"
Depth 71'-5"

LOFT
11-6x21-6

SLOPE CLG   SLOPE CLG

SLOPE CLG

DN

ATTIC

GARAGE
11 FT CLG

COPYRIGHT LARRY E BELK

DN

PORCH

Design 8241

Square Footage: 1,993
Unfinished Loft: 307 square feet

■ A gabled roof, flanked by attractive dormers, tops the welcoming covered front porch of this country charmer. Inside, a formal dining room opens directly off the foyer, announced by decorative columns. The nearby living room offers a warming fireplace and access to the rear covered porch. Angled counters in the kitchen contribute to easy food preparation, while a snack counter accommodates quick meals. Nestled in its own wing, the master suite opens through double doors from a private vestibule and offers a relaxing retreat for the homeowner. On the other side of the plan, two family bedrooms share a full hall bath. Please specify crawlspace or slab foundation when ordering.

PORCH
29-0x10-6

BRKFST
13-8x10-2
9 FT CLG

UP

UTILITY

BDRM 3
13-8x12-4
9 FT CLG

SLOPE CLG

LIVING
15-4x19-8
12 FT CLG

42" LEDGE

FP

KITCH
11-8x
14-8
9 FT CLG

MASTER
BEDROOM
13-4x16-2
9 FT CLG

BATH 2

BDRM 2
14-4x11-8
9 FT CLG

FOYER
9 FT CLG

DINING
14-2x10-10
9 FT CLG

LINEN

KS

MASTER
BATH
9 FT CLG

SEAT

PORCH
35-4x8-4

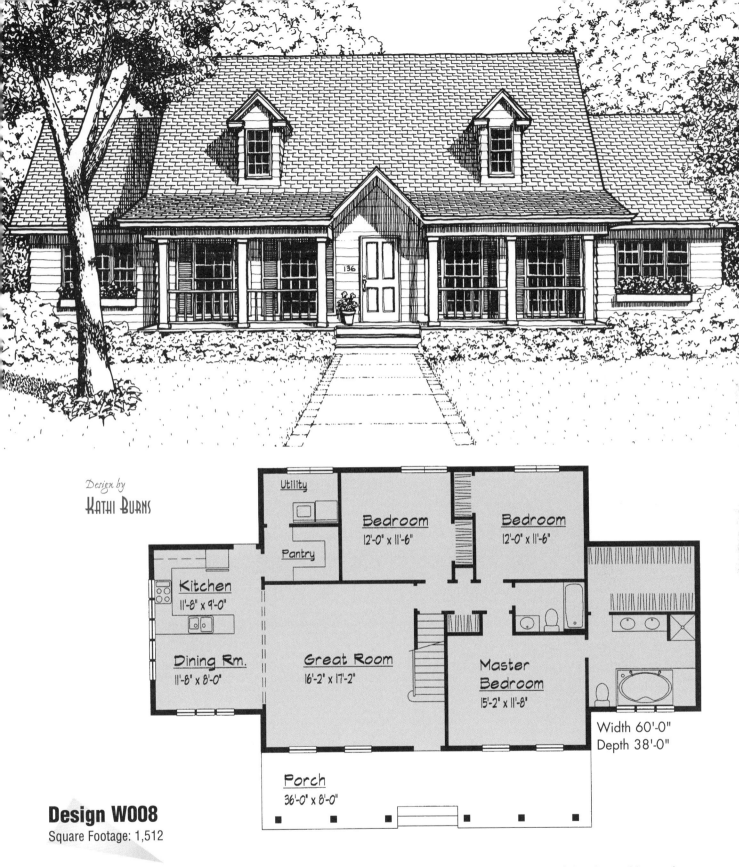

Design by
Kathi Burns

Utility

Bedroom
12'-0" x 11'-6"

Bedroom
12'-0" x 11'-6"

Pantry

Kitchen
11'-8" x 9'-0"

Dining Rm.
11'-8" x 8'-0"

Great Room
16'-2" x 17'-2"

Master Bedroom
15'-2" x 11'-8"

Width 60'-0"
Depth 38'-0"

Porch
36'-0" x 8'-0"

Design W008
Square Footage: 1,512

■ Perfectly symmetrical on the outside, this appealing home has an equally classic floor plan on the inside. A covered porch featuring full, multi-paned windows opens directly to the spacious great room. It is open to the dining room and U-shaped kitchen for convenience and gracious entertaining. The kitchen connects to a roomy utility room with loads of counterspace and windows overlooking the rear yard. The master bedroom lies to the front of the plan and has a view of the covered porch. Its bath features a whirlpool tub, separate shower and two sinks. A room-sized walk-in closet is an added amenity. Two family bedrooms reside to the rear of the plan. Each has a window with backyard views. The upstairs is unfinished but can add 555 square feet of usable space when needed.

135

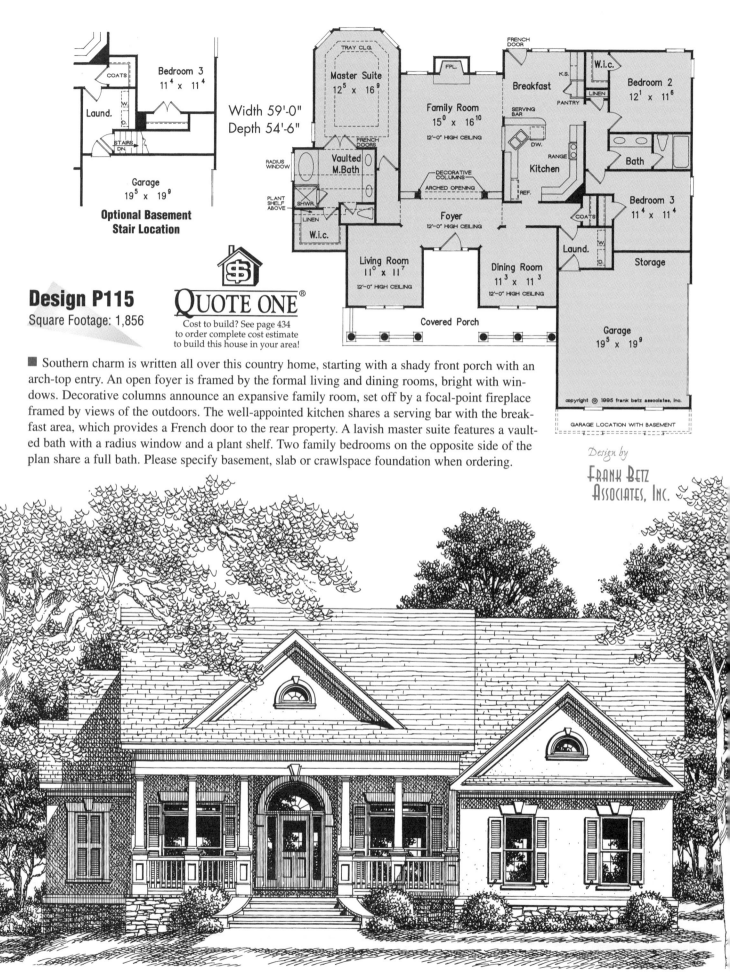

Bedroom 3
11⁴ x 11⁴

COATS

Laund.

STAIRS DN.

Garage
19⁵ x 19⁹

Width 59'-0"
Depth 54'-6"

**Optional Basement
Stair Location**

TRAY CLG.

Master Suite
12⁵ x 16⁹

FRENCH DOORS

RADIUS WINDOW

Vaulted M.Bath

PLANT SHELF ABOVE

SHWR.

LINEN

W.i.c.

Living Room
11⁰ x 11⁷
12'-0" HIGH CEILING

FRENCH DOOR

FPL.

Family Room
15⁰ x 16¹⁰
12'-0" HIGH CEILING

DECORATIVE COLUMNS

ARCHED OPENING

Foyer
12'-0" HIGH CEILING

SERVING BAR

DW.

Kitchen

RANGE

REF.

Breakfast

K.S.

PANTRY

LINEN

W.i.c.

Bedroom 2
12¹ x 11⁶

Bath

Bedroom 3
11⁴ x 11⁴

COATS

Laund.

Dining Room
11³ x 11³
12'-0" HIGH CEILING

Storage

Garage
19⁵ x 19⁹

Covered Porch

copyright © 1995 frank betz associates, inc.

GARAGE LOCATION WITH BASEMENT

Design P115
Square Footage: 1,856

QUOTE ONE®
Cost to build? See page 434
to order complete cost estimate
to build this house in your area!

■ Southern charm is written all over this country home, starting with a shady front porch with an arch-top entry. An open foyer is framed by the formal living and dining rooms, bright with windows. Decorative columns announce an expansive family room, set off by a focal-point fireplace framed by views of the outdoors. The well-appointed kitchen shares a serving bar with the breakfast area, which provides a French door to the rear property. A lavish master suite features a vaulted bath with a radius window and a plant shelf. Two family bedrooms on the opposite side of the plan share a full bath. Please specify basement, slab or crawlspace foundation when ordering.

Design by
FRANK BETZ
ASSOCIATES, INC.

B. NATHAN

Design 7645

Square Footage: 1,903

■ This symmetrical Folk Victorian combines the charm of yesteryear with a plan designed for today's family. Accented by columns, the great room with a fireplace is vaulted, while the foyer, dining room, kitchen, breakfast bay and bedroom/study boast impressive ten-foot ceilings. With double door entry, the secluded master suite features a tray ceiling, walk-in closet and private, skylit bath. Three additional bedrooms are located on the opposite side of the house and share a full bath with linen closet. Note that the front and back porches extend the living space to the outdoors.

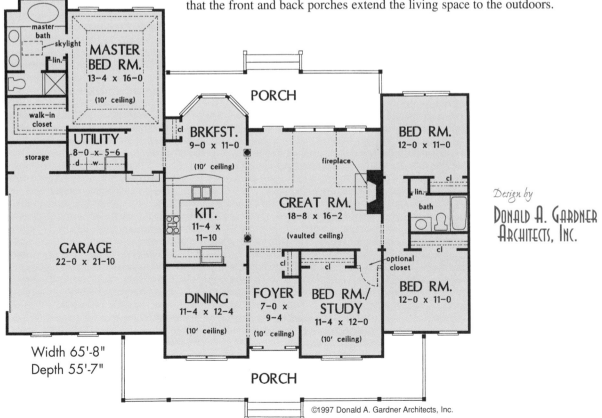

master bath
skylight
lin.

MASTER BED RM.
13-4 x 16-0
(10' ceiling)

walk-in closet

storage

UTILITY
8-0 x 5-6
d w

GARAGE
22-0 x 21-10

Width 65'-8"
Depth 55'-7"

cl

BRKFST.
9-0 x 11-0
(10' ceiling)

KIT.
11-4 x 11-10

DINING
11-4 x 12-4
(10' ceiling)

PORCH

fireplace

GREAT RM.
18-8 x 16-2
(vaulted ceiling)

FOYER
7-0 x 9-4
(10' ceiling)

cl

BED RM./ STUDY
11-4 x 12-0
(10' ceiling)

cl

BED RM.
12-0 x 11-0

lin.
bath
cl

optional closet

BED RM.
12-0 x 11-0

PORCH

Design by
Donald A. Gardner Architects, Inc.

137

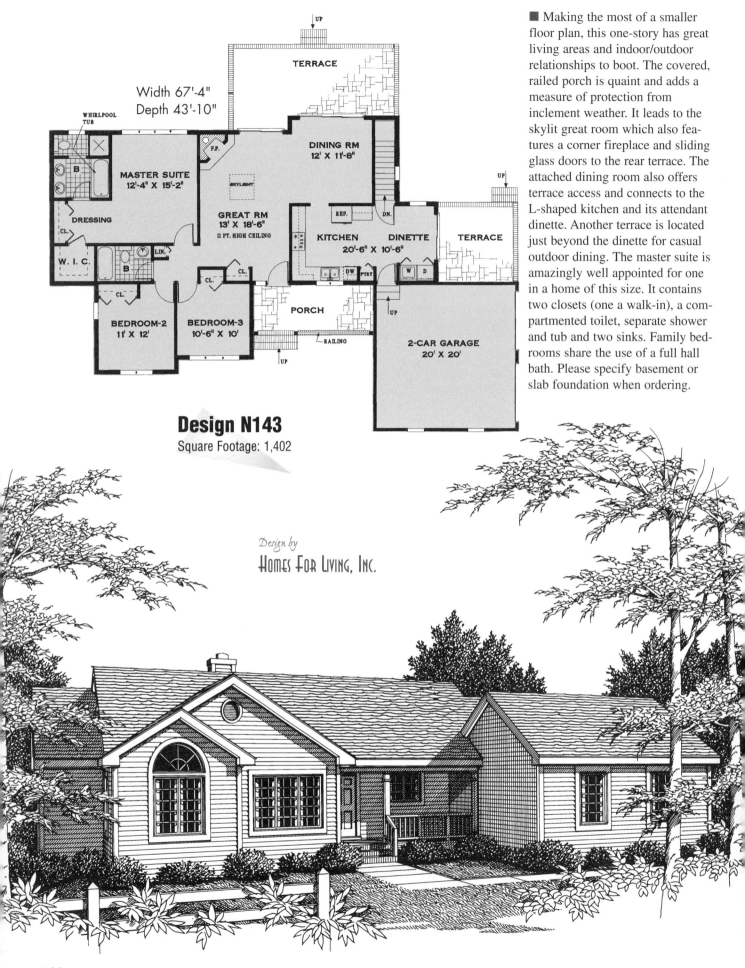

Width 67'-4"
Depth 43'-10"

WHIRLPOOL TUB

MASTER SUITE
12'-4" X 15'-2"

F.P.

DINING RM
12' X 11'-8"

UP

TERRACE

DRESSING

SKYLIGHT

GREAT RM
13' X 18'-6"
11 FT. HIGH CEILING

CL.

W. I. C.

B

LIN.

REF.

DN.

UP

CL.

CL.

KITCHEN
20'-6" X 10'-6"

DINETTE

TERRACE

CL.

W   D

PNTRY

BEDROOM-2
11' X 12'

BEDROOM-3
10'-6" X 10'

PORCH

UP

RAILING

UP

2-CAR GARAGE
20' X 20'

Design N143
Square Footage: 1,402

Design by
HOMES FOR LIVING, INC.

Making the most of a smaller floor plan, this one-story has great living areas and indoor/outdoor relationships to boot. The covered, railed porch is quaint and adds a measure of protection from inclement weather. It leads to the skylit great room which also features a corner fireplace and sliding glass doors to the rear terrace. The attached dining room also offers terrace access and connects to the L-shaped kitchen and its attendant dinette. Another terrace is located just beyond the dinette for casual outdoor dining. The master suite is amazingly well appointed for one in a home of this size. It contains two closets (one a walk-in), a compartmented toilet, separate shower and tub and two sinks. Family bedrooms share the use of a full hall bath. Please specify basement or slab foundation when ordering.

■ Special touches add so much to the exterior of this home: fan detailing over two windows and the front entry, a barrel-vaulted covered porch, graceful columns and shuttered windows. The floor plan offers touches of its own to appreciate. Both formal living and dining rooms are defined by columned entries—one at the foyer and one at the central hall. The family room has a focal-point fireplace and sliding glass doors leading to the rear yard. The casual dining area is delightfully shaped with windows all around and a tray ceiling. Three bedrooms are found to the left of the plan. The master suite has a bath with whirlpool tub, walk-in closet and double sinks. Family bedrooms share a hall bath. The two-car garage offers a large area for storage or workshop space.

Design C149
Square Footage: 2,278

Design by
James Fahy Design

Width 76'-0"
Depth 58'-0"

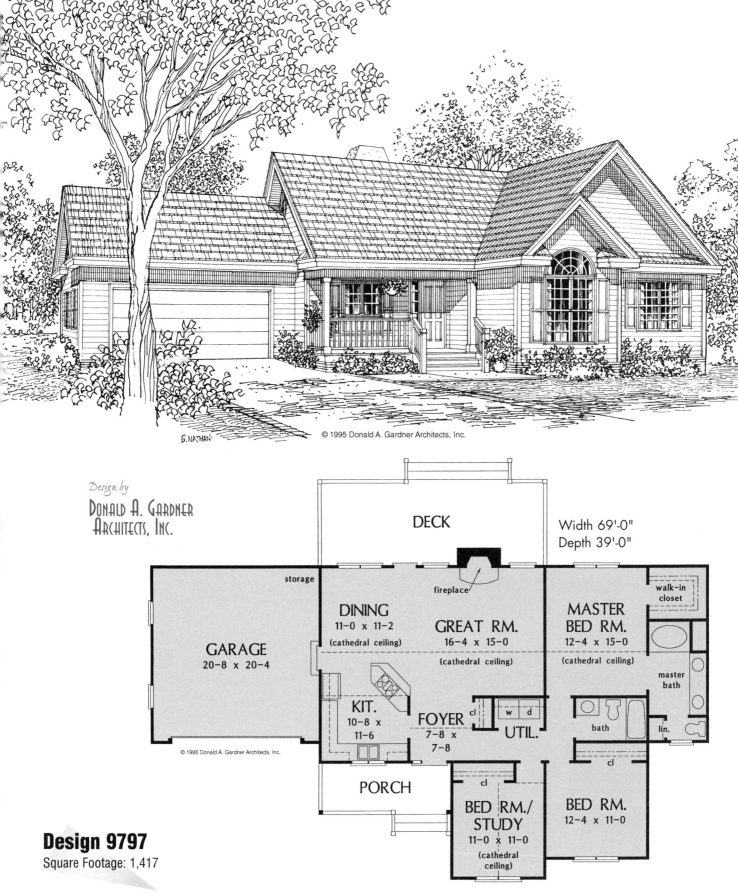

B. NATHAN
© 1995 Donald A. Gardner Architects, Inc.

Design by
DONALD A. GARDNER
ARCHITECTS, INC.

DECK

Width 69'-0"
Depth 39'-0"

storage

GARAGE
20-8 x 20-4

DINING
11-0 x 11-2
(cathedral ceiling)

fireplace

GREAT RM.
16-4 x 15-0
(cathedral ceiling)

MASTER
BED RM.
12-4 x 15-0
(cathedral ceiling)

walk-in
closet

master
bath

KIT.
10-8 x
11-6

FOYER
7-8 x
7-8

cl

w d

UTIL.

bath

lin.

cl

© 1995 Donald A. Gardner Architects, Inc.

PORCH

BED RM./
STUDY
11-0 x 11-0
(cathedral
ceiling)

cl

BED RM.
12-4 x 11-0

Design 9797

Square Footage: 1,417

■ A wide-open floor plan puts the emphasis on family living in this modest, single-story home. A cathedral ceiling stretches the length of the plan, stylishly topping the dining room, great room and master bedroom. Cooks will enjoy working in the presentation kitchen that's open to the dining room and great room. The master suite has a walk-in closet and a compartmented bath with a garden tub and twin vanities. One of the two family bedrooms has a cathedral ceiling as well, making it an optional study. A full hall bath and a convenient hallway laundry center complete this plan.

140

■ You'll love the ceiling treatments in the special rooms of this home. They are made possible by a volume roofline that adds appeal to the exterior as well. Both the foyer and the great room feature vaulted ceilings while the formal dining room has a step ceiling and the casual dining area has a tray ceiling. The master bedroom is graced by a cathedral ceiling, just one of many details that make it luxurious. Family bedrooms are split away from the master suite for privacy; they share a hall bath. The two-car garage connects conveniently to the main house via a service entry that also leads to the laundry area and the island kitchen. Double doors at this point lead to the master suite and keep it private.

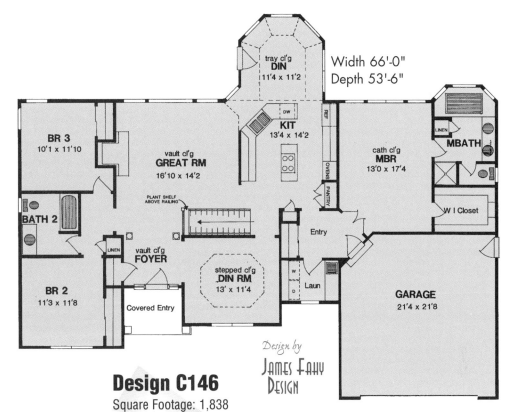

Width 66'-0"
Depth 53'-6"

Design C146
Square Footage: 1,838

Design by
James Fahy Design

Alternate Elevation A   **Alternate Elevation B**

B. NATHAN

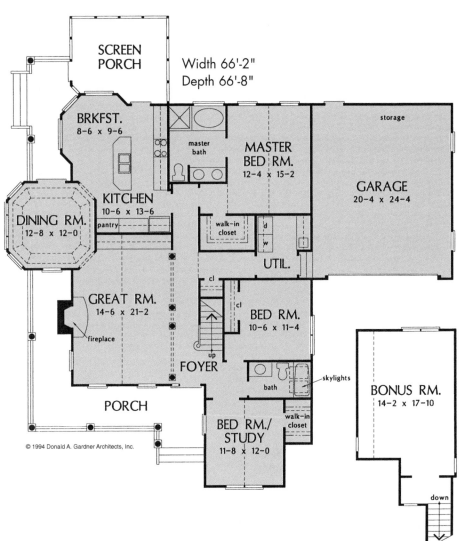

SCREEN PORCH

Width 66'-2"
Depth 66'-8"

BRKFST.
8-6 x 9-6

master bath

MASTER BED RM.
12-4 x 15-2

storage

KITCHEN
10-6 x 13-6

pantry

DINING RM.
12-8 x 12-0

GARAGE
20-4 x 24-4

walk-in closet

d w

UTIL.

GREAT RM.
14-6 x 21-2

fireplace

cl

cl

BED RM.
10-6 x 11-4

up

FOYER

PORCH

bath

skylights

BONUS RM.
14-2 x 17-10

BED RM./ STUDY
11-8 x 12-0

walk-in closet

down

Design 7601

Square Footage: 1,787
Bonus Room: 326 square feet

■ A neighborly porch as friendly as a handshake wraps around this charming country home, warmly greeting family and friends alike. Inside, cathedral ceilings promote a feeling of spaciousness. To the left of the foyer, the great room is enhanced with a fireplace and built-in bookshelves. A uniquely shaped formal dining room separates the kitchen and breakfast area. Outdoor pursuits—rain or shine—will be enjoyed from the screen porch. The master suite is located at the rear of the plan for privacy and features a walk-in closet and a luxurious bath. Two additional bedrooms, one with a walk-in closet, share a skylit bath. A second-floor bonus room is available to develop later as a study, home office or play area. Please specify basement or crawlspace foundation when ordering.

Design by
DONALD A. GARDNER
ARCHITECTS, INC.

■ This popular and economic one-story country design is easy to build. The entrance, sheltered by the front porch, opens to an imposing living room with high ceiling and heat-circulating fireplace. The formal dining room features a full wall of windows facing the front porch. The fully equipped kitchen and dinette combination access a rear terrace through 6-foot sliding glass doors. The spacious master bedroom suite provides a large dressing area with a walk-in closet plus two linear closets and space for a vanity. One side of the bedroom contains a media wall with ample space for a TV, VCR, stereo speakers, CD player and more. Please specify basement or slab foundation when ordering.

Design N119
Square Footage: 1,367

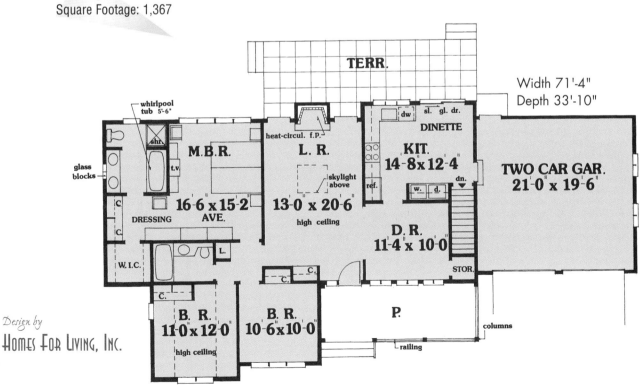

Width 71'-4"
Depth 33'-10"

Design by
Homes For Living, Inc.

143

Design 7351

Square Footage: 1,815

■ Stone and siding come together and further combine with a front porch to lend beautiful detailing to this ranch home. A cathedral ceiling in the great room complements its fireplace. The dining room has a ten-foot ceiling and is just across the hall from the L-shaped kitchen for convenience. The breakfast nook has a sunny covered porch and wide windows for light. Bedrooms 2 and 3 sit to the far right of the plan and share the use of a full bath. The master suite is on the left; note the walk-in closet and separate tub and shower here.

Design by
DESIGN BASICS, INC.

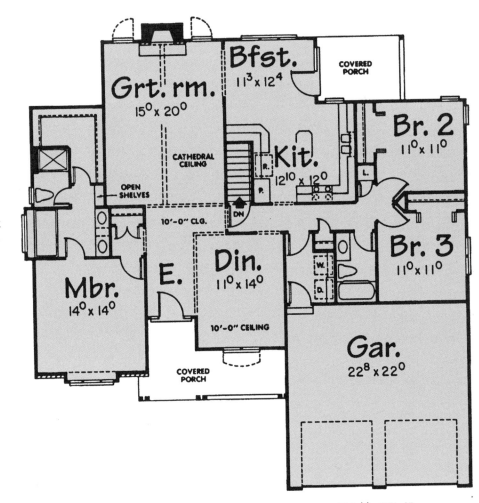

Width 55'-4"
Depth 56'-0"

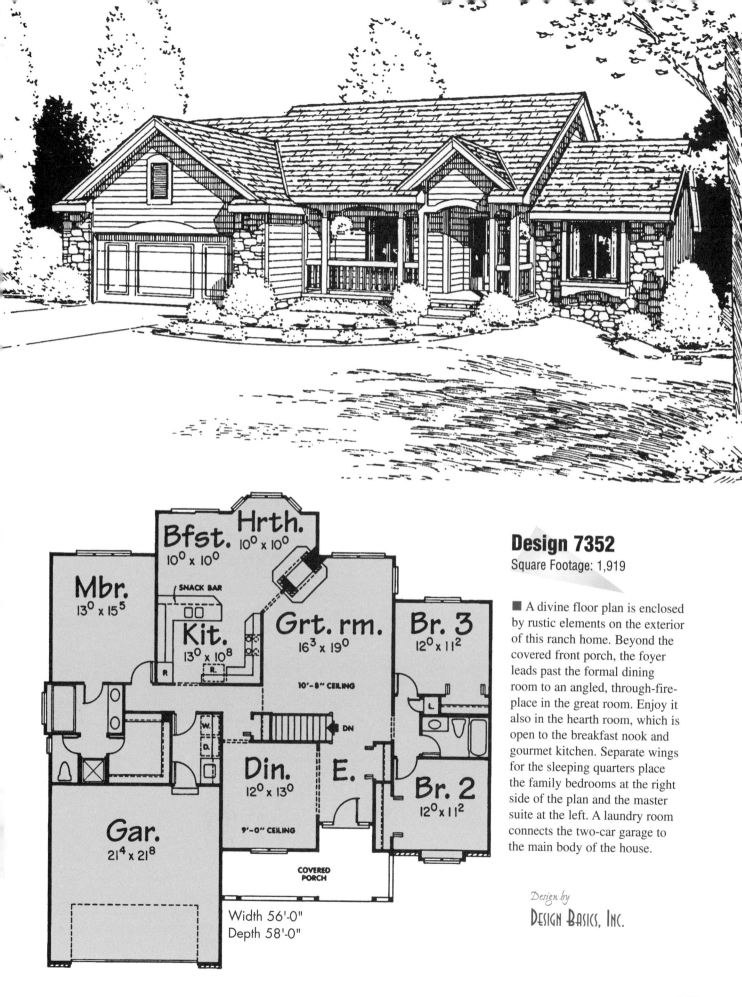

Design 7352

Square Footage: 1,919

■ A divine floor plan is enclosed by rustic elements on the exterior of this ranch home. Beyond the covered front porch, the foyer leads past the formal dining room to an angled, through-fireplace in the great room. Enjoy it also in the hearth room, which is open to the breakfast nook and gourmet kitchen. Separate wings for the sleeping quarters place the family bedrooms at the right side of the plan and the master suite at the left. A laundry room connects the two-car garage to the main body of the house.

Design by
DESIGN BASICS, INC.

Width 56'-0"
Depth 58'-0"

Floor plan labels:

Mbr. 13⁰ x 15⁵
Bfst. 10⁰ x 10⁰
Hrth. 10⁰ x 10⁰
SNACK BAR
Kit. 13⁰ x 10⁸
Grt. rm. 16³ x 19⁰
Br. 3 12⁰ x 11²
10'-8" CEILING
Gar. 21⁴ x 21⁸
Din. 12⁰ x 13⁰
9'-0" CEILING
E.
Br. 2 12⁰ x 11²
COVERED PORCH

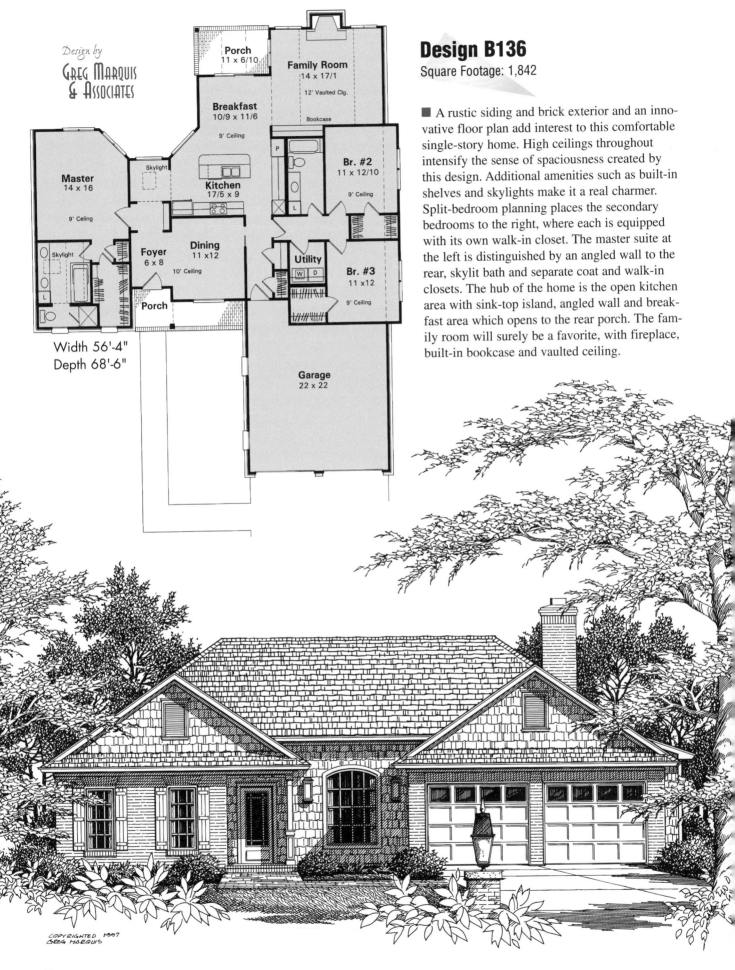

Design by
Greg Marquis
& Associates

Porch
11 x 6/10

Family Room
14 x 17/1

12' Vaulted Clg.

Breakfast
10/9 x 11/6

9' Ceiling

Bookcase

Skylight

P

Br. #2
11 x 12/10

9' Ceiling

L

Master
14 x 16

9' Celing

Kitchen
17/5 x 9

Skylight

L

Foyer
6 x 8

Dining
11 x12

10' Ceiling

Utility
W D

Br. #3
11 x12

9' Ceiling

Porch

Garage
22 x 22

Width 56'-4"
Depth 68'-6"

Design B136
Square Footage: 1,842

■ A rustic siding and brick exterior and an innovative floor plan add interest to this comfortable single-story home. High ceilings throughout intensify the sense of spaciousness created by this design. Additional amenities such as built-in shelves and skylights make it a real charmer. Split-bedroom planning places the secondary bedrooms to the right, where each is equipped with its own walk-in closet. The master suite at the left is distinguished by an angled wall to the rear, skylit bath and separate coat and walk-in closets. The hub of the home is the open kitchen area with sink-top island, angled wall and breakfast area which opens to the rear porch. The family room will surely be a favorite, with fireplace, built-in bookcase and vaulted ceiling.

Design 3498

Square Footage: 2,135

■ You'll savor the timeless style of this charming bungalow design. With pleasing proportions, it welcomes all onto its expansive front porch—perfect for quiet conversations. Inside, livability excels with a side facing family kitchen. Here, an interesting bumped-out nook facilitates the placement of a built-in table and bench seats. A formal dining room rests to the rear of the plan and enjoys direct access to a back porch. The parlor, with a central fireplace, also has access to this outdoor living area. The master bedroom is just a step away from the living room. It offers large dimensions and a private bath with a walk-in closet, dual lavs and a bumped-out tub. An additional bedroom may also serve as a study.

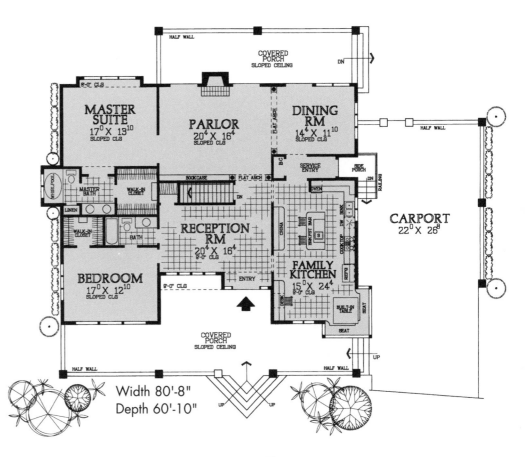

Width 80'-8"
Depth 60'-10"

Design by
HOME PLANNERS

QUOTE ONE®

Cost to build? See page 434
to order complete cost estimate
to build this house in your area!

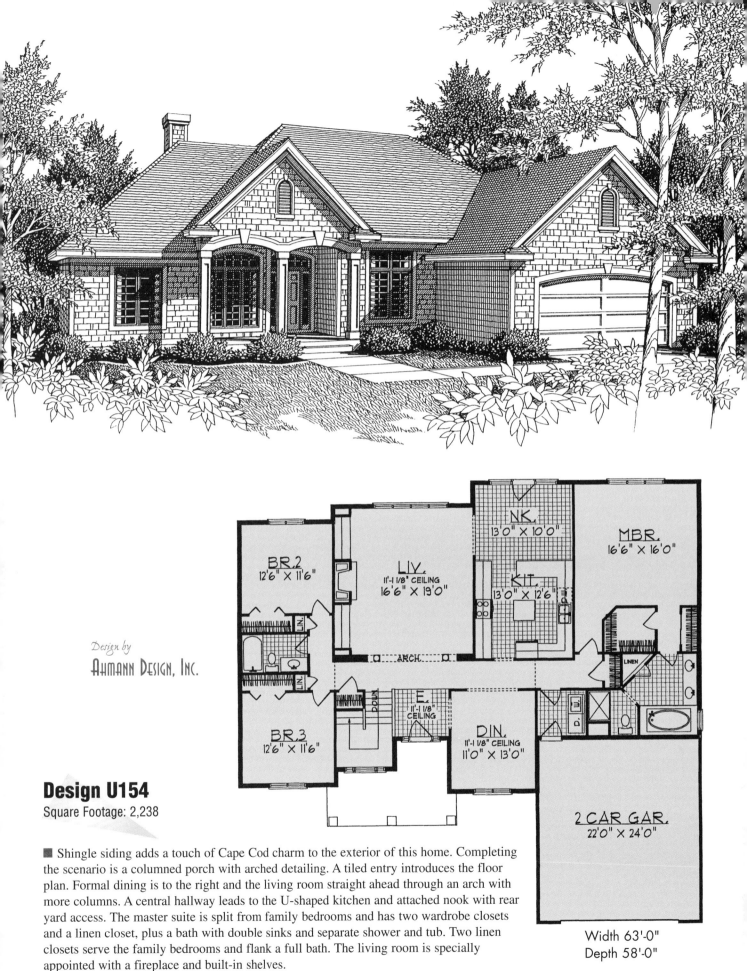

Design by
Ahmann Design, Inc.

Floor plan labels:

BR.2 12'6" X 11'6"

LIV. 11'-1 1/8" CEILING 16'6" X 19'0"

NK. 13'0" X 10'0"

MBR. 16'6" X 16'0"

KIT. 13'0" X 12'6"

LIN.

LINEN

BR.3 12'6" X 11'6"

ARCH.

DOWN

E. 11'-1 1/8" CEILING

DIN. 11'-1 1/8" CEILING 11'0" X 13'0"

2 CAR GAR. 22'0" X 24'0"

Design U154

Square Footage: 2,238

■ Shingle siding adds a touch of Cape Cod charm to the exterior of this home. Completing the scenario is a columned porch with arched detailing. A tiled entry introduces the floor plan. Formal dining is to the right and the living room straight ahead through an arch with more columns. A central hallway leads to the U-shaped kitchen and attached nook with rear yard access. The master suite is split from family bedrooms and has two wardrobe closets and a linen closet, plus a bath with double sinks and separate shower and tub. Two linen closets serve the family bedrooms and flank a full bath. The living room is specially appointed with a fireplace and built-in shelves.

Width 63'-0"
Depth 58'-0"

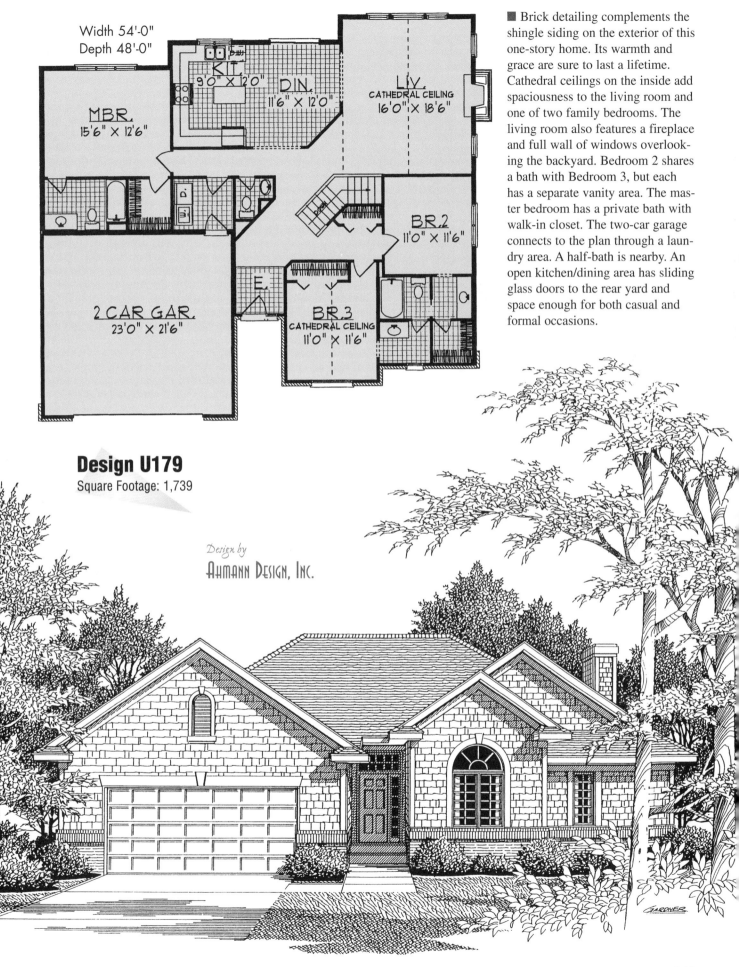

Width 54'-0"
Depth 48'-0"

MBR.
15'6" X 12'6"

KIT.
9'0" X 12'0"

DIN.
11'6" X 12'0"

LIV.
CATHEDRAL CEILING
16'0" X 18'6"

2 CAR GAR.
23'0" X 21'6"

BR.2
11'0" X 11'6"

BR.3
CATHEDRAL CEILING
11'0" X 11'6"

Design U179
Square Footage: 1,739

Design by
Ahmann Design, Inc.

■ Brick detailing complements the shingle siding on the exterior of this one-story home. Its warmth and grace are sure to last a lifetime. Cathedral ceilings on the inside add spaciousness to the living room and one of two family bedrooms. The living room also features a fireplace and full wall of windows overlooking the backyard. Bedroom 2 shares a bath with Bedroom 3, but each has a separate vanity area. The master bedroom has a private bath with walk-in closet. The two-car garage connects to the plan through a laundry area. A half-bath is nearby. An open kitchen/dining area has sliding glass doors to the rear yard and space enough for both casual and formal occasions.

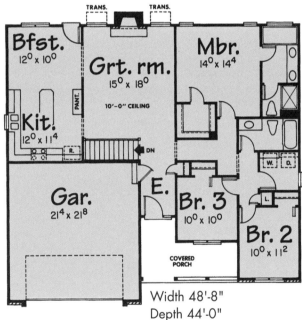

Width 48'-8"
Depth 44'-0"

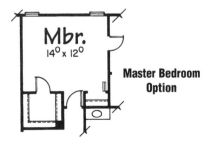

Master Bedroom Option

Design by
DESIGN BASICS, INC.

Design 7373

Square Footage: 1,453

■ With two gables, a hip roof and a covered front porch, this petite three bedroom home is sure to please. A spacious great room features a warming fireplace flanked by transom windows. In the kitchen, an island counter is available for added space to prepare meals. A large breakfast area is adjacent to this room. Two secondary bedrooms share a full bath as well as easy access to the laundry room. The master bedroom offers a walk-in closet and a private bath. Note the option for a second closet in the bedroom.

Design by
HOME PLANNERS

QUOTE ONE®

Cost to build? See page 434
to order complete cost estimate
to build this house in your area!

Width 75'-0"
Depth 47'-5"

Design 3804

Square Footage: 2,034

L

■ Horizontal siding, multi-pane windows and a simple balustrade lend a Prairies 'N' Plains flavor to this traditional, three bedroom home. A roomy foyer with a sloped ceiling leads through a tiled vestibule with built-in shelves to the spacious gathering room, complete with a warming fireplace. An angled kitchen with a snack bar easily serves the formal dining room, which leads outdoors to the rear entertainment terrace. The luxurious master suite has its own door to the terrace as well as a fabulous private bath with a windowed whirlpool tub. Two additional bedrooms share a full bath and a hall that offers more wardrobe space.

■ A porch with column detailing covers the entry to this single-story American classic. Inside, the foyer opens to the living room with a wall of windows and French doors that lead outside. A splendid colonnade defines the banquet-sized dining room. To the right, the spacious kitchen with work island opens to a sunlit breakfast area and a keeping room featuring a warming hearth and doors to the rear deck. A hallway just off the foyer leads to the double doors of the master suite. Inside, the special shape of the suite and mirrored ceiling detail make this room unique. The bath accommodates every need with His and Hers vanities, a garden tub and walk-in closet. Two additional bedrooms with spacious closets, common bath with dual vanities, and individual tub and water closet complete the main level. This home is designed with a basement foundation.

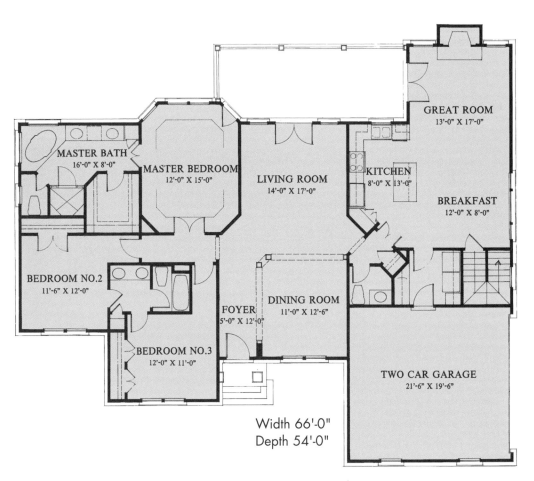

MASTER BATH
16'-0" X 8'-0"

MASTER BEDROOM
12'-0" X 15'-0"

LIVING ROOM
14'-0" X 17'-0"

GREAT ROOM
13'-0" X 17'-0"

KITCHEN
8'-0" X 13'-0"

BREAKFAST
12'-0" X 8'-0"

BEDROOM NO.2
11'-6" X 12'-0"

BEDROOM NO.3
12'-0" X 11'-0"

FOYER
5'-0" X 12'-0"

DINING ROOM
11'-0" X 12'-6"

TWO CAR GARAGE
21'-6" X 19'-6"

Width 66'-0"
Depth 54'-0"

Design T072
Square Footage: 2,078

Design by
DESIGN TRADITIONS

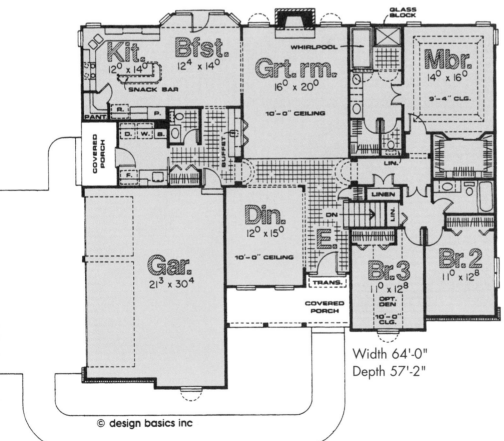

Width 64'-0"
Depth 57'-2"

Design 7332

Square Footage: 2,311

■ Interesting details on the front porch add to the appeal of this ranch home. The great room is highlighted by a pass-through wet bar/buffet and sits just across the hall from the formal dining room. A well-planned kitchen features a walk-in pantry and L-shaped island snack bar. The bedrooms are found in a cluster to the right of the home; a master suite, and two family bedrooms sharing a full bath. The master suite has a shower with glass-block detailing, a whirlpool tub and dual vanities. A three-car garage attaches to the main house via a service entrance.

Design by
Design Basics, Inc.

Design E103

Square Footage: 2,355

■ Round columns and arched windows grace the elegant entry of this Savannah cottage. Front and rear porches offer plenty of room to sit and relish a sweet breeze on a warm summer evening—and further embellish an easy-care stucco exterior. Inside, delightful views of the rear courtyard abound. The breakfast area, family room and master suite all enjoy this amenity. Raised ceilings in these last two rooms expand the plan and add drama to the interior. The convenient kitchen/breakfast area, just off the family room, features a snack bar and a view to the rear yard. Please specify crawlspace or slab foundation when ordering.

Design by
CHATHAM HOME
PLANNING, INC.

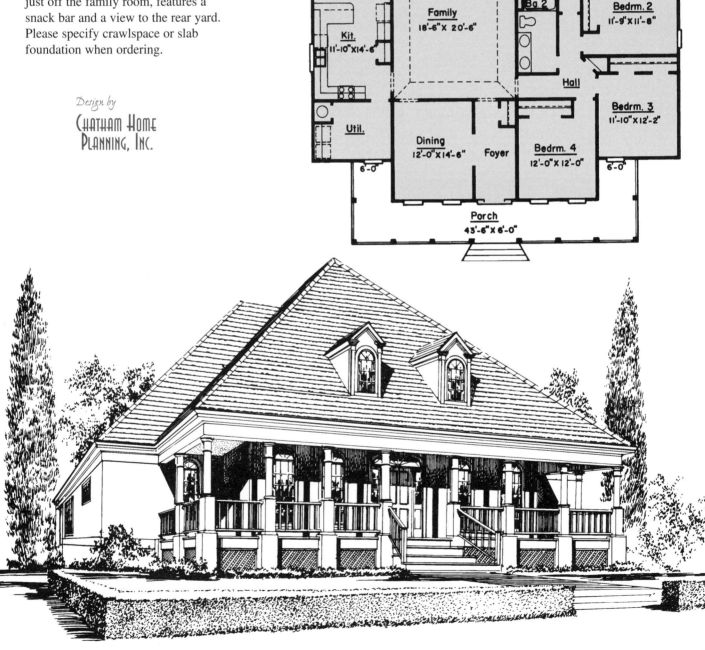

154

Design E106
Square Footage: 1,704

Stor 5'

Carport 20' X 20'

Porch

Bedroom 16' X 13'- 2"

Bath

Ba

Living 16' X 18'- 6"

Breakfast 9'- 2" X 9'- 8"

Kit 9'- 2" X 13'- 2"

Bedroom 10' X 12'- 6"

Bedroom 10' X 12'- 6"

9' CLG. **Foy.**

Dining 12' X 12'- 6"

Utility 7' X 10'

Porch 47' X 6'

Width 47'-0"
Depth 66'-0"

■ This Southern cottage provides spacious front and rear porches—plus a whole lot more. The side-lit entry leads to the formal dining room on the right and a grand living space with tray ceiling just beyond. The open kitchen and breakfast areas allow courtyard views and connect directly to the living areas. The large master suite features separate walk-in closets and a bath with two lavatories, a whirlpool tub and a separate shower. Two family bedrooms share a full bath. This home includes a nine-foot ceiling in the foyer and raised ceilings in the living room and master bedroom. Please specify crawlspace or slab foundation when ordering.

Design by
CHATHAM HOME
PLANNING, INC.

Design T194

Square Footage: 2,485

■ The most inviting amenity of this country plan has to be its extra-wide, side-wrap porch from which three entrances to the home open. The notable great room has a formal ceiling detail, fireplace, built-ins and French doors to the rear porch. Casual entertaining will surely revolve around activity in the open country kitchen. The master bedroom enjoys a lush bath, walk-in closet and private French doors to the rear porch. Two secondary bedrooms share a private bath. A full two-car garage is joined to the rear of the home, out of sight so that the home's curb appeal is not compromised. This house is designed with a basement foundation.

Design by
DESIGN TRADITIONS

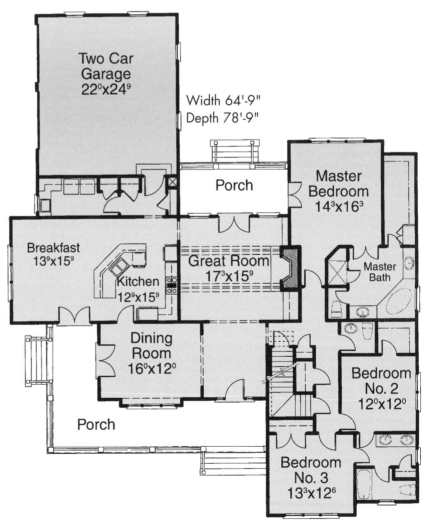

Two Car Garage 22⁰x24⁹

Width 64'-9"
Depth 78'-9"

Porch

Master Bedroom 14³x16³

Breakfast 13⁹x15⁹

Kitchen 12⁹x15⁹

Great Room 17³x15⁹

Master Bath

Dining Room 16⁰x12⁰

Bedroom No. 2 12⁰x12⁰

Porch

Bedroom No. 3 13³x12⁶

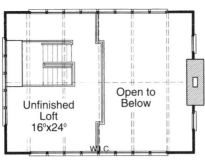

Unfinished
Loft
16⁰x24⁰

Open to
Below

W.I.C.

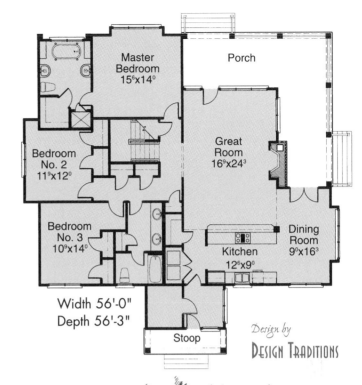

Master
Bedroom
15⁶x14⁰

Porch

Bedroom
No. 2
11⁹x12⁰

Great
Room
16⁹x24³

Bedroom
No. 3
10⁹x14⁰

Kitchen
12⁶x9⁰

Dining
Room
9⁰x16³

Width 56'-0"
Depth 56'-3"

Stoop

Design by
DESIGN TRADITIONS

Design T183

Square Footage: 2,019
Loft: 384 square feet

■ This design takes inspiration from the casual fishing cabins of the Pacific Northwest and interprets it for modern livability. It offers three options for a main entrance. One door opens onto a mud porch, where a small hall leads to a galley kitchen and the vaulted great room. Two French doors on the side porch open into a dining room with bay-window seating. Another porch entrance opens directly into the great room. The great room is centered around a massive stone fireplace and is accented with a beautiful wall of windows. The secluded master bedroom features a master bath with a claw-foot tub and twin pedestal sinks, as well as a separate shower and walk-in closet. Two more bedrooms share a spacious bath. Ideal for a lounge or extra sleeping space, an unfinished loft looks over the great room.

© Design Traditions

157

Design B130

Square Footage: 1,507

■ Up the steps, through the foyer and step into a welcoming family room with fireplace and double doors which open onto the long covered front porch. This compact three-bedroom country cottage features lots of closet space and a master suite with nine-foot ceiling in the bedroom and dual vanities in the master bath. The dining room with built-in pantry and china cabinet is open to the family room and the island kitchen. A laundry room is tucked into the center of the home. The kitchen has access to the rear patio.

Design by
Greg Marquis & Associates

Width 49'-0"
Depth 80'-0"

Garage
22 x 22

Patio

Master
16 x 13
9' CLG.

Kitchen
14 x 10/7

9' Ceiling

Dining
14 x 10

BR. #2
10 x 11

Pantry

China Cab.

BR. #3
11 x 10/8

Family Room
15 x 19/6
10' CLG.

Foyer

Porch
6 x 27/8

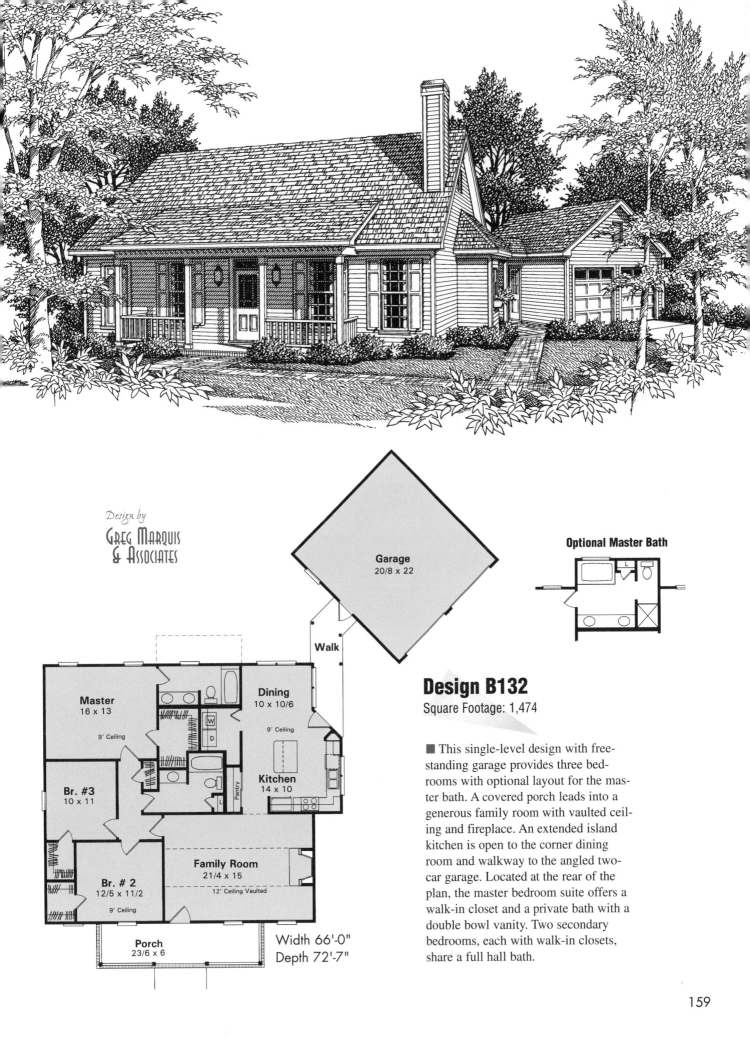

Design by
Greg Marquis & Associates

Garage
20/8 x 22

Optional Master Bath

Walk

Master
16 x 13

9' Ceiling

Dining
10 x 10/6

9' Ceiling

W
D

Kitchen
14 x 10

Pantry

Br. #3
10 x 11

Family Room
21/4 x 15

12' Ceiling Vaulted

Br. # 2
12/5 x 11/2

9' Ceiling

Porch
23/6 x 6

Width 66'-0"
Depth 72'-7"

Design B132
Square Footage: 1,474

■ This single-level design with free-standing garage provides three bedrooms with optional layout for the master bath. A covered porch leads into a generous family room with vaulted ceiling and fireplace. An extended island kitchen is open to the corner dining room and walkway to the angled two-car garage. Located at the rear of the plan, the master bedroom suite offers a walk-in closet and a private bath with a double bowl vanity. Two secondary bedrooms, each with walk-in closets, share a full hall bath.

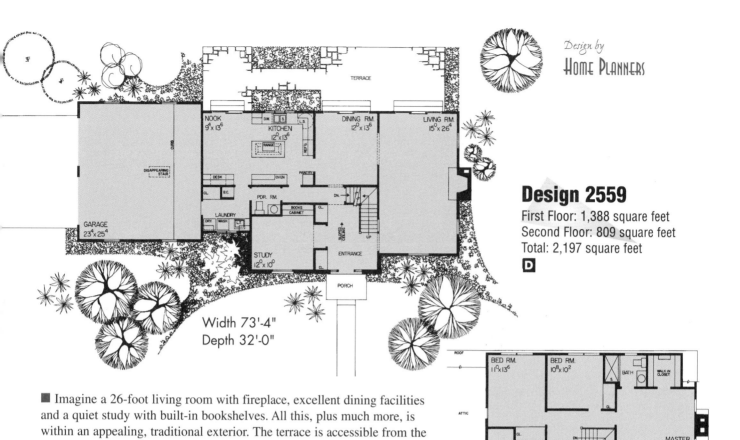

Design by
HOME PLANNERS

Width 73'-4"
Depth 32'-0"

Design 2559

First Floor: 1,388 square feet
Second Floor: 809 square feet
Total: 2,197 square feet

D

■ Imagine a 26-foot living room with fireplace, excellent dining facilities and a quiet study with built-in bookshelves. All this, plus much more, is within an appealing, traditional exterior. The terrace is accessible from the living room, dining room and breakfast nook. Upstairs, the master bedroom offers a private bath, a walk-in closet and access to attic storage. Two family bedrooms share a bath that has a double-bowl vanity. More attic storage is located above the garage.

*This home, as shown in the photograph, may differ from the actual blueprints.
For more detailed information, please check the floor plans carefully.*

Photo by Bob Greenspan

Design 9686

Square Footage: 1,980

■ Providing the utmost in flexible outdoor living, this home is graced with a covered front porch and generous rear deck. On the interior is a floor plan that is a pleasure to live in. The great room has a fireplace, cathedral ceiling and sliding glass doors with an arched window above to admit natural light. Impressive round columns promote a sense of elegance in the dining room. The master suite boasts a large master bedroom with two walk-in closets and a well-organized master bath with double-bowl vanity and a whirlpool tub. Two more bedrooms are located at the opposite end of the house for privacy. The garage is connected to the house with a breezeway. Please specify basement or crawlspace foundation when ordering.

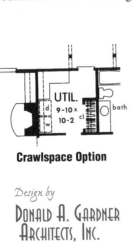

Crawlspace Option

Design by
Donald A. Gardner Architects, Inc.

Width 63'-10"
Depth 73'-4"

161

Design 9049

Square Footage: 1,891

■ This cozy one-story Victorian provides a wealth of architectural and design details that make it a pleasure to come home to. Begin with the veranda which wraps around three sides of the home, then investigate the raised-foyer entry which introduces the intriguing floor plan. From the formal dining room to the kitchen/breakfast room and ample living room, amenities abound: ten- and twelve-foot ceilings, numerous built-ins, French doors, a fireplace, a wet bar, a work island in the kitchen and a bay-windowed breakfast area. The bedrooms and baths are no less well appointed: large closets, double vanities, corner windows and built-ins.

QUOTE ONE®

Cost to build? See page 434 to order complete cost estimate to build this house in your area!

Design by
LARRY W. GARNETT & ASSOCIATES

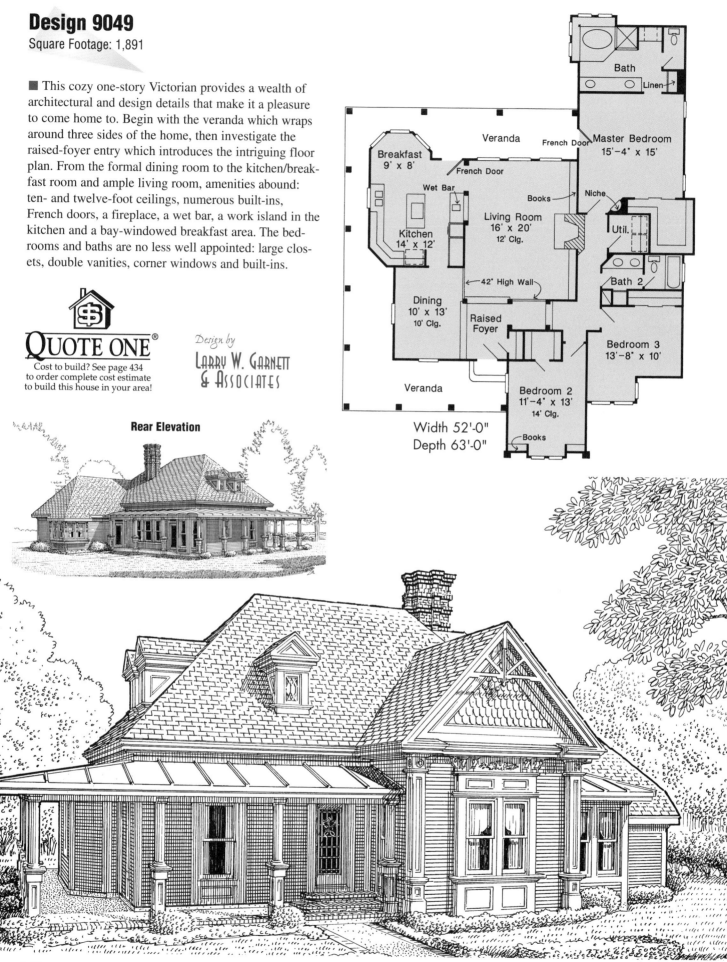

Rear Elevation

Veranda
Breakfast 9' x 8'
French Door
Wet Bar
Kitchen 14' x 12'
Living Room 16' x 20' 12' Clg.
Books
French Door
Master Bedroom 15'-4" x 15'
Bath
Linen
Niche
Util.
Bath 2
Dining 10' x 13' 10' Clg.
42" High Wall
Raised Foyer
Bedroom 3 13'-8" x 10'
Veranda
Bedroom 2 11'-4" x 13' 14' Clg.
Books
Books

Width 52'-0"
Depth 63'-0"

Design 3496

Square Footage: 2,033

L

■ Get more out of your homebuilding dollars with this unique one-story bungalow. A covered front porch provides sheltered entry into a spacious living room. A bookshelf and a column are special touches. The dining room enjoys a sloped ceiling, a wet bar and direct access to the rear covered patio. In the nearby kitchen, a breakfast bar accommodates quick meals. The adjacent family room rounds out this casual living area. The large master suite pampers with a sitting area, patio access and a luxurious bath which features a corner tub, a separate shower and dual lavatories. Two secondary bedrooms share a full hall bath.

QUOTE ONE®

Cost to build? See page 434 to order complete cost estimate to build this house in your area!

Width 47'-6"
Depth 61'-6"

Design by
HOME PLANNERS

Design M113

Square Footage: 2,277

Design by
Fillmore Design Group

■ A covered front porch, spindled columns and Victorian accents project country style with a capital C! Farmhouse living is easy, as this floor plan demonstrates. To the left of the entry, a formal dining room easily converts to a study—or with its front porch access—a home office. An expansive living room features a cathedral ceiling, an entertainment center, a fireplace bordered by windows and patio access. U-shaped for efficiency, the island kitchen opens to a bright breakfast room that also provides passage to the covered patio. Split planning places two family bedrooms—each with a walk-in closet—and a shared bath to the left of the home and the secluded master suite to the right. A private covered patio is accessed from the master bedroom, inviting romantic nights and light breezes. Two large walk-in closets precede a master bath designed for relaxation. Details for a full basement, a crawlspace and a slab foundation are included with the blueprints.

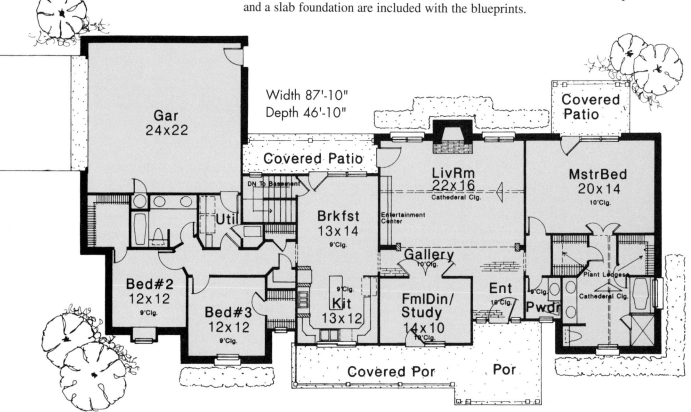

Width 87'-10"
Depth 46'-10"

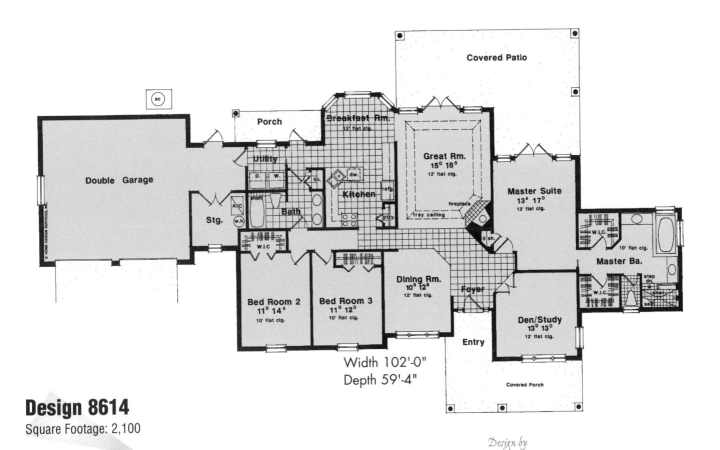

Width 102'-0"
Depth 59'-4"

Design 8614

Square Footage: 2,100

■ Gingerbread trim crowns the roof of this Victorian-inspired plan, enhanced by an intricate facade with high-ceilinged spaces. The covered porch gives way to a tiled foyer. Double doors on the right open to a den or study with a twelve-foot ceiling. The splendid great room sports a tray ceiling, corner fireplace and French doors to a covered patio. The pass-through kitchen serves the front-facing dining room and bayed breakfast room with equal ease. Bedrooms include a master suite with patio access and a sunken shower, and two secondary bedrooms which share a bath.

Design by
Home Design Services

Design by
HOME PLANNERS

COVERED PATIO

SEAT

SEAT

SPA

SUN TERRACE

LOW WALL

BATH

LINEN

BEDRM
12² x 10⁴
9'-0" CLG

VESTIBULE

MORNING ROOM
11⁶ x 13⁶
9'-0" CLG

BEDRM
12² x 11¹⁰
9'-0" CLG

POWDER RM

RAILING

GARDEN TUB

SHWR

LOW WALL

WALK-IN CLOSET

PLANT SHELF ABV

MEDIA SHELF

MASTER BATH

LINEN

PLANT SHELF ABV

NICHE

GREAT RM
19⁰ x 13⁰
SLOPED CLG

SNACK BAR

HOME CENTER

BROOM CLOSET

HVAC

WH

UTILITY SINK

W

D

HVAC

GARAGE
21⁸ x 20⁰

KIT
11⁶ x 18⁰
9'-0" CLG

PANTRY

OVN

COOK TOP

LAUNDRY ROOM

SLOPES CLG

LOW WALL

REFG

DW

B

MASTER SUITE
14⁰ x 12²
SLOPED CLG

FOYER

PLANT SHELF ABV

DINING RM
11⁴ x 11⁶
SLOPED CLG

COVERED PORCH

RAILING

QUOTE ONE®

Cost to build? See page 434
to order complete cost estimate
to build this house in your area!

Design 3676

Square Footage: 2,090

L D

■ Artistic angles and arches provided in the floor plan of this traditional design give it a special appeal. Elegant curves lead you from the foyer to the private master bedroom on the left or through a nine-foot arch to the corner dining room on the right. The great room features an angled fireplace with a built-in media shelf connecting to the raised hearth. The kitchen, in the center of the home, provides lots of counter space and a wonderful curved snack bar. Its close proximity to both the dining room and the morning room make it ideal. Two family bedrooms share a full bath and easy access to the rear sun porch.

Width 76'-0"
Depth 64'-0"

Design V006

Square Footage: 1,527

■ Three dormers, horizontal siding and a covered front porch welcome friends and family to this three-bedroom country home. Inside, the entry opens directly into the great room, where a warming fireplace waits for those cool evenings. Angles dress up the kitchen, which offers a workspace island/snack counter and access to the sunny keeping room. Two family bedrooms share a hall bath, while the master bedroom features a tray ceiling, walk-in closet and a private bath. The attached two-car garage easily shelters the family fleet.

Design by
UNITED DESIGN
ASSOCIATES, INC.

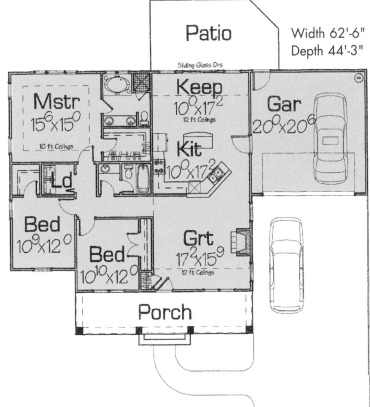

Width 62'-6"
Depth 44'-3"

Patio

Sliding Glass Drs

Keep
10⁰x17²
12 ft Ceilings

Gar
20⁰x20⁶

Mstr
15⁶x15⁰
10 ft Ceilings

Kit
10⁰x17²

Ld

Bed
10⁹x12⁰

Bed
10¹⁰x12⁰

Grt
17²x15⁹
12 ft Ceilings

Porch

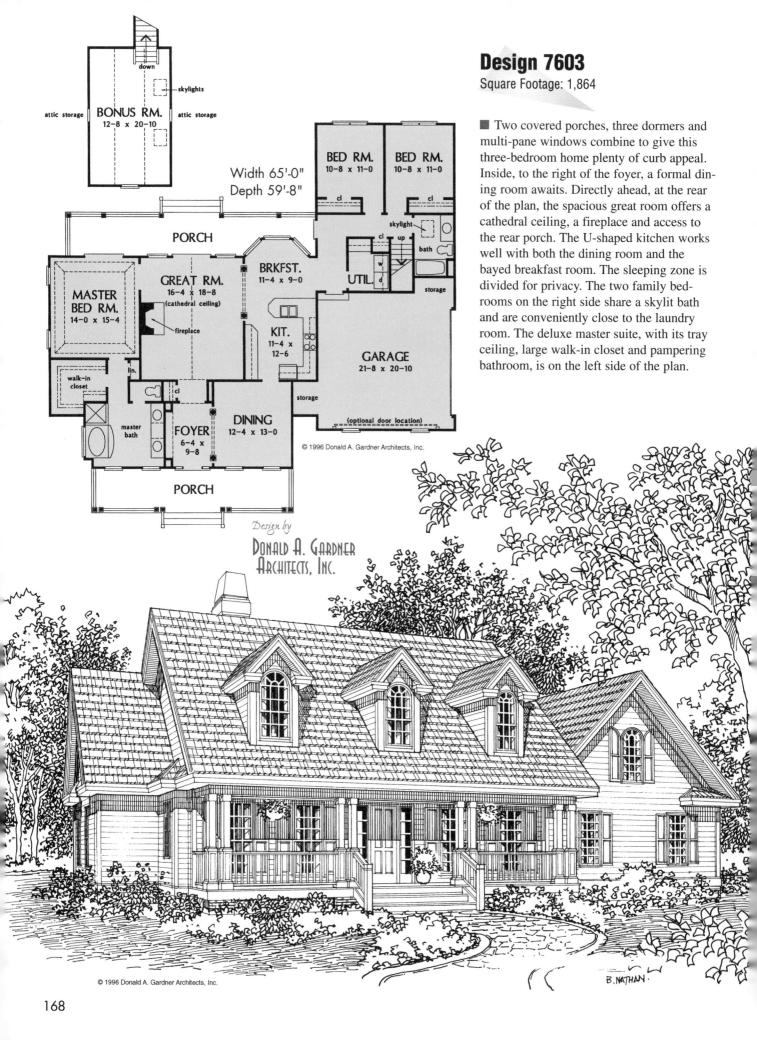

BONUS RM.
12-8 x 20-10

down

skylights

attic storage   attic storage

Width 65'-0"
Depth 59'-8"

BED RM.
10-8 x 11-0

BED RM.
10-8 x 11-0

cl   cl

skylight

PORCH

cl   up

bath

UTIL.

w
d

storage

GREAT RM.
16-4 x 18-8
(cathedral ceiling)

BRKFST.
11-4 x 9-0

MASTER
BED RM.
14-0 x 15-4

fireplace

lin.

KIT.
11-4 x
12-6

GARAGE
21-8 x 20-10

walk-in
closet

cl

storage

master
bath

FOYER
6-4 x
9-8

DINING
12-4 x 13-0

(optional door location)

PORCH

© 1996 Donald A. Gardner Architects, Inc.

Design by
DONALD A. GARDNER
ARCHITECTS, INC.

Design 7603

Square Footage: 1,864

■ Two covered porches, three dormers and multi-pane windows combine to give this three-bedroom home plenty of curb appeal. Inside, to the right of the foyer, a formal dining room awaits. Directly ahead, at the rear of the plan, the spacious great room offers a cathedral ceiling, a fireplace and access to the rear porch. The U-shaped kitchen works well with both the dining room and the bayed breakfast room. The sleeping zone is divided for privacy. The two family bedrooms on the right side share a skylit bath and are conveniently close to the laundry room. The deluxe master suite, with its tray ceiling, large walk-in closet and pampering bathroom, is on the left side of the plan.

B. NATHAN.

B.NATHAN.

Design 7658

Square Footage: 1,899
Bonus Room: 315 square feet

■ Country charm in a one-story home—but it looks like a two-story. The upper-level dormers provide light to the floor plan and add detailing to the exterior. A covered porch wraps around three sides of the plan and is accessed at two separate points. Both the great room and the master bedroom have cathedral ceilings, while the formal dining room has a vaulted ceiling. A screen porch to the rear can be reached from the breakfast room (note the bay window here). The plan calls for three bedrooms, but one may be used as a study or home office if you choose. The two-car garage sits to the rear of the plan, taking nothing away from the beauty of the facade. Appointments in the master suite include a bath with vaulted ceiling, garden whirlpool and compartmented toilet. A bonus room over the garage allows space to expand.

Design by

DONALD A. GARDNER
ARCHITECTS, INC.

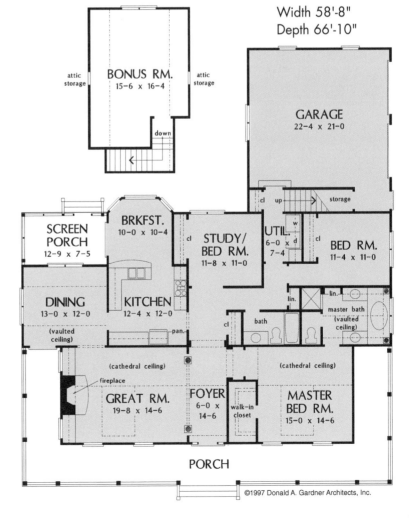

Width 58'-8"
Depth 66'-10"

169

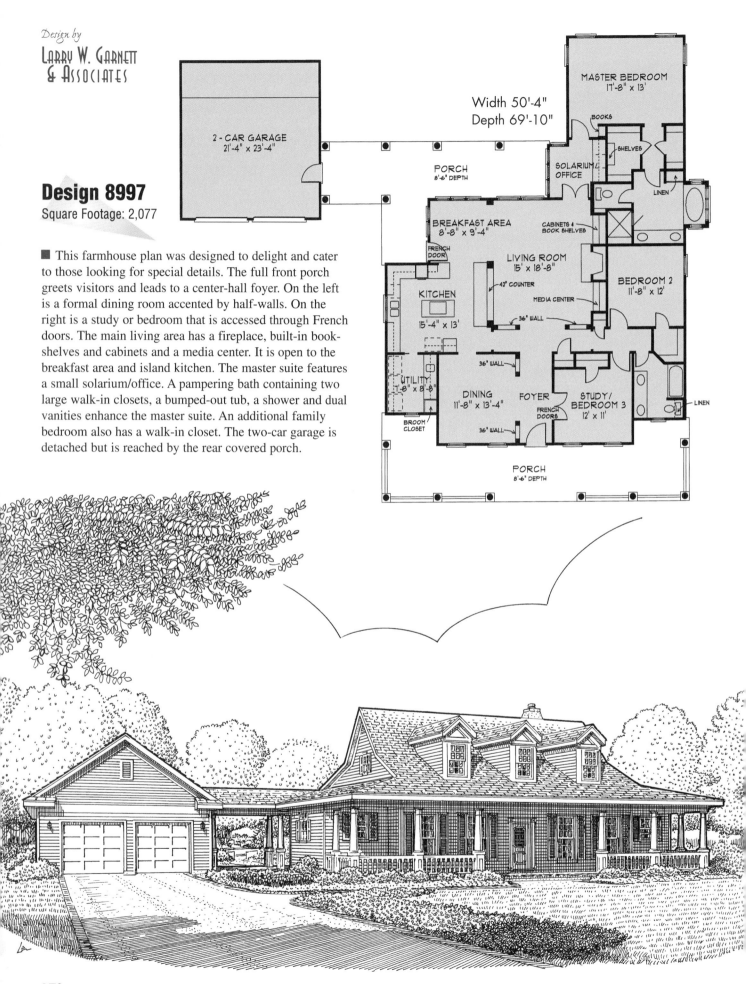

Design by

LARRY W. GARNETT & ASSOCIATES

2 - CAR GARAGE
21'-4" x 23'-4"

Width 50'-4"
Depth 69'-10"

Design 8997

Square Footage: 2,077

■ This farmhouse plan was designed to delight and cater to those looking for special details. The full front porch greets visitors and leads to a center-hall foyer. On the left is a formal dining room accented by half-walls. On the right is a study or bedroom that is accessed through French doors. The main living area has a fireplace, built-in bookshelves and cabinets and a media center. It is open to the breakfast area and island kitchen. The master suite features a small solarium/office. A pampering bath containing two large walk-in closets, a bumped-out tub, a shower and dual vanities enhance the master suite. An additional family bedroom also has a walk-in closet. The two-car garage is detached but is reached by the rear covered porch.

MASTER BEDROOM
17'-8" x 13'

BOOKS

SHELVES

SOLARIUM/
OFFICE

LINEN

PORCH
8'-6" DEPTH

BREAKFAST AREA
8'-8" x 9'-4"

CABINETS &
BOOK SHELVES

FRENCH
DOOR

LIVING ROOM
15' x 18'-8"

42" COUNTER

BEDROOM 2
11'-8" x 12'

KITCHEN
15'-4" x 13'

MEDIA CENTER

36" WALL

UTILITY
7'-6" x 8'-8"

36" WALL

DINING
11'-8" x 13'-4"

FOYER

STUDY/
BEDROOM 3
12' x 11'

LINEN

BROOM
CLOSET

36" WALL

FRENCH
DOORS

PORCH
8'-6" DEPTH

Design 7616

Square Footage: 2,450

■ A handsome display of columns
frames the porch of this gracious
Southern home. The foyer opens to the
dining room and to a study, which could
also be an additional bedroom. The
open living room and family room are
joined under a dramatic cathedral ceiling, divided with a showpiece fireplace
that opens to both rooms. The efficient
corner kitchen has a handy breakfast
nook that opens to a morning porch and
a work island with a cooktop and
curved snack bar. The master suite has a
stylish tray ceiling, twin walk-in closets
and a compartmented bath with an elegant bumped-out tub.

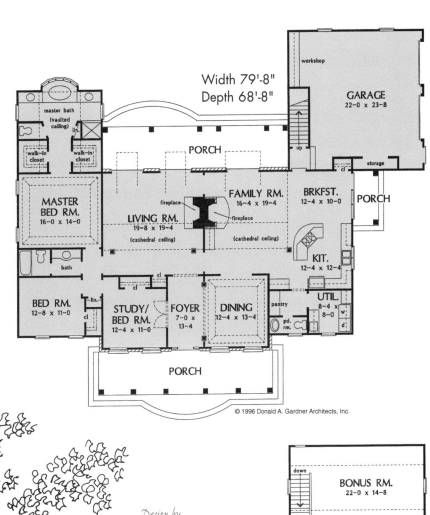

Width 79'-8"
Depth 68'-8"

© 1996 Donald A. Gardner Architects, Inc.

Design by
Donald A. Gardner
Architects, Inc.

© 1996 Donald A. Gardner Architects, Inc.   B. NATHAN

Design B100

Square Footage: 2,988

■ This large, rambling country home offers all of its amenities on one level, providing plenty of convenience. The living room, with a fireplace, and the dining room open onto a large rear porch with skylights. The porch can also be accessed from the equally spacious master suite, which offers a roomy master bath and a walk-in closet and is located away from the other bedrooms. The huge kitchen and breakfast/keeping room with a fireplace are a definite magnet for entertaining. From the two-car garage, the large utility room/mud room leads to a full bath, making clean-up a breeze.

Width 92'-0"
Depth 78'-0"

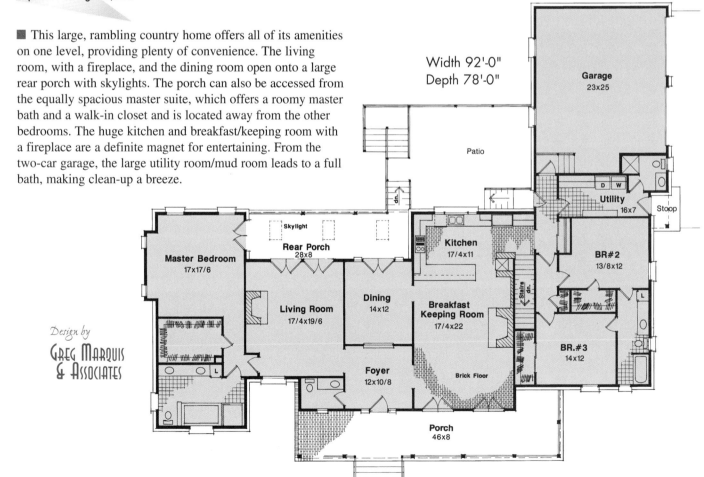

Design by
GREG MARQUIS
& ASSOCIATES

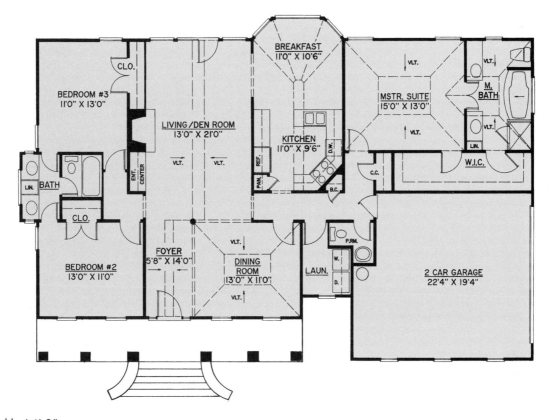

Width 64'-0"
Depth 40'-6"

Design by
Archival Designs

Design S126

Square Footage: 1,751

■ This raised-porch farmhouse holds all the charisma of others of its style, but boasts a one-story floor plan. A huge living area dominates the center of the plan. It features a vaulted ceiling, built-ins and a warming fireplace. The formal dining room is across the hall and open to the foyer and the living area, defined by a single column at its corner. Casual dining takes place in a light-filled breakfast room, attached to the designer kitchen. A spectacular master suite sits behind the two-car garage. It has a tray ceiling, enormous walk-in closet and well-appointed bath. Family bedrooms are at the other end of the hallway and share a jack-and-jill bath with separate vanity area.

© Design Traditions

Design T187

Square Footage: 2,721

■ In this design, equally at home in the country or at the coast, classic elements play against a rustic shingle-and-stone exterior. Doric porch columns provide the elegance, while banks of cottage-style windows let in lots of natural light. The symmetrical layout of the foyer and formal dining room blend easily with the cozy great room. Here, a fireplace creates a welcome atmosphere that invites you to select a novel from one of the built-in bookcases and curl up in your favorite easy chair. The adjacent U-shaped kitchen combines with a sunny breakfast room that opens onto a rear porch, making casual meals a plea-sure. Split away from family bedrooms for privacy, the master suite occupies the right side of the house and enjoys a dramatic master bath. The left wing contains two secondary bedrooms that share a bath with compartmentalized vanity/dressing areas. This home is designed with a basement foundation.

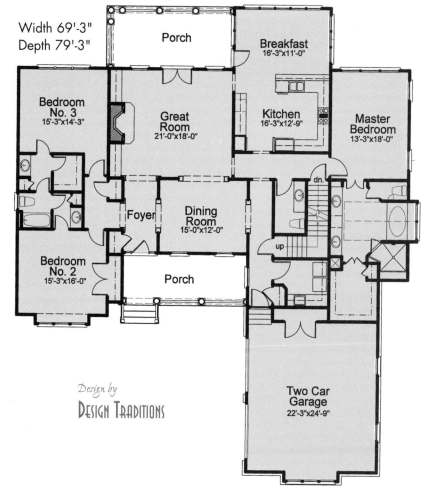

Width 69'-3"
Depth 79'-3"

Porch

Breakfast
16'-3"x11'-0"

Bedroom
No. 3
15'-3"x14'-3"

Great
Room
21'-0"x18'-0"

Kitchen
16'-3"x12'-9"

Master
Bedroom
13'-3"x18'-0"

Foyer

Dining
Room
15'-0"x12'-0"

dn.

up

Bedroom
No. 2
15'-3"x16'-0"

Porch

Two Car
Garage
22'-3"x24'-9"

Design by
DESIGN TRADITIONS

174

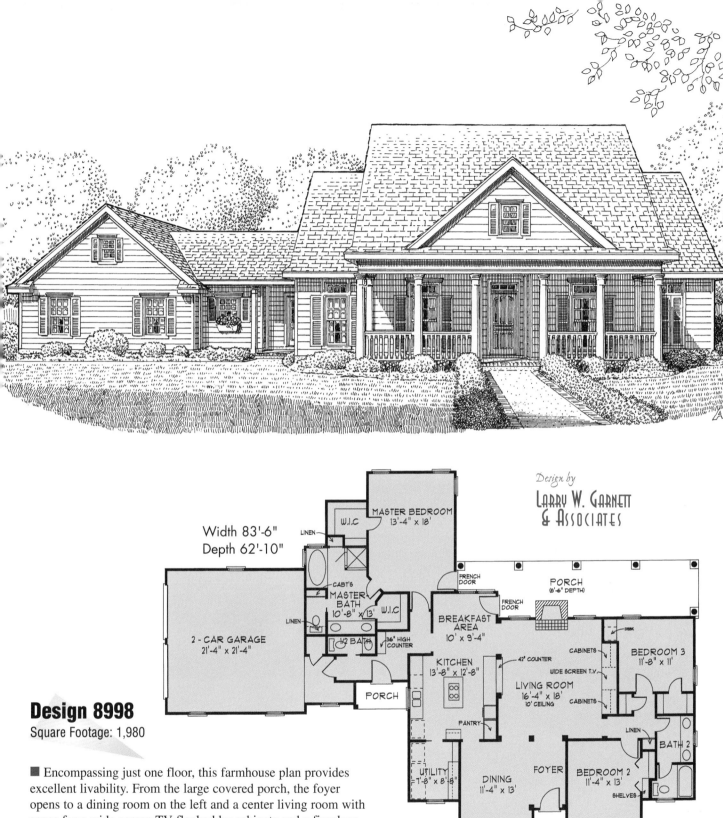

Width 83'-6"
Depth 62'-10"

Design by
Larry W. Garnett
& Associates

MASTER BEDROOM
13'-4" x 18'

W.I.C

LINEN

CABT'S

MASTER BATH
10'-8" x 13'

W.I.C

LINEN

1/2 BATH

36" HIGH COUNTER

PORCH
(8'-6" DEPTH)

FRENCH DOOR

FRENCH DOOR

BREAKFAST AREA
10' x 9'-4"

DESK

2 - CAR GARAGE
21'-4" x 21'-4"

KITCHEN
13'-8" x 12'-8"

42" COUNTER

CABINETS

WIDE SCREEN T.V.

BEDROOM 3
11'-8" x 11'

LIVING ROOM
16'-4" x 18'
10' CEILING

CABINETS

PANTRY

PORCH

LINEN

BATH 2

UTILITY
7'-8" x 8'-8"

DINING
11'-4" x 13'

FOYER

BEDROOM 2
11'-4" x 13'

SHELVES

PORCH
(8'-6" DEPTH)

Design 8998
Square Footage: 1,980

■ Encompassing just one floor, this farmhouse plan provides excellent livability. From the large covered porch, the foyer opens to a dining room on the left and a center living room with space for a wide-screen TV flanked by cabinets and a fireplace with a scenic view on each side. The large kitchen sports an island cooktop and easy accessibility to the rear breakfast area, the utility room, and the dining room. While the family bedrooms reside on the right side of the plan and share a full bath with twin vanities, the master bedroom takes advantage of its secluded rear location. It features twin walk-in closets and vanities, a windowed corner tub, a separate shower and private access to the rear covered porch.

DECK

DECK

BEDROOM
11'-0'' x 10'-0''

LIVING ROOM
16'-0'' x 14'-0''

FP

KITCHEN
12'-0'' x 14'-0''

MASTER BEDROOM
16'-0'' x 14'-0''

WIC

BATH

VAULTED CEILING

Design by
R.L Pfotenhauer

BATH

VAULTED CEILING

FAMILY ENTRY

DN

BEDROOM
11'-0'' x 10'-0''

DINING ROOM
12'-0'' x 14'-0''

LAUNDRY

TWO-CAR GARAGE
21'-0'' x 21'-0''

ENTRY FOYER

W   D

Design F147

Square Footage: 1,550

PORCH

Width 62'-9"
Depth 36'-1"

■ If you like the rustic appeal of ranch-style homes, you'll love this version. Both horizontal and vertical siding appear on the exterior and are complemented by a columned covered porch and a delightful cupola as accent. The entry opens to a huge open living/dining room combination. A fireplace in the living area is flanked by windows and doors to one of two rear decks. A vaulted ceiling runs the width of this area. The kitchen also accesses the deck and features counterspace galore. Look for a private deck behind the master suite. A vaulted ceiling graces the master bedroom. Two family bedrooms have good closet space and share a full bath at the opposite end of the hall.

Design 7372

Square Footage: 1,433

■ This home is simplicity personified and tidy in its exterior approach with horizontal wood siding. But its size makes it the perfect starter or empty-nester plan. The covered porch is what you'll notice first—it leads to a central entry hall opening to a large great room. Look for a fireplace flanked by windows overlooking the rear yard and a twelve-foot ceiling here. The breakfast room is nearby, sharing a snack bar with the convenient kitchen. Two family bedrooms (or make one a den) and the master suite are to the right of the plan. The master suite is well appointed with a walk-in closet and bath with double sinks and separate tub and shower. A laundry room off the kitchen leads to the two-car garage.

Design by
DESIGN BASICS, INC.

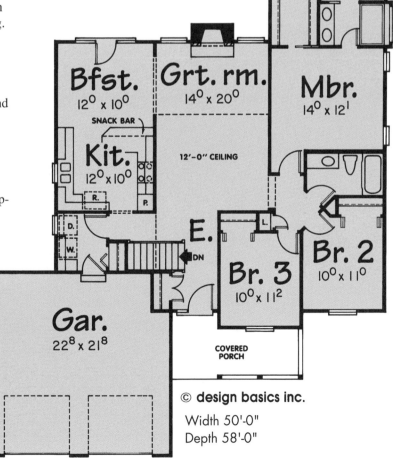

Bfst.
$12^0 \times 10^0$

SNACK BAR

Kit.
$12^0 \times 10^0$

R.

D.

W.

Grt. rm.
$14^0 \times 20^0$

12'-0" CEILING

E.

DN

Mbr.
$14^0 \times 12^1$

L.

Br. 3
$10^0 \times 11^2$

Br. 2
$10^0 \times 11^0$

Gar.
$22^8 \times 21^8$

COVERED PORCH

© design basics inc.

Width 50'-0"
Depth 58'-0"

Design B107

Square Footage: 1,475

■ This home-sweet-home features a welcoming front porch across it's entire length. Once you enter, you'll be greeted by ten-foot ceilings in the large family room and a cozily angled fireplace. The vaulted eat-in kitchen with its popular L-shape and work island includes an ample pantry and a laundry room. But there's more to this easy-to-build house. Note the large master bedroom with a walk-in closet. Each of the other two bedrooms also have walk-in closets. Out back, a covered walk runs next to the deck and connects the angled two-car garage with the living space in a most charming way. Details for both a crawlspace and slab foundation are included in the blueprints.

Design by
Greg Marquis
& Associates

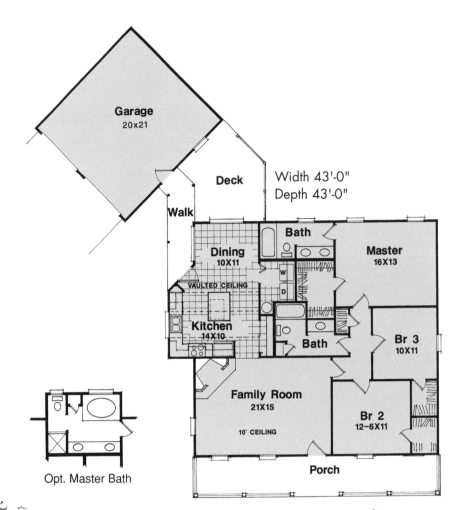

Opt. Master Bath

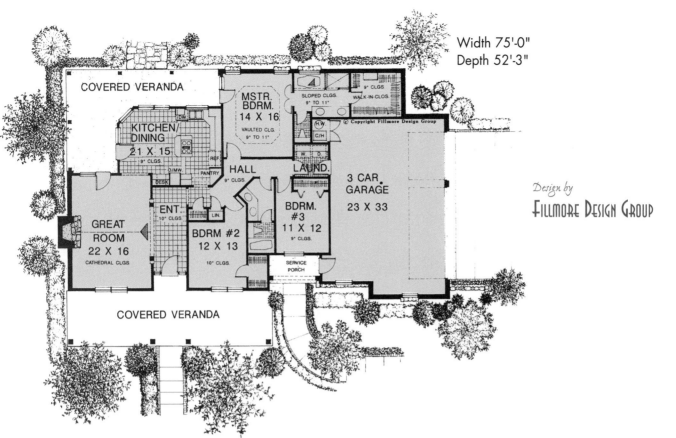

Width 75'-0"
Depth 52'-3"

COVERED VERANDA

MSTR. BDRM. 14 X 16
VAULTED CLG. 9" TO 11"

SLOPED CLGS. 9" TO 11"

WALK-IN-CLOS.

9" CLGS.

© Copyright Fillmore Design Group

KITCHEN/DINING 21 X 15
9" CLGS.

H.W.
C/H

W.D.

HALL 9" CLGS.

LAUND.

3 CAR GARAGE 23 X 33

Design by
FILLMORE DESIGN GROUP

PANTRY

DESK

ENT. 10" CLGS.

LIN.

BDRM. #3 11 X 12
9" CLGS.

GREAT ROOM 22 X 16
CATHEDRAL CLGS.

BDRM #2 12 X 13
10" CLGS.

SERVICE PORCH

COVERED VERANDA

Design M117

Square Footage: 1,830

■ Characteristics that include a cupola, shutters, arched transoms and an exterior of combined stone and lap siding give this one-story home its country identity. To the left of the entry is the great room. Here, a cathedral ceiling and a fireplace extend an invitation for family and friends alike to relax and enjoy themselves. The kitchen and dining room are located nearby. Kitchen amenities include an island cooktop, a built-in planning desk and a pantry,

while the multi-windowed dining room overlooks and provides access to the covered veranda. A hall leads to sleeping quarters that include two secondary bedrooms and a luxurious master suite. Conveniently situated to serve the entire household is a laundry room. Room for the family fleet is provided by the three-car garage. Details for both a crawlspace and a slab foundation are included in the blueprints.

Alternate Elevation

Design 3460

Square Footage: 1,389

L

■ A double dose of charm, this special farmhouse plan offers two elevations in its blueprint package. Though rooflines and porch options are different, the floor plan is basically the same and very livable. A formal living room has a warming fireplace and a delightful bay window. The kitchen separates this area from the more casual family room. Three bedrooms include two family bedrooms served by a full, shared bath and a lovely master suite with its own private bath. Each room has a vaulted ceiling and large windows to let the outdoors in beautifully.

Design by
Home Planners

Width 44'-8"
Depth 54'-6"

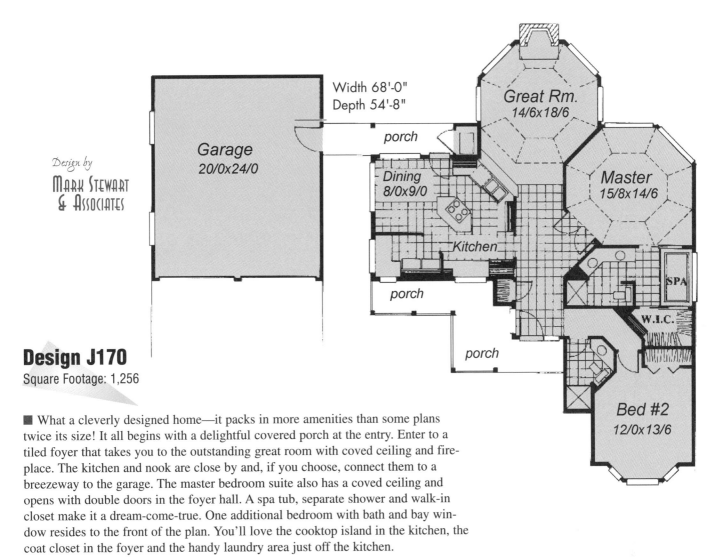

Width 68'-0"
Depth 54'-8"

Garage
20/0x24/0

Design by
Mark Stewart
& Associates

porch

Great Rm.
14/6x18/6

Dining
8/0x9/0

Master
15/8x14/6

Kitchen

porch

SPA

W.I.C.

porch

Bed #2
12/0x13/6

Design J170
Square Footage: 1,256

■ What a cleverly designed home—it packs in more amenities than some plans twice its size! It all begins with a delightful covered porch at the entry. Enter to a tiled foyer that takes you to the outstanding great room with coved ceiling and fireplace. The kitchen and nook are close by and, if you choose, connect them to a breezeway to the garage. The master bedroom suite also has a coved ceiling and opens with double doors in the foyer hall. A spa tub, separate shower and walk-in closet make it a dream-come-true. One additional bedroom with bath and bay window resides to the front of the plan. You'll love the cooktop island in the kitchen, the coat closet in the foyer and the handy laundry area just off the kitchen.

© design basics inc.

Design 7333

Square Footage: 1,554

■ A lovely corner wrapping porch provides a focal point for this cozy ranch design. The entry opens to a great room with cathedral ceiling and to a formal dining room with a ten-foot-high ceiling. The spacious kitchen features a corner sink and a built-in bookcase and shares a snack bar with the breakfast area. The bedroom wing has convenient laundry access. Choose the formal dining room or, if needed, make this room into a third bedroom. The master suite opens with French doors. Amenities here include a volume ceiling, mirrored walk-in closet doors and a sunny whirlpool bath.

Design by
DESIGN BASICS, INC.

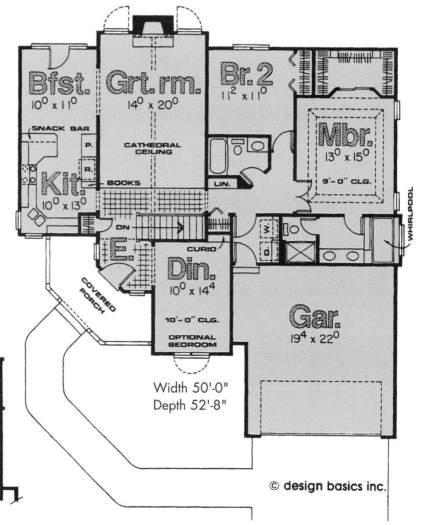

Bfst.
10⁰ x 11⁰

Grt. rm.
14⁰ x 20⁰

Br. 2
11² x 11⁰

SNACK BAR

CATHEDRAL CEILING

P.
R.

Kit.
10⁰ x 13⁰

BOOKS

LIN.

Mbr.
13⁰ x 15⁰
9'-0" CLG.

WHIRLPOOL

ON

CURIO

COVERED PORCH

Din.
10⁰ x 14⁴
10'-0" CLG.
OPTIONAL BEDROOM

Gar.
19⁴ x 22⁰

Width 50'-0"
Depth 52'-8"

© design basics inc.

ON

Br. 3
10⁰ x 12⁰

10'-0" CLG.

Traditional Americana:
One-story homes found in your neighborhood

Design 7003
Square Footage: 1,971

■ Symmetry with just a touch of variance makes the exterior of this home a standout. The entry is offset just a bit from center and reached by a curving walk to a covered stoop. A large, arched window must be passed and looks into the formal dining area. Graced by a servery that separates it from the kitchen and hearth room, the dining room becomes a fine center of formal entertaining. Two living areas, the hearth room and the great room, are separated by a three-sided fireplace. A U-shaped kitchen includes a snack bar, beyond which is the cozy breakfast nook. Three bedrooms include two family bedrooms and a master suite. Look for luxurious appointments in the master bath: a walk-in closet, whirlpool tub and double sinks for convenience.

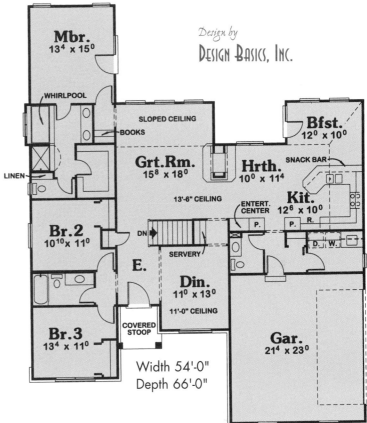

Design by
DESIGN BASICS, INC.

Mbr.
13^4 x 15^0

WHIRLPOOL

SLOPED CEILING

BOOKS

Bfst.
12^0 x 10^0

LINEN

Grt.Rm.
15^8 x 18^0

Hrth.
10^0 x 11^4

SNACK BAR

13'-6" CEILING

ENTERT. CENTER

Kit.
12^6 x 10^0

P.

P.

R.

Br.2
10^{10} x 11^0

DN

SERVERY

D. W.

E.

Din.
11^0 x 13^0

11'-0" CEILING

Br.3
13^4 x 11^0

COVERED STOOP

Gar.
21^4 x 23^0

Width 54'-0"
Depth 66'-0"

DESIGNERS' INK

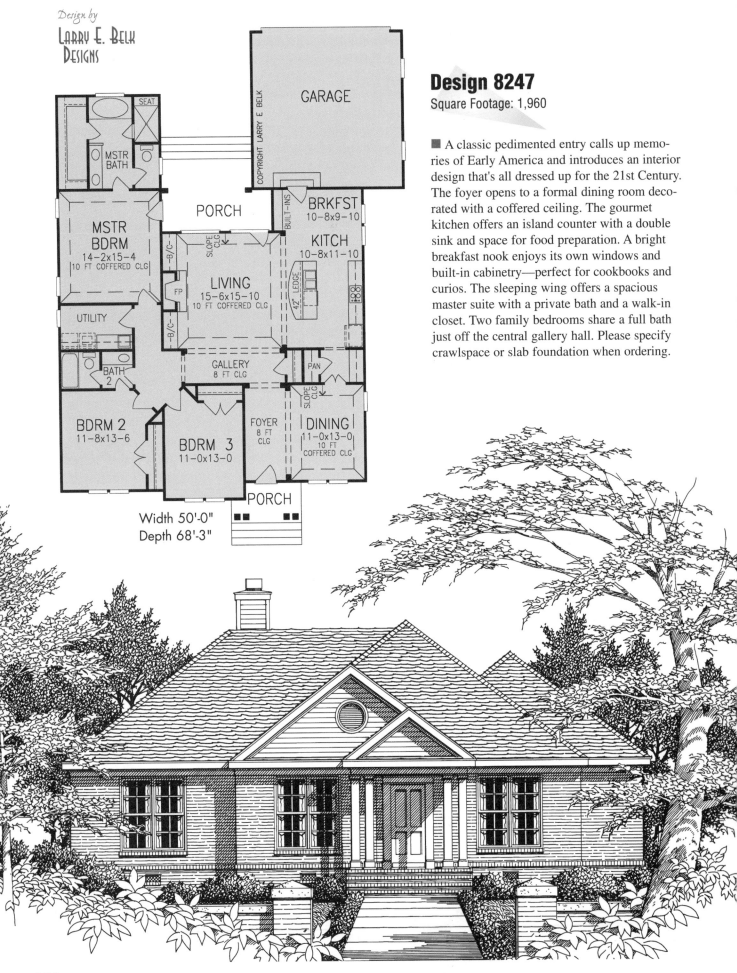

Design by
LARRY E. BELK
DESIGNS

GARAGE

COPYRIGHT LARRY E BELK

SEAT

MSTR BATH

PORCH

BRKFST
10-8x9-10

MSTR BDRM
14-2x15-4
10 FT COFFERED CLG

KITCH
10-8x11-10

SLOPE CLG

B/C

LIVING
15-6x15-10
10 FT COFFERED CLG

FP

42" LEDGE

BUILT-INS

UTILITY

B/C

GALLERY
8 FT CLG

PAN

BATH 2

BDRM 2
11-8x13-6

BDRM 3
11-0x13-0

FOYER
8 FT CLG

SLOPE CLG

DINING
11-0x13-0
10 FT COFFERED CLG

PORCH

Width 50'-0"
Depth 68'-3"

Design 8247
Square Footage: 1,960

■ A classic pedimented entry calls up memories of Early America and introduces an interior design that's all dressed up for the 21st Century. The foyer opens to a formal dining room decorated with a coffered ceiling. The gourmet kitchen offers an island counter with a double sink and space for food preparation. A bright breakfast nook enjoys its own windows and built-in cabinetry—perfect for cookbooks and curios. The sleeping wing offers a spacious master suite with a private bath and a walk-in closet. Two family bedrooms share a full bath just off the central gallery hall. Please specify crawlspace or slab foundation when ordering.

Design 9567

Square Footage: 1,644
Lower Level: 1,012 square feet

■ The character of this home is purely traditional. At the forefront is an elegant dining room open to the great room. The spacious kitchen is centered around a cooktop island. Double doors lead to a rear deck. The main-level master suite also opens to this area. A den or bedroom faces the front and is not far from a full bath, making it an ideal guest room. On the lower level, a games room and two more bedrooms reside. Built-ins and outdoor access make the games room versatile.

MASTER
13/0 X 16/0
(10'-4" CLG.)

GREAT RM.
17/2 X 16/0
(10'-4" CLG.)

18/6 X 13/8

PANT. REF.

W. D.

DN.

SPA

GARAGE
19/4 X 21/8 +/-

DINING
10/8 X 13/2
(10'-4" CLG.)

LIN.

DEN/ BR. 2
13/0 X 10/0 +

Width 52'-0"
Depth 55'-0"

Design by
Alan Mascord
Design Associates, Inc.

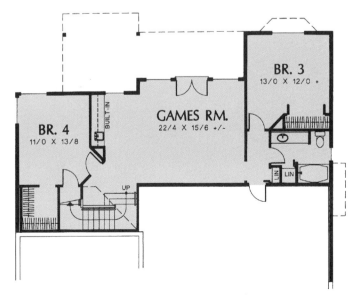

BR. 4
11/0 X 13/8

BUILT-IN

GAMES RM.
22/4 X 15/6 +/-

BR. 3
13/0 X 12/0 +

LIN LIN

UP

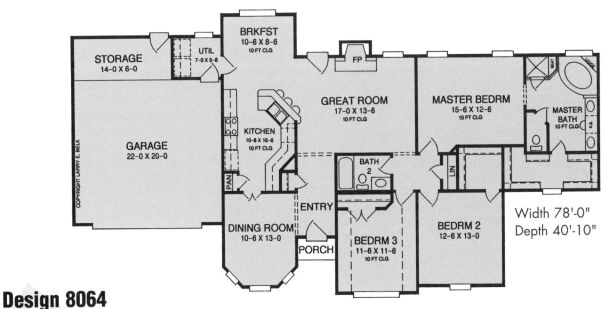

Design 8064

Square Footage: 1,742

■ This traditional design warmly welcomes both family and visitors with a delightful bay window, a Palladian window and shutters. The entry introduces a beautiful interior plan, starting with the formal dining room and the central great room with fireplace, and views and access to outdoor spaces. Ten-foot ceilings in the major living areas give the home an open, spacious feel. The kitchen features an angled eating bar, a pantry and lots of cabinet and counter space. Comfort and style abound in the distinctive master suite, offering a high ceiling, corner whirlpool tub, knee-space vanity and compartmented toilet. An ample walk-in closet with a window for natural light completes this owner's retreat. Bedrooms 2 and 3 are nearby and share a hall bath, and Bedroom 3 offers a raised ceiling. Please specify basement or crawlspace foundation when ordering.

Design by
LARRY E. BELK
DESIGNS

Design U178

Square Footage: 2,234

■ This brick one-story home says "welcome home" in so many ways. Its traditional facade has a classic appeal that will impress all in the neighborhood. Its floor plan will prove to be both livable and versatile enough to meet the needs of your family. Note the extended ceilings in the dining room, great room and entry. They add a sense of spaciousness to these areas. The great room is graced by a warming fireplace flanked by windows that overlook the backyard. The master bedroom has a bay window with a similar view. Another bay window in the nook allows light filled casual meals—or choose to dine al fresco on the covered patio outside. Two family bedrooms complement the master and share a full bath with a separate dressing/vanity area.

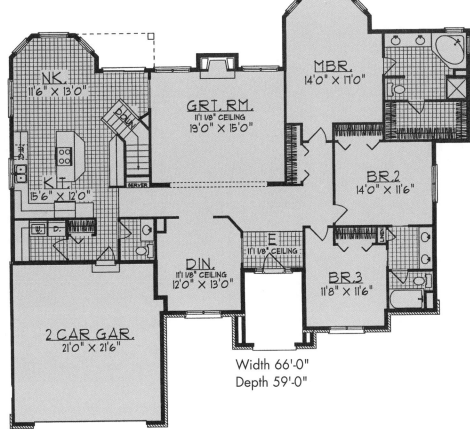

NK.
11'6" X 13'0"

GRT. RM.
11'1 1/8" CEILING
19'0" X 15'0"

MBR.
14'0" X 17'0"

KT.
15'6" X 12'0"

BR.2
14'0" X 11'6"

DIN.
11'1 1/8" CEILING
12'0" X 13'0"

E
11'1 1/8" CEILING

BR.3
11'8" X 11'6"

2 CAR GAR.
21'0" X 21'6"

Width 66'-0"
Depth 59'-0"

Design by

Ahmann Design, Inc.

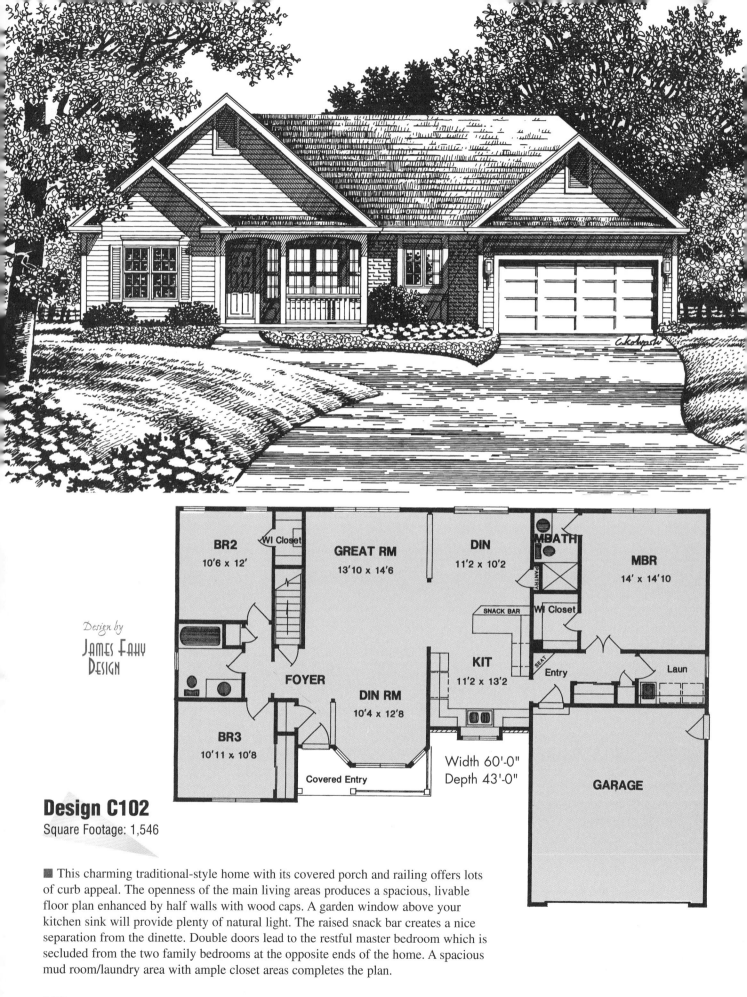

Design by
James Fahy Design

BR2
10'6 x 12'

WI Closet

GREAT RM
13'10 x 14'6

DIN
11'2 x 10'2

MBATH

PANTRY

MBR
14' x 14'10

SNACK BAR

WI Closet

FOYER

KIT
11'2 x 13'2

SEAT

Entry

Laun

DIN RM
10'4 x 12'8

BR3
10'11 x 10'8

Covered Entry

Width 60'-0"
Depth 43'-0"

GARAGE

Design C102

Square Footage: 1,546

■ This charming traditional-style home with its covered porch and railing offers lots of curb appeal. The openness of the main living areas produces a spacious, livable floor plan enhanced by half walls with wood caps. A garden window above your kitchen sink will provide plenty of natural light. The raised snack bar creates a nice separation from the dinette. Double doors lead to the restful master bedroom which is secluded from the two family bedrooms at the opposite ends of the home. A spacious mud room/laundry area with ample closet areas completes the plan.

Design T235

Square Footage: 3,063

■ Though all on one level, the floor plan for this home defines masterful design. Open planning is evident, though there are spaces for privacy as well. The great room and dining room are separated only by well-placed columns, yet each is distinct in its purpose and structure. Similarly, the keeping room is open to the breakfast area and kitchen, but retains a sense of solitude with a cozy fireplace and built-ins. The kitchen is all a gourmet might ever ask for, with a huge storage pantry, butler's pantry connecting it to the dining room and an island cooktop. Each bedroom has its own bath—take a close look at the master bath and its superb amenities. A rear covered porch is accessed through the great room, the keeping room and the master bedroom. The two-car garage holds a bit of extra space for storage or a workshop bench.

Master Bedroom
13⁸ x 17²

Covered Porch

Great Room
15⁸ x 11⁸

Great Room
15⁸ x 18⁶

Breakfast
16⁰ x 11⁸

Kitchen
16⁸ x11⁸

Bedroom #2
12⁰ x 14⁶

Foyer

Dining Room
13⁴ x 13⁷

Bedroom #3
14⁶ x 13²

Width 68'-0"
Depth 80'-0"

Two Car Garage
24⁴ x 23²

Design by
DESIGN TRADITIONS

© Design Traditions

Design P294

Square Footage: 1,232

■ Gabled rooflines, shutters and siding—all elements of a fine facade, and the floor plan inside equals this quality. The foyer opens directly into the vaulted great room, where a fireplace waits to warm cool winter evenings. Nearby, the efficient kitchen has easy access to the dining room. Two secondary bedrooms share a full hall bath with a linen closet nearby. The deluxe master bedroom suite, with a tray ceiling, offers a vaulted master bath and a spacious walk-in closet. A laundry room is located in between the master suite and the two-car garage.

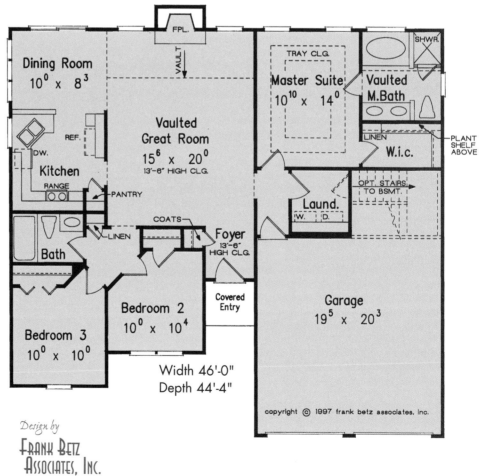

Dining Room
10⁰ x 8³

FPL.

VAULT

Vaulted Great Room
15⁶ x 20⁰
13'-6" HIGH CLG.

TRAY CLG.

Master Suite
10¹⁰ x 14⁰

Vaulted M.Bath

SHWR.

LINEN

PLANT SHELF ABOVE

REF.

DW.

Kitchen

RANGE

PANTRY

W.i.c.

LINEN

Bath

COATS

Foyer
13'-6" HIGH CLG.

Laund.
W. D.

OPT. STAIRS TO BSMT.

Bedroom 2
10⁰ x 10⁴

Covered Entry

Garage
19⁵ x 20³

Bedroom 3
10⁰ x 10⁰

Width 46'-0"
Depth 44'-4"

copyright © 1997 frank betz associates, inc.

Design by
FRANK BETZ ASSOCIATES, INC.

190

Design S131

Square Footage: 1,670

■ With an offset entrance, this home adds interest and charm to any neighborhood. Enter into a spacious family room, with a galley kitchen nearby offering easy access to the sunny breakfast room. Bedrooms 2 and 3 each have walk-in closets and share a full hall bath. Bedroom 2, which opens off the family room, could also be used as a den. The formal dining room separates the master bedroom from the rest of the home, providing pleasant privacy. The master suite features many amenities, including a walk-in closet, a private bath and access to a private courtyard.

Design by

ARCHIVAL DESIGNS

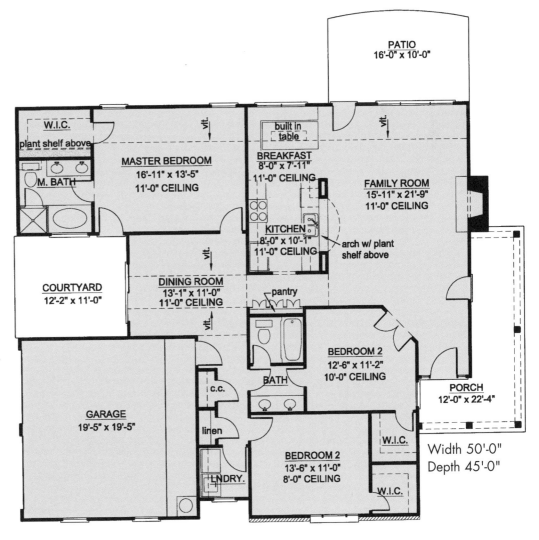

PATIO
16'-0" x 10'-0"

W.I.C.
plant shelf above

M. BATH

MASTER BEDROOM
16'-11" x 13'-5"
11'-0" CEILING

built in table

BREAKFAST
8'-0" x 7'-11"
11'-0" CEILING

FAMILY ROOM
15'-11" x 21'-9"
11'-0" CEILING

KITCHEN
8'-0" x 10'-1"
11'-0" CEILING

arch w/ plant shelf above

COURTYARD
12'-2" x 11'-0"

DINING ROOM
13'-1" x 11'-0"
11'-0" CEILING

pantry

GARAGE
19'-5" x 19'-5"

c.c.

BATH

BEDROOM 2
12'-6" x 11'-2"
10'-0" CEILING

PORCH
12'-0" x 22'-4"

linen

LNDRY.

BEDROOM 2
13'-6" x 11'-0"
8'-0" CEILING

W.I.C.

W.I.C.

Width 50'-0"
Depth 45'-0"

Design 9735

Square Footage: 2,625
Bonus Room: 447 square feet

■ This stately brick facade features a columned, covered porch that ushers visitors in to the large foyer. An expansive great room with a fireplace and access to a covered rear porch awaits. The centrally located kitchen is within easy reach of the great room, formal dining room and skylit breakfast area. Split-bedroom planning places the master bedroom and elegant master bath to the right of the home. Two bedrooms with abundant closet space are placed to the left, while an optional bedroom or study with a Palladian window faces the front. A large bonus room is located above the garage.

Design by
DONALD A. GARDNER
ARCHITECTS, INC.

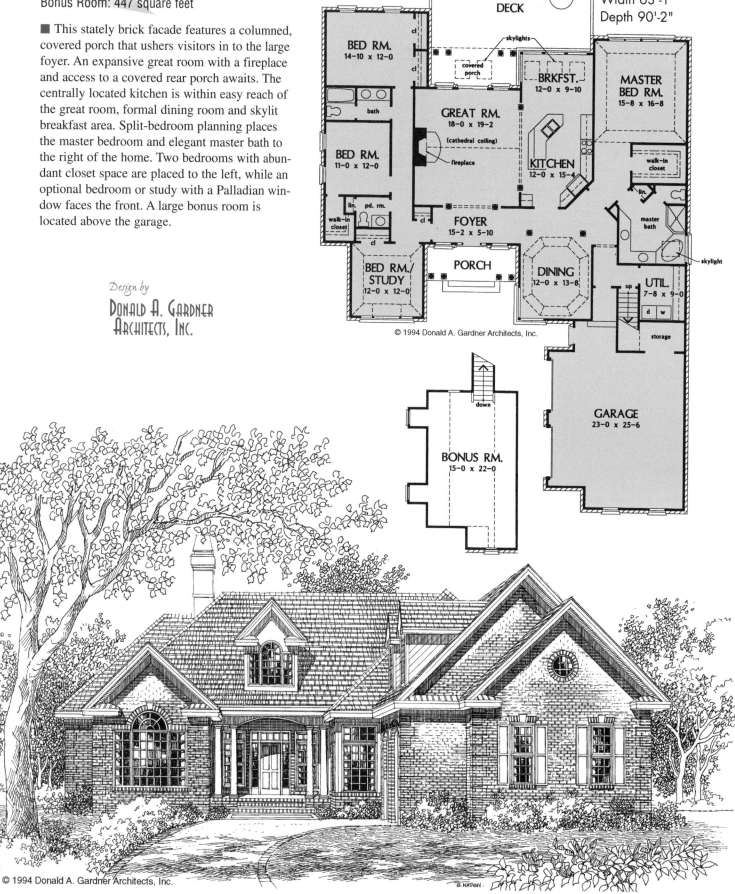

Width 63'-1"
Depth 90'-2"

© 1994 Donald A. Gardner Architects, Inc.

B. NATHAN

Design 7009
Square Footage: 1,806

■ This is up-to-date floor planning at its best—open, airy and allowing for plenty of options. The main living area is casual, but is complemented by a formal dining room for special occasions. Both rooms sport ten-foot ceilings. The great room has a focal-point fireplace. To make serving easy, the dining room connects to the kitchen via a servery. You'll also appreciate the peninsula snack bar in the kitchen that divides it from the breakfast room. A door here leads to a covered porch for outdoor meals. The master suite also has a ten-foot ceiling. Its bath is complete with a corner whirlpool tub, separate shower, compartmented toilet and walk-in closet. Family bedrooms share the use of a full bath with double sinks. A three-car garage guarantees you never lack for vehicle parking space again.

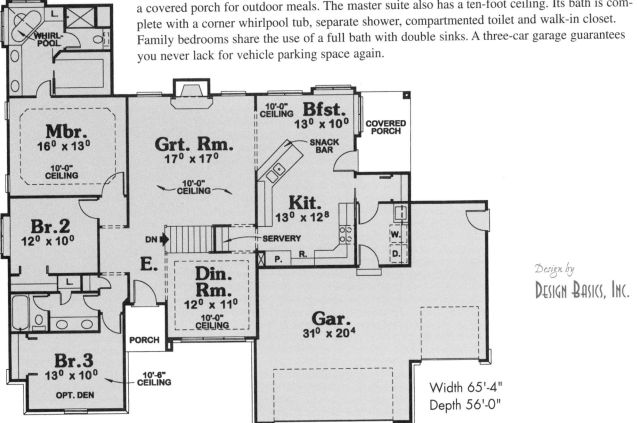

WHIRL-POOL

Mbr.
16⁰ x 13⁰
10'-0"
CEILING

Grt. Rm.
17⁰ x 17⁰
10'-0"
CEILING

10'-0"
CEILING
Bfst.
13⁰ x 10⁰

COVERED
PORCH

SNACK
BAR

Kit.
13⁰ x 12⁸

Br. 2
12⁰ x 10⁰

DN   SERVERY

E.   W.   D.

Din.
Rm.
12⁰ x 11⁰
10'-0"
CEILING

P.   R.

PORCH

Gar.
31⁰ x 20⁴

Br. 3
13⁰ x 10⁰
10'-6"
CEILING

OPT. DEN

Design by
Design Basics, Inc.

Width 65'-4"
Depth 56'-0"

DESIGNERS' INK

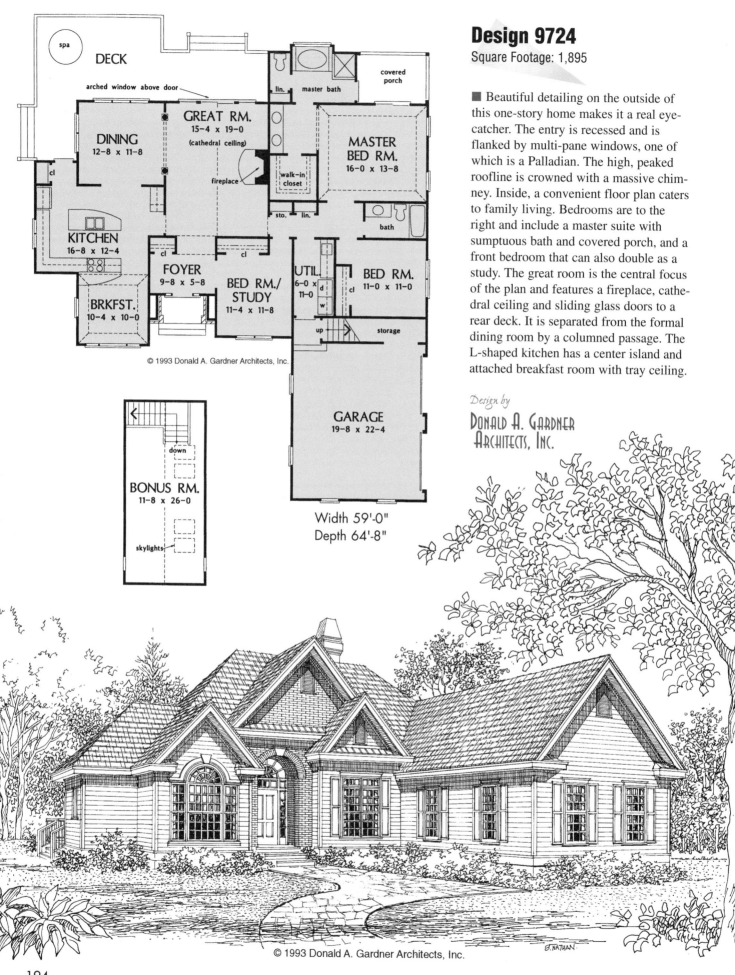

DECK

spa

arched window above door

DINING
12-8 x 11-8

GREAT RM.
15-4 x 19-0
(cathedral ceiling)

fireplace

master bath

lin.

covered porch

MASTER BED RM.
16-0 x 13-8

walk-in closet

sto. lin.

bath

cl

KITCHEN
16-8 x 12-4

cl

FOYER
9-8 x 5-8

cl

UTIL.
6-0 x 11-0

d

w

cl

BED RM.
11-0 x 11-0

BRKFST.
10-4 x 10-0

BED RM./ STUDY
11-4 x 11-8

up

storage

© 1993 Donald A. Gardner Architects, Inc.

GARAGE
19-8 x 22-4

down

BONUS RM.
11-8 x 26-0

skylights

Width 59'-0"
Depth 64'-8"

Design 9724

Square Footage: 1,895

■ Beautiful detailing on the outside of this one-story home makes it a real eye-catcher. The entry is recessed and is flanked by multi-pane windows, one of which is a Palladian. The high, peaked roofline is crowned with a massive chimney. Inside, a convenient floor plan caters to family living. Bedrooms are to the right and include a master suite with sumptuous bath and covered porch, and a front bedroom that can also double as a study. The great room is the central focus of the plan and features a fireplace, cathedral ceiling and sliding glass doors to a rear deck. It is separated from the formal dining room by a columned passage. The L-shaped kitchen has a center island and attached breakfast room with tray ceiling.

Design by

Donald A. Gardner Architects, Inc.

© 1993 Donald A. Gardner Architects, Inc.

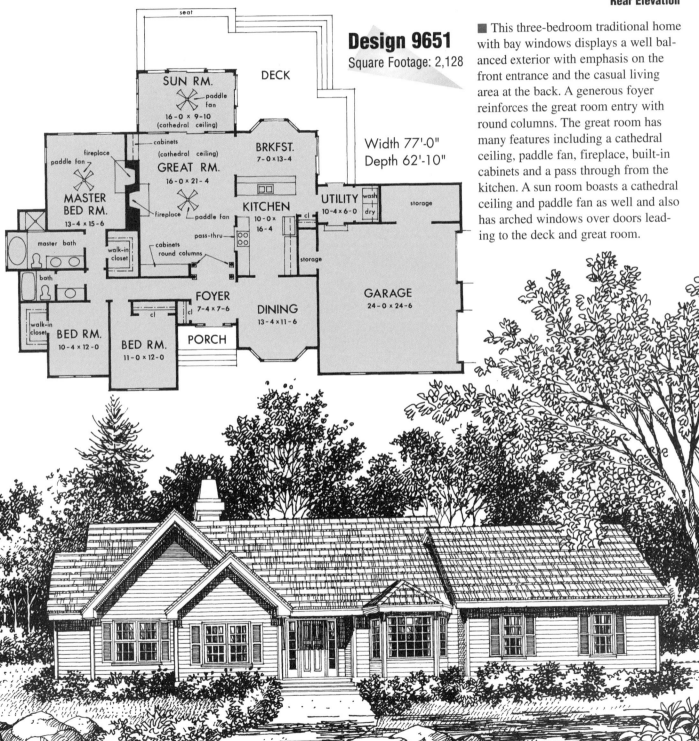

Rear Elevation

Design by

Donald A. Gardner Architects, Inc.

seat

Design 9651
Square Footage: 2,128

DECK

SUN RM.
paddle fan
16-0 × 9-10
(cathedral ceiling)

cabinets
(cathedral ceiling)
GREAT RM.
16-0 × 21-4

BRKFST.
7-0 × 13-4

Width 77'-0"
Depth 62'-10"

fireplace
paddle fan

MASTER
BED RM.
13-4 × 15-6

fireplace
paddle fan

KITCHEN
10-0 ×
16-4

UTILITY
10-4 × 6-0

wash
dry

storage

master bath

walk-in
closet

cabinets
round columns

pass-thru

cl

storage

GARAGE
24-0 × 24-6

bath

walk-in
closet

BED RM.
10-4 × 12-0

BED RM.
11-0 × 12-0

cl   cl

FOYER
7-4 × 7-6

PORCH

DINING
13-4 × 11-6

■ This three-bedroom traditional home with bay windows displays a well balanced exterior with emphasis on the front entrance and the casual living area at the back. A generous foyer reinforces the great room entry with round columns. The great room has many features including a cathedral ceiling, paddle fan, fireplace, built-in cabinets and a pass through from the kitchen. A sun room boasts a cathedral ceiling and paddle fan as well and also has arched windows over doors leading to the deck and great room.

B. NATHAN

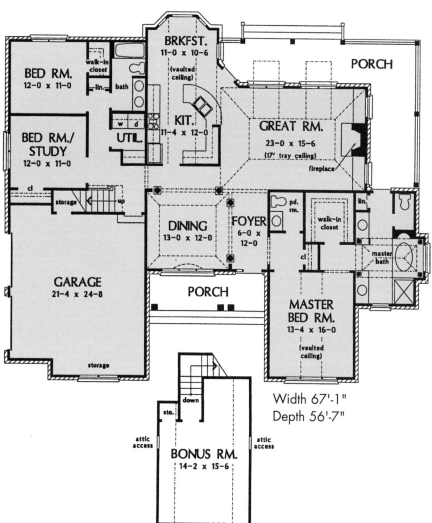

BED RM.
12-0 x 11-0

walk-in closet

lin.

bath

BRKFST.
11-0 x 10-6
(vaulted ceiling)

PORCH

BED RM./
STUDY
12-0 x 11-0

w   d

UTIL.

KIT.
11-4 x 12-0

GREAT RM.
23-0 x 15-6
(17' tray ceiling)

fireplace

cl

storage   up

DINING
13-0 x 12-0

FOYER
6-0 x 12-0

pd. rm.

walk-in closet

lin.

cl

master bath

GARAGE
21-4 x 24-8

PORCH

MASTER
BED RM.
13-4 x 16-0
(vaulted ceiling)

storage

down

sto.

attic access

attic access

Width 67'-1"
Depth 56'-7"

BONUS RM.
14-2 x 15-6

seat

Design 7657

Square Footage: 2,198
Bonus Room: 325 square feet

■ If you find that the great livability in this one-story home is not quite enough, you can develop the bonus room into a home office, guest suite or hobby room, how and when you choose. In the meantime, you'll find that the main floor plan holds superior spaces: a formal dining room, a great room (both with tray ceilings), a gourmet-style kitchen with attached breakfast room, and three bedrooms with two full baths. The comfortable wrap-around porch at the rear of the plan extends its invitation to the master suite, great room and breakfast room, for all to enjoy. Vaulted ceilings in the breakfast room and master bedroom open these areas to new heights. One of the family bedrooms sports a walk-in closet.

Design by
DONALD A. GARDNER
ARCHITECTS, INC.

Design 7624

Square Footage: 1,800

Design by
DONALD A. GARDNER
ARCHITECTS, INC.

■ A covered front porch and plenty of windows give this elevation a lot of charm. The floor plan is attractive, too, for empty-nesters or those just starting out. A front bedroom could serve as a study, leaving another family bedroom and, on the other side of the house, a secluded master suite. With a tray ceiling, skylit bath and walk-in closet, this bedroom is sure to please. The spacious foyer provides two closets and an arched opening into the great room that fills the middle of the home. Highlighted by a fireplace and cathedral ceiling, this room offers access to the back patio and opens into the breakfast room/kitchen area. Located at the front of the house, the charming dining room is also easily accessible from the kitchen.

PATIO

MASTER BED RM.
13-4 x 14-8

skylight

master bath

BED RM.
11-4 x 12-0

GREAT RM.
15-4 x 18-6
(cathedral ceiling)

fireplace

BRKFST.
11-4 x 9-4

w d

walk-in closet

storage

bath

lin.

cl

KIT.
11-4 x 11-8

GARAGE
20-0 x 19-8

FOYER
8-2 x 6-2

cl cl

BED RM./ STUDY
11-4 x 11-4

PORCH

DINING
11-4 x 12-6

storage

Width 62'-2"
Depth 53'-5"

© 1996 Donald A. Gardner Architects, Inc.

Rear Elevation

B. NATHAN.

© 1996 Donald A. Gardner Architects, Inc.

Design 7004

Square Footage: 2,750

■ This is a grand design—much more than the typical ranch-style home. It speaks of tradition and classic planning. First is the quaint covered porch with an elegant entry and sidelites. The main foyer opens on the right to a dining room with tray ceiling or straight ahead to the spacious great room with fireplace. The kitchen has more-than-adequate details: a snack bar, walk-in pantry, planning desk and attached breakfast room with extended ceiling. Choose three family bedrooms or two and a den. Two full baths are found here. The master suite is at the opposite end of the plan for privacy. A massive walk-in closet, corner whirlpool tub and compartmented toilet are among its many appointments. Don't miss the convenience of the three-car garage.

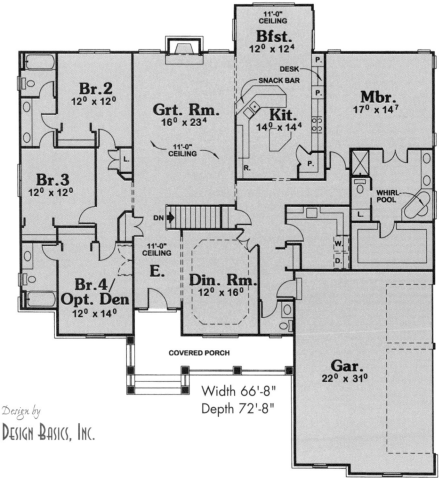

Design by
Design Basics, Inc.

Rear Elevation

Design 7308

Square Footage: 2,186

■ Brick columns and a tall, gabled entry create a prominent elevation with brick-and-siding accents. A bright twelve-foot entry enjoys interior vistas of the expansive great room, which offers a fireplace with an extended hearth and opens to the formal dining room. The nearby gourmet island kitchen with a service bar and lots of wrapping counters is well integrated with the bayed breakfast and dining areas. A spacious and secluded master suite boasts a lavish whirlpool bath, a U-shaped walk-in closet and ten-foot ceilings. The utility corridor leads to a laundry and to a convenient computer area, which could also be developed as an oversized walk-in pantry. A sunlit shop area highlights the three-car garage.

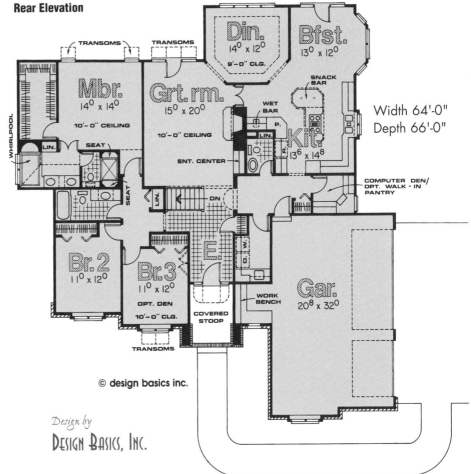

Width 64'-0"
Depth 66'-0"

Design by
DESIGN BASICS, INC.

© design basics inc.

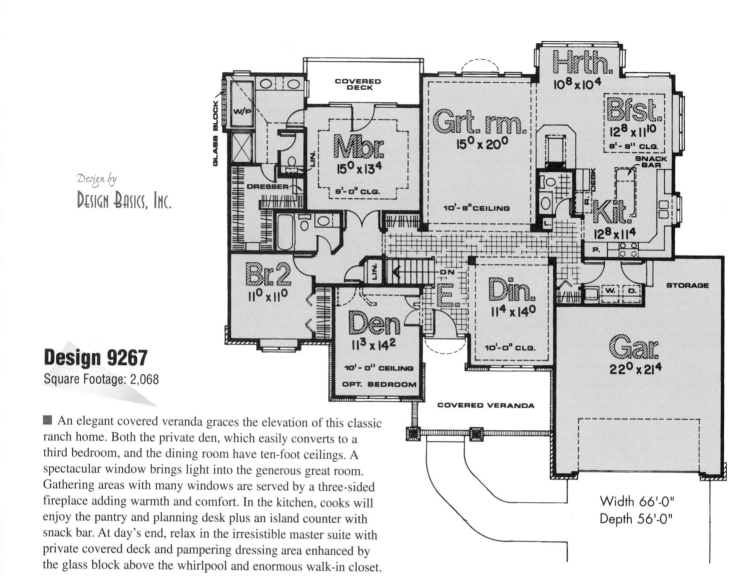

Design by
Design Basics, Inc.

Design 9267
Square Footage: 2,068

■ An elegant covered veranda graces the elevation of this classic ranch home. Both the private den, which easily converts to a third bedroom, and the dining room have ten-foot ceilings. A spectacular window brings light into the generous great room. Gathering areas with many windows are served by a three-sided fireplace adding warmth and comfort. In the kitchen, cooks will enjoy the pantry and planning desk plus an island counter with snack bar. At day's end, relax in the irresistible master suite with private covered deck and pampering dressing area enhanced by the glass block above the whirlpool and enormous walk-in closet.

Width 66'-0"
Depth 56'-0"

Design 9305

Square Footage: 2,015

■ Romantic appeal radiates from the elegant covered porch and gracious features of this ranch home. A formal dining room with bright windows is viewed from the entry. In the great room, featuring an entertainment center and bookcases, warmth emanates from the three-sided fireplace. Homeowners will enjoy the cozy retreat of the bay-windowed hearth room with its ten-foot ceiling. Near the hearth is an open breakfast area and kitchen with snack bar, pantry and ample counter space. A window seat framed by closets highlights Bedroom 2. The third bedroom easily converts to an optional den for quiet study. Designed for privacy, the master suite enjoys a boxed ceiling, skylit dressing area, corner whirlpool and large walk-in closet.

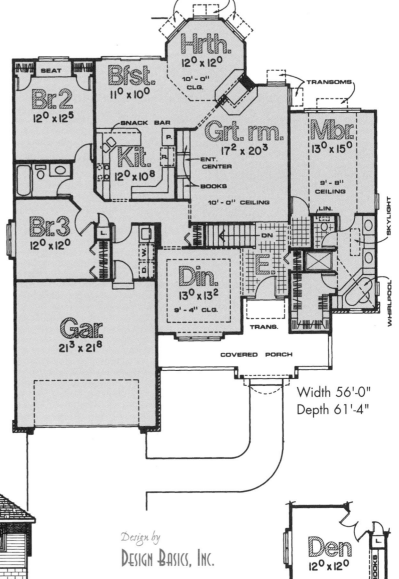

Width 56'-0"
Depth 61'-4"

Design by
Design Basics, Inc.

Rear Elevation

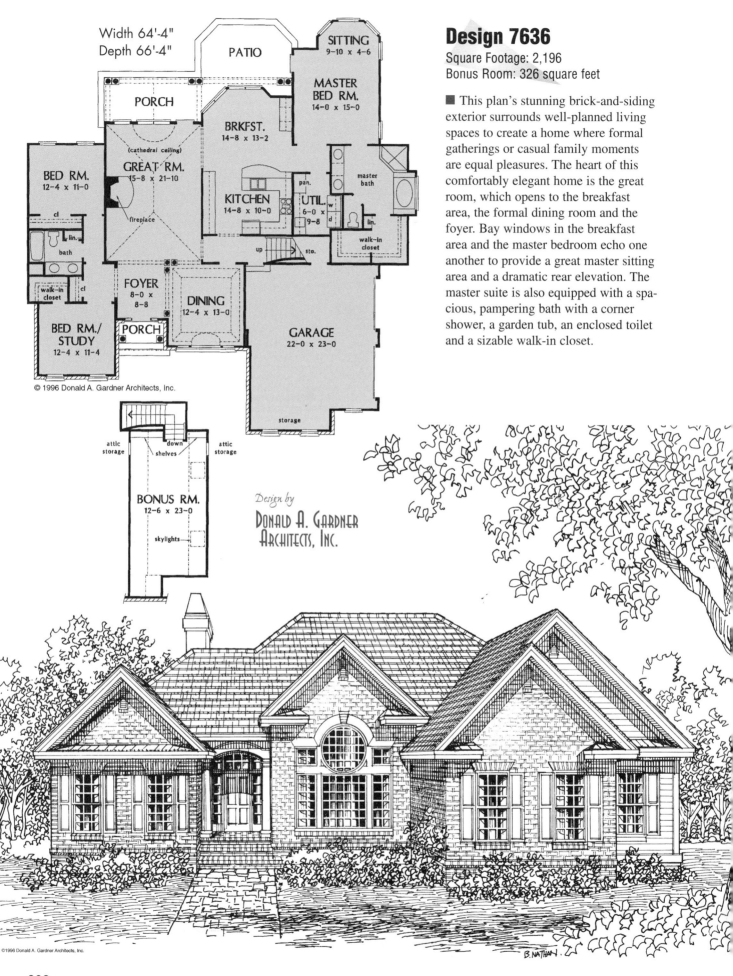

Width 64'-4"
Depth 66'-4"

PATIO

PORCH

SITTING
9-10 x 4-6

MASTER
BED RM.
14-0 x 15-0

BRKFST.
14-8 x 13-2

(cathedral ceiling)

GREAT RM.
15-8 x 21-10

BED RM.
12-4 x 11-0

cl

lin.

bath

fireplace

KITCHEN
14-8 x 10-0

pan.

UTIL.
6-0 x
9-8

w
d

master
bath

lin.

walk-in
closet

walk-in
closet

cl

up

sto.

BED RM./
STUDY
12-4 x 11-4

FOYER
8-0 x
8-8

PORCH

DINING
12-4 x 13-0

GARAGE
22-0 x 23-0

storage

© 1996 Donald A. Gardner Architects, Inc.

attic
storage

down

shelves

attic
storage

BONUS RM.
12-6 x 23-0

skylights

Design by
DONALD A. GARDNER
ARCHITECTS, INC.

Design 7636

Square Footage: 2,196
Bonus Room: 326 square feet

■ This plan's stunning brick-and-siding exterior surrounds well-planned living spaces to create a home where formal gatherings or casual family moments are equal pleasures. The heart of this comfortably elegant home is the great room, which opens to the breakfast area, the formal dining room and the foyer. Bay windows in the breakfast area and the master bedroom echo one another to provide a great master sitting area and a dramatic rear elevation. The master suite is also equipped with a spacious, pampering bath with a corner shower, a garden tub, an enclosed toilet and a sizable walk-in closet.

B. NATHAN

202

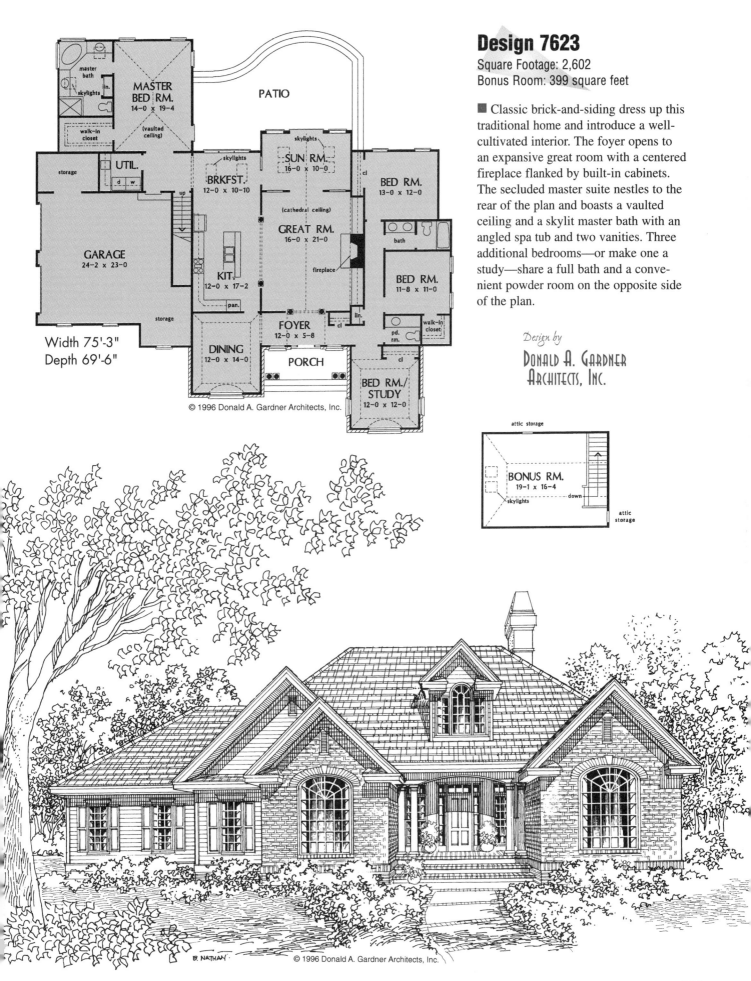

Design 7623

Square Footage: 2,602
Bonus Room: 399 square feet

■ Classic brick-and-siding dress up this traditional home and introduce a well-cultivated interior. The foyer opens to an expansive great room with a centered fireplace flanked by built-in cabinets. The secluded master suite nestles to the rear of the plan and boasts a vaulted ceiling and a skylit master bath with an angled spa tub and two vanities. Three additional bedrooms—or make one a study—share a full bath and a convenient powder room on the opposite side of the plan.

Design by
Donald A. Gardner
Architects, Inc.

Width 75'-3"
Depth 69'-6"

© 1996 Donald A. Gardner Architects, Inc.

MASTER BED RM.
14-0 x 19-4
(vaulted ceiling)

master bath
skylights
walk-in closet
storage
UTIL.
GARAGE
24-2 x 23-0
storage

PATIO

BRKFST.
12-0 x 10-10
SUN RM.
16-0 x 10-0
GREAT RM.
16-0 x 21-0
(cathedral ceiling)
KIT.
12-0 x 17-2
fireplace
pan.
FOYER
12-0 x 5-8
DINING
12-0 x 14-0
PORCH

BED RM.
13-0 x 12-0
bath
BED RM.
11-8 x 11-0
pd. rm.
walk-in closet
BED RM./STUDY
12-0 x 12-0

attic storage
BONUS RM.
19-1 x 16-4
skylights
down
attic storage

B. NATHAN
© 1996 Donald A. Gardner Architects, Inc.

203

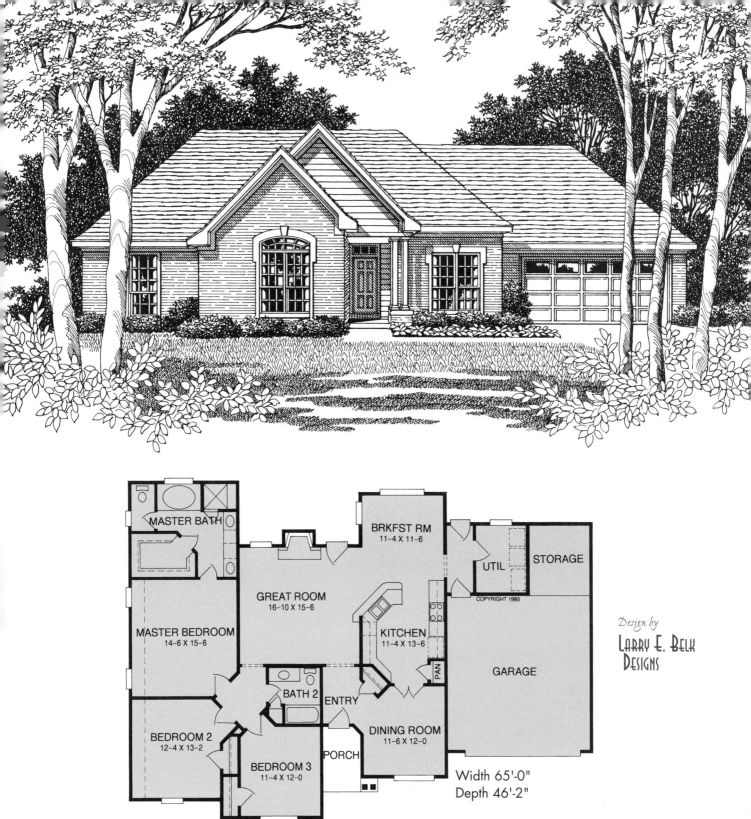

MASTER BATH

BRKFST RM
11-4 X 11-6

UTIL

STORAGE

GREAT ROOM
16-10 X 15-6

COPYRIGHT 1993

Design by
LARRY E. BELK
DESIGNS

MASTER BEDROOM
14-6 X 15-6

KITCHEN
11-4 X 13-6

PAN

GARAGE

BATH 2

ENTRY

BEDROOM 2
12-4 X 13-2

DINING ROOM
11-6 X 12-0

PORCH

BEDROOM 3
11-4 X 12-0

Width 65'-0"
Depth 46'-2"

Design 8180
Square Footage: 1,862

■ This charming traditional has all the amenities of a larger plan in a compact layout. Ten-foot ceilings give this home an expansive feel. An angled eating bar separates the kitchen and great room while leaving these areas open to one another for family gatherings and entertaining. The master bedroom includes a huge walk-in closet and a superior master bath with a whirlpool tub and separate shower. A large utility room and an oversized storage area are located near the secondary entrance to the home. Two additional bedrooms and a bath finish the plan. Please specify crawlspace or slab foundation when ordering.

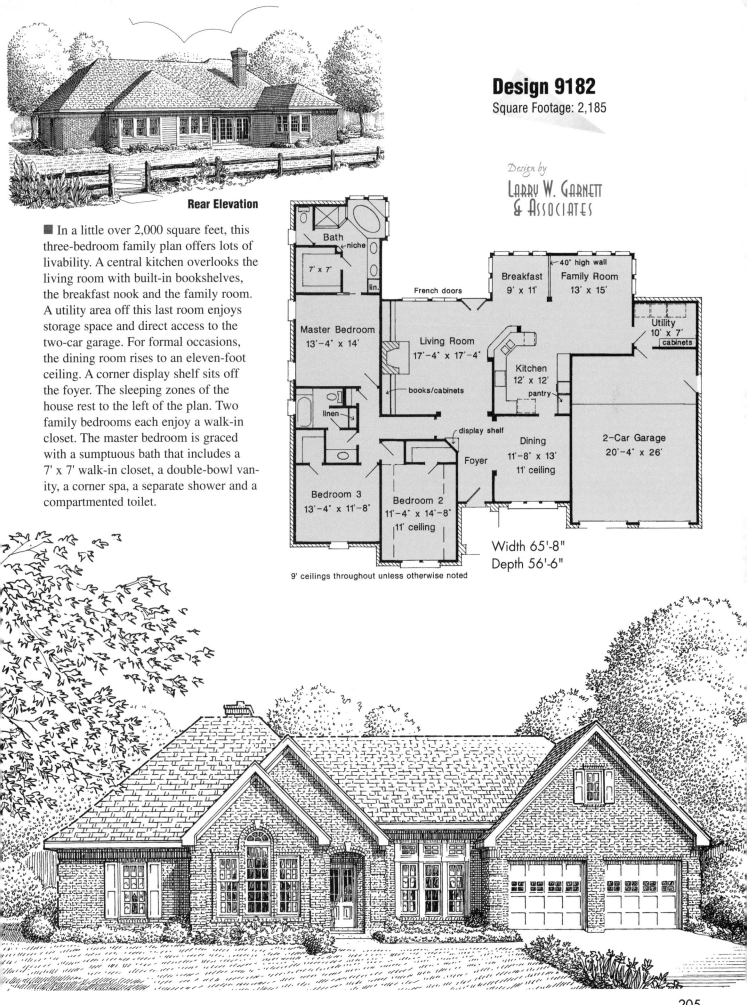

Rear Elevation

Design 9182
Square Footage: 2,185

Design by
Larry W. Garnett & Associates

In a little over 2,000 square feet, this three-bedroom family plan offers lots of livability. A central kitchen overlooks the living room with built-in bookshelves, the breakfast nook and the family room. A utility area off this last room enjoys storage space and direct access to the two-car garage. For formal occasions, the dining room rises to an eleven-foot ceiling. A corner display shelf sits off the foyer. The sleeping zones of the house rest to the left of the plan. Two family bedrooms each enjoy a walk-in closet. The master bedroom is graced with a sumptuous bath that includes a 7' x 7' walk-in closet, a double-bowl vanity, a corner spa, a separate shower and a compartmented toilet.

Bath

niche

7' x 7'

lin.

Master Bedroom
13'-4" x 14'

French doors

Breakfast
9' x 11'

Family Room
13' x 15'

40" high wall

Living Room
17'-4" x 17'-4"

Utility
10' x 7'

cabinets

books/cabinets

Kitchen
12' x 12'

linen

pantry

display shelf

Dining
11'-8" x 13'
11' ceiling

2-Car Garage
20'-4" x 26'

Foyer

Bedroom 3
13'-4" x 11'-8"

Bedroom 2
11'-4" x 14'-8"
11' ceiling

Width 65'-8"
Depth 56'-6"

9' ceilings throughout unless otherwise noted

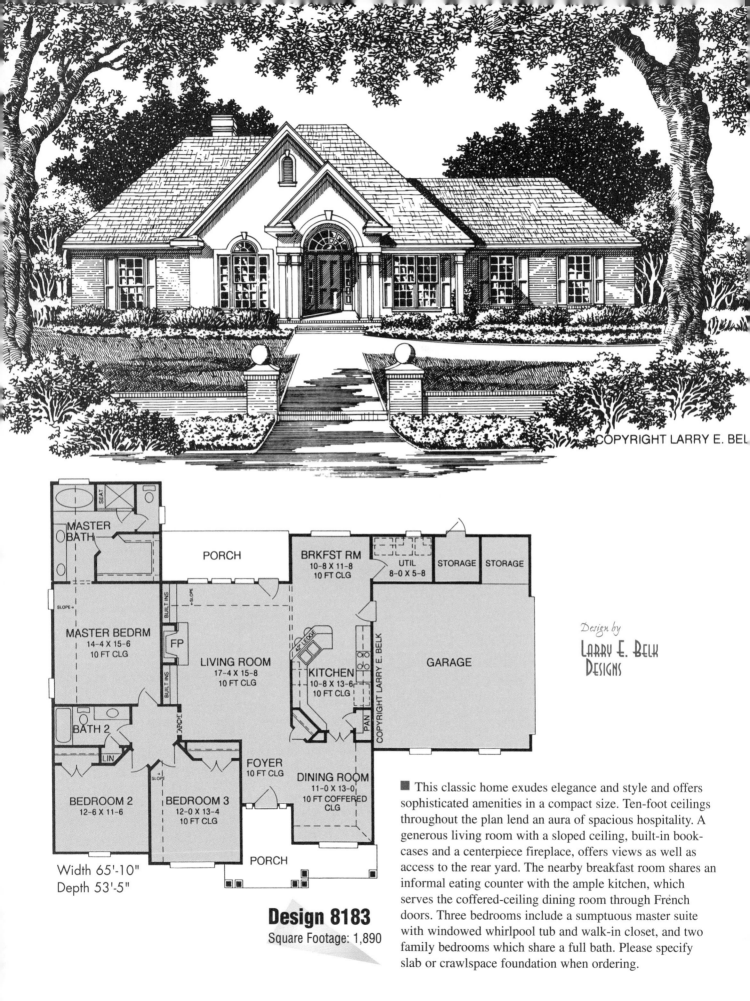

COPYRIGHT LARRY E. BEL

MASTER BATH

SEAT

MASTER BEDRM
14-4 X 15-6
10 FT CLG

SLOPE→

FP

BUILT INS

BATH 2

LIN

BEDROOM 2
12-6 X 11-6

BEDROOM 3
12-0 X 13-4
10 FT CLG

SLOPE→

ARCH

PORCH

LIVING ROOM
17-4 X 15-8
10 FT CLG

BUILT INS

+SLOPE→

42 LEDGE

KITCHEN
10-8 X 13-6
10 FT CLG

PAN

FOYER
10 FT CLG

DINING ROOM
11-0 X 13-0
10 FT COFFERED
CLG

PORCH

BRKFST RM
10-8 X 11-8
10 FT CLG

UTIL
8-0 X 5-8

STORAGE

STORAGE

GARAGE

COPYRIGHT LARRY E. BELK

Design by

LARRY E. BELK
DESIGNS

Width 65'-10"
Depth 53'-5"

Design 8183
Square Footage: 1,890

■ This classic home exudes elegance and style and offers sophisticated amenities in a compact size. Ten-foot ceilings throughout the plan lend an aura of spacious hospitality. A generous living room with a sloped ceiling, built-in bookcases and a centerpiece fireplace, offers views as well as access to the rear yard. The nearby breakfast room shares an informal eating counter with the ample kitchen, which serves the coffered-ceiling dining room through French doors. Three bedrooms include a sumptuous master suite with windowed whirlpool tub and walk-in closet, and two family bedrooms which share a full bath. Please specify slab or crawlspace foundation when ordering.

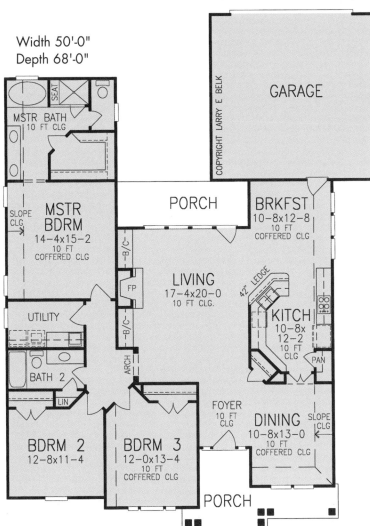

Width 50'-0"
Depth 68'-0"

GARAGE

MSTR BATH
10 FT CLG

SEAT

SLOPE
CLG

MSTR
BDRM
14-4x15-2
10 FT
COFFERED CLG

PORCH

BRKFST
10-8x12-8
10 FT
COFFERED CLG

LIVING
17-4x20-0
10 FT. CLG.

FP

42" LEDGE

KITCH
10-8x
12-2
10 FT
CLG

UTILITY

PAN

BATH 2

LIN

ARCH

BDRM 2
12-8x11-4

BDRM 3
12-0x13-4
10 FT
COFFERED CLG

FOYER
10 FT
CLG

DINING
10-8x13-0
10 FT
COFFERED CLG

SLOPE
CLG

PORCH

Design 8244

Square Footage: 1,948

■ A mock portico with twin sets of
columns introduces you to this fine
European-flavored design, and ushers
you into the foyer. A formal dining
room with a coffered ceiling will handle
traditional occasions, while a spacious
living room offers a warming fireplace.
An angled kitchen with a 42" ledge
enjoys natural light from an adjacent
breakfast area. The master suite is
designed to pamper with a coffered ceiling, a walk-in closet and a deluxe master bath. Two family bedrooms share a
full hall bath. Please specify crawlspace
or slab foundation when ordering.

Design by
LARRY E. BELK
DESIGNS

Keeping Room
13³ x 13⁹

Porch

Master Bedroom
13³ x 15⁶

Breakfast
11³ x 10⁰

Dining Room
11⁶ x 13⁰

Great Room
16⁰ x 15³

Kitchen
14⁹ x 11⁰

Bedroom #3
11⁹ x 12⁰

Width 63'-0"
Depth 59'-6"

Bedroom #2
11⁴ x 12⁰

Two Car Garage
21⁴ x 21⁴

Design by
DESIGN TRADITIONS

© Design Traditions

Design T213
Square Footage: 2,165

■ With a brick facade and captivating adornments, this one-story plan stands out as a perennial favorite. The raised front porch opens to an entry hall separated from the main living area by classic columns. Columns also define the formal dining area which shares views of the covered rear porch with the great room. If you choose, Bedroom 2 might become a den—change its entry from the secluded hall to the entry hall. A grand kitchen features an island workspace and attaches to a breakfast room and hearth-warmed keeping room beyond. Bedrooms are to the right of the plan and include a master suite with a tray ceiling, walk-in closet and corner whirlpool tub. The two-car garage protects the main house from street noise and traffic.

© Design Traditions

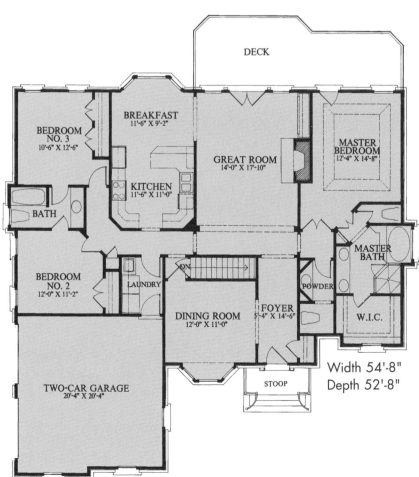

DECK

BREAKFAST
11'-6" X 9'-2"

BEDROOM
NO. 3
10'-6" X 12'-6"

GREAT ROOM
14'-0" X 17'-10"

MASTER
BEDROOM
12'-4" X 14'-8"

KITCHEN
11'-6" X 11'-0"

BATH

MASTER
BATH

BEDROOM
NO. 2
12'-0" X 11'-2"

LAUNDRY

DN

POWDER

W.I.C.

DINING ROOM
12'-0" X 11'-0"

FOYER
5'-4" X 14'-6"

TWO-CAR GARAGE
20'-4" X 20'-4"

STOOP

Width 54'-8"
Depth 52'-8"

Design T091

Square Footage: 1,850

■ A side-loaded garage helps maintain a beautiful facade for this brick one-story. The recessed entry opens to a central foyer that leads to the dining room on the left and the great room to the rear. A lovely deck is found beyond the great room and is also accessed from the master suite. The large kitchen has an attached breakfast room with bay window and is just across the hall from the service entrance with laundry. Two secondary bedrooms have plenty of closet space and share a compartmented full bath. This home is designed with a basement foundation.

Design by

DESIGN TRADITIONS

Design T215

Square Footage: 1,733

■ Count on the center-hall design and open floor planning of this design to meet your livability needs for years to come. The great room serves both informal and formal occasions and is close enough to the formal dining room and the less formal breakfast room to make entertaining easy. Further enhancements in the great room include a fireplace and double doors opening to the rear deck. The breakfast room has a bay-style window for sunny morning coffee. Bedrooms are split with two family bedrooms and a full bath on the left and the master suite on the right. The master bedroom features a tray ceiling and a bath with plenty of closet space, a garden whirlpool and double sinks. The two-car garage has extra room for storage or a workbench.

Design by
DESIGN TRADITIONS

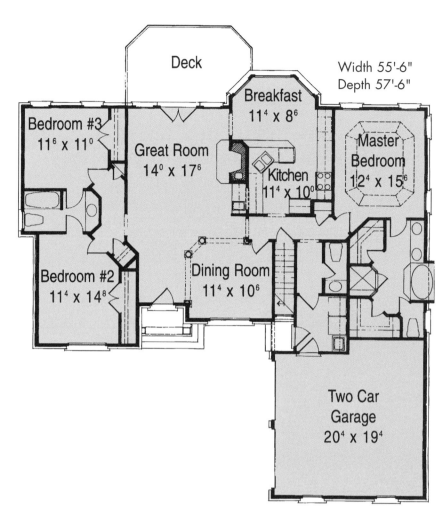

Deck

Width 55'-6"
Depth 57'-6"

Bedroom #3
11⁶ x 11⁰

Great Room
14⁰ x 17⁶

Breakfast
11⁴ x 8⁶

Kitchen
11⁴ x 10⁰

Master Bedroom
12⁴ x 15⁶

Bedroom #2
11⁴ x 14⁸

Dining Room
11⁴ x 10⁶

Two Car Garage
20⁴ x 19⁴

Design T110
Square Footage: 1,815

PORCH

BREAKFAST
10'-0" X 10'-0"

GREAT ROOM
16'-0" X 18'-0"

MASTER BEDROOM
15'-0" X 14'-0"

W.I.C.

MASTER BATH

KITCHEN
14'-0" X 11'-4"

POWDER

FOYER
5'-0" X 9'-0"

DINING ROOM
10'-6" X 13'-0"

BEDROOM
NO. 3
10'-6" X 10'-0"

BEDROOM NO. 2
11'-2" X 11'-0"

BATH

LAUND
5'-2" X
10'-6"

DN.

TWO CAR GARAGE
20'-4" X 19'-4"

Width 60'-0"
Depth 60'-6"

Design by
DESIGN TRADITIONS

■ With zoned living at the core of this floor plan, livability takes a convenient turn. Living areas are to the left of the plan; sleeping areas to the right. The formal dining room is open to the central hallway and foyer, and features graceful columned archways to define its space. The great room has angled corners and a magnificent central fireplace and offers ample views to the rear grounds. Steps away is a well-lit breakfast room with private rear-porch access and an adjoining U-shaped kitchen with unique angled counter space and sink. Sleeping quarters are clustered around a private hallway which offers a guest bath. The master suite includes a resplendent bath with garden tub, dual lavatories and walk-in closet. Two family bedrooms share a full bath with compartmented toilet and tub. This home is designed with a basement foundation.

© Design Traditions

211

COPYRIGHT LARRY E. BELK

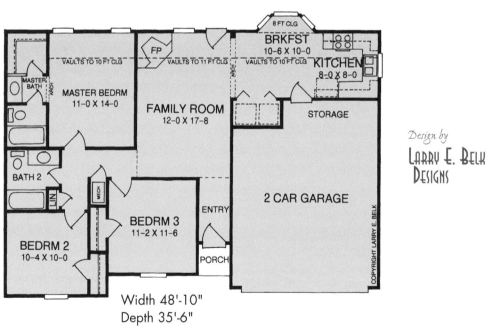

8 FT CLG

BRKFST
10-6 X 10-0

KITCHEN
8-0 X 8-0

FP

VAULTS TO 10 FT CLG   VAULTS TO 11 FT CLG   VAULTS TO 10 FT CLG

MASTER
BATH

MASTER BEDRM
11-0 X 14-0

FAMILY ROOM
12-0 X 17-8

STORAGE

ARCH

BATH 2

2 CAR GARAGE

LIN   MECH

BEDRM 3
11-2 X 11-6

ENTRY

BEDRM 2
10-4 X 10-0

PORCH

COPYRIGHT LARRY E. BELK

Width 48'-10"
Depth 35'-6"

Design by
LARRY E. BELK
DESIGNS

Design 8198
Square Footage: 1,142

■ This three-bedroom home will be a delight to come home to. Two family bedrooms share a full hall bath and provide plenty of space for growing kids or for overnight guests. The master bedroom features a walk-in closet and a full bath. The large central family room, with its corner fireplace and outdoor access, will be the perfect spot for sharing special occasions. A bayed breakfast room and a counter-filled kitchen with garage access complete this wonderful plan. Please specify crawlspace or slab foundation when ordering.

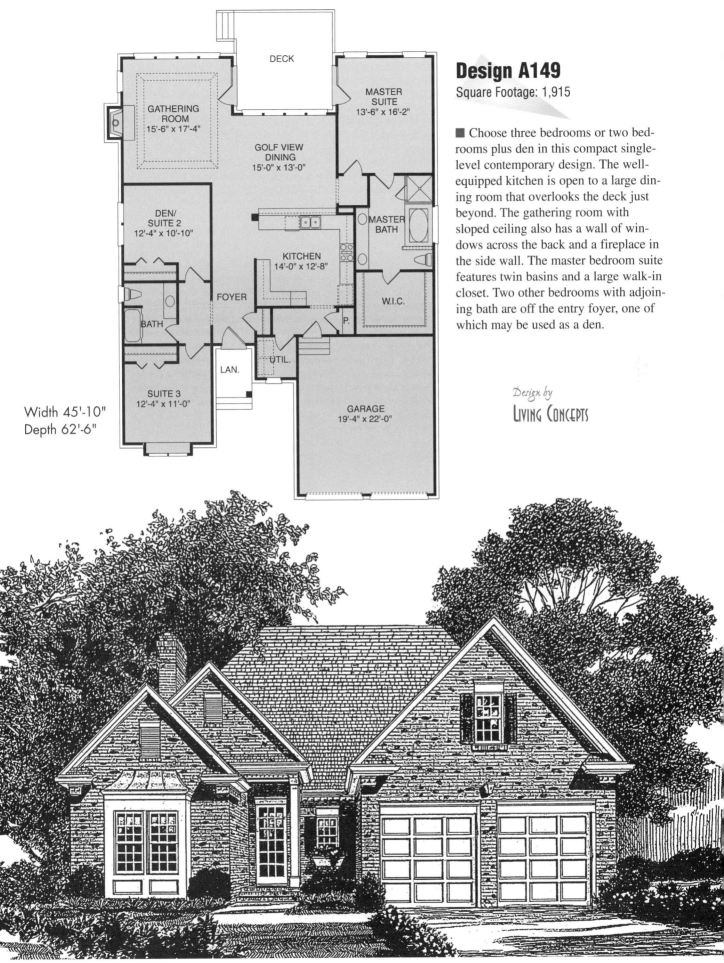

DECK

GATHERING
ROOM
15'-6" x 17'-4"

MASTER
SUITE
13'-6" x 16'-2"

GOLF VIEW
DINING
15'-0" x 13'-0"

DEN/
SUITE 2
12'-4" x 10'-10"

MASTER
BATH

BATH

FOYER

KITCHEN
14'-0" x 12'-8"

W.I.C.

P.

UTIL.

LAN.

SUITE 3
12'-4" x 11'-0"

GARAGE
19'-4" x 22'-0"

Width 45'-10"
Depth 62'-6"

Design A149

Square Footage: 1,915

■ Choose three bedrooms or two bedrooms plus den in this compact single-
level contemporary design. The well-
equipped kitchen is open to a large dining room that overlooks the deck just
beyond. The gathering room with
sloped ceiling also has a wall of windows across the back and a fireplace in
the side wall. The master bedroom suite
features twin basins and a large walk-in
closet. Two other bedrooms with adjoining bath are off the entry foyer, one of
which may be used as a den.

Design by
LIVING CONCEPTS

Design P295

Square Footage: 1,425

■ The floor plan of this beautifully styled traditional home leaves room for many options. For instance, Bedroom 2, with its vaulted ceiling, would make a fine home office or den. Plant shelves throughout the plan allow you to indulge your hobby as an indoor gardener, or to display fine collectibles or art objects. Living spaces are open and graced with extended ceilings. The family room features a corner fireplace and shares with the dining room a serving bar in the kitchen. A nearby breakfast room has a vaulted ceiling also and a wall of windows overlooking the rear yard. The master suite is truly luxurious. It is appointed with a tray ceiling and has a vaulted master bath with a huge whirlpool tub, walk-in closet with built-in linen storage and double sink. The two-car garage contains extra storage space.

Design by

Frank Betz
Associates, Inc.

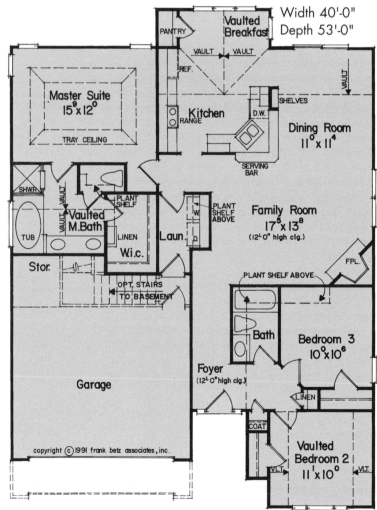

Width 40'-0"
Depth 53'-0"

Master Suite 15⁹ x 12⁰
TRAY CEILING

PANTRY

Vaulted Breakfast
VAULT VAULT

REF.

Kitchen
RANGE D.W.

SHELVES

VAULT

Dining Room 11⁰ x 11⁴

SERVING BAR

SHWR

VAULT

Vaulted M.Bath

PLANT SHELF

TUB

LINEN

Wi.c.

Laun.

PLANT SHELF ABOVE

W D

Family Room 17⁵ x 13⁸
(12'-0" high clg.)

FPL.

Stor.

OPT. STAIRS TO BASEMENT

PLANT SHELF ABOVE

Bath

Bedroom 3 10⁰ x 10⁶

Garage

copyright © 1991 frank betz associates, inc.

Foyer (12'-0" high clg.)

LINEN

COAT

Vaulted Bedroom 2 11¹ x 10⁰
VLT. VLT.

214

Design A246

Square Footage: 1,913

■ This traditional home begins with a stylish columned lanai, which leads to a spacious foyer and hall that opens to all areas. The kitchen overlooks a central formal dining room with views and access to the rear deck. An open, spacious gathering room shares the glow of an extended-hearth fireplace with the dining area and kitchen. The master suite opens from a private vestibule and offers a deluxe bath with a garden tub, a separate shower and a U-shaped walk-in closet. Two additional suites share a full bath on the other side of the plan. One of these rooms could serve as a den or study. A service entrance from the two-car garage leads to a pantry area and to the laundry.

Design by
LIVING CONCEPTS

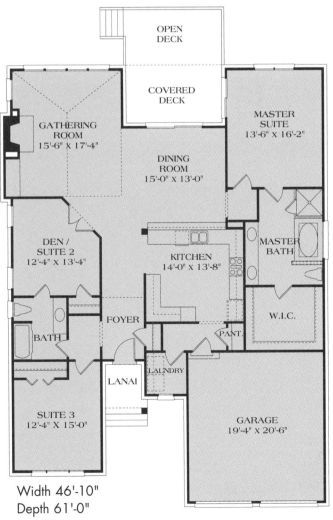

Width 46'-10"
Depth 61'-0"

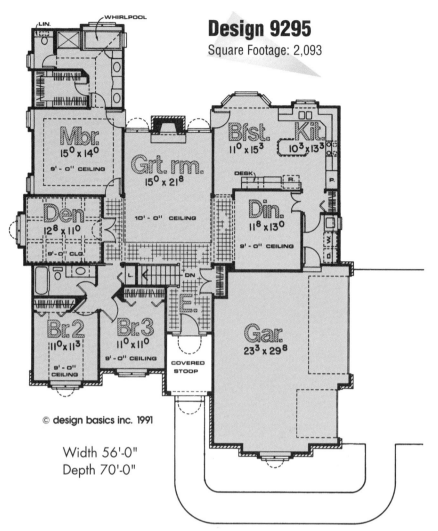

Design 9295

Square Footage: 2,093

Mbr.
15⁰ x 14⁰
9'-0" CEILING

Grt. rm.
15⁰ x 21⁸
10'-0" CEILING

Bfst.
11⁰ x 15³

Kit.
10³ x 13³

Den
12⁸ x 11⁰
9'-0" CLG.

DESK

Din.
11⁸ x 13⁰
9'-0" CEILING

Br.2
11⁰ x 11³
9'-0" CEILING

Br.3
11⁰ x 11⁰
9'-0" CEILING

COVERED STOOP

Gar.
23³ x 29⁸

WHIRLPOOL

LIN.

© design basics inc. 1991

Width 56'-0"
Depth 70'-0"

■ Repeating rooflines and arched windows complement this ranch home with three-car garage. A straight view from the entry reveals a ten-foot ceiling in the great room which is appointed with two windows with arched transoms and a raised-hearth fireplace. French doors off the great room access the den. This private room features a nine-foot spider-beam ceiling for added effect. In the island kitchen are special extras such as the desk, pantry and Lazy Susan. The bright dinette retains outdoor access. A front secondary bedroom includes an arched window, while the other bedroom contains a boxed window. Both are conveniently located near the bath. Enhancements in the master suite are a boxed ceiling, a walk-in closet and a whirlpool tub. The bedrooms are segregated from the primary living spaces.

Design by
DESIGN BASICS, INC.

G. MacDonald

Width 65'-0"
Depth 49'-6"

PATIO
13'-1" x 10'-5"

BREAKFAST
11'-10" x 8'-0"

breakfast bar

KEEPING ROOM
13'-7" x 17'-2"
vlt.   vlt.

dw.

ref.

LIVING ROOM
14'-0" x 16'-10"
11'-0" Ceiling

MASTER BEDROOM
14'-1" x 15'-8"

trey ceiling

W.I.C.

lin.   vlt.

MASTER BATH
vlt.

W.I.C.

LAUNDRY
w.   d.

KITCHEN

w.h.

lin.

BATH

lin.   clo.

FOYER

cc   clo.

DINING
11'-6" x 14'-0"
11'-0" Ceiling

ENTRY

BEDROOM
12'-5" x 11'-10"
vlt.   vlt.

BEDROOM
11'-9" x 13'-8"

GARAGE
21'-4" x 21'-4"

Design S129
Square Footage: 2,054

■ Defined by an elegant column, the covered entrance to this three bedroom home welcomes friends and family. Inside, a formal dining room and formal living room, also defined by a graceful column, are open to one another, providing a wonderful entertaining area. The kitchen, enhanced by angles, features a work island and a breakfast bar. The nearby keeping room offers a vaulted ceiling and a warming fireplace. Two secondary bedrooms share a hall bath, while the master bedroom is complete with many amenities. Here, a tray ceiling, two walk-in closets and a vaulted bath are sure to please.

Design by
ARCHIVAL DESIGNS

Design 9264

Square Footage: 2,355

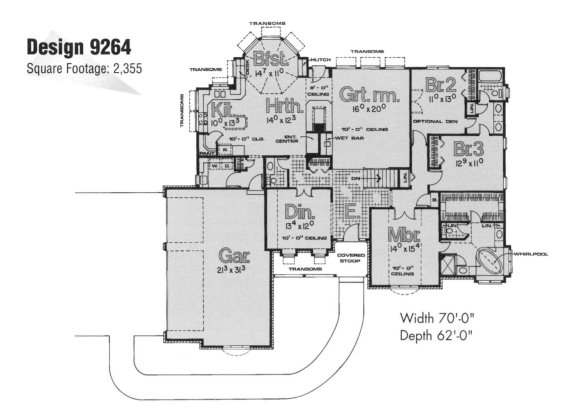

Width 70'-0"
Depth 62'-0"

■ This home presents a facade of simple, timeless elegance. The vaulted entry paves the way to views of the stairway and great room beyond. The three-sided fireplace serves as a focal point for both the great room and the adjacent hearth room. The formal dining room has ten-foot ceilings and boxed windows. A breakfast room with gazebo ceiling is convenient for more casual dining. The home's sleeping wing includes two family bedrooms that share a full bath. A luxurious master suite is highlighted by a dressing area with twin vanities, an angled oval whirlpool tub and a large walk-in closet.

Design by
DESIGN BASICS, INC.

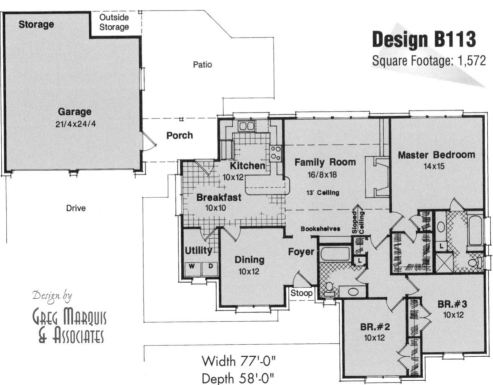

Storage

Outside
Storage

Patio

Garage
21/4x24/4

Porch

Drive

Kitchen
10x12

Family Room
16/8x18

13' Ceiling

Master Bedroom
14x15

Breakfast
10x10

Bookshelves

Sloped
Ceiling

Utility

W D

Dining
10x12

Foyer

L

L

Stoop

BR.#3
10x12

BR.#2
10x12

Design B113
Square Footage: 1,572

Width 77'-0"
Depth 58'-0"

Design by
GREG MARQUIS
& ASSOCIATES

■ This house has real curb appeal, and the inside's just as pleasing! The large family room with warming fireplace vaults to thirteen feet for added drama. The open kitchen and breakfast area with eat-in bar make casual meals a breeze. The nearby formal dining room easily accommodates dinner parties. And take a look at the large utility room. In the sleeping zone, two family bedrooms have access to a full hall bath, while the master bedroom pampers with a private bath and a large walk-in closet. The detached garage connects via a covered walk and accommodates the family fleet.

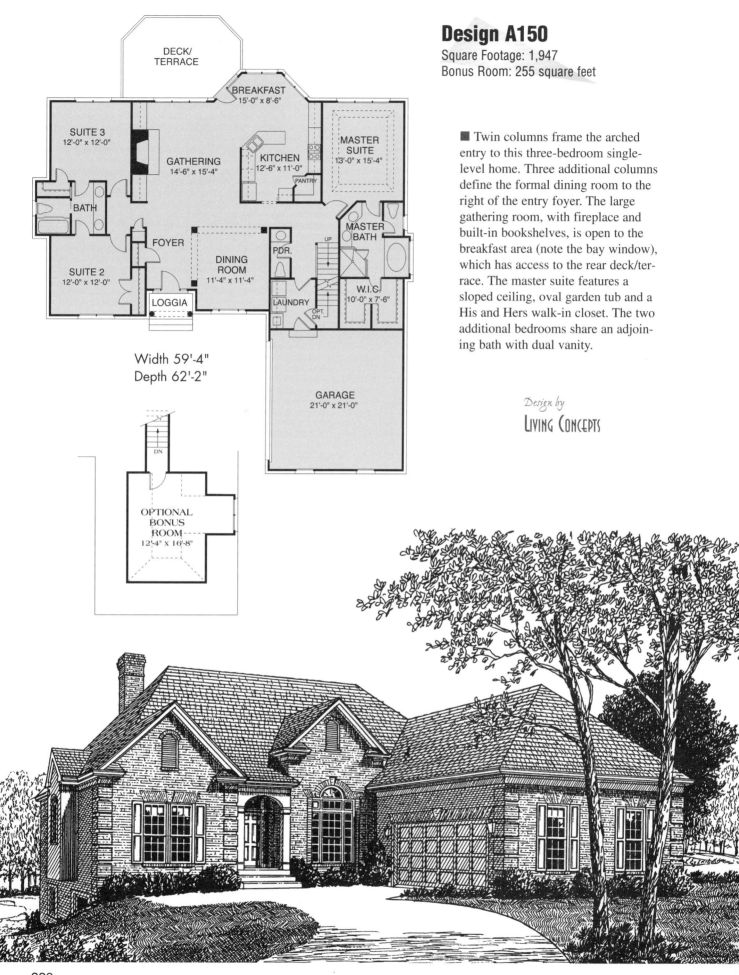

Design A150

Square Footage: 1,947
Bonus Room: 255 square feet

DECK/
TERRACE

BREAKFAST
15'-0" x 8'-6"

SUITE 3
12'-0" x 12'-0"

GATHERING
14'-6" x 15'-4"

KITCHEN
12'-6" x 11'-0"

PANTRY

MASTER
SUITE
13'-0" x 15'-4"

BATH

FOYER

DINING
ROOM
11'-4" x 11'-4"

PDR.

UP

MASTER
BATH

SUITE 2
12'-0" x 12'-0"

LOGGIA

LAUNDRY

OPT.
DN

W.I.C.
10'-0" x 7'-6"

GARAGE
21'-0" x 21'-0"

Width 59'-4"
Depth 62'-2"

DN

OPTIONAL
BONUS
ROOM
12'-4" x 16'-8"

■ Twin columns frame the arched entry to this three-bedroom single-level home. Three additional columns define the formal dining room to the right of the entry foyer. The large gathering room, with fireplace and built-in bookshelves, is open to the breakfast area (note the bay window), which has access to the rear deck/terrace. The master suite features a sloped ceiling, oval garden tub and a His and Hers walk-in closet. The two additional bedrooms share an adjoining bath with dual vanity.

Design by
Living Concepts

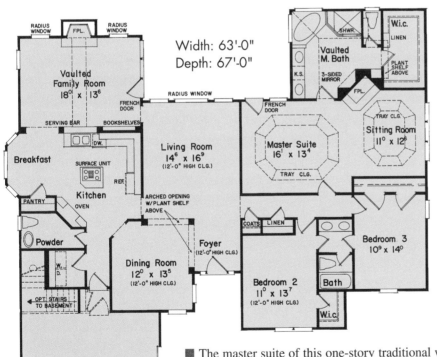

RADIUS WINDOW · FPL. · RADIUS WINDOW

Vaulted Family Room
18⁰ x 13⁶

SERVING BAR · BOOKSHELVES

Breakfast

SURFACE UNIT

Kitchen

PANTRY · OVEN

Powder

W. D.

OPT. STAIRS TO BASEMENT

Dining Room
12⁰ x 13⁵
(12'-0" HIGH CLG.)

Garage

copyright (c) 1993 frank betz associates, inc.

FRENCH DOOR

RADIUS WINDOW

Living Room
14⁶ x 16⁹
(12'-0" HIGH CLG.)

ARCHED OPENING W/PLANT SHELF ABOVE

Foyer
(12'-0" HIGH CLG.)

COATS · LINEN

Bedroom 2
11⁰ x 13⁷
(12'-0" HIGH CLG.)

W.i.c.

Width: 63'-0"
Depth: 67'-0"

W.i.c. · LINEN

SHWR.

Vaulted M. Bath

K.S. · 3-SIDED MIRROR

PLANT SHELF ABOVE

FRENCH DOOR

Master Suite
16' x 13⁴
TRAY CLG.

FPL.

TRAY CLG.

Sitting Room
11⁰ x 12⁶

Bedroom 3
10⁹ x 14⁰

Bath

Design P126

Square Footage: 2,236

Design by

FRANK BETZ
ASSOCIATES, INC.

■ The master suite of this one-story traditional will be a haven for any homeowner. Separate tray ceilings split a generous sitting room from the main bedroom while a fireplace warms both areas. The vaulted master bath includes a three-sided mirror, a corner whirlpool tub, His and Hers sinks and a walk-in closet with built-in linen storage. The master suite also includes French-door access to the rear yard. The rest of the home is equally impressive. Radius windows highlight the central living room, arches create a dramatic entrance to the dining room and the open kitchen area includes a cooktop island, a sunny breakfast area and a serving bar to the vaulted family room with its cozy fireplace. Two bedrooms and a full bath with dual basins complete this amenity-filled design. Please specify basement or crawlspace foundation when ordering.

Design 6659

Square Footage: 2,659

L

■ Varied roof lines, multi-pane windows and elegant pillars combine to present a fine traditional family home. Through double entry doors, columns frame the foyer, creating arches that lead to the formal dining room and grand room. The central living area boasts a wall of sliding glass doors to the rear veranda, a fireplace and built-ins. Off the leisure room, three family bedrooms—each with ample closet space—share a full bath with twin vanities, while the deluxe master suite nestles in a private wing of the plan.

Design by
The Sater Design Collection

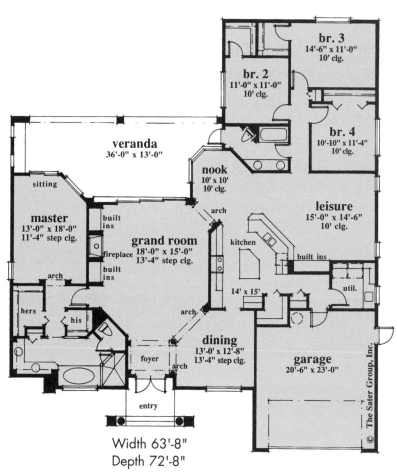

Width 63'-8"
Depth 72'-8"

222

Design 7315

Square Footage: 1,782

■ Symmetrical gables offset a hip roof and arch-top windows and complement a stately brick exterior with this traditional design. Inside, the formal dining room opens from an elegant tiled entry and offers space for quiet, planned occasions as well as traditional festivities. The casual living area shares a three-sided fireplace with the breakfast area and hearth room, while the kitchen offers a convenient snack bar for easy meals. A nine-foot ceiling enhances the master suite, which features a whirlpool tub, twin vanities, an ample walk-in closet and a compartmented toilet. Split sleeping quarters offer privacy to both the master and the family bedrooms, which share a full bath.

Design by
Design Basics, Inc.

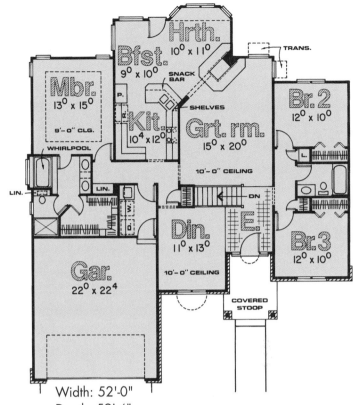

Width: 52'-0"
Depth: 59'-4"

Rear Elevation

223

Design 7345

Square Footage: 2,504

■ Brick detail and interesting window treatments create a dramatic exterior on this traditional one-story home. Inside, formal living and dining rooms share a through-fireplace. Additionally, transom windows and French doors open the formal living area to the outside. A nearby kitchen provides a snack bar, an island counter, easy access to the dining room and a cathedral ceiling. A perfect retreat, the master suite is highlighted by French doors, matching vanities, a walk-in closet and an oval whirlpool tub.

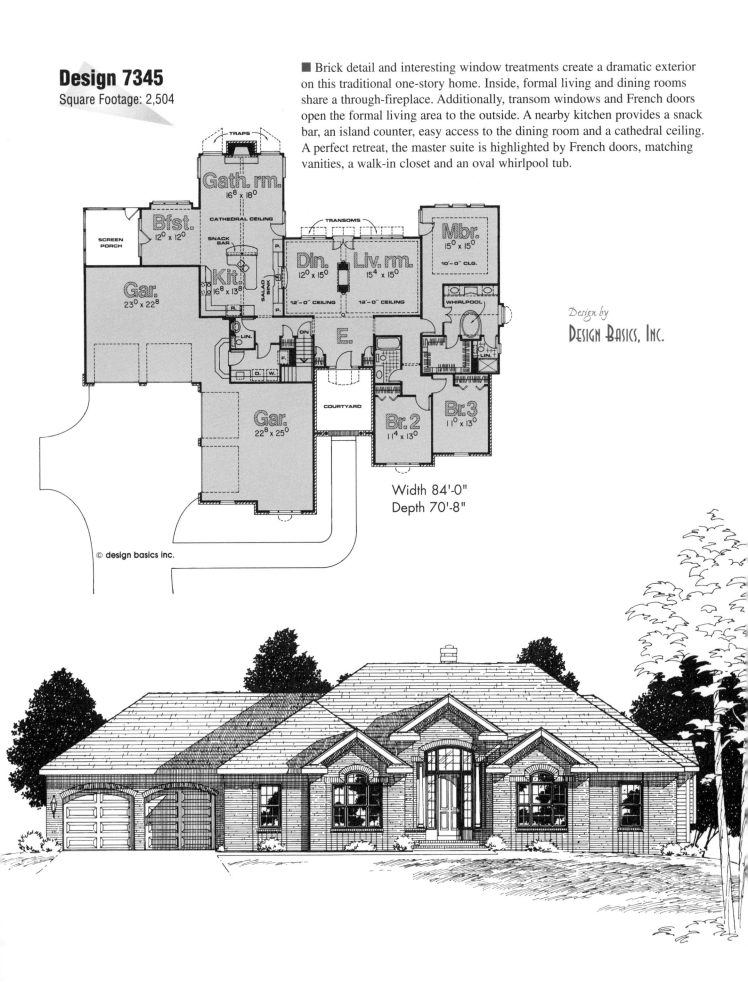

Design by
DESIGN BASICS, INC.

Width 84'-0"
Depth 70'-8"

© design basics inc.

Design 9396

Square Footage: 2,775

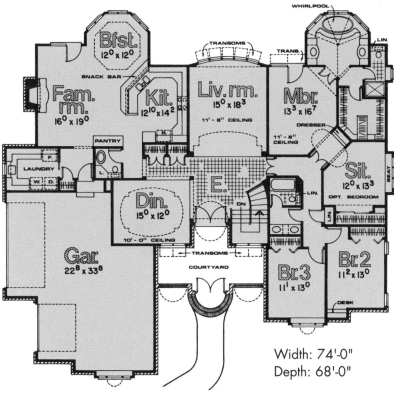

Width: 74'-0"
Depth: 68'-0"

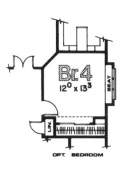

Design by
DESIGN BASICS, INC.

■ An impressive wrought iron-accented entry introduces a captivating courtyard. The dignified surroundings of the formal dining room enhance entertaining. Family living is highlighted in the integrated design of the kitchen, breakfast bay and family room. The huge laundry room is well planned and placed for efficiency and convenience. For maximum privacy, double doors seclude the bedroom wing from the rest of the house. The master suite includes a built-in dresser, outdoor access and a private sitting room. The master bath with dual lavatories and an extra-large oval whirlpool is distinguished by a multi-faceted sloped ceiling.

■ Stately brick detailing embellishes this European-style ranch home. The entry allows a lovely view of the fireplace in the great room, framed by handsome windows and transoms. The living room offers a ten-foot ceiling and is located conveniently across the foyer from the formal dining room. If you choose, the living room may be made into a fourth bedroom. Bowed windows in the breakfast area and a snack bar peninsula in the kitchen serve to dress up this casual living space. The master suite features a ten-foot ceiling and access to a private deck. Look for a corner whirlpool tub, His and Hers vanities and a large walk-in closet in the master bath. Secondary bedrooms are in a separate wing for privacy. They share a full bath. The three-car garage is a side-load style.

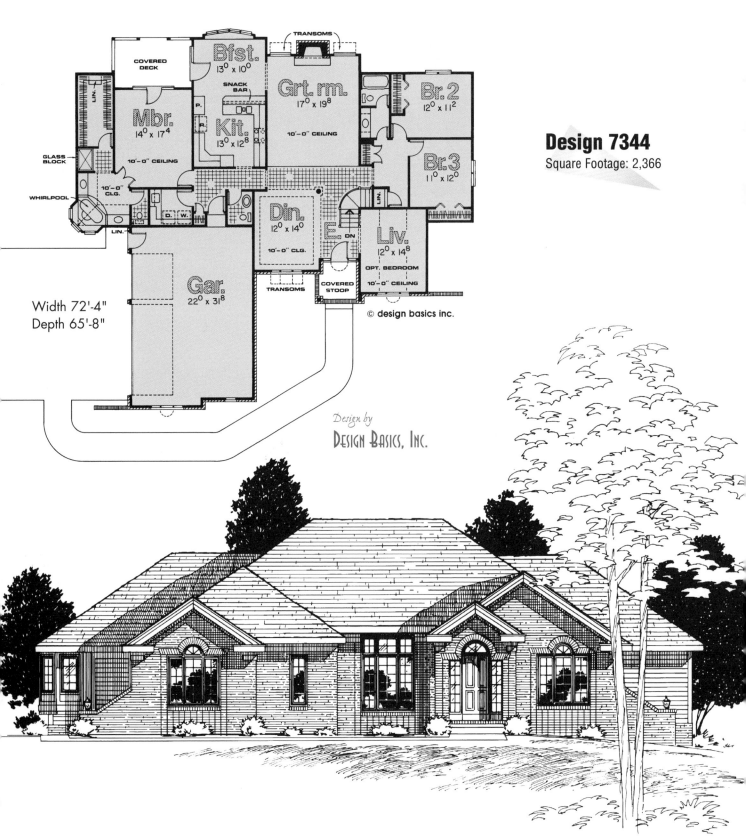

Design 7344
Square Footage: 2,366

Width 72'-4"
Depth 65'-8"

Design by
Design Basics, Inc.

© design basics inc.

Design 7318
Square Footage: 2,187

Design by
DESIGN BASICS, INC.

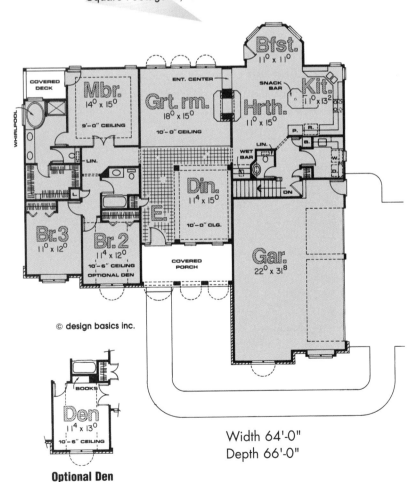

© design basics inc.

Width 64'-0"
Depth 66'-0"

Optional Den

■ Multiple arches adorn the covered front porch of this volume three-bedroom home. Inside, an elegant formal dining room is located immediately to the right of the foyer, separated from the large and inviting great room by graceful columns. The great room and the hearth room share a through-fireplace. The large island kitchen is a gourmet's delight, with plenty of cabinet and counter space available. The adjacent bayed breakfast nook offers direct access to the rear yard and is sure to please. The sleeping zone consists of two secondary bedrooms (or make one a cozy study with built-ins) that share a full hall bath, and a lavish master bedroom suite. The amenities are many in this sumptuous suite, ranging from a tray ceiling, a large walk-in closet and a luxurious bath, to a private covered deck.

Rear Elevation

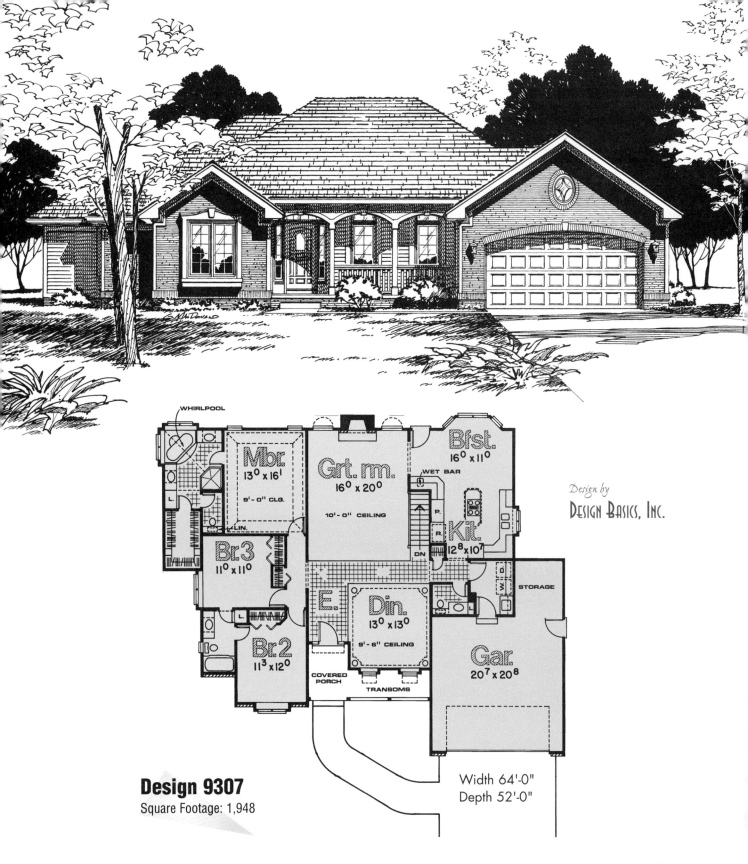

Design 9307
Square Footage: 1,948

Width 64'-0"
Depth 52'-0"

Design by
DESIGN BASICS, INC.

■ Wood and brick details along with an elegant porch highlight the elevation of this special design. A ten-foot-high entry views the open dining room with tapered columns. Gourmet cooks will delight in the island kitchen with pantry and wrapping wet bar/servery. Outdoor access is available from the sunny bayed dinette. In the great room, a cozy fireplace is flanked by large windows with arched transoms above. Two secondary bedrooms share a Hollywood bath with a linen cabinet. At night, the lucky homeowners can retreat to the elegant master suite complete with vaulted ceilings and a pampering master bath. Special amenities include His and Hers vanities, linen closet, corner whirlpool, special shower and roomy walk-in closet. Truly, this home is delightful inside and out.

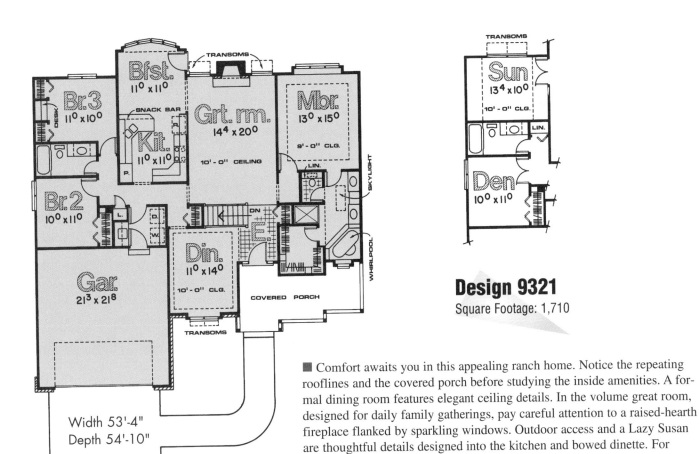

Br. 3
11⁰ x 10⁰

Bfst.
11⁰ x 11⁰

SNACK BAR

Kit.
11⁰ x 11⁰

Grt. rm.
14⁴ x 20⁰
10' - 0" CEILING

Mbr.
13⁰ x 15⁰
9' - 0" CLG.

TRANSOMS

Br. 2
10⁰ x 11⁰

SKYLIGHT

LIN.

Gar.
21³ x 21⁸

Din.
11⁰ x 14⁰
10' - 0" CLG.

DN

WHIRLPOOL

COVERED PORCH

TRANSOMS

Width 53'-4"
Depth 54'-10"

TRANSOMS

Sun
13⁴ x 10⁰
10' - 0" CLG.

LIN.

Den
10⁰ x 11⁰

Design 9321
Square Footage: 1,710

■ Comfort awaits you in this appealing ranch home. Notice the repeating rooflines and the covered porch before studying the inside amenities. A formal dining room features elegant ceiling details. In the volume great room, designed for daily family gatherings, pay careful attention to a raised-hearth fireplace flanked by sparkling windows. Outdoor access and a Lazy Susan are thoughtful details designed into the kitchen and bowed dinette. For added flexibility, two secondary bedrooms can be easily converted to a sun room with French doors and an optional den. The secluded master suite is enhanced by a boxed ceiling and deluxe skylit dressing room.

Design by
Design Basics, Inc.

Design 9450

Square Footage: 2,378

■ Spacious living all on one story—this traditional design has a place for everything. A large central kitchen with an island serves the dining room, living room, nook and family room all with ease. Note the fireplace and vaulted ceiling in the family room. Four bedrooms, or three bedrooms and a den, occupy the right wing of the house. The master suite with vaulted ceiling comes in two versions—the choice is up to you.

Design by

ALAN MASCORD
DESIGN ASSOCIATES, INC.

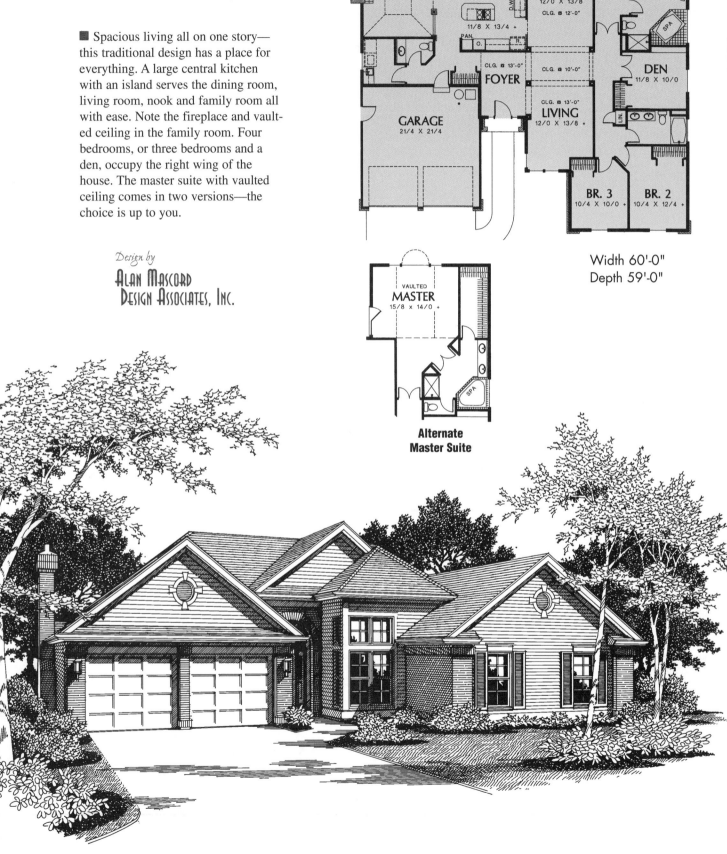

VAULTED
MASTER
16/8 X 14/0

NOOK
8/10 X 8/0

VAULTED
FAMILY
12/10 X 17/0

DINING
12/0 X 13/8

CLG. @ 12'-0"

11/8 X 13/4 +

SPA

PAN.

DEN
11/8 X 10/0

CLG. @ 13'-0"

CLG. @ 10'-0"

FOYER

CLG. @ 13'-0"

GARAGE
21/4 X 21/4

LIVING
12/0 X 13/8 +

LIN

BR. 3
10/4 X 10/0 +

BR. 2
10/4 X 12/4 +

Width 60'-0"
Depth 59'-0"

VAULTED
MASTER
15/8 X 14/0 +

SPA

**Alternate
Master Suite**

Design 9328

Square Footage: 1,496

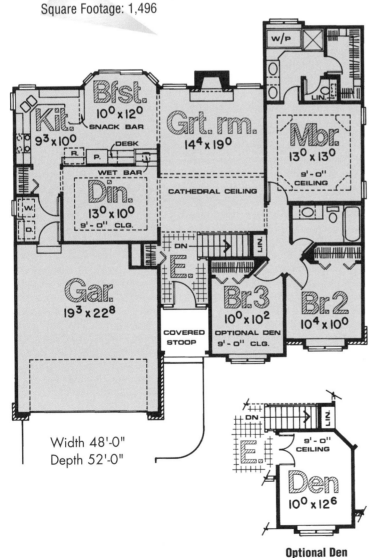

Bfst. 10⁰ x 12⁰
SNACK BAR

Kit. 9³ x 10⁰

DESK

Grt. rm. 14⁴ x 19⁰

Mbr. 13⁰ x 13⁰
9'-0" CEILING

Din. 13⁰ x 10⁰
9'-0" CLG.

WET BAR

R. P.

W.

D.

W/P

LIN

CATHEDRAL CEILING

LIN

DN

Gar. 19³ x 22⁸

Br. 3 10⁰ x 10²
OPTIONAL DEN
9'-0" CLG.

Br. 2 10⁴ x 10⁰

COVERED STOOP

E.

Width 48'-0"
Depth 52'-0"

DN

LIN

9'-0" CEILING

E.

Den 10⁰ x 12⁶

Optional Den

■ Sleek rooflines, lap siding and brick accents highlight the exterior of this three-bedroom ranch home. A tiled entry views the spacious great room featuring a sloping cathedral ceiling and window-framed fireplace. Note the strategic location of the dining room (with nine-foot boxed ceiling and wet bar/servery) which accommodates formal entertaining and family gatherings. Natural light and warmth add comfort to the bayed breakfast area with pantry, handy planning desk and the peninsula kitchen. Well-segregated sleeping quarters add to the flexibility of this modern floor plan. Both secondary bedrooms share a full bath and linen closet. Bedroom 3 is easily converted to a den or home office. With the nine-foot high boxed ceiling, walk-in closet, sunlit whirlpool tub and double vanities, the master suite is soothing and luxurious.

Design by
DESIGN BASICS, INC.

231

Design 7365
Square Footage: 1,729

Design by
Design Basics, Inc.

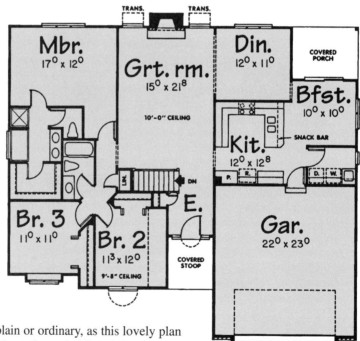

Width 55'-4"
Depth 48'-4"

■ Simple, single-level design need not be plain or ordinary, as this lovely plan proves. Its facade is well managed, with horizontal wood siding, brick accents and an arched window under a gabled pediment. The floor plan is accommodating, with well-defined living and sleeping areas. A large great room with ten-foot ceiling dominates the center of the plan, with a smaller dining room, a light-filled breakfast room and a U-shaped kitchen falling to the right. On the left are two family bedrooms which have use of a full bath. The master suite stands alone and is graced by a walk-in closet, separate shower and tub and dual lavatories. A two-car garage is the icing on this ranch-style cake.

Design 7012

Square Footage: 1,894

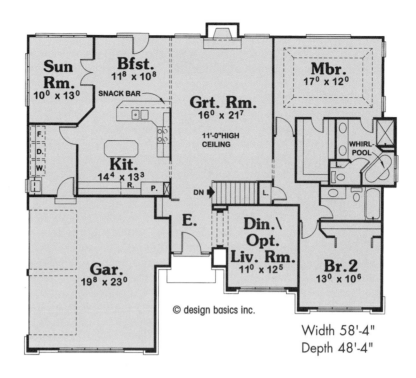

Sun Rm. 10⁰ x 13⁰

Bfst. 11⁸ x 10⁸

SNACK BAR

Grt. Rm. 16⁰ x 21⁷

11'-0"HIGH CEILING

Mbr. 17⁰ x 12⁰

WHIRL-POOL

Kit. 14⁴ x 13³

DN

Dined.\Opt.Liv. Rm. 11⁰ x 12⁵

E.

Br.2 13⁰ x 10⁶

Gar. 19⁸ x 23⁰

Design by
Design Basics, Inc.

© design basics inc.

Width 58'-4"
Depth 48'-4"

■ Special enhancements turn on the appeal of this quaint ranch home. A sun room warms and lights up the breakfast room and kitchen while a handy snack bar here is perfect for quick, light meals. The great room features an eleven-foot ceiling and window-framed fireplace. A formal dining room can be devised into a formal living area if you'd prefer. Look to the master suite for true luxury. It has a tray ceiling, corner whirlpool tub, compartmented toilet, separate shower and double sinks. Bedroom 2 has its own bath. The two-car garage is connected to the main house via a service entrance that passes through a convenient laundry area with space for a washer, dryer, freezer and work sink.

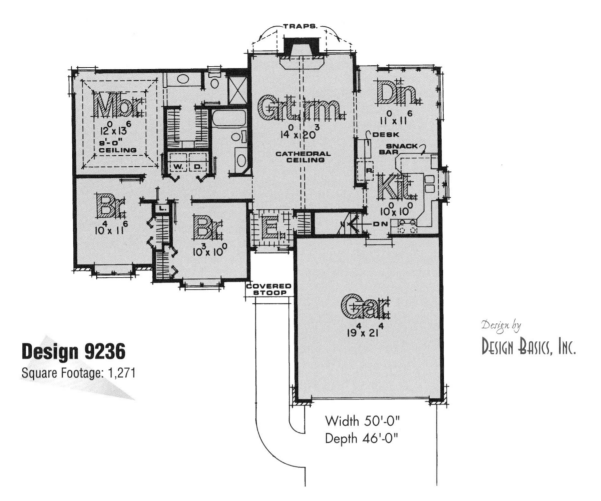

Design 9236

Square Footage: 1,271

Design by
DESIGN BASICS, INC.

Width 50'-0"
Depth 46'-0"

■ This charmingly snug three-bedroom home offers all the features you've been looking for in a family home. The great room has a lovely cathedral ceiling and a fireplace surrounded by windows. Nearby is the dining area and efficient kitchen with a window box, planning desk, Lazy Susan and snack bar counter. Intriguing ceiling treatment dominates the master bedroom where you'll also find corner windows, a dressing area with large vanity and a walk-in closet. Two family bedrooms share a full bath and are located near the laundry room.

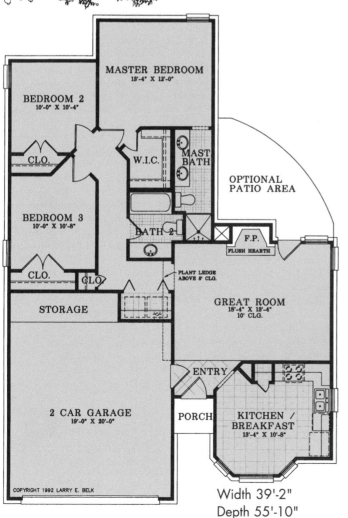

MASTER BEDROOM
18'-4" X 12'-0"

BEDROOM 2
10'-0" X 10'-4"

CLO.

W.I.C.

MAST BATH

OPTIONAL PATIO AREA

BEDROOM 3
10'-0" X 10'-8"

BATH 2

CLO.

CLO.

F.P.
FLUSH HEARTH

STORAGE

PLANT LEDGE ABOVE 8' CLG.

GREAT ROOM
18'-4" X 18'-4"
10' CLG.

2 CAR GARAGE
19'-0" X 20'-0"

ENTRY

PORCH

KITCHEN / BREAKFAST
18'-4" X 10'-8"

Width 39'-2"
Depth 55'-10"

Design 8197

Square Footage: 1,178

■ This cozy traditional charmer is set off by a bay window and asymmetrical gables. The inviting entry leads to a spacious great room, complete with a fireplace as well as access to an optional patio area. The front bay window brings in natural light to the kitchen/breakfast room with an ample pantry and wrapping counters. A gallery hall connects the sleeping quarters, which include two family bedrooms sharing a full bath, and a generous master suite with a private bath. Please specify crawlspace or slab foundation when ordering.

Design by
LARRY E. BELK
DESIGNS

Design C151

Square Footage: 1,840
Optional Master Bath: 105 square feet

■ Gabled rooflines, a bay window and a covered front porch combine to give this home plenty of curb appeal. Inside, cathedral ceilings throughout the home promote a spacious feeling. If entertaining is your forte, you'll love the way the large great room opens to the bayed family dining room, providing tons of casual space. The formal dining room echoes the bay window and offers easy access to the efficient kitchen. Separated for privacy, two secondary bedrooms reside to the right rear of the home and share a full bath, while the master suite is located on the left side of the plan. Here, a walk-in closet and a private bath await to pamper the homeowner. Also on this side of the home is a cozy study. Note the alternate option for the master bath.

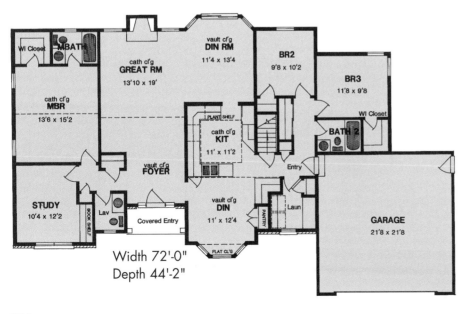

Width 72'-0"
Depth 44'-2"

Design by
James Fahy Design

Optional Master Bath

Design by

FRANK BETZ
ASSOCIATES, INC.

Design P233

Square Footage: 1,671

■ Asymmetrical gables, a columned porch and an abundance of windows brighten the exterior of this compact home. An efficient kitchen boasts a pantry and a serving bar that it shares with the formal dining room and the vaulted family room. A sunny breakfast room and nearby laundry room complete the living zone. Be sure to notice extras such as the focal-point fireplace in the family room and a plant shelf in the laundry room. The sumptuous master suite offers a door to the backyard, a vaulted sitting area and a pampering bath. Two family bedrooms share a hall bath. Please specify basement, crawlspace or slab foundation when ordering.

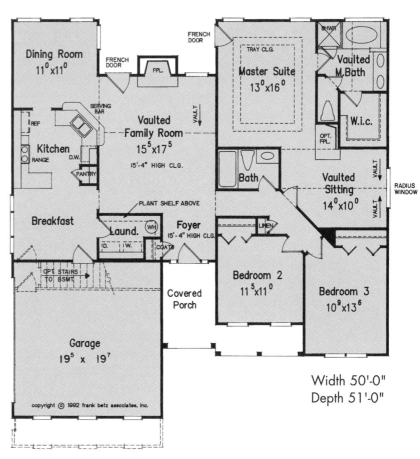

QUOTE ONE®

Cost to build? See page 434
to order complete cost estimate
to build this house in your area!

Width 50'-0"
Depth 51'-0"

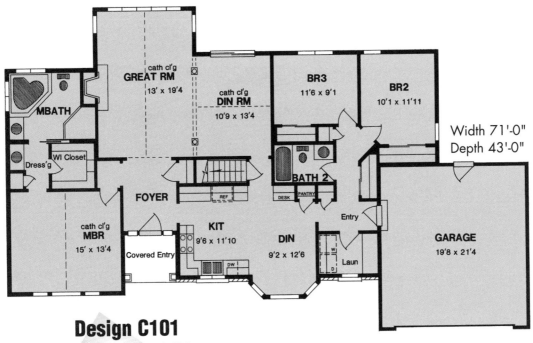

Design C101
Square Footage: 1,724

■ Gables along the roofline enhance this traditional ranch. Inside, the foyer receives the spacious great room and formal dining room soaring with cathedral ceilings and lots of glass, creating a dramatic impact. The front kitchen and dinette are conveniently located for your family's living needs while the formal entertaining areas are located at the rear of the home.

Your guests will dine with warmth from the fireplace. Natural light is abundant throughout the entire house. The master bedroom featuring a cathedral ceiling is tucked away to the left of the foyer. Every amenity from a corner whirlpool tub, glass corner shower, and His and Hers vanities is found in the adjoining master bath.

Design by
James Fahy Design

Design 7619

Square Footage: 1,912
Bonus Room: 398 square feet

■ An appealing blend of stone, siding and stucco announces a 21st-Century floor plan. A formal dining area defined by decorative columns opens to a grand great room with a centered hearth. The gourmet kitchen overlooks the great room, and enjoys natural light brought in by the bayed breakfast nook. The sleeping wing, to the right of the plan, includes a sumptuous master suite with a tray ceiling and a skylit bath with twin vanities. A secluded study is near a family bedroom and shares its bath.

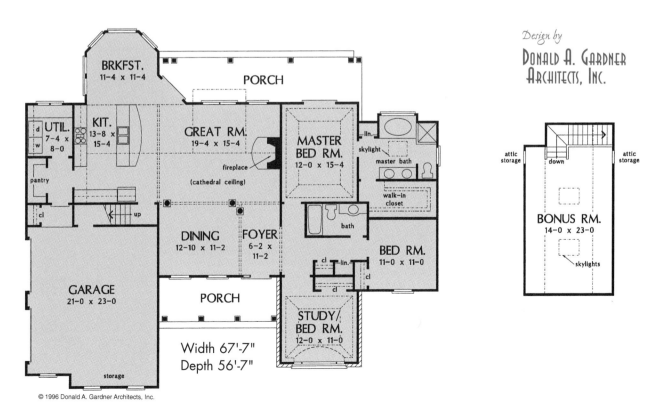

Design by
Donald A. Gardner Architects, Inc.

Rear Elevation

Design 9716
Square Footage: 2,097

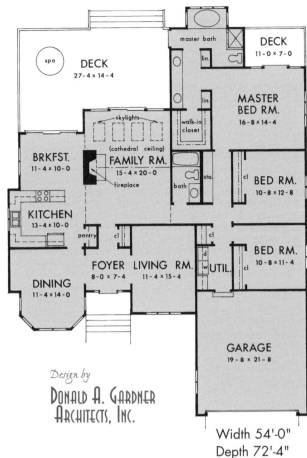

■ A bank of ventilating skylights flood the large family room with natural light and fresh air in this three-bedroom ranch. Many other special features—uncommon in a home this size—make an appearance. For example, the breakfast area, family room and master bath open to a spacious deck with a spa area. In the family room you'll find a cathedral ceiling and a fireplace. The plan provides both formal living and dining rooms. The U-shaped kitchen epitomizes the best in efficiency. The large master bedroom has a private deck and pampers with a whirlpool tub, a separate shower and a double-bowl vanity. Two secondary bedrooms each find ample closet space and share a full hall bath.

Design by
Donald A. Gardner Architects, Inc.

Width 54'-0"
Depth 72'-4"

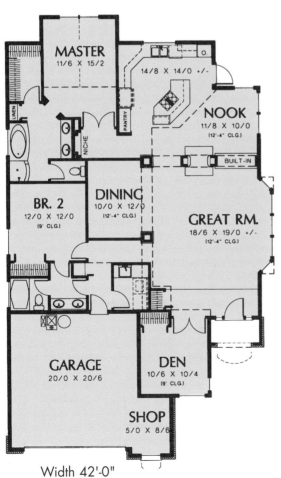

MASTER
11/6 X 15/2

14/8 X 14/0 +/-

NOOK
11/8 X 10/0
(12'-4" CLG.)

LINEN

NICHE

PANTRY

BUILT-IN

BR. 2
12/0 X 12/0
(9' CLG.)

DINING
10/0 X 12/0
(12'-4" CLG.)

GREAT RM.
18/6 X 19/0 +/-
(12'-4" CLG.)

GARAGE
20/0 X 20/6

DEN
10/6 X 10/4
(9' CLG.)

SHOP
5/0 X 8/6

Width 42'-0"
Depth 68'-0"

Design 7449

Square Footage: 1,864

■ With an offset front entry and brick-and-siding detail, this home is the model of sheltered style. The entry opens directly into the large great room, but a secluded den is just to the left through double doors. A through-fireplace serves both the great room and nook; columns separate the formal dining room from the great room. A lovely island kitchen features everything the gourmet might request: pantry, abundant counterspace, an over-the-sink window and outdoor access. Both bedrooms have private baths. The master bath is a study in indulgence with a whirlpool tub, separate shower, compartmented toilet, double sink and huge walk-in closet. The two-car garage has space enough for a workshop.

Design by

Alan Mascord
Design Associates, Inc.

Design 3345

Square Footage: 1,738

 L

■ This quaint shingled cottage offers an unexpected amount of living space in just over 1,700 square feet. The large gathering room with fireplace, dining room with covered porch, and kitchen with breakfast room handle formal parties as easily as they do the casual family get-together. Three bedrooms, one that could also serve as a study, are found in a separate wing of the house. Special note should be taken of all the storage space provided in this home as well as the extra touches that set it apart from many homes of equal size.

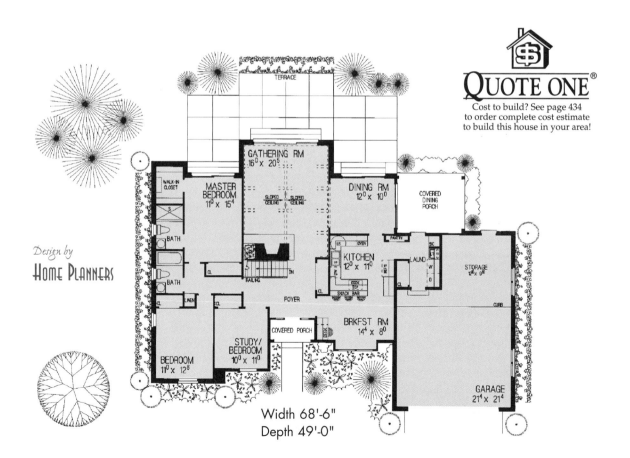

QUOTE ONE®

Cost to build? See page 434
to order complete cost estimate
to build this house in your area!

Design by
HOME PLANNERS

Width 68'-6"
Depth 49'-0"

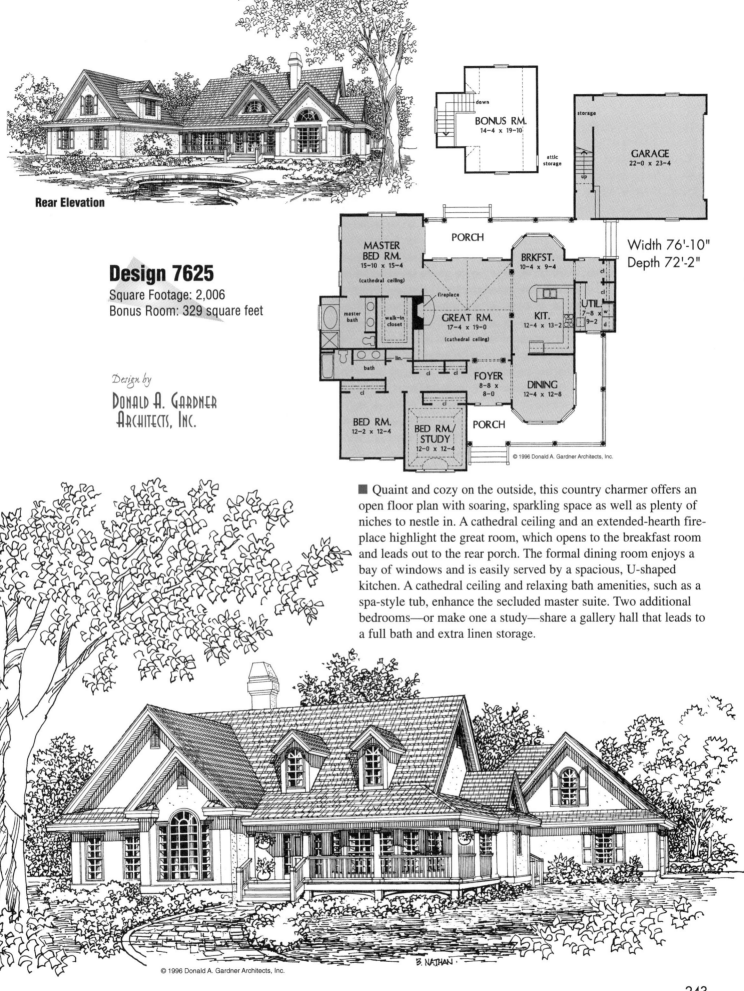

Rear Elevation

BONUS RM.
14-4 x 19-10

down

attic storage

storage

GARAGE
22-0 x 23-4

up

Width 76'-10"
Depth 72'-2"

Design 7625

Square Footage: 2,006
Bonus Room: 329 square feet

Design by

DONALD A. GARDNER ARCHITECTS, INC.

PORCH

MASTER BED RM.
15-10 x 15-4
(cathedral ceiling)

master bath

walk-in closet

BRKFST.
10-4 x 9-4

fireplace

GREAT RM.
17-4 x 19-0
(cathedral ceiling)

KIT.
12-4 x 13-2

UTIL.
7-8 x
9-2

bath

lin.

FOYER
8-8 x
8-0

DINING
12-4 x 12-8

BED RM.
12-2 x 12-4

BED RM./
STUDY
12-0 x 12-4

PORCH

© 1996 Donald A. Gardner Architects, Inc.

■ Quaint and cozy on the outside, this country charmer offers an open floor plan with soaring, sparkling space as well as plenty of niches to nestle in. A cathedral ceiling and an extended-hearth fireplace highlight the great room, which opens to the breakfast room and leads out to the rear porch. The formal dining room enjoys a bay of windows and is easily served by a spacious, U-shaped kitchen. A cathedral ceiling and relaxing bath amenities, such as a spa-style tub, enhance the secluded master suite. Two additional bedrooms—or make one a study—share a gallery hall that leads to a full bath and extra linen storage.

B. NATHAN

Design T233
Square Footage: 2,204

Design by
DESIGN TRADITIONS

Master Bath

Master Bedroom
13⁸ x 18⁰

Great Room
19⁵ x 16⁰

Breakfast
11⁸ x 8⁰

Keeping Room
11⁸ x 10⁰

Kitchen
11⁸ x 11¹⁰

Bedroom #3
12⁰ x 12⁰

Bedroom #2
12⁸ x 12⁸

Foyer

Dining Room
11⁹ x 13⁰

Covered Porch

Two Car Garage
23⁴ x 21⁴

Width 71'-2"
Depth 49'-7"

■ A bay window is accented by a gracefully covered porch on this three bedroom home. If entertaining is your hobby, note how the great room and the formal dining room are only separated by elegant columns, providing ease for any gathering you wish. The large U-shaped kitchen is sure to please also, with a worktop island, plenty of counter and cabinet space and an adjacent breakfast room. Two secondary bedrooms—one with a bay window—share a full bath, while the master suite is full of amenities. From the two walk-in closets, the lavish bath and the bayed sitting area, this room is a haven for any homeowner.

© Design Tr

244

Design 3487

Square Footage: 1,835

L

Design by
HOME PLANNERS

Width 71'-0"
Depth 43'-5"

■ Country living is the focus of this charming design. A cozy covered porch invites you into the foyer with the sleeping area on the right and the living area straight ahead. From the windowed front-facing breakfast room, enter the efficient kitchen with its corner laundry room, large pantry, snack-bar pass-through to the gathering room, and passage to the dining room. The massive gathering room and dining room feature sloped ceilings, an impressive fireplace and access to the rear terrace. Terrace access is also available from the master bedroom with its sloped ceiling and a master bath that includes a whirlpool tub, a separate shower and a separate vanity area. A study at the front of the house can also be converted into a third bedroom.

QUOTE ONE®

Cost to build? See page 434 to order complete cost estimate to build this house in your area!

KOIZUMI/BUTLER

Design 3489

Square Footage: 2,415

L D

■ This traditional design incorporates the perfect floor plan for a large family. Privacy is assured with three family bedrooms and a strategically placed laundry on the left side of the home, and a large master bedroom with a luxurious bath and spacious walk-in closet on the right side. A comfortable covered porch welcomes you to the living areas. The family room looks out to the covered porch and continues on to the efficient kitchen with a writing desk, a large pantry and access to the dining room. The kitchen also features a snack bar that provides a perfect opportunity to chat with folks in the large gathering room with its warming fireplace and access to the backyard terrace. Sloped ceilings in the living areas and the master bedroom, and nine-foot ceilings in the other bedrooms, give this home a spacious, airy feel.

Width 74'-0"
Depth 54'-0"

QUOTE ONE®

Cost to build? See page 434 to order complete cost estimate to build this house in your area!

Design by
HOME PLANNERS

Design 3491

Square Footage: 2,098

L **D**

■ This is a fine home for a young family or for empty-nesters. The versatile bedroom/study offers room for growth or a quiet haven for reading. The U-shaped kitchen includes a handy nook with a snack bar and easy accessibility to the dining room or the gathering room—perfect for entertaining. The master bedroom includes its own private outdoor retreat, a walk-in closet and an amenity-filled bathroom. An additional bedroom and a large laundry room with an adjacent, walk-in pantry complete the plan.

Design by
Home Planners

Quote One®

Cost to build? See page 434
to order complete cost estimate
to build this house in your area!

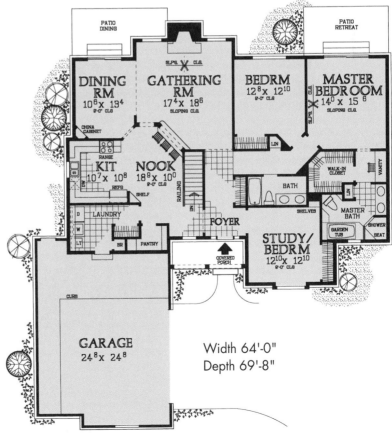

Width 64'-0"
Depth 69'-8"

Design 3490

Square Footage: 1,970

L D

A projecting two-car garage narrows the overall width of this house, thus permitting the utilization of a smaller, less expensive building site. Efficient traffic patterning characterizes the interior. Open planning results in a spacious kitchen area with a convenient U-shaped work space and a generous informal eating area. A study may function as a home office or sewing room. In the master bedroom, a sloped ceiling and sliding glass doors to the patio will be appreciated. In the master bath, a garden tub, a stall shower, two lavatories, a walk-in closet and a linen closet assure fine livability.

QUOTE ONE®

Cost to build? See page 434 to order complete cost estimate to build this house in your area!

Design by
HOME PLANNERS

Width 58'-4"
Depth 62'-0"

Design 3710
Square Footage: 1,452

Basic Plan

■ This unique ranch home designed for warm climates has built-in charm and affordability. Included in this home are three bedrooms and two full size baths, one in the master bedroom and the other adjacent to the remaining two bedrooms. As you enter this home through the foyer, you have access to a large living room and a formal dining room. The kitchen adjoins a family room for your entertaining needs. A two-car garage, standard or double-size deck and a fireplace are optional. The blueprints for this house show how to build both the basic, low-cost version and the enhanced, upgraded version.

Design by
HOME PLANNERS

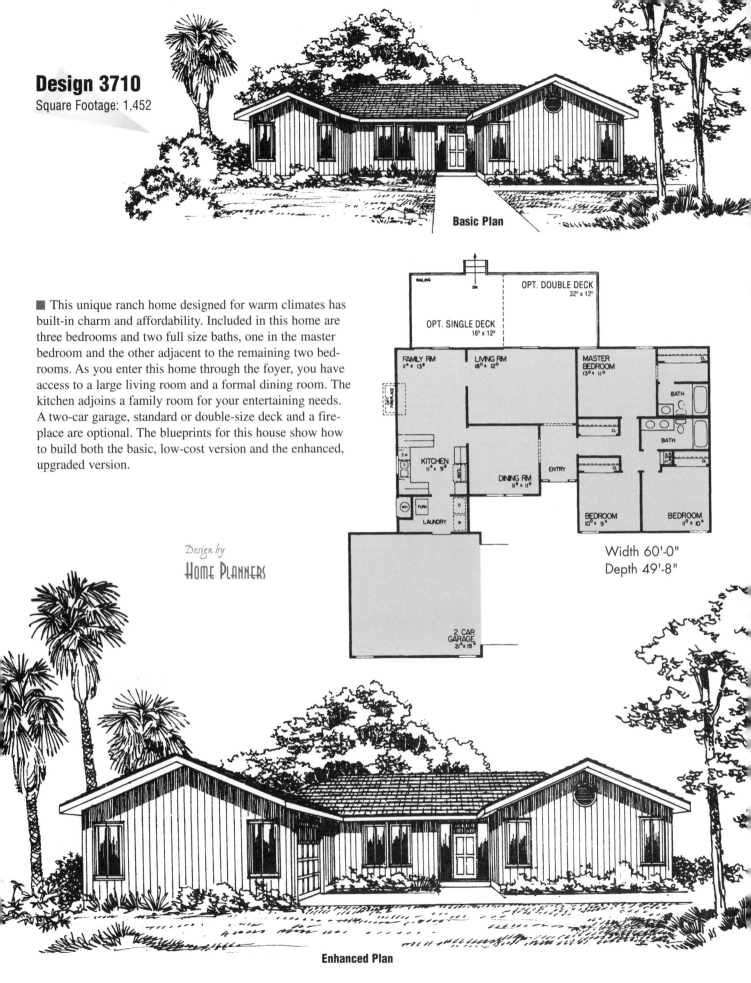

RAILING · DN

OPT. DOUBLE DECK
32⁰ x 12⁰

OPT. SINGLE DECK
16⁰ x 12⁰

FAMILY RM
11⁴ x 13⁸

LIVING RM
18⁰ x 12⁰

MASTER BEDROOM
13⁰ x 11⁰

OPT. FIREPLACE

BATH

KITCHEN
11⁴ x 9⁸

DINING RM
11⁸ x 11⁰

ENTRY

BATH

LAUNDRY

BEDROOM
10⁰ x 9⁴

BEDROOM
11⁰ x 10⁴

2 CAR GARAGE
21⁴ x 19⁰

Width 60'-0"
Depth 49'-8"

Enhanced Plan

Design 7300

Square Footage: 1,842

■ Shutters, double-hung windows and a pleasant covered porch coax visitors and family alike to call this house a home. Entertaining is made easy with the proximity of the dining room to the large great room. The U-shaped kitchen is a pleasure to work in with its central island, pantry and a nearby breakfast nook—which offers access to the rear yard. The master suite is designed to pamper. From its luxurious bath which contains twin vanities, a separate toilet and shower room and a spa tub, to its large walk-in closet, this is surely a peaceful retreat. Two secondary bedrooms and a hall bath complete this attractive one-story home.

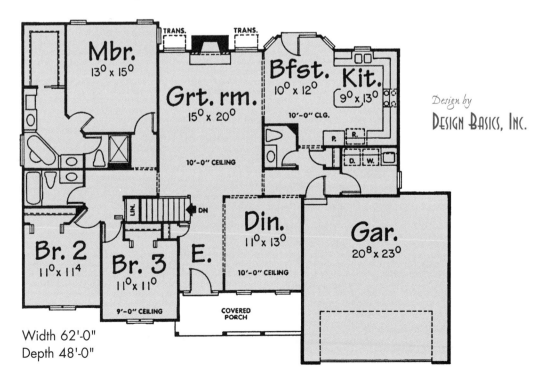

Width 62'-0"
Depth 48'-0"

Design by
DESIGN BASICS, INC.

Design 3350

Square Footage: 1,777

L D

■ Though smaller in size, this traditional one-story home provides a family-oriented floor plan that leaves nothing out. Besides the formal living room (or study if you prefer) and dining room, there's a gathering room with fireplace, snack bar and sliding glass doors to the rear terrace. The U-shaped kitchen is in close proximity to the handy utility area. Of particular note is the grand master bedroom with garden whirlpool tub, walk-in closet and private terrace. The sleeping area is completed with two family bedrooms to the front.

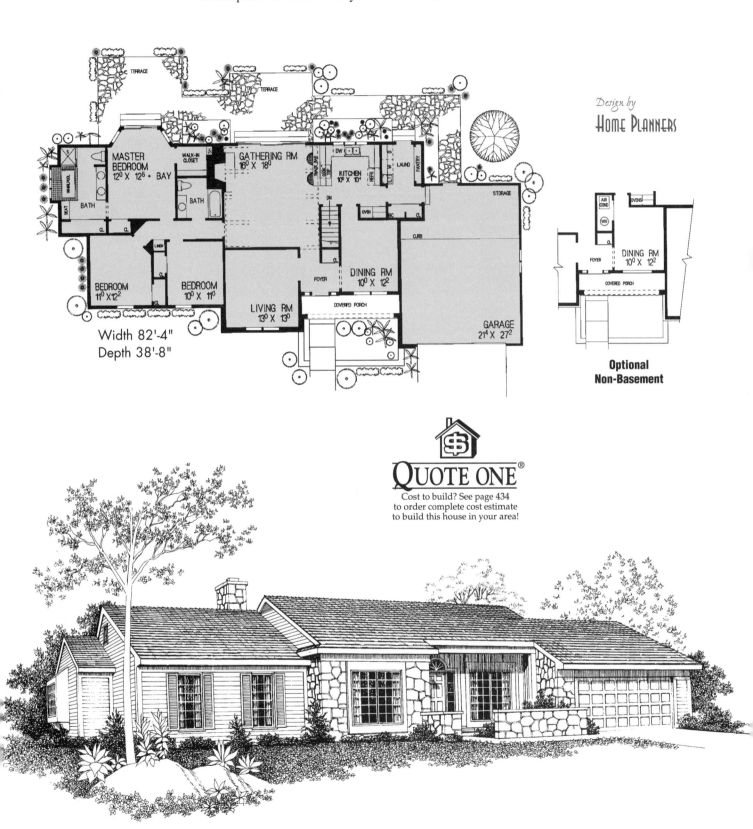

Width 82'-4"
Depth 38'-8"

Design by
Home Planners

**Optional
Non-Basement**

QUOTE ONE®
Cost to build? See page 434
to order complete cost estimate
to build this house in your area!

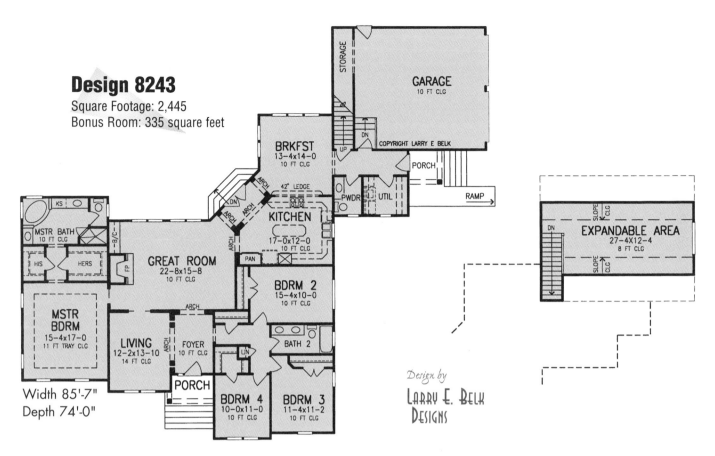

Design 8243

Square Footage: 2,445
Bonus Room: 335 square feet

GARAGE
10 FT CLG

STORAGE

DN

UP

COPYRIGHT LARRY E. BELK

PORCH

RAMP

BRKFST
13-4x14-0
10 FT CLG

DN

ARCH

ARCH

ARCH

42" LEDGE

PWDR

UTIL

KITCHEN
17-0x12-0
10 FT CLG

MSTR BATH
10 FT CLG

KS

HIS

HERS

B/C

FP

PAN

GREAT ROOM
22-8x15-8
10 FT CLG

ARCH

BDRM 2
15-4x10-0
10 FT CLG

MSTR BDRM
15-4x17-0
11 FT TRAY CLG

LIVING
12-2x13-10
14 FT CLG

ARCH

FOYER
10 FT CLG

LIN

BATH 2

EXPANDABLE AREA
27-4x12-4
8 FT CLG

DN

SLOPE CLG

SLOPE CLG

Width 85'-7"
Depth 74'-0"

PORCH

BDRM 4
10-0x11-0
10 FT CLG

BDRM 3
11-4x11-2
10 FT CLG

Design by
LARRY E. BELK DESIGNS

■ An arch-top muntin window sets off a refined blend of natural materials on this traditional exterior, while staggered gables give it an eclectic splash. A dazzling arched foyer leads to the formal living room and to the expansive great room, complete with a focal-point fireplace. French doors framed by dramatic archways open to the rear property and set an elegant tone for the interior. A split bedroom plan places the master suite in the left wing. A corner whirlpool tub, a knee-space vanity and two walk-in closets highlight the master bath. Three family bedrooms share a private hall and a full bath.

COPYRIGHT LARRY E. BELK

Design 8229

Square Footage: 1,955

MASTER BEDRM
12-8 X 14-6
10 FT CLG

MASTER BATH
10 FT CLG

BATH 2

BEDRM 2
11-0 X 13-6

LIN

BEDRM 3
12-6 X 13-4

FOYER
10 FT CLG

FP

GREAT ROOM
18-6 X 15-6
10 FT CLG

BRKFST RM
12-0 X 10-0
10 FT CLG

42" LEDGE

KITCHEN
12-6 X 14-0
10 FT CLG

UTIL
6-8 X 8-6

PAN

DINING ROOM
12-2 X 14-0
10 FT CLG

PORCH

GARAGE

COPYRIGHT LARRY E. BELK

Width 65'-0"
Depth 58'-8"

■ A finely detailed covered porch and arch-topped windows announce a scrupulously designed interior, replete with amenities. A grand foyer with 10-foot ceiling and columned archways set the pace for the entire floor plan. Clustered sleeping quarters to the left feature a luxurious master suite with a sloped ceiling, corner whirlpool bath and walk-in closet, and two family bedrooms which share a bath. Picture windows flanking a centered fireplace lend plenty of natural light to the great room, which is open through grand, columned archways to the formal dining area and the bay-windowed breakfast room. The kitchen, conveniently positioned between the dining and breakfast rooms, shares an informal eating counter with the great room. A utility room and walk-in pantry are tucked neatly to the side of the plan. Please specify crawlspace or slab foundation when ordering.

Design by

Larry E. Belk
Designs

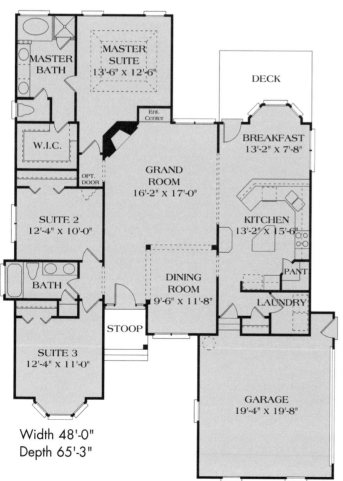

MASTER BATH

MASTER SUITE
13'-6" x 12'-6"

W.I.C.

Ent.
Center

GRAND
ROOM
16'-2" x 17'-0"

OPT.
DOOR

SUITE 2
12'-4" x 10'-0"

BATH

DINING
ROOM
9'-6" x 11'-8"

STOOP

SUITE 3
12'-4" x 11'-0"

DECK

BREAKFAST
13'-2" x 7'-8"

KITCHEN
13'-2" x 15'-6"

PANT

LAUNDRY

GARAGE
19'-4" x 19'-8"

Width 48'-0"
Depth 65'-3"

Design A245
Square Footage: 1,734

■ Master planning makes the most of the smaller square footage of this one-story home. The raised porch allows entry to a short hallway, open through columns to the formal dining room and the large grand room beyond. The grand room is graced by a corner fireplace and entertainment center built right in. On the right is the island kitchen and bay-windowed breakfast nook with deck access. At the other end, the kitchen connects to the two-car garage through a laundry area with broom closet. The master suite is at the rear of the plan for privacy. Its tray ceiling and elegant bath make it a standout. You may wish to include a door from the master suite directly into Suite 2 (perfect for a nursery) or choose the more private option, with both family suites opening from their own hallway. Suite 3 has a lovely bay window overlooking the front yard.

Design by
LIVING CONCEPTS

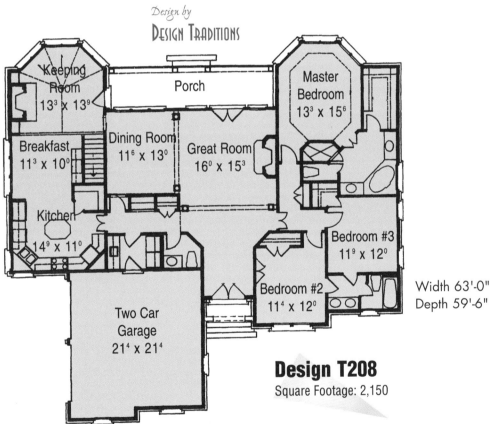

Design by
DESIGN TRADITIONS

Keeping Room
13³ x 13⁹

Porch

Master Bedroom
13³ x 15⁶

Breakfast
11³ x 10⁰

Dining Room
11⁶ x 13⁰

Great Room
16⁰ x 15³

Kitchen
14⁹ x 11⁰

Bedroom #3
11⁹ x 12⁰

Bedroom #2
11⁴ x 12⁰

Width 63'-0"
Depth 59'-6"

Two Car Garage
21⁴ x 21⁴

Design T208
Square Footage: 2,150

■ This attractive brick cottage home with an arched covered entry makes visitors feel warmly welcomed. The jack-arch window detailing adds intrigue to the exterior. The foyer, dining room and great room are brought together, defined by decorative columns. To the right of the foyer, a bedroom with a complete bath could double as a home office or children's den. The spacious kitchen has a centered work island and an adjacent keeping room with a fireplace—ideal for families that like to congregate at meal times. The abundance of windows throughout the back of the home provides a grand view of the back property. The master suite enjoys privacy to the rear of the home. A garden tub, large walk-in closet and two vanities make a perfect homeowner retreat. This home is designed with a basement foundation.

Design T237

Square Footage: 2,919

■ This plan was made for entertaining. Its entry and center hall are lined with columns that help define, but not limit, the great room, dining room and bedroom wing. A beamed ceiling, a fireplace and covered rear porch access are highlights in the great room. It also is open to a sun room and the bay-windowed breakfast room. A large, gourmet-styled kitchen is a great work center. Bedrooms include two family suites with shared bath and private vanity areas and a master suite with tray ceiling in the bedroom. The master bath has His and Hers walk-in closets, a garden whirlpool, separate shower, compartmented toilet and make-up vanity. A powder room in the central hall and a convenient laundry room round out the interior spaces. The two-car garage sits to the front to screen street noise. It features storage or work-bench space.

Width 70'-10"
Depth 66'-6"

Design by
DESIGN TRADITIONS

© Design Traditions

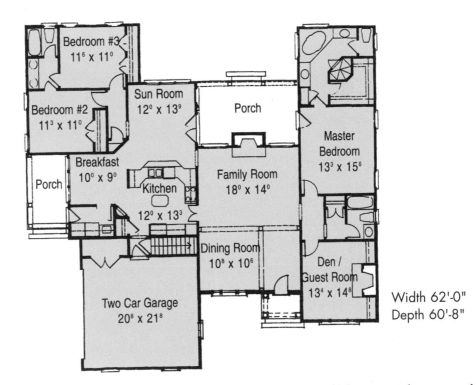

Design T212
Square Footage: 2,140

Design by
DESIGN TRADITIONS

Bedroom #3
11⁶ x 11⁰

Bedroom #2
11³ x 11⁰

Sun Room
12⁰ x 13⁹

Porch

Master Bedroom
13³ x 15⁶

Breakfast
10⁰ x 9⁰

Porch

Kitchen
12⁰ x 13³

Family Room
18⁰ x 14⁰

Dining Room
10⁸ x 10⁶

Den / Guest Room
13⁴ x 14⁸

Two Car Garage
20⁸ x 21⁸

Width 62'-0"
Depth 60'-8"

■ Decorative columns define the formal dining room of this lovely traditional home and announce casual living space that features a fireplace and porch access. Split sleeping quarters allow the master suite a private wing which includes a den or guest room with its own fireplace and full bath. An angled, oversized shower, a compartmented toilet and a corner whirlpool tub highlight the master bath. The gourmet kitchen overlooks the sun room, which opens to the rear porch through French doors. A covered side porch invites morning meals outdoors, while the breakfast room offers a casual dining area inside. Each of the family bedrooms has its own access to the shared bath, which offers a compartmented, double-bowl vanity. This home is designed with a basement foundation.

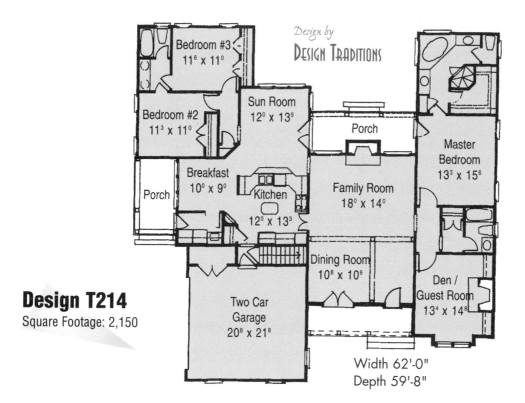

Design by
DESIGN TRADITIONS

Bedroom #3
11^6 x 11^0

Bedroom #2
11^3 x 11^0

Sun Room
12^0 x 13^9

Porch

Master Bedroom
13^3 x 15^6

Porch

Breakfast
10^0 x 9^0

Kitchen
12^0 x 13^3

Family Room
18^0 x 14^0

Design T214
Square Footage: 2,150

Two Car Garage
20^8 x 21^8

Dining Room
10^8 x 10^6

Den / Guest Room
13^4 x 14^8

Width 62'-0"
Depth 59'-8"

■ Open, casual living space is offset by a quiet den or study with its own fireplace in this casual Colonial-style home. A bright sunroom opens to the covered rear porch through French doors. The gourmet kitchen enjoys a breakfast area convenient to the family bedrooms. A corner whirlpool tub and an angled shower highlight the master suite, which also has a walk-in closet and separate lavatories. This home is designed with a basement foundation.

© Design Traditions

Design E116

Square Footage: 2,318

■ The stately brick facade of this traditional home conceals a stylish, entirely livable, interior plan. A stunning living room with a centered fireplace and patio access is further enhanced by a raised ceiling. Amenities abound in the fashionable kitchen, complete with a sit-down bar and a large pantry. Sleeping quarters, including a fabulous master suite, are conveniently clustered around the living area. Find a good book and relax awhile in the secluded study. Please specify crawlspace or slab foundation when ordering.

Design by

CHATHAM HOME
PLANNING, INC.

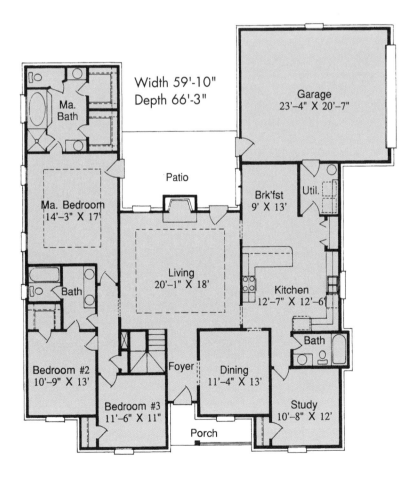

Width 59'-10"
Depth 66'-3"

Ma. Bath

Garage
23'-4" X 20'-7"

Patio

Brk'fst
9' X 13'

Util.

Ma. Bedroom
14'-3" X 17'

Living
20'-1" X 18'

Kitchen
12'-7" X 12'-6"

Bath

Bedroom #2
10'-9" X 13'

Foyer

Dining
11'-4" X 13'

Bath

Bedroom #3
11'-6" X 11'

Study
10'-8" X 12'

Porch

Design 9184

Square Footage: 2,325
Future Room: 377 square feet

Rear Elevation

■ For fine traditional living, look no further than this delightful one-story home. The front entry opens with an elegant view to the dining room and living room. Half walls, a tiered ceiling, a fireplace and French doors opening to a rear covered porch all add distinction to the latter. In the kitchen, efficient planning includes an island work space and a pass-through to the breakfast area. A utility room leads to the two-car garage with storage. Three bedrooms include two secondary bedrooms with walk-in closets and bookshelves. The master bedroom is sure to please with its fireplace and private bath. There's also room to grow with a future room located over the garage. It provides a full bath and lots of privacy.

Design by
Larry W. Garnett & Associates

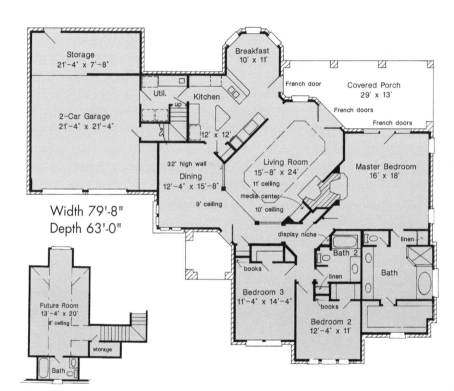

Width 79'-8"
Depth 63'-0"

Design 9205
Square Footage: 2,254

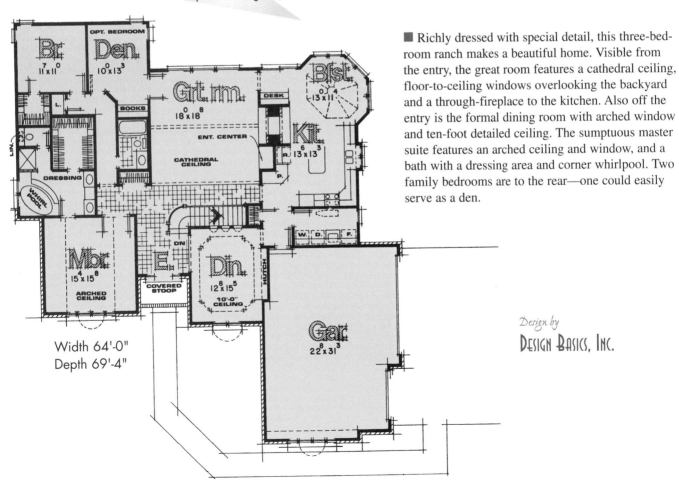

Width 64'-0"
Depth 69'-4"

■ Richly dressed with special detail, this three-bed-room ranch makes a beautiful home. Visible from the entry, the great room features a cathedral ceiling, floor-to-ceiling windows overlooking the backyard and a through-fireplace to the kitchen. Also off the entry is the formal dining room with arched window and ten-foot detailed ceiling. The sumptuous master suite features an arched ceiling and window, and a bath with a dressing area and corner whirlpool. Two family bedrooms are to the rear—one could easily serve as a den.

Design by
DESIGN BASICS, INC.

Design E112

Square Footage: 2,547

Width 63'-10"
Depth 77'-5"

Ext. Storage

Garage
22'-11" x 20'-0"

Study
15'-4" x 13'-0"

Bath

Kitchen
10'-6" x 11'-0"

Breakfast
13'-1" x 8'-4"

Utility

Patio

Cov. Porch
19'-10" x 8'-0"

Living
21'-8" x 19'-6"

Dining
11'-11" x 13'-6"

Foyer

Bedroom
11'-11" x 11'-0"

Hall

Bath

Bath

Bedroom
16'-10" x 15'-0"

Bath

Bedroom
13'-1" x 12'-0"

Porch
32'-0" x 6'-0"

■ This stately Southern exterior welcomes guests in style with a raised porch displaying decorative columns and lovely arched windows. Ten-foot ceilings prevail downstairs, enhancing the foyer and the formal dining room, as well as the central living area with a welcoming fireplace and views to the rear yard. The magnificent foyer announces the living and dining areas with stunning decorative columns. The perfect marriage of style and comfort was made in the plush master suite, highlighted by a raised ceiling and voluminous bath with twin corner walk-in closets and separate dual lavatories. The spacious kitchen shares a corner of the plan with a sunlit informal eating area and allows access to the rear of the home, where a quiet study and guest bath await. Please specify crawlspace or slab foundation when ordering.

Design by
CHATHAM HOME
PLANNING, INC.

European Inspiration:
One-story homes with Old-World tastes

Design M104
Square Footage: 2,696

■ A brick archway covers the front porch of this European-style home, creating a truly grand entrance. Situated beyond the entry, the living room takes center-stage with a fireplace flanked by tall windows that overlook the backyard. To the right is a bayed eating area, reserved for casual meals, and an efficient kitchen. Steps away is the formal dining room for holidays and special occasions. Skillful planning creates flexibility for the master suite. If you wish, use Bedroom 2 as a secondary bedroom or guest room with the adjacent study accessible to everyone. Or if you prefer, combine the master suite with the study, using it as a private retreat and Bedroom 2 as a nursery, creating a wing that provides complete privacy. Completing this clever plan are two family bedrooms—each with a walk-in closet—a powder room and a utility room.

Design by
FILLMORE DESIGN GROUP

Width 80'-0"
Depth 64'-1"

Design F131

Square Footage: 2,529

Design by
R.L. Pfotenhauer

Width 78'-2"
Depth 50'-2"

SCREENED IN PORCH 19'-4" x 14'-0"

MASTER BEDROOM 15'-5" x 15'-8"
TRAY CEILING

PORCH

BREAKFAST 9'-0" x 10'-0"

WIP

BATH

W   D
MUD ROOM

WIC

MASTER BATH

FP

GREAT ROOM 23'-0" x 15'-6"

KITCHEN 10'-8" x 12'-0"

DN

THREE CAR GARAGE 21'-11" x 31'-10"

BATH

LIN

DEN/BEDROOM 12'-0" x 12'-9"

DINING ROOM 14'-4" x 12'-9"

BEDROOM 15'-5" x 10'-6"

VAULTED CEILING

■ This charming home grabs attention with a beautiful facade including corner quoins, symmetrical design and a lovely roofline. The floor plan holds great livability. A central great room connects to the breakfast room and galley-style kitchen. A formal dining room, just off the foyer, has a huge wall of windows for elegant dining. A complementary room to the left of the foyer serves as a den or guest bedroom as needed. The master bedroom features a tray ceiling and wonderfully appointed bath. A family bedroom to the front of the plan has a vaulted ceiling. Don't miss the screened porch to the rear of the plan.

Design 8056

Square Footage: 3,426

Design by
LARRY E. BELK DESIGNS

■ One-story living takes off in this brick traditional home. Formal living areas flanking the entry are enhanced with ten-foot ceilings and open views to the great room. The great room has a twelve-foot ceiling and is accented by a fireplace and expansive windows. The island kitchen has a sunny breakfast nook and easy passage to the dining room. A luxurious master bedroom has a spa-style bath with a raised corner whirlpool tub and a special exercise room. Three bedrooms share a full hall bath. Please specify crawlspace or slab foundation when ordering.

Width 78'-6"
Depth 82'-4"

265

FREILING

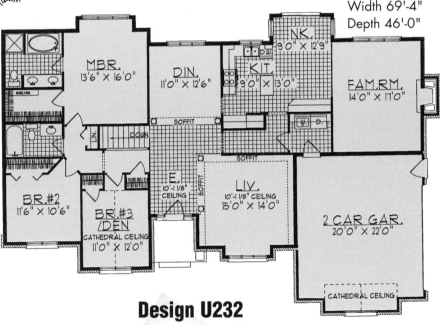

Width 69'-4"
Depth 46'-0"

MBR.
13'6" X 16'0"

DIN.
11'0" X 12'6"

NK.
9'0" X 12'9"

KIT.
9'0" X 13'0"

FAM.RM.
14'0" X 11'0"

BR. #2
11'6" X 10'6"

BR. #3
/DEN
CATHEDRAL CEILING
11'0" X 12'0"

E.
10'-1 1/8"
CEILING

LIV.
10'-1 1/8" CEILING
15'0" X 14'0"

2 CAR GAR.
20'0" X 22'0"

CATHEDRAL CEILING

SOFFIT

Design U232

Square Footage: 1,984

■ Bowing to the demands of formal entertaining, yet including casual living spaces as well, this is one versatile plan. Formal spaces are open and shaped primarily by columns and soffits at their boundaries. The family room, by contrast, is more private and cozy with a fireplace and proximity to the breakfast nook. The island kitchen is also nearby and has access to the two-car garage through the laundry room.

Choose three bedrooms or two and a den. Bedroom 3 (the den) has a cathedral ceiling and an arch-top window. The master suite features all you might ask for: box bay window, huge walk-in closet with built-in shelves, separate shower and whirlpool tub and double sinks. A handy linen closet boosts storage for the two full baths.

Design by
AHMANN DESIGN, INC.

Design U258

Square Footage: 1,756

■ Large living spaces make the smaller footprint of this plan seem bigger than it is. The family room serves as both a formal and casual space and is spacious at almost 16' x 22'. Its fireplace will be welcome to warm cool nights and wintery days. The nearby dining room and attached kitchen are joined with an expanse of tiled floor. A cozy eating bar separates the two spaces and serves snacks and quick meals. The two family bedrooms are split from the master suite. They share a full bath. A walk-in closet and bath with double sinks enhance the master bedroom. Pass through the laundry area, close to the kitchen and the master suite for convenience, to access the two-car garage.

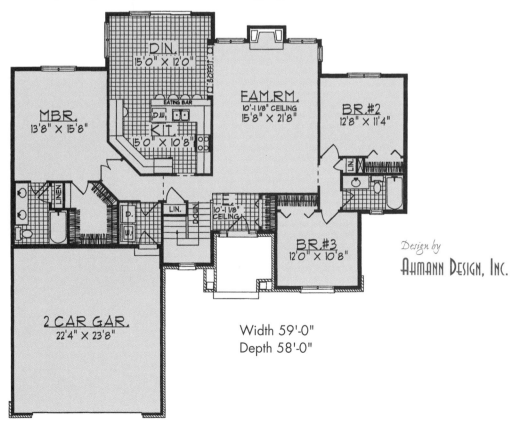

Width 59'-0"
Depth 58'-0"

Design by
Ahmann Design, Inc.

Design A132

Square Footage: 2,774
Bonus Room: 367 square feet

■ Warm and welcoming, this compact single-level, three-bedroom has an optional bonus room in the attic. Three bay windows across the back offer a special feeling to the master bedroom, breakfast nook and large gathering room with fireplace. A center kitchen easily serves the formal dining room, the grand room with octagonal tray ceiling and dinette. Two additional bedroom suites have private baths and large closets. The master suite features His and Hers walk-in closets, dual vanities and an oval garden tub.

Design by
LIVING CONCEPTS

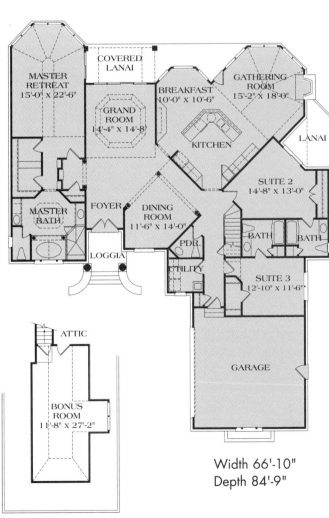

Design 9656

Square Footage: 2,099

Design by

Donald A. Gardner
Architects, Inc.

Rear Elevation

■ By putting the garage to the rear of this plan, nothing is taken away from the beautiful stone and stucco facade. Access from the garage is enhanced by a covered breezeway which passes the rear covered porch and connects to the home at the utility room. A great room with cathedral ceiling and fireplace has sliding glass doors to the rear deck and access to the skylit sunroom which also opens to the deck. The master bath connects to the sunroom as well. It is the perfect complement to the private master bedroom. Choose two styles of dining: the formal dining room with columned entrance to the great room, or the sunny breakfast room, attached to the U-shaped kitchen. Two additional bedrooms are at the right side of the plan and share a full bath with linen storage.

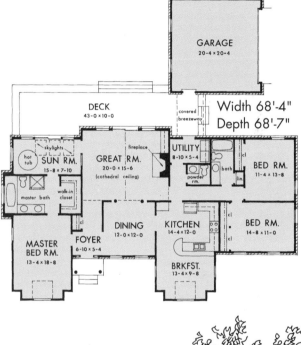

GARAGE
20-4 × 20-4

Width 68'-4"
Depth 68'-7"

DECK
43-0 × 10-0

covered breezeway

skylights

hot tub

SUN RM.
15-8 × 7-10

GREAT RM.
20-0 × 15-6
(cathedral ceiling)

fireplace

UTILITY
8-10 × 5-4

bath

powder rm.

BED RM.
11-4 × 13-8

master bath

walk-in closet

DINING
12-0 × 12-0

KITCHEN
14-4 × 12-0

BED RM.
14-8 × 11-0

MASTER BED RM.
13-4 × 18-8

FOYER
6-10 × 5-4

BRKFST.
13-4 × 9-8

Design 3810
Square Footage: 2,393

QUOTE ONE®

Cost to build? See page 434
to order complete cost estimate
to build this house in your area!

Width 79'-7"
Depth 71'-7"

■ Corner quoins, hipped rooflines and a well-designed floor plan make this three-bedroom home highly desirable. From the media room to the family room with its fireplace, this house can be built with the family in mind. The formal dining room and living room work well together for entertaining needs. The large kitchen will easily serve a banquet, while also accommodating intimate meals. Two family bedrooms share a full hall bath with a double-bowl vanity. The master bedroom features a large walk-in closet, a compartmented shower and toilet and a garden tub. A two-car garage easily handles the family fleet.

Design by
Home Planners

Design M102
Square Footage: 2,888

■ Alternate exteriors—both European style! Stone quoins and shutters give one elevation the appearance of a French country cottage. The other, with keystone window treatment and a copper roof over the bay window creates the impression of a stately French chateau. From the entry, formal living areas are accessed through graceful columned openings—living room to the left and dining room to the right. Straight ahead, the comfortable family room awaits with its warming fireplace and cathedral ceiling, offering room to relax and enjoy casual gatherings. The private master suite features a pullman ceiling, a luxurious bath and twin walk-in closets. A private lanai is accessed from the master bath. Located nearby, Bedroom 2 serves nicely as a guest room or easily converts to a nursery or study. Two family bedrooms with a connecting bath, a handy kitchen and breakfast room, and a utility room complete the floor plan.

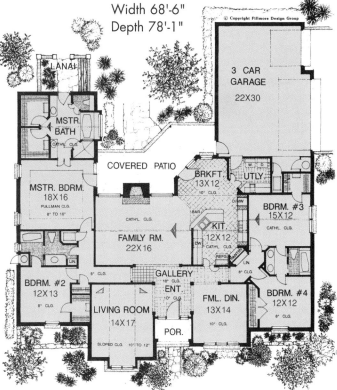

Width 68'-6"
Depth 78'-1"

© Copyright Fillmore Design Group

LANAI

3 CAR GARAGE
22X30

MSTR. BATH
CATH'L CLG.

COVERED PATIO

BRKFT.
13X12
10" CLG.

UTLY

W D

MSTR. BDRM.
18X16
PULLMAN CLG.
8' TO 10'

BAR

KIT.
12X12
CATH'L CLG.

BDRM. #3
15X12
CATH'L CLG.

FAMILY RM.
22X16
CATH'L CLG.

GALLERY
10" CLG.

ENT.
10" CLG.

BDRM. #2
12X13
8' CLG.

LIVING ROOM
14X17
SLOPED CLG. 10' TO 12'

FML. DIN.
13X14
10" CLG.

BDRM. #4
12X12
8' CLG.

POR.

Design by
Fillmore Design Group

Alternate Elevation

Design B112

Square Footage: 2,215
Bonus Room: 253 square feet

■ This symmetrical design offers single-story convenience with an optional bonus room over the garage—great for a home office! A formal living room could also be used as a fourth bedroom. The columned dining room opens into a spacious family room with a fireplace and built-in shelves, plus a nice view of the rear porch through a series of French doors. The master suite also accesses the porch and features a tray ceiling, twin walk-in closets and separate lavatories. Two family bedrooms share a full hall bath. A large laundry room with a built-in sink makes chores easier. And there's even extra storage in the garage.

Design by
Greg Marquis & Associates

Width 63'-0"
Depth 61'-0"

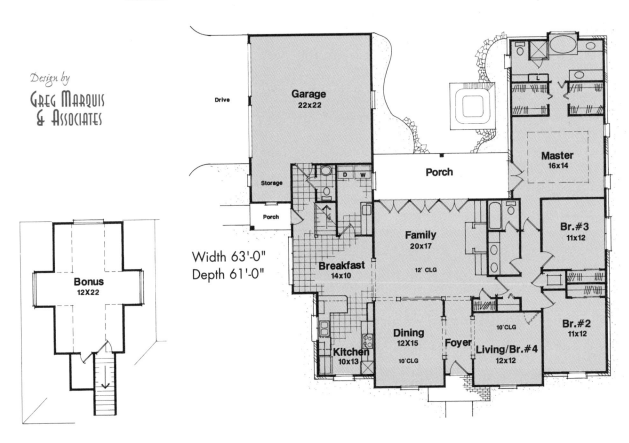

Design 9451

Square Footage: 2,089

■ This one-story design gives a sense of space with dramatic raised ceilings in the entry, master suite, living room and family room. Formal living dominates the front of the plan, but flows gracefully to more casual family living at the rear. Corner fireplaces in both areas add warmth and coziness. Three bedrooms include twin secondary bedrooms—each with a linen closet just outside the door. A skylight brightens the hallway here. The master suite sports a skylight in its private, luxurious bath.

Design by
ALAN MASCORD
DESIGN ASSOCIATES, INC.

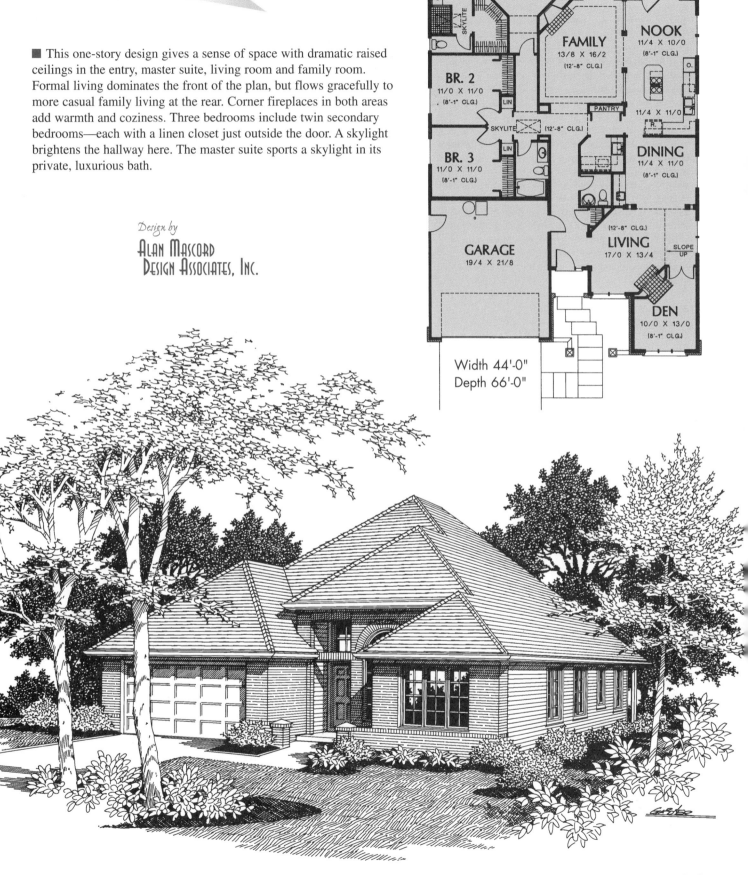

SPA

MASTER
VAULTED
16/0 X 12/6

FAMILY
13/8 X 16/2
(12'-8" CLG.)

NOOK
11/4 X 10/0
(8'-1" CLG.)

BR. 2
11/0 X 11/0
(8'-1" CLG.)

11/4 X 11/0

SKYLITE (12'-8" CLG.)

PANTRY

BR. 3
11/0 X 11/0
(8'-1" CLG.)

DINING
11/4 X 11/0
(8'-1" CLG.)

GARAGE
19/4 X 21/8

(12'-8" CLG.)

LIVING
17/0 X 13/4

SLOPE UP

DEN
10/0 X 13/0
(8'-1" CLG.)

Width 44'-0"
Depth 66'-0"

Design A157

Square Footage: 2,500

■ Triple dormers highlight the roofline of this distinctive single-level French country design. Double doors enhance the covered entryway leading to a grand open area with graceful columns outlining the dimensions of the formal living room and dining room. The large family room with fireplace opens through double doors to the rear terrace. An L-shaped island kitchen opens into a breakfast area with bay window. The master bedroom suite fills one wing and features a bay window, vaulted ceilings and access to the terrace. Two additional bedrooms on the opposite side of the house share a full bath.

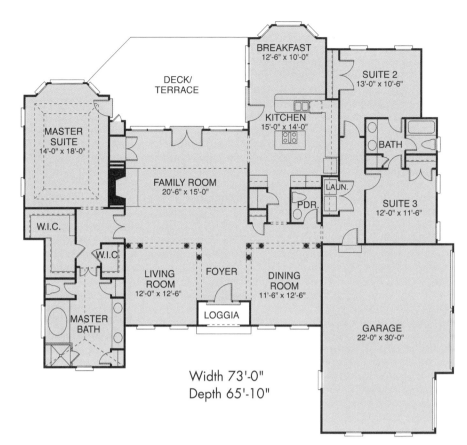

BREAKFAST
12'-6" x 10'-0"

SUITE 2
13'-0" x 10'-6"

DECK/
TERRACE

KITCHEN
15'-0" x 14'-0"

BATH

MASTER
SUITE
14'-0" x 18'-0"

FAMILY ROOM
20'-6" x 15'-0"

LAUN.

PDR.

SUITE 3
12'-0" x 11'-6"

W.I.C.

W.I.C.

LIVING
ROOM
12'-0" x 12'-6"

FOYER

DINING
ROOM
11'-6" x 12'-6"

MASTER
BATH

LOGGIA

GARAGE
22'-0" x 30'-0"

Width 73'-0"
Depth 65'-10"

Design by
Living Concepts

Deck

Brk
$11^0 x 12^4$

Width 75'-3"
Depth 57'-7"

Mstr
$16^2 x 16^0$

Bed
$12^8 x 11^0$

Grt
$24^0 x 24^0$

Kit
$12^6 x 12^4$

Design V005
Square Footage: 2,688

Bed
$14^8 x 12^0$

Study
$11^6 x 14^0$

Foy

Din
$16^0 x 14^0$

Gar
$20^0 x 20^0$

Design by
UNITED DESIGN
ASSOCIATES, INC.

■ What a unique one-story design. By raising it just a bit and adding a volume roof, it takes on all the character of a 1½- or even two-story home. The floor plan pinpoints the great room as the hub of the plan, around which all other rooms revolve. It is grand in style with a fireplace flanked by two doors opening to a rear deck. The formal dining room is defined by columns at the entry foyer and also has access to the kitchen and attached breakfast nook. A study sits at the opposite side of the foyer, but opens from a door in the bedroom-wing hallway. Note the placement of the master suite on the right side of the plan. Separating it from family bedrooms keeps it private. You'll love the amenities in the master bath: double sinks, walk-in closet and separate tub and shower. Family bedrooms share a full bath in their wing.

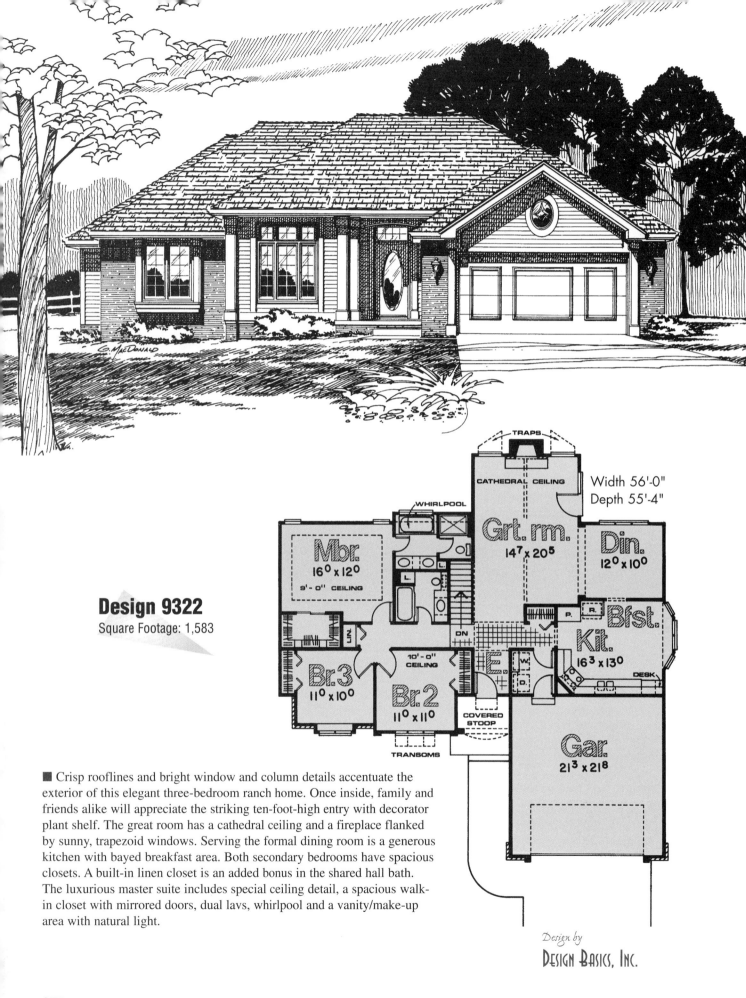

Design 9322

Square Footage: 1,583

Width 56'-0"
Depth 55'-4"

Mbr.
16⁰ x 12⁰
9'-0" CEILING

Grt. rm.
14⁷ x 20⁵

Din.
12⁰ x 10⁰

WHIRLPOOL

Bfst.

Kit.
16³ x 13⁰

DESK

10'-0" CEILING

Br.3
11⁰ x 10⁰

Br.2
11⁰ x 11⁰

DN

LIN

COVERED STOOP

TRANSOMS

TRAPS

CATHEDRAL CEILING

Gar.
21³ x 21⁸

■ Crisp rooflines and bright window and column details accentuate the exterior of this elegant three-bedroom ranch home. Once inside, family and friends alike will appreciate the striking ten-foot-high entry with decorator plant shelf. The great room has a cathedral ceiling and a fireplace flanked by sunny, trapezoid windows. Serving the formal dining room is a generous kitchen with bayed breakfast area. Both secondary bedrooms have spacious closets. A built-in linen closet is an added bonus in the shared hall bath. The luxurious master suite includes special ceiling detail, a spacious walk-in closet with mirrored doors, dual lavs, whirlpool and a vanity/make-up area with natural light.

Design by
DESIGN BASICS, INC.

276

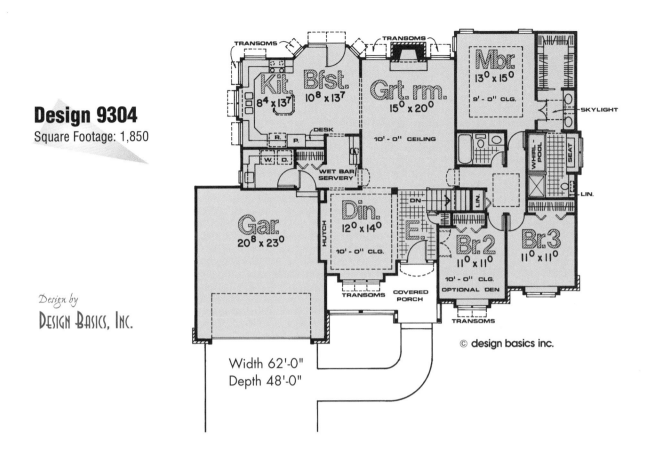

Design 9304

Square Footage: 1,850

Kit. 8⁴ x 13⁷

Bfst. 10⁸ x 13⁷

Grt. rm. 15⁰ x 20⁰
10'-0" CEILING

Mbr. 13⁰ x 15⁰
9'-0" CLG.

SKYLIGHT

TRANSOMS

DESK

WET BAR SERVERY

WHIRL POOL

SEAT

LIN.

Gar. 20⁸ x 23⁰

Din. 12⁰ x 14⁰
10'-0" CLG.

HUTCH

DN

LIN.

Br.2 11⁰ x 11⁰
10'-0" CLG.
OPTIONAL DEN

Br.3 11⁰ x 11⁰

TRANSOMS

COVERED PORCH

TRANSOMS

Design by
Design Basics, Inc.

Width 62'-0"
Depth 48'-0"

© design basics inc.

European style influences the elevation of this distinctive ranch home. Appealing rooflines and a covered porch with repeating arches provide stunning curb appeal. Inside, an impressive ten-foot-high entry greets family and friends. An open concept pervades the kitchen/dinette area. Picture your family enjoying the bayed eating area, wrapping counters, desk, island and wet bar/servery ideal for entertaining. The decorative hutch space adds appeal to a formal dining room.

Bright windows frame a fireplace in the great room. Sure to please is the service entry to the laundry/mud room with soaking sink and counter space. Bedroom 2 can easily be converted into a private den. A boxed ceiling decorates the master suite, while three windows provide natural lighting. Dual lavs, a walk-in closet, whirlpool and cedar-lined window seat enhance the master bath.

Design 6607
Square Footage: 2,200

sunning deck

verandah
63'-0" x 10'-0"

nook
12'-6" x 8'-0"
9' flat clg.

grill

master suite
14'-0" x 16'-8"
9' flat clg.

high glass

great room
18'-8" x 16'-8" avg.
vaulted ceiling

kitchen
10' x 14'

br. 2
12'-0" x 12'-0"
9' flat clg.

foyer

dining
11'-4" x 13'-8"
9' flat clg.

utility

br. 3
12'-0" x 11'-4"
9' flat clg.

study
11'-6" x 11'-4"
11' flat clg.

entry porch

Width 63'-0"
Depth 79'-0"

Design by
THE SATER DESIGN COLLECTION

garage
21'-0" x 35'-0"

■ A joyful marriage of indoor-outdoor living relationships endures in this spirited brick home. An abundance of windows and double doors to the rear of the plan allows clear, warming sunlight to flood the rooms. All rooms to the rear offer access to a full length veranda and a sunning deck, perfect for enjoying evening's cooling breezes and beautiful sunsets. An airy, open feeling greets you with the combination of the formal dining room (divided from the foyer by a half-wall), the spacious great room and the charming kitchen, complete with a walk-in pantry and bayed breakfast nook. Split sleeping quarters contain the master wing to the left and two secondary bedrooms to the right. The secluded master suite is highlighted by a double walk-in closet, a relaxing garden tub with a privacy wall, a separate shower and a double-bowl vanity.

Quote One®
Cost to build? See page 434 to order complete cost estimate to build this house in your area!

Design 7447

Square Footage: 1,790

■ With horizontal wood siding and brick accents, this clever design offers exterior charm. The floor plan is practical, but contains many amenities to boost livability, as well. A central hall unites the living areas and defines formal from informal spaces. The living and dining rooms are graced with columns and ten-foot ceilings. The family room also has a ten-foot ceiling, plus it features a warming fireplace and media center. An island kitchen and breakfast nook are close by. The nook has sliding glass doors to the rear yard. The bedrooms are aligned along the left side of the plan, behind the two-car garage. One of the family bedrooms sports a walk-in closet. The master suite is to the rear and has a tray ceiling and walk-in closet. Its bath bows to graciousness with a large spa tub, separate shower and double sinks.

Width 44'-0"
Depth 68'-0"

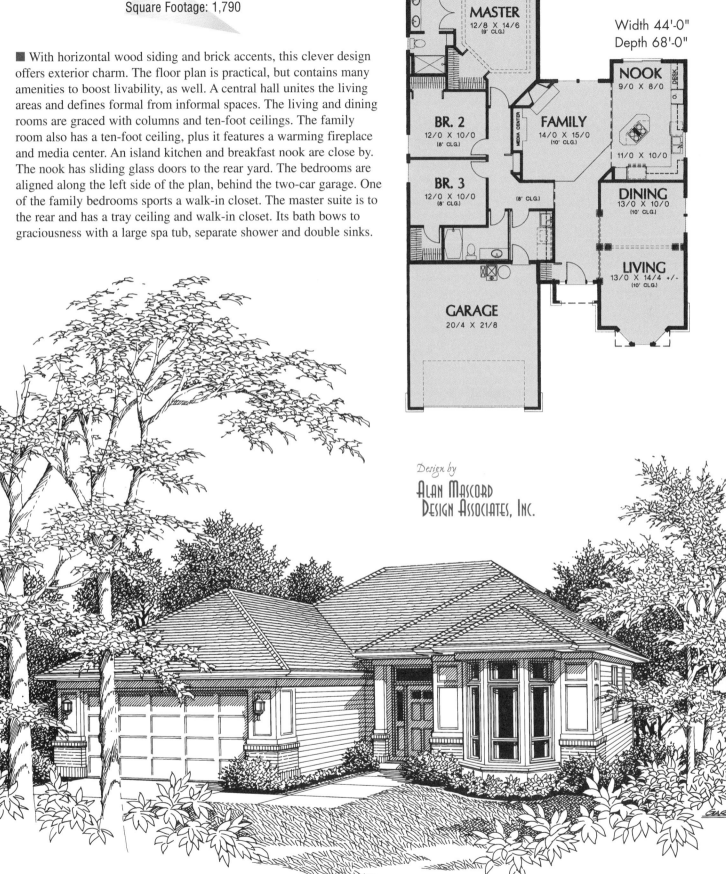

Design by
Alan Mascord
Design Associates, Inc.

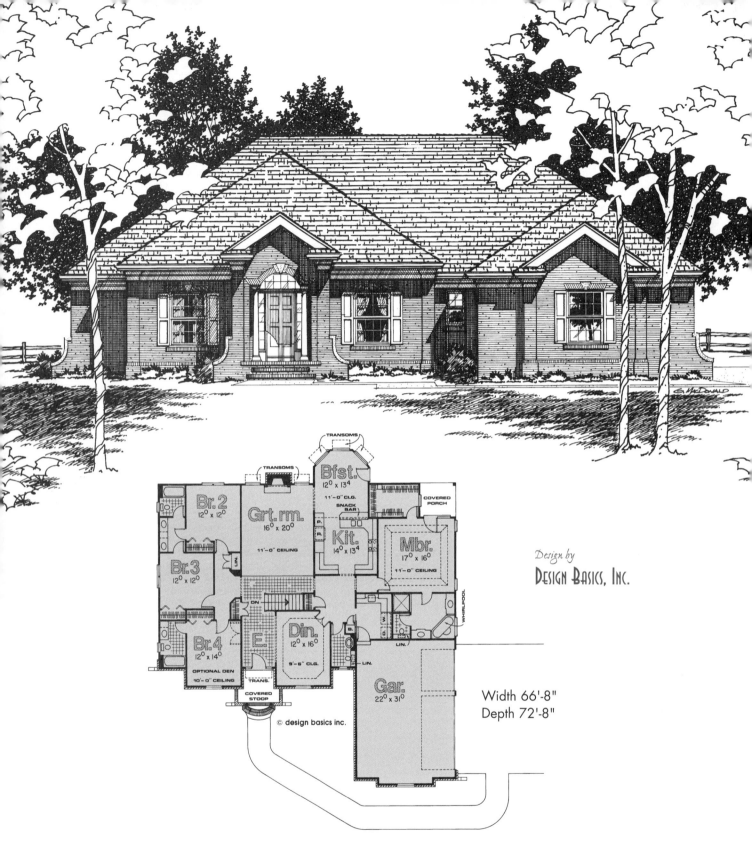

Design 7341
Square Footage: 2,655

■ Brick provides a polished, stately exterior on this outstanding one-story home. Natural light fills the interior via transom windows that showcase a fireplace in the great room and the bay-windowed breakfast area. An angled whirlpool tub, two vanities, a walk-in closet and a covered porch highlight the master suite. Secondary sleeping quarters include two family bedrooms that share a full bath, while an additional bedroom or guest suite has its own bath.

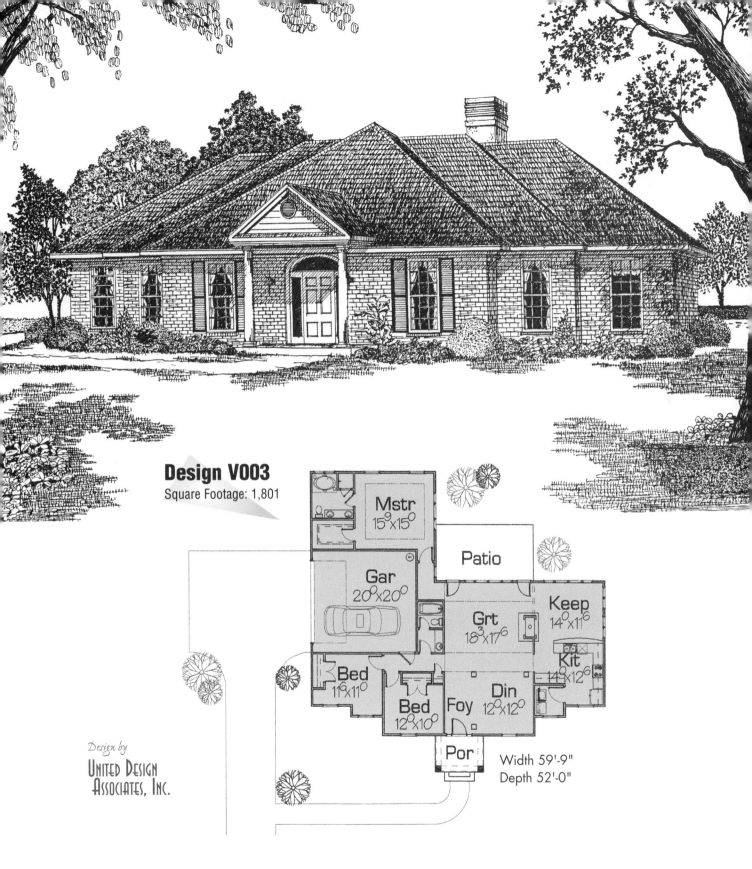

Design V003
Square Footage: 1,801

Mstr
15⁹x15⁰

Gar
20⁰x20⁰

Patio

Grt
18³x17⁶

Keep
14⁰x11⁶

Kit
14⁰x12⁶

Bed
11⁰x11⁰

Bed
12⁰x10⁰

Foy

Din
12⁰x12⁰

Por

Width 59'-9"
Depth 52'-0"

Design by
UNITED DESIGN
ASSOCIATES, INC.

■ This plan has some interesting surprises. For instance, the garage is set into the floor plan, to keep the footprint narrow and provide noise shelter for the master bedroom. The columned entry opens directly into the formal dining room—defined only by three columns. The great room is large and enhanced by double doors to the rear patio and a through-fireplace to the keeping room. The kitchen serves all areas easily and has access to the laundry area featuring space for a washer and dryer. Two family bedrooms sit in front of the garage and share a full bath in the hall. The master suite has a tray ceiling, walk-in closet and full bath with spa tub. An abundance of windows throughout the plan creates a sunny, airy ambience.

Design 9333

Square Footage: 2,470

■ This dynamic elevation, with its brick detailing, promises luxury in its three-bedroom design. The volume entry opens to the dining room on the left and the great room to the rear. A gigantic hearth room with a snack bar contains a door to the covered veranda. The full-sized kitchen and sunny dinette are also great for informal family gatherings. The three-car garage gains access to both the kitchen area and the outdoors. Secondary bedrooms share a full bath while the master suite features its own spa bath. This room excels with its use of French doors to a dressing area and a luxurious bath.

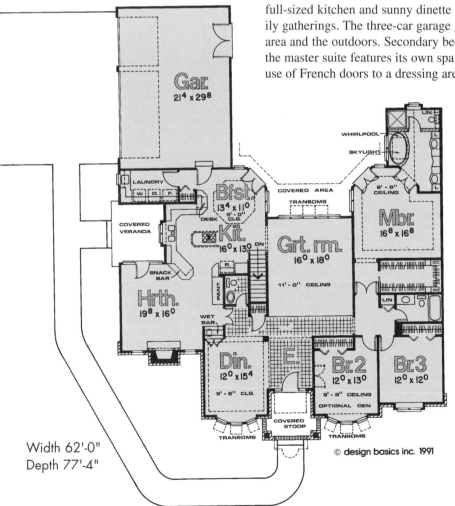

Design by
DESIGN BASICS, INC.

Width 62'-0"
Depth 77'-4"

© design basics inc. 1991

MBR.
17'x14'

KIT.
11'6"x12'

NK.
10'x12'

FAM. RM.
10'-1 1/8" CEILING
17'x21'

BR.3
12'x11'

DESK

PANTRY

DOWN

DIN.
11'6"x12'6"

LIV.
CATHEDRAL CEILING
14'x16'6"

E.

BR.2
12'x12'

3 CAR GAR.
22'x32'

Width 71'-0"
Depth 65'-4"

Design U248
Square Footage: 2,380

■ If you find that the formal living and dining rooms in this home are not sufficient to handle your entertaining needs, you can simply move the festivities to the immense family room! You'll love the special details that have been included: columns separating the living and dining rooms, a cathedral ceiling in the living room, a window-framed hearth in the family room, a butler's pantry connecting the dining room to the kitchen and a three-car garage. The kitchen and nook are fully tiled. The kitchen has a workspace island, a planning desk and an over-the-sink window. A rich master suite is separated from the secondary bedrooms and features a bath with an oversized walk-in closet, spa tub, garden whirlpool and two sinks. Family bedrooms share a full bath at the other side of the plan.

Design by
Ahmann Design, Inc.

Design V001
Square Footage: 1,597

■ Compact but commodious, this one-story home offers a wealth of open living in just under 1600 square feet. The great room is the focal point of the plan and serves as the hub of livability. It is open to the dining room and the U-shaped kitchen and, with just a few short feet down two separate hallways, to the bedrooms. The kitchen accesses a deck to the side of the plan—alfresco dining space in the warm months.

The family bedrooms feature one with a large walk-in closet and both share a full bath with separate vanity area. A private master suite also has a walk-in closet and a private bath with a spa tub, separate shower and large vanity area. The laundry room connects the main plan to the two-car garage. Note the large pantry in the kitchen and the linen closet in the hall bath.

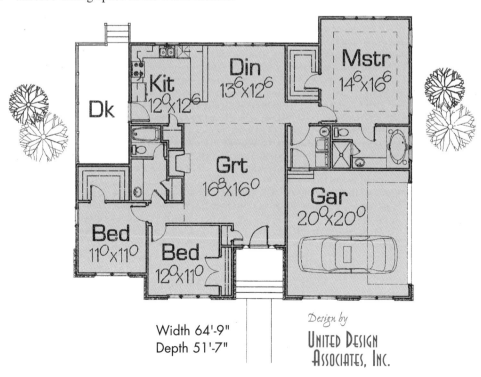

Width 64'-9"
Depth 51'-7"

Design by
UNITED DESIGN
ASSOCIATES, INC.

Design V008

Square Footage: 1,460

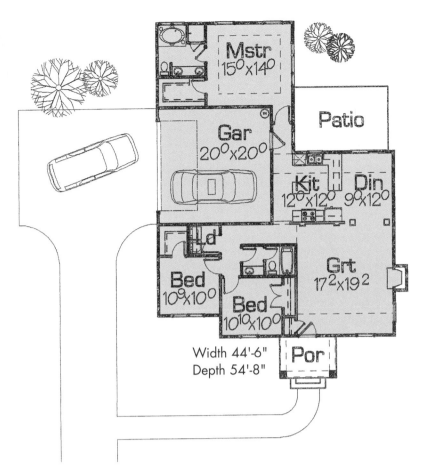

Width 44'-6"
Depth 54'-8"

■ Clever designing keeps this floor plan compact, but does not inhibit the great livability of its structure. The great room, with warming fireplace, is predominant at the entry and opens, through columns, to the dining room. A rear patio beyond the dining room offers space for outdoor dining. The two-car garage is set into the plan, making the width smaller and protecting the master suite behind it. Don't miss the fine amenities in the master bath: spa tub, separate shower and two sinks. Family bedrooms are at the front of the plan and share the use of a full bath. Both the master suite and one of the family bedrooms have walk-in closets. There is also a laundry room in the hall near the secondary bedrooms.

Design by
United Design
Associates, Inc.

Design U135

Square Footage: 2,121

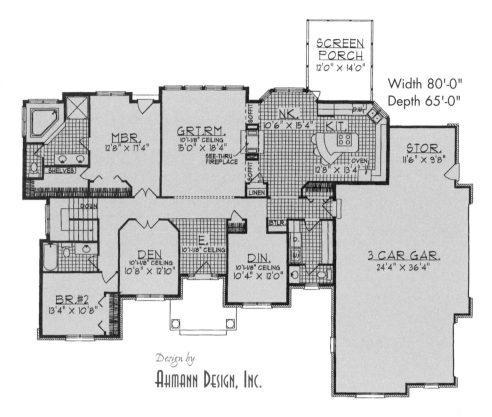

SCREEN PORCH
12'0" X 14'0"

Width 80'-0"
Depth 65'-0"

MBR.
12'8" X 17'4"

GRT. RM.
10'1-1/8" CEILING
15'0" X 18'4"

SEE-THRU FIREPLACE

NK.
10'6" X 15'4"

KIT.
12'8" X 13'4"

OVEN

STOR.
11'6" X 9'8"

SHELVES

LINEN

DOWN

DEN
10'1-1/8" CEILING
10'8" X 12'10"

F.
10'1-1/8" CEILING

DIN.
10'1-1/8" CEILING
10'4" X 12'0"

BTLR.

3 CAR GAR.
24'4" X 36'4"

BR. #2
13'4" X 10'8"

Design by
Ahmann Design, Inc.

■ A touch of Tudor dresses up this fine two-bedroom home, portraying the flavor of the Old World. Inside, a tiled foyer leads to the spacious great room which features a see-thru fireplace and a wall of windows. The large kitchen/nook area is designed for convenience, with a cooktop snack bar, an adjacent screen porch and plenty of counter space. The master bedroom suite is made to pamper and includes two closets (one a walk-in!), a corner whirlpool tub and separate shower and direct access to the rear yard. A cozy den waits across the hall and can be used as a home office or media room. A three-car garage easily shelters the family fleet.

Width 66'-6"
Depth 62'-0"

Bedroom No. 2
11³ x 13⁰

Porch

Breakfast
13⁰ x 10⁰

Master Bedroom
15³ x 16³

Family Room
16³ x 20⁰

Bedroom No. 3
11³ x 13⁰

Kitchen
13⁶ x 12³

Two Car Garage
22⁰ x 23⁶

Dining Room
11⁹ x 17⁶

Foyer

Study
12⁶ x 13⁶

Design by
DESIGN TRADITIONS

Design T236
Square Footage: 2,648

■ With brick and siding, a hipped roofline, a covered porch accented by columns and two fireplaces, this three-bedroom home is a perfect example of Old-World class. Inside, the foyer is flanked by a formal dining room and a cozy study. Directly ahead is the family room, complete with a fireplace, built-ins and French doors to the rear deck. Nearby, the elegant kitchen is full of amenities, including a snack bar, a pantry and the adjacent bayed breakfast area. Sleeping quarters consist of two family bedrooms which share a bath, and a deluxe master suite. Here, the homeowner will relish such amenities as a large walk-in closet, a separate tub and shower and direct access to the rear deck. This home is designed with a basement foundation.

© Design Traditions

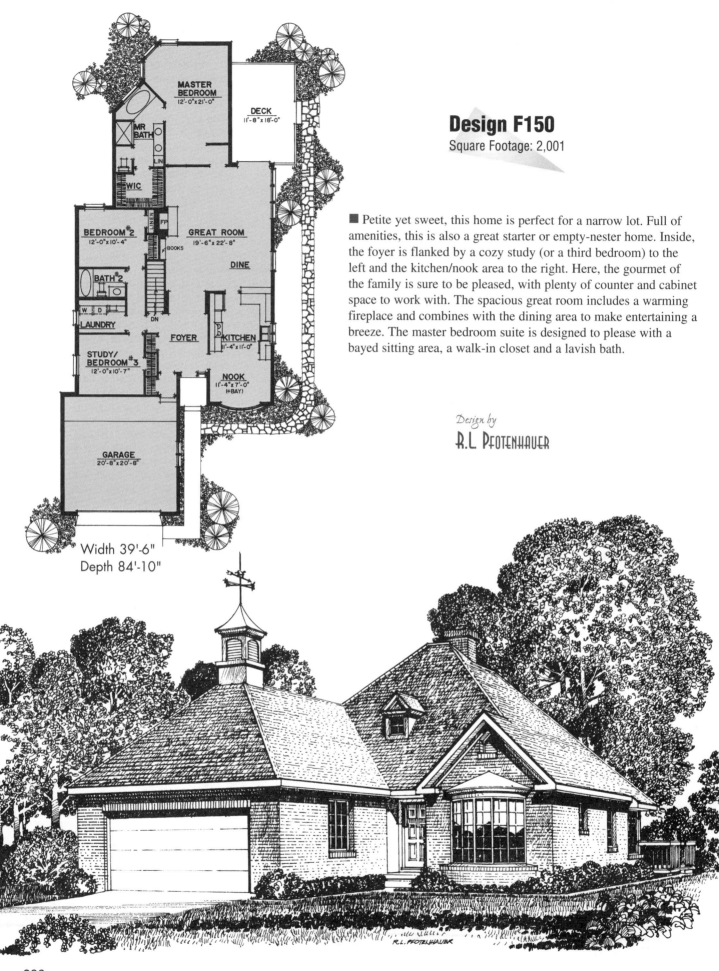

MASTER
BEDROOM
12'-0"x21'-0"

DECK
11'-8"x18'-0"

MR
BATH

LIN

WIC

LINEN

BEDROOM #2
12'-0"x10'-4"

FP

GREAT ROOM
19'-6"x22'-8"

BOOKS

DINE

BATH #2

W D

DN

LAUNDRY

FOYER

KITCHEN
11'-4"x11'-0"

STUDY/
BEDROOM #3
12'-0"x10'-7"

NOOK
11'-4"x7'-0"
(+BAY)

GARAGE
20'-8"x20'-6"

Width 39'-6"
Depth 84'-10"

Design F150

Square Footage: 2,001

■ Petite yet sweet, this home is perfect for a narrow lot. Full of amenities, this is also a great starter or empty-nester home. Inside, the foyer is flanked by a cozy study (or a third bedroom) to the left and the kitchen/nook area to the right. Here, the gourmet of the family is sure to be pleased, with plenty of counter and cabinet space to work with. The spacious great room includes a warming fireplace and combines with the dining area to make entertaining a breeze. The master bedroom suite is designed to please with a bayed sitting area, a walk-in closet and a lavish bath.

Design by
R.L. Pfotenhauer

R.L. PFOTENHAUER

© Design Traditions

Design T043

Square Footage: 2,090

■ Grace and elegance in one-story living abound in this traditional English country home. It contains all the necessary elements of a convenient floor plan as well: great room with fireplace, formal dining room, kitchen with attached breakfast nook, guest room/office, three bedrooms including a master suite. Here, amenities abound and include two walk-in closets and a lavish bath. A large, unfinished basement area allows for future expansion.

Design by
DESIGN TRADITIONS

Width 61'-0"
Depth 72'-6"

Quote One®

Cost to build? See page 434 to order complete cost estimate to build this house in your area!

MASTER BATH

MASTER BEDRDOOM
16'-4" X 13'-6"

PORCH

BREAKFAST
13'-4" X 9'-0"

BEDROOM/OFFICE
10'-4" X 11'-7"

KITCHEN
13'-4" X 10'-6"

GREAT ROOM
17'-0" X 17'-8"

BEDROOM NO. 2
10'-4" X 12'-0"

BATH

LAUNDRY

DN

BATH

DINING ROOM
11'-4" X 12'-10"

BEDROOM/STUDY
11'-2" X 12'-0"

TWO CAR GARAGE
20'-6" X 19'-6"

STOOP

PATIO

FUTURE GUEST BEDROOM
16'-2" X 14'-6"

FUTURE BATH

STORAGE/WORKSHOP
12'-8" X 11'-0"

FUTURE GAME ROOM
13'-4" X 19'-4"

FUTURE FAMILY ROOM
14'-8" X 18'-0"

FUTURE MEDIA ROOM
16'-0" X 18'-0"

MECHANICAL

UP

Unfinished Basement

STORAGE

Design C147

Square Footage: 2,095

A hipped and gabled roofline, together with corner quoins, calls out the influence of Europe on this two-bedroom ranch home. Inside, the floor plan is designed for efficiency, with the spacious great room opening into the formal dining room, making entertaining a breeze. Skylights in the breakfast room flood the area with natural light, which is shared with the large kitchen. A cozy study—or make it a third bedroom—is located at the front of the home and features built-ins. The master bedroom suite, entered through double doors, is complete with a walk-in closet and a lavish bath. A secondary bedroom, full hall bath and a laundry room finish out this efficient plan.

Design by
James Fahy
Design

MBATH

MBR
16'2 x 15'4

DIN
vault cl'g

DIN RM
13'6 x 11'8
high cl'g

BATH2

Laun

KIT
11'8 x 12'

GREAT RM
15'4 x 20'4
tray cl'g

BR2
10'4 x 10'4

Entry

FOYER
vault cl'g

STUDY
12' x 13'6

Porch

GARAGE

Width 55'-4"
Depth 62'-4"

Design 9203
Square Footage: 2,422

■ You can't help but feel spoiled by this amenity-filled plan. A tiled entry and open stairwell with dome ceiling greet visitors to this unusual home. Just off the entry is a den or optional bedroom, an open dining room with hutch space and an enormous great room with arched windows. An open-hearth fireplace serves both the great room and kitchen, creating a hearth room on the kitchen side. A large work area in the kitchen caters to the resident gourmet. The spacious master suite includes ten-foot ceilings, a whirlpool with dome ceiling and an enormous walk-in closet.

Width 72'-0"
Depth 55'-8"

Design by
DESIGN BASICS, INC.

Rear Elevation

291

Tall hipped rooflines, corner quoins and brick detailing are just the beginning of class for this three-bedroom home. Inside, compact doesn't mean cramped, with the living room opening to the dining area, giving a spacious feeling to the layout. Here also is a warming fireplace, waiting to add cheer to chilly winter evenings. Two family bedrooms—or make one a comfortable study—share a full hall bath. The master bedroom suite is full of amenities, including a large walk-in closet, a lavish bath and direct access to the rear covered patio. A two-car garage easily shelters the family fleet.

Design F149
Square Footage: 1,527

Design by
R.L Pfotenhauer

Width 55'-1"
Depth 51'-1"

Design 7320

Square Footage: 2,057

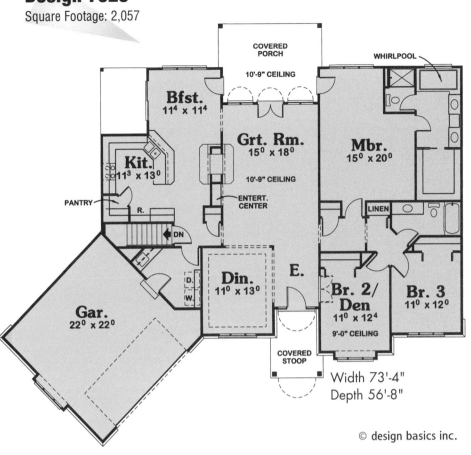

COVERED PORCH
10'-9" CEILING

WHIRLPOOL

Bfst.
11⁴ x 11⁴

Grt. Rm.
15⁰ x 18⁰

10'-9" CEILING

Mbr.
15⁰ x 20⁰

Kit.
11³ x 13⁰

PANTRY

R.

DN

ENTERT. CENTER

LINEN

D.
W.

Din.
11⁰ x 13⁰

E.

Br. 2/ Den
11⁰ x 12⁴

9'-0" CEILING

Br. 3
11⁰ x 12⁰

Gar.
22⁰ x 22⁰

COVERED STOOP

Width 73'-4"
Depth 56'-8"

© design basics inc.

Design by
DESIGN BASICS, INC.

■ This artful design speaks volumes about European charm, with a stucco veneer and an arch-top entry. A central great room features French doors to the back covered porch and a see-through fireplace it shares with the kitchen, which boasts a walk-in pantry. An elegant formal dining room opens to the great room and enjoys easy access from the kitchen. The master suite provides a whirlpool bath and private access to the back covered porch. One of two additional bedrooms to the front of the plan offers the option of a den, which would expand the living space of the home.

Design by

FRANK BETZ ASSOCIATES, INC.

Design P109

Square Footage: 1,670

■ A grand front window display illumi-nates the formal dining room and the great room in this country French charmer. Open planning allows for easy access between the formal dining room, great room, vaulted breakfast nook and kitchen. Extra amenities include a deco-rative column, fireplace and an optional bay window in the breakfast nook. The elegant master suite is fashioned with a tray ceiling in the bedroom, a vaulted master bath and a walk-in closet. Two family bedrooms are designated in a pocket-door hall and share a large hall bath. Please specify basement, crawl-space or slab foundation when ordering.

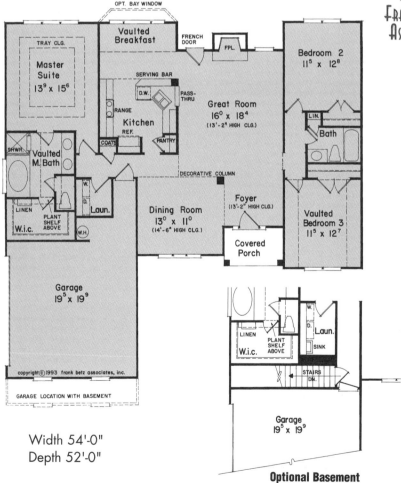

OPT. BAY WINDOW

Vaulted Breakfast

FRENCH DOOR

FPL.

TRAY CLG.

Master Suite
13⁹ x 15⁶

SERVING BAR

D.W.

PASS-THRU

Bedroom 2
11⁵ x 12⁸

Great Room
16⁰ x 18⁴
(13'-2" HIGH CLG.)

RANGE

Kitchen

REF.

COATS

PANTRY

L.IN.

Bath

SHWR.

Vaulted M. Bath

LINEN

W.

D.

Laun.

W.H.

DECORATIVE COLUMN

PLANT SHELF ABOVE

W.i.c.

Dining Room
13⁰ x 11⁰
(14'-6" HIGH CLG.)

Foyer
(13'-2" HIGH CLG.)

Vaulted Bedroom 3
11⁵ x 12⁷

Covered Porch

Garage
19⁵ x 19⁹

copyright © 1993 frank betz associates, inc.

GARAGE LOCATION WITH BASEMENT

Width 54'-0"
Depth 52'-0"

LINEN

W.i.c.

PLANT SHELF ABOVE

W.

D.

Laun.

SINK

STAIRS DN.

Garage
19⁵ x 19⁹

Optional Basement Stair Location

QUOTE ONE®

Cost to build? See page 434 to order complete cost estimate to build this house in your area!

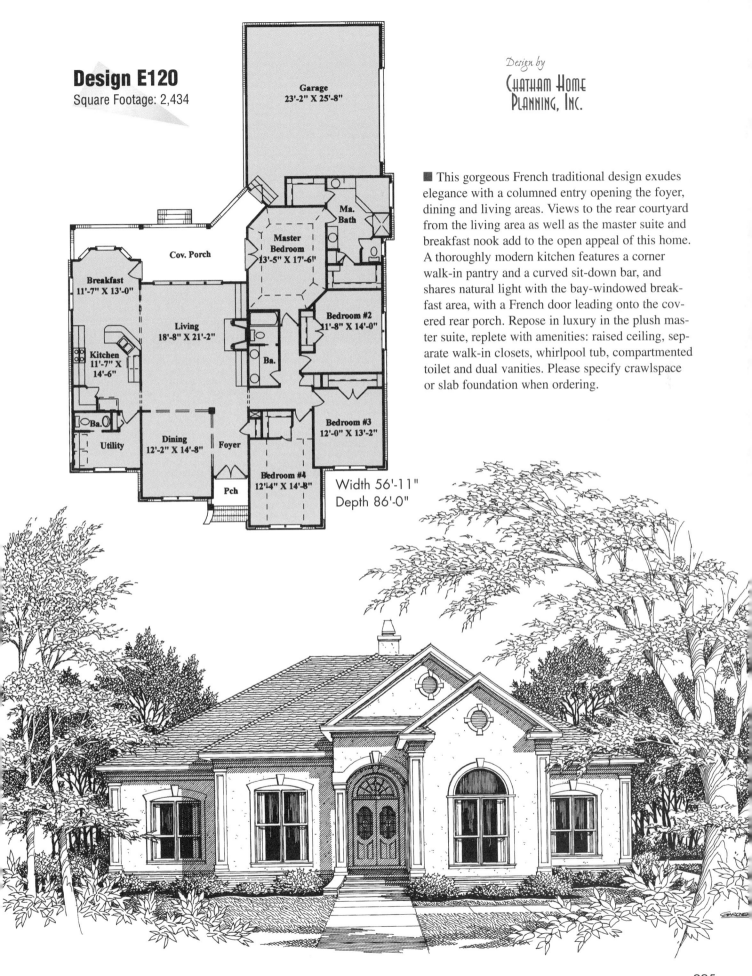

Design E120
Square Footage: 2,434

Design by
Chatham Home Planning, Inc.

Garage
23'-2" X 25'-8"

Cov. Porch

Ma. Bath

Master Bedroom
13'-5" X 17'-6"

Breakfast
11'-7" X 13'-0"

Living
18'-8" X 21'-2"

Bedroom #2
11'-8" X 14'-0"

Kitchen
11'-7" X 14'-6"

Ba.

Ba.

Bedroom #3
12'-0" X 13'-2"

Utility

Dining
12'-2" X 14'-8"

Foyer

Bedroom #4
12'-4" X 14'-8"

Pch

Width 56'-11"
Depth 86'-0"

■ This gorgeous French traditional design exudes elegance with a columned entry opening the foyer, dining and living areas. Views to the rear courtyard from the living area as well as the master suite and breakfast nook add to the open appeal of this home. A thoroughly modern kitchen features a corner walk-in pantry and a curved sit-down bar, and shares natural light with the bay-windowed breakfast area, with a French door leading onto the covered rear porch. Repose in luxury in the plush master suite, replete with amenities: raised ceiling, separate walk-in closets, whirlpool tub, compartmented toilet and dual vanities. Please specify crawlspace or slab foundation when ordering.

Design by

FRANK BETZ
ASSOCIATES, INC.

QUOTE ONE®

Cost to build? See page 434
to order complete cost estimate
to build this house in your area!

Design P123

Square Footage: 1,715

A grand double bank of windows looking in on the formal dining room mirrors the lofty elegance of the extra-tall vaulted ceiling inside. From the foyer, an arched entrance to the great room visually frames the fireplace on the back wall. The wraparound kitchen has plenty of counter and cabinet space, along with a handy serving bar. The luxurious master suite features a front sitting room for quiet times and a large spa-style bath. Two family bedrooms are split from the master for privacy and share a hall bath. Please specify basement, crawl-space or slab foundation when ordering.

Width 55'-0"
Depth 51'-6"

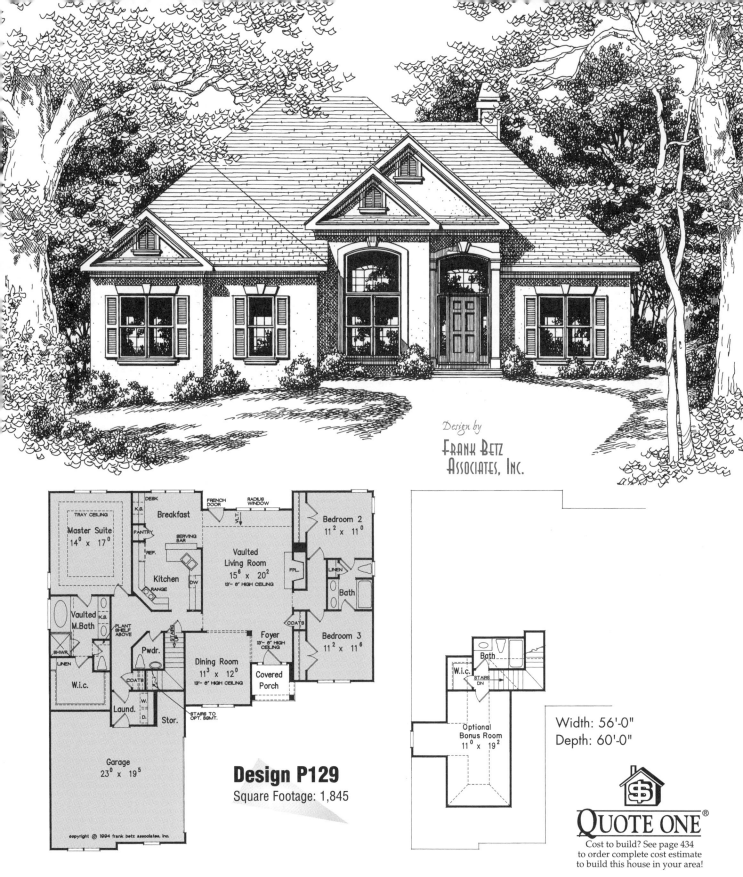

Design by

FRANK BETZ
ASSOCIATES, INC.

Floor Plan Labels

Left plan:
- TRAY CEILING
- Master Suite 14⁰ x 17⁰
- Vaulted M.Bath
- SHWR
- LINEN
- W.i.c.
- Laund.
- Stor.
- Garage 23⁰ x 19⁵
- PWDR.
- COATS
- STAIRS
- PLANT SHELF ABOVE
- Kitchen
- RANGE
- DW
- REF.
- PANTRY
- DESK
- Breakfast
- SERVING BAR
- FRENCH DOOR
- RADIUS WINDOW
- VLT.
- Vaulted Living Room 15⁶ x 20² 13'- 6" HIGH CEILING
- FPL.
- Bedroom 2 11² x 11⁰
- LINEN
- Bath
- Foyer 13'- 6" HIGH CEILING
- COATS
- Bedroom 3 11² x 11⁶
- Dining Room 11³ x 12⁰ 13'- 6" HIGH CEILING
- Covered Porch
- STAIRS TO OPT. BSMT.

copyright © 1994 frank betz associates, inc.

Design P129
Square Footage: 1,845

Right plan:
- Bath
- W.i.c.
- STAIRS DN
- Optional Bonus Room 11⁰ x 19²

Width: 56'-0"
Depth: 60'-0"

$ QUOTE ONE®

Cost to build? See page 434
to order complete cost estimate
to build this house in your area!

■ The stucco exterior and combination roof lines give a stately appearance to this traditional home. Inside, the well-lit foyer leads to an elegant living room with a vaulted ceiling, a fireplace, a radius window and a French door leading to the rear yard. Two family bedrooms share a full bath on the right side of the home, while an impressive master suite is located on the left side for privacy. The master suite includes a tray ceiling and a vaulted master bath with dual sinks, a separate tub and shower and a walk-in closet. A formal dining room and an open kitchen area with plenty of counter space and a serving bar complete this plan. An optional bonus room with a full bath, perfect for a college student, could be added later. Please specify basement or crawlspace foundation when ordering.

Design A163

Square Footage: 2,677
Bonus Room: 319 square feet

■ A beautiful cove entry with double doors opens onto a foyer with unobstructed views to the grand room. A formal dining room with tray ceiling is to the right and the master suite fills the wing to the left. A sitting area with bay window and entrance to the deck highlight the master bedroom. A garden tub in its own bay window and large walk-in closet enhance this area. A breakfast nook occupies a third bay window just off the U-shaped kitchen with pass-through window to the deck. The island cooktop borders the keeping den with sloped ceiling and fireplace. Two additional bedrooms each have their own bath.

Design by
LIVING CONCEPTS

Width 63'-10"
Depth 80'-4"

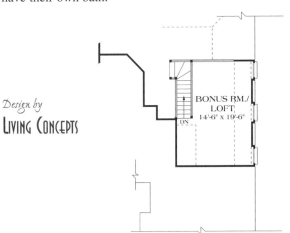

BONUS RM./LOFT
14'-6" x 19'-6"

Design A131

Square Footage: 2,765
Bonus Room: 367 square feet

■ Moulded window facades and corner quoins join with triple gables to decorate the exterior of this three-bedroom plus attic bonus room plan. Entertain in the formal dining room, the grand room or the gracious gathering room with wraparound windows and fireplace. Breakfast in the bay window breakfast nook that faces the covered lanai. The master bedroom suite stretches along the left wing of the house and features His and Hers walk-in closets, toilet compartment and garden tub. Two additional bedrooms on the other side of the house share a full bath.

Design by
LIVING CONCEPTS

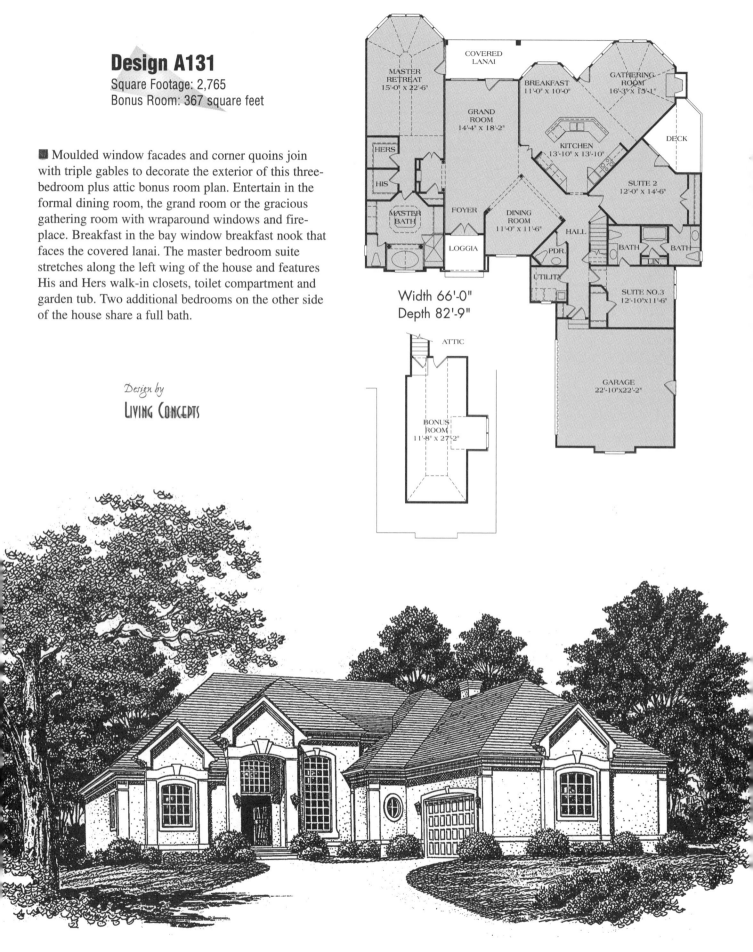

MASTER RETREAT
15'-0" x 22'-6"

COVERED LANAI

BREAKFAST
11'-0" x 10'-0"

GATHERING ROOM
16'-3" x 15'-1"

GRAND ROOM
14'-4" x 18'-2"

KITCHEN
13'-10" x 13'-10"

DECK

HERS

HIS

MASTER BATH

FOYER

DINING ROOM
11'-0" x 11'-6"

HALL

SUITE 2
12'-0" x 14'-6"

LOGGIA

PDR.

BATH

BATH

LIN.

UTILITY

SUITE NO.3
12'-10"x11'-6"

Width 66'-0"
Depth 82'-9"

ATTIC

BONUS ROOM
11'-8" x 27'-2"

GARAGE
22'-10"x22'-2"

Design P122

Square Footage: 1,884

■ Keystones above the windows and stately corner quoins are just a hint of the attention to detail this well-crafted plan offers. Arched openings, decorative columns and elegant ceiling detail throughout highlight the very livable floor plan. The large country kitchen has a spacious work area, prep island and breakfast nook. The dining room is set to the rear for gracious entertaining and opens to the great room. The master suite is beautifully appointed with a compartmented bath and walk-in closet. Two family bedrooms share a private compartmented bath. Please specify basement, crawlspace or slab foundation when ordering.

Design by

Frank Betz Associates, Inc.

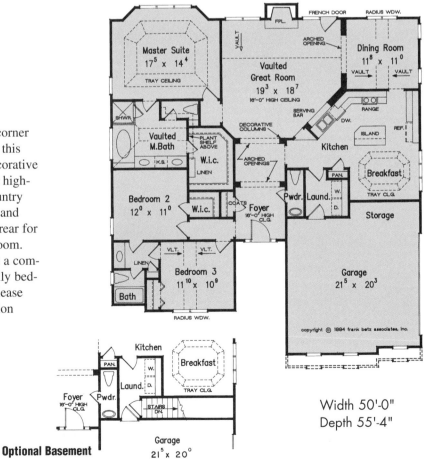

Optional Basement
Stair Location

Width 50'-0"
Depth 55'-4"

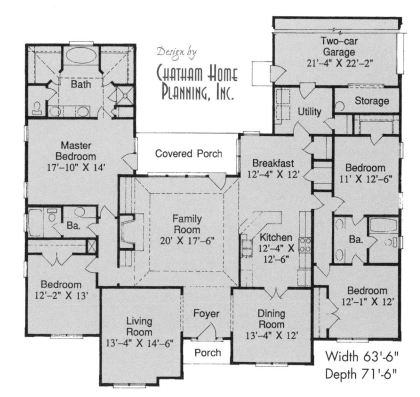

Design by
Chatham Home Planning, Inc.

Two-car Garage
21'-4" X 22'-2"

Utility

Storage

Bath

Master Bedroom
17'-10" X 14'

Covered Porch

Breakfast
12'-4" X 12'

Bedroom
11' X 12'-6"

Design E138
Square Footage: 2,558

Ba.

Family Room
20' X 17'-6"

Kitchen
12'-4" X 12'-6"

Ba.

Bedroom
12'-2" X 13'

Living Room
13'-4" X 14'-6"

Foyer

Dining Room
13'-4" X 12'

Bedroom
12'-1" X 12'

Porch

Width 63'-6"
Depth 71'-6"

■ Heavy corner quoins make a rustic impression that is dressed up by a subtly asymmetrical design and arches on the windows. The floor plan is almost labyrinthine, sprawling over 2,500 square feet in a single story. The centerpiece of the home is a magnificent family room with tray ceiling, fireplace, built-in shelves and access to the rear covered porch. Adjacent are the breakfast room and the kitchen, which serves

the formal dining room through elegant double doors. Two secondary bedrooms are secluded on the far right of the plan, each having private access to a full bath with twin vanities. To the far left are a third bedroom and the spacious master suite, which features His and Hers walk in closets, an oval tub, a separate shower, compartmented toilet and twin vanities.

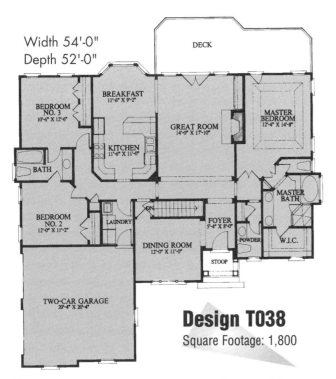

Width 54'-0"
Depth 52'-0"

DECK

BEDROOM NO. 3
10'-6" X 12'-6"

BREAKFAST
11'-6" X 9'-2"

GREAT ROOM
14'-0" X 17'-10"

MASTER BEDROOM
12'-4" X 14'-8"

KITCHEN
11'-6" X 11'-0"

BATH

MASTER BATH

BEDROOM NO. 2
12'-0" X 11'-2"

LAUNDRY

DN.

FOYER
5'-4" X 8'-0"

POWDER

W.I.C.

DINING ROOM
12'-0" X 11'-0"

STOOP

TWO-CAR GARAGE
20'-4" X 20'-4"

Design T038

Square Footage: 1,800

CRAWL SPACE

FUTURE FAMILY ROOM
14'-0" X 16'-8"

FUTURE GUEST BEDROOM
12'-4" X 14'-8"

WET BAR

UP.

FUTURE BATH

STORAGE

MECHANICAL

SLAB ON GRADE

STOOP ABOVE

Unfinished Basement

■ This European-inspired cottage contains one of the most efficient floor plans available. From the formal dining room at the front of the plan to the commodious great room at the rear, it accommodates various lifestyles in less than 2,000 square feet. An opulent master suite with deck access and grand bath dominates the right wing of the house. Two family bedrooms and a full bath are found to the left. There's even a powder room for guests. The gourmet-style kitchen has an attached breakfast area with glassed bay for sunny brunches. Bonus space in the basement allows for future development.

Design by
DESIGN TRADITIONS

© Design Traditions

302

Patio
23'11" x 9'3"

Covered Porch
23'11" x 6'

Living
25'2" x 16'6"

Master Bath

Master Bedroom
13'10" x 15'

Breakfast
9'3" x 12'

Kitchen
11'7" x 12'

Bedroom
11'4" x 11'

Dining
11'6" x 14'

Utility
9' x 9'8"

Bath

Foyer

Garage
21' x 21'8"

Porch

Bedroom
11'4" x 11'6"

Width 79'-3"
Depth 40'-10"

Design E140
Square Footage: 2,184

■ Delicate molded arches adorn this pretty single-story home. The thoughtful floor plan makes the most of a narrow lot and includes many special amenities. The double-door entry is beautifully covered by a double arch and fanlight and opens to a long, elegant foyer. The right side of the plan is devoted to sleeping quarters, with the master suite at the rear. The master bedroom offers a tray ceiling and double doors to the master bath with separate twin vanities, oval tub and separate toilet and shower compartment. The dining room also features a tray ceiling and is isolated from the kitchen for formal entertaining. Another tray ceiling crowns the enormous living room, which offers a corner fireplace and access to the covered porch and patio at the rear.

Design by
CHATHAM HOME
PLANNING, INC.

Design S130

Square Footage: 1,661

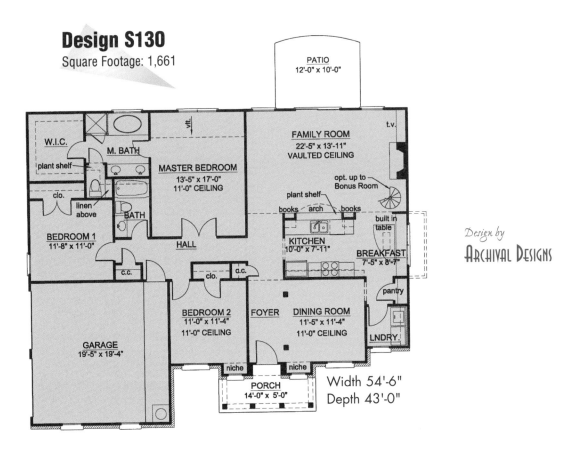

PATIO
12'-0" x 10'-0"

W.I.C.

plant shelf

M. BATH

clo.

linen above

BATH

BEDROOM 1
11'-8" x 11'-0"

c.c.

MASTER BEDROOM
13'-5" x 17'-0"
11'-0" CEILING

HALL

clo.

c.c.

FAMILY ROOM
22'-5" x 13'-11"
VAULTED CEILING

t.v.

opt. up to
Bonus Room

plant shelf

books   arch   books

built in
table

KITCHEN
10'-0" x 7'-11"

BREAKFAST
7'-5" x 8'-7"

pantry

BEDROOM 2
11'-0" x 11'-4"
11'-0" CEILING

FOYER

DINING ROOM
11'-5" x 11'-4"
11'-0" CEILING

LNDRY.

GARAGE
19'-5" x 19'-4"

niche   niche

PORCH
14'-0" x 5'-0"

Width 54'-6"
Depth 43'-0"

Design by
ARCHIVAL DESIGNS

■ European accents grace the facade of this delightful plan and include an arched entry, circle detailing and a columned overhang. The floor plan is classically rendered as well, though with a nod to less formal living. The entry opens with a dining room on the right, defined by two columns at the foyer. The kitchen and breakfast room separate the dining room from the gigantic family room with its built-in shelves,

fireplace, spiral staircase to a small loft and access to the rear patio. There are three bedrooms in the plan—or make one into a cozy den if you choose. The master bedroom connects to a truly luxurious bath with spa tub, walk-in closet, separate shower and compartmented bath. The hall bath serves both family bedrooms.

Design P236

Square Footage: 1,978

■ A glass-paneled entry poses an inviting complement to stucco cornices and double-hung windows, and adds a generous dash of European spirit to this stunning country home. Inside, vaulted ceilings and radius windows inspire a broader sense of space and help bring in the outdoors. Arched openings decorate the interior, while an unrestrained floor plan provides a plentitude of well-lit bays and niches. Casual living space enjoys a wide serving bar, served by the gourmet kitchen and warmed by a centered hearth in the family room. A tray ceiling, a sunlit sitting area and a vaulted bath highlight the master suite, which enjoys a secluded wing to the rear of the plan. Two family bedrooms share a hall bath to the right of the breakfast/kitchen area. Please specify basement or crawlspace foundation when ordering.

Design by
**FRANK BETZ
ASSOCIATES, INC.**

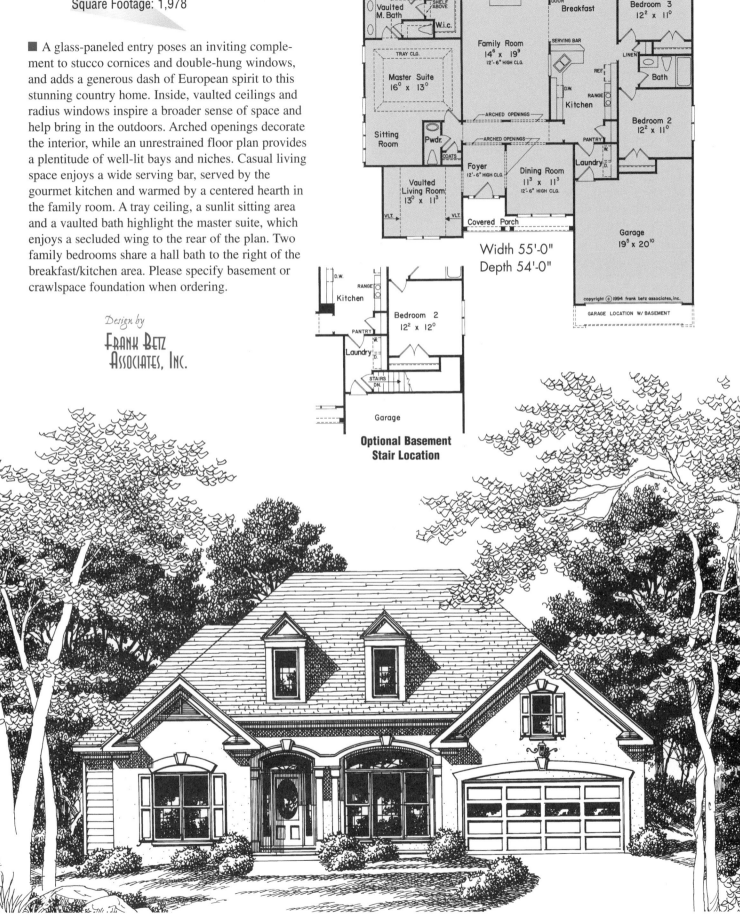

Width 55'-0"
Depth 54'-0"

copyright © 1994 frank betz associates, inc.

GARAGE LOCATION W/ BASEMENT

**Optional Basement
Stair Location**

305

Width 57'-0"
Depth 56'-4"

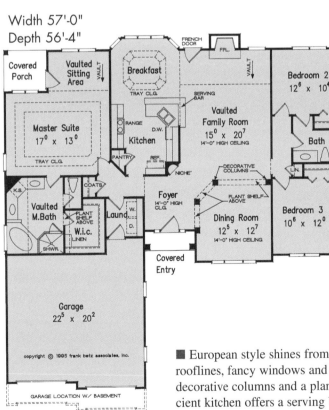

Optional Basement Stair Location

Design P191

Square Footage: 1,779

Design by

FRANK BETZ ASSOCIATES, INC.

■ European style shines from this home's facade in the form of its stucco detailing, hipped rooflines, fancy windows and elegant entryway. Inside, the formal dining room is defined by decorative columns and a plant shelf, and works well with the vaulted family room. The efficient kitchen offers a serving bar to both the family room and the deluxe breakfast room. Located apart from the family bedrooms for privacy, the master suite is sure to please with its many amenities, including a vaulted sitting area and a private covered porch. The two secondary bedrooms share a full hall bath. Please specify basement or crawlspace foundation when ordering.

Design S128

Square Footage: 2,588

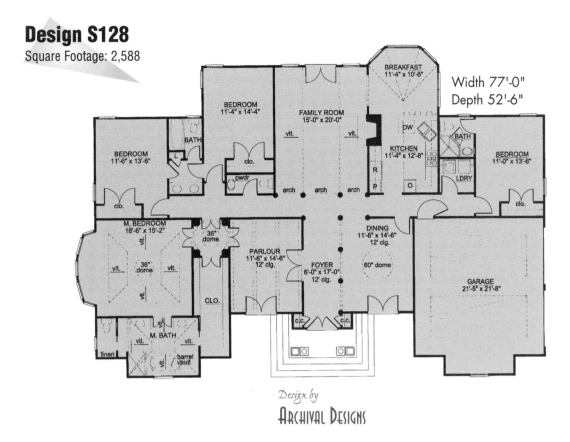

Width 77'-0"
Depth 52'-6"

BREAKFAST 11'-4" x 10'-6"

BEDROOM 11'-4" x 14'-4"

FAMILY ROOM 15'-0" x 20'-0"

BEDROOM 11'-6" x 13'-6"

BATH

DW

BATH

KITCHEN 11'-4" x 12'-8"

BEDROOM 11'-0" x 13'-6"

clo.

pwdr

LDRY

arch   arch   arch

M. BEDROOM 18'-6" x 15'-2"

36" dome

DINING 11'-6" x 14'-6" 12' clg.

36" dome

PARLOUR 11'-6" x 14'-6" 12' clg.

FOYER 6'-0" x 17'-0" 12' clg.

60" dome

GARAGE 21'-5" x 21'-8"

CLO.

M. BATH

linen

barrel vault

c.c.   c.c.

Design by
ARCHIVAL DESIGNS

■ A Mediterranean mansion or an Italian villa—these are the influences on the exterior of this grand one-story. The floor plan was designed for royalty, as well. Double doors open to an elegant entry foyer which opens on the left to the formal parlor and to the right to the formal dining room, accented with columns. The family room is also introduced by columns and is further enhanced by a fireplace and double doors to the rear yard. The kitchen area is large and magnified by a break-

fast room full of light. A guest bedroom, or private suite, is down the hall behind the garage and has a private bath. Two family bedrooms are at the other end of the hall and share a bath. The master suite may be accessed through a private foyer, either at the hall or from the parlor. Its bath is superb with a gigantic walk-in closet, His and Hers sinks, a garden whirlpool and separate shower.

Design J123

Square Footage: 2,485

■ This plan is a stunning one-story with today's active family in mind. Unique rooflines provide curb appeal and give interesting ceiling treatments to almost every room in the house. Formal entertaining is easy in the open living room/dining room area, with large windows for natural light and a fireplace for warmth. The family room has a second fireplace and skylights, and is conveniently close to the spacious kitchen and sunny breakfast nook. For quieter moments, the den is separated from the main living areas. Three large bedrooms, including a deluxe master suite, are grouped to the right of the plan, with the laundry room nearby.

Design by

MARK STEWART & ASSOCIATES

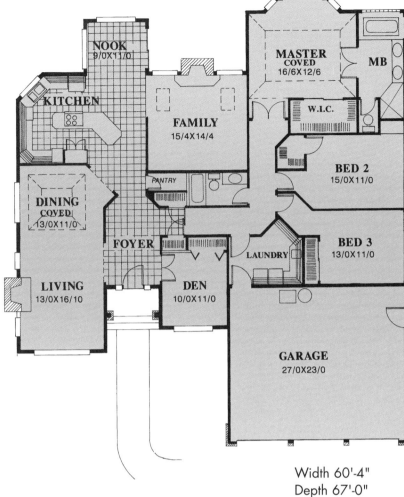

NOOK
9/0X11/0

KITCHEN

MASTER
COVED
16/6X12/6

MB

FAMILY
15/4X14/4

W.I.C.

BED 2
15/0X11/0

DINING
COVED
13/0X11/0

PANTRY

FOYER

LAUNDRY

BED 3
13/0X11/0

LIVING
13/0X16/10

DEN
10/0X11/0

GARAGE
27/0X23/0

Width 60'-4"
Depth 67'-0"

Design 7634

Square Footage: 1,699
Bonus Room: 386 square feet

■ Keystone arches, asymmetrical gables and a stunning stucco exterior lend European sophistication to this great plan. The interior starts with an expansive great room, which features an extended-hearth fireplace and views to the outdoors. The U-shaped kitchen serves a spectacular dining room, with bay-window views that feast the soul. A private master suite nestles to the rear of the plan and offers a tray ceiling and a lavish bath with a garden tub, twin vanities and a corner whirlpool tub. Two additional bedrooms share a full bath nearby, while upstairs bonus space is available for future development.

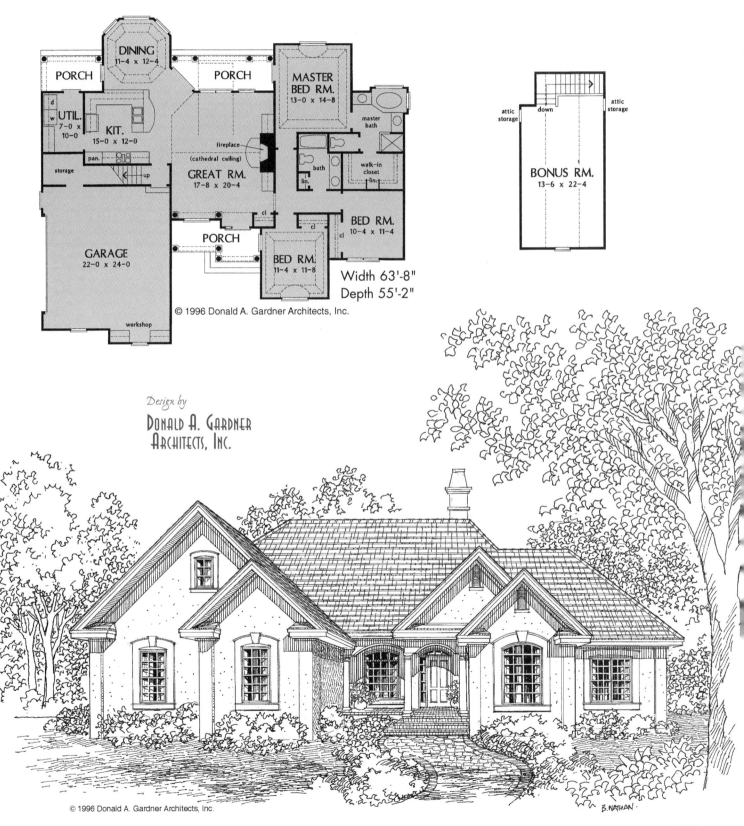

Width 63'-8"
Depth 55'-2"

© 1996 Donald A. Gardner Architects, Inc.

Design by

DONALD A. GARDNER
ARCHITECTS, INC.

© 1996 Donald A. Gardner Architects, Inc.

B. NATHAN

Design T211

Square Footage: 2,174

Design by
DESIGN TRADITIONS

Width 63'-0"
Depth 59'-6"

■ With the blending of stucco and stone, this home draws its inspiration from country French tradition. Beginning at the dramatic entrance, the open floor plan flows gracefully from room to room. From the foyer and across the great room, French doors and large side windows give a generous view of the rear porch. The adjoining dining room is subtly defined by columns and a large triple window. The accommodating kitchen, with its generous work island, adjoins the breakfast area and keeping room. The bedroom at the front of the home has direct access to a full bath, which makes it a good choice as guest quarters or a children's den. The master suite features a bay window, a garden tub and separate vanities. This home is designed with a basement foundation.

© Design Traditions

Design T209
Square Footage: 2,140

Bedroom #3
11⁶ x 11⁰

Bedroom #2
11³ x 11⁰

Sun Room
12⁰ x 13⁹

Porch

Porch

Master Bedroom
13³ x 15⁶

Breakfast
10⁰ x 9⁰

Kitchen
12⁰ x 13³

Great Room
18⁰ x 14⁰

Dining Room
10⁷ x 10⁷

Den/ Guest Room
13⁴ x 14⁸

Two Car Garage
20⁸ x 21⁸

Width 62'-0"
Depth 60'-6"

■ Imagine the luxurious living you'll enjoy in this beautiful home! The natural beauty of stone combined with sophisticated window detailing represent the good taste you'll find carried throughout the design. Common living areas occupy the center of the plan and include a family room with fireplace, sun room and breakfast area, plus rear and side porches. A second fireplace is located in the front den. The master suite features private access to the rear porch and a wonderfully planned bath. This home is designed with a basement foundation.

Design by
DESIGN TRADITIONS

Design U217

Square Footage: 1,817

Width 57'-0"
Depth 56'-0"

BR. #2
10'8" X 10'4"

NK.
9'8" X 9'4"

MBR.
14'0" X 14'0"

GRT. RM.
12'-1 1/8" CEILING
18'8" X 18'6"

KIT.
9'8" X 13'2"

BR. #3
10'8" X 11'4"

12'-1 1/8" CEILING

DOWN

PANTRY

DIN.
12'-1 1/8" CEILING
12'0" X 11'8"

LINEN

2 CAR GAR.
21'8" X 21'8"

Design by
Ahmann Design, Inc.

■ Grand proportions decorate the entry of this home and lend elegance to its dimensions. From the columned front porch, step into a tiled entry with a formal dining room immediately on the right. A great room with corner fireplace and snack counter is straight on from the foyer. It attaches to the breakfast room and the gourmet-style kitchen. The master suite has two closets—one a walk-in—and a bath with everything you might require. Family bedrooms are at the other end of the plan and include a full bath with double sinks. A laundry with plenty of workspace connects the main home to the two-car garage. Note the box-bay window in the dining room and patio access in the breakfast nook.

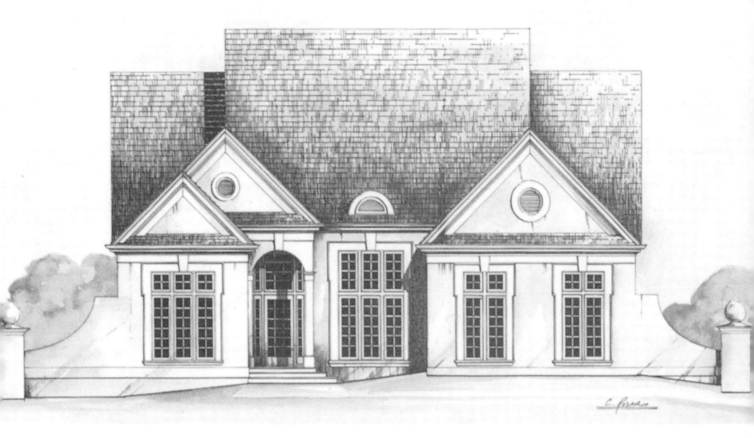

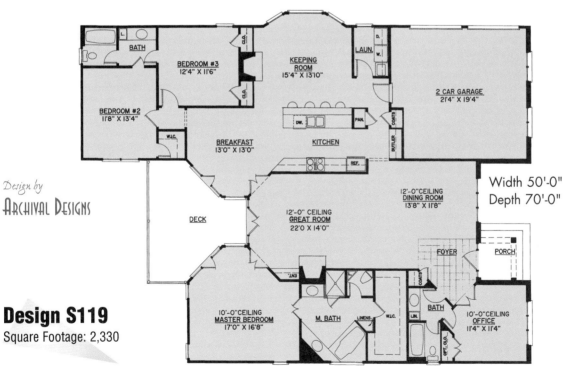

Design S119
Square Footage: 2,330

Width 50'-0"
Depth 70'-0"

■ This plan almost looks like it has two stories—but the floor plan reveals that it is conveniently laid out on just one level. But what a level! A huge great room/dining room combination dominates the front of the plan and has handy access to the galley kitchen and the breakfast room at two points. At one end, the great room has double doors to a deck. Nearby is a warming hearth and built-in shelves. For casual occasions, consider the keeping room. It features a bay window and a fireplace, plus a snack counter for easy meals. For those who work at home, there is a wonderful office just off the entry. It doubles as a guest room, as it includes a full bath. The master suite is delightful and graced with deck access and a pampering bath. Two additional bedrooms—one with walk-in closet —share a full bath.

Design T234
Square Footage: 2,494

Porch

Breakfast
11⁶ x 9⁰

Master
Bedroom
13³ x 19⁰

Great
Room
15⁰ x 18⁰

Bedroom
#2
12³ x 12³

Kitchen
11³ x 13³

Master
Bath

Bedroom
#3
12⁹ x 13⁰

Dining
Room
12⁰ x 13³

Foyer

Two Car
Garage
24⁹ x 21⁹

Living
Room
15⁰ x 15⁰

Width 65'-4"
Depth 61'-8"

■ Stucco-and-stone, multi-pane windows, a covered porch—all elements to a fine European-flavored home. Inside, the foyer is flanked by formal living and dining rooms, and leads back to more casual areas. Here, a great room with a warming fireplace is framed by windows, with a nearby kitchen and breakfast room finishing off gathering areas. Two family bedrooms reside to the right and share a full bath with two vanities. The master suite is sure to please with a large walk-in closet and a sumptuous master bath.

Design by
DESIGN TRADITIONS

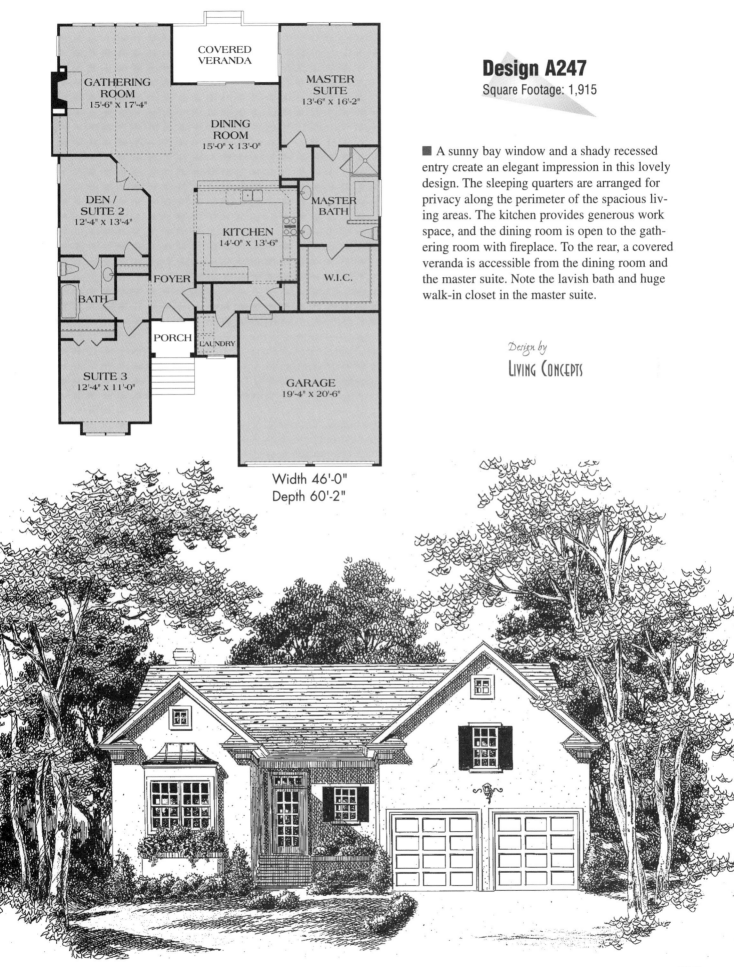

GATHERING ROOM
15'-6" x 17'-4"

COVERED VERANDA

MASTER SUITE
13'-6" x 16'-2"

DINING ROOM
15'-0" x 13'-0"

DEN / SUITE 2
12'-4" x 13'-4"

MASTER BATH

KITCHEN
14'-0" x 13'-6"

FOYER

W.I.C.

BATH

PORCH

LAUNDRY

SUITE 3
12'-4" x 11'-0"

GARAGE
19'-4" x 20'-6"

Width 46'-0"
Depth 60'-2"

Design A247
Square Footage: 1,915

■ A sunny bay window and a shady recessed entry create an elegant impression in this lovely design. The sleeping quarters are arranged for privacy along the perimeter of the spacious living areas. The kitchen provides generous work space, and the dining room is open to the gathering room with fireplace. To the rear, a covered veranda is accessible from the dining room and the master suite. Note the lavish bath and huge walk-in closet in the master suite.

Design by
LIVING CONCEPTS

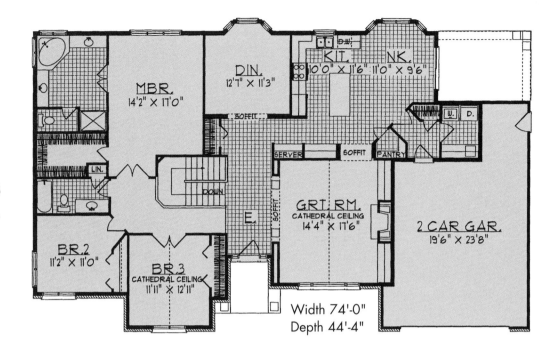

Design U152

Square Footage: 2,286

MBR.
14'2" X 17'0"

DIN.
12'7" X 11'3"

KIT.
10'0" X 11'6"

NK.
11'0" X 9'6"

SOFFIT

SERVER   SOFFIT   PANTRY

GRT. RM.
CATHEDRAL CEILING
14'4" X 17'6"

2 CAR GAR.
19'6" X 23'8"

DOWN

E.

BR.2
11'2" X 11'0"

BR.3
CATHEDRAL CEILING
11'11" X 12'11"

Width 74'-0"
Depth 44'-4"

■ One of the first things you'll notice about this design is the magnificent window which is in the great room. It echoes the lines of the entry and beckons a warm welcome. A tiled entry foyer continues through to the kitchen and nook with stops along the way at a formal dining room with bay window and a servery. Enhancing the kitchen area are an island workcenter, a walk-in pantry and a bay window in the breakfast room.

Continue on and you'll find a large laundry with service entrance to the two-car garage. The opposite end of the plan holds three bedrooms—one with cathedral ceiling. The master suite includes a bath that is almost as large as the bedroom and features a corner whirlpool tub, separate shower and twin sinks. There is also a huge walk-in closet.

Design by
AHMANN DESIGN, INC.

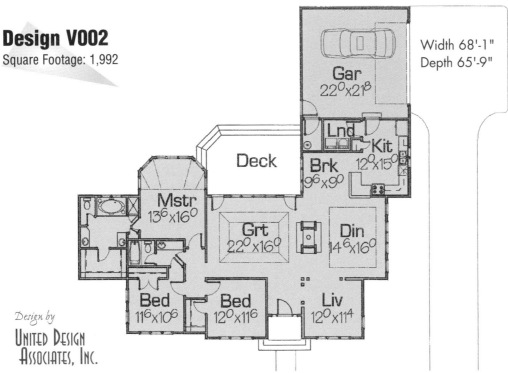

Design V002

Square Footage: 1,992

Width 68'-1"
Depth 65'-9"

Gar
22⁰x21⁸

Lnd

Kit
12⁰x15⁰

Deck

Brk
9⁶x9⁰

Mstr
13⁶x16⁰

Grt
22⁰x16⁰

Din
14⁶x16⁰

Bed
11⁶x10⁶

Bed
12⁰x11⁶

Liv
12⁰x11⁴

Design by
United Design
Associates, Inc.

■ This is a lovely plan and the perfect size for just about any family. It has the right mix of formal and informal areas and good outdoor livability. The great room, dining room and formal living room form a triangle of living space just beyond the entry. Separating the dining room and great room is a wonderful through-fireplace. To the rear of the plan is a U-shaped kitchen with smaller breakfast area. Note the location in juxtaposition to the garage. Three bedrooms are included in the plan. Two share a full bath at the end of the hall. The master suite has a gorgeous window treatment and a bath that is amenity filled. The rear deck is accessed from the great room through two separate doors.

© Design Traditions

Design T042

Square Footage: 2,120

■ As quaint as the European countryside, this charming cottage boasts a unique interior. Living patterns revolve around the central family room—notice the placement of the formal dining room, kitchen with attached breakfast nook and sun room. Family bedrooms are tucked quietly away to the rear, while the master suite maintains privacy at the opposite end of the plan. A den with fireplace attaches to the master bedroom or can be accessed from the entry foyer. Bonus space in the basement can be developed later.

Width 62'-0"
Depth 62'-6"

Design by
DESIGN TRADITIONS

Unfinished Basement

Design M131
Square Footage: 2,590

■ With a solid exterior of rough cedar and stone, this new country French design will stand the test of time. A wood-paneled study on the front features a large bay window. The heart of the house is found in a large, open great room with built-in entertainment center. The spacious master bedroom features a corner reading area and access to an adjacent covered patio. A three-car garage and three additional bedrooms complete this generous family home.

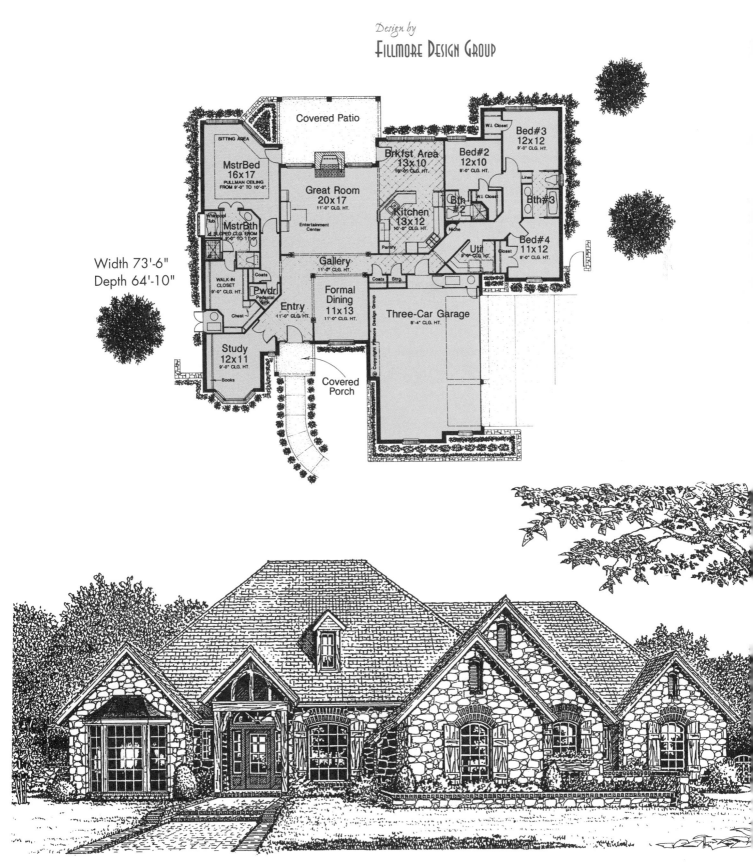

Design by
FILLMORE DESIGN GROUP

Width 73'-6"
Depth 64'-10"

© Copyright Fillmore Design Group

319

© Design Traditions

Design T207

Square Footage: 1,751

Design by

DESIGN TRADITIONS

Deck

Breakfast
11⁴ x 8⁶

Bedroom #3
11⁶ x 11⁰

Great Room
14⁰ x 17⁶

Master
Bedroom
12⁴ x 15⁶

Kitchen
11⁴ x 10⁰

Bedroom
#2
11⁴ x 14⁸

Dining Room
11⁴ x 10⁶

Two Car
Garage
20⁴ x 19⁴

Width 55'-6"
Depth 59'-6"

■ A brick facade and central gable with an arched window introduce this English cottage design. The double-hung windows are crested by jack arches. The foyer opens to a large great room, emphasizing the open and airy floor plan, with French doors that lead to a back deck for a warm, inviting feeling. Convenient to both the great room and dining room, the kitchen opens to an attractive breakfast area with a bay window. To the left of the kitchen, two bedrooms—each with a walk-in closet—share a bath area. The luxurious master suite is located to the rear of the home, offering comfort and a peaceful retreat. The master bath contains a garden tub, a separate shower and double vanities. This home is designed with a basement foundation.

Design U214

Square Footage: 1,912

■ This lovely stone cottage with jack-arch detailing begins with a columned entry and opens to a wonderful floor plan. The tiled foyer has an open staircase to the basement level then leads on to a huge great room with a tray ceiling, fireplace and built-ins. Columns divide this room from the formal dining room. An L-shaped kitchen has an island workcounter and an attached nook with access to a private covered porch. The pantry in the kitchen is stupendous. The bedrooms reside to the right of the plan and consist of two family bedrooms with a shared bath and a master suite that features a bedroom with cathedral ceiling and bath with huge walk-in closet, spa tub and separate shower. The two-car garage opens to the side to take nothing away from the attractive facade.

DIN.
12'8" X 12'8"

GRT. RM.
TRAY CEILING
11'-1 1/8" CEILING
14'0" X 20'0"

MBR.
CATHEDRAL CEILING
15'0" X 13'8"

NK.
19'4" X 11'0"

KIT.

PANTRY

11'-1 1/8" CEILING

BR. #2
11'0" X 10'4"

BR. #3
CATHEDRAL CEILING
11'0" X 10'8"

2 CAR GAR.
19'4" X 23'8"

Width 52'-0"
Depth 65'-0"

Design by
Ahmann Design, Inc.

■ Radiant fanlights are echoed in oval windows, while the columns supporting the covered front porch create an interplay of vertical lines in the tall triple windows of this one-story home. High ceilings throughout and a flowing layout give a feeling of luxurious expansiveness. The bedrooms are arranged for privacy, separated by living areas. The breakfast room, open to the kitchen, and the master bedroom have views of the covered rear porch, while the family room is warmed by a fireplace and lit by tall windows.

Design B137

Square Footage: 1,849

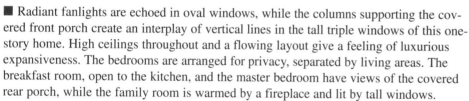

Design by
GREG MARQUIS
& ASSOCIATES

Width 66'-5"
Depth 60'-0"

Design T054

Square Footage: 2,935

MASTER BATH · **SITTING RM.** 11'-6" X 10'-0" · **DECK** · **KEEPING ROOM** 15'-3" X 15'-3" · VLT. CLG.

MASTER SUITE 18'-0" X 16'-0" · **W.I.C.** · **GREAT ROOM** 15'-6" X 17'-3" · **KITCHEN** 14'-0" X 13'-3" · **BREAKFAST** 14'-0" X 13'-0"

BEDROOM NO. 3 12'-0" X 12'-0" · **W.I.C.** · **W.I.C.** · DN. · **LAUNDRY** · **POWDER**

BATH · **BEDROOM NO. 2** 13'-3" X 11'-6" · **FOYER** · **DINING ROOM** 13'-3" X 18'-6"

STOOP · VLT. CLG. · **2-CAR GARAGE** 21'-6" X 21'-6"

Width 71'-0"
Depth 66'-0"

■ This spacious one-story easily accommodates a large family, providing all the luxuries and necessities for gracious living. For formal occasions, there is a grand dining room just off the entry foyer. It features a vaulted ceiling and is just across the hall from the gourmet kitchen. The great room offers a beautiful ceiling treatment and access to the rear deck. For more casual times, the breakfast nook and adjoining keeping room with a fireplace fill the bill. The master suite is spacious and filled with amenities that include sitting room, a walk-in closet and access to the rear deck. Two family bedrooms share a full bath. Each of these bedrooms has its own lavatory. This home is designed with a basement foundation.

Design by
DESIGN TRADITIONS

323

■ The favorite gathering place of this beautiful home is certain to be its sun-filled breakfast and keeping room complemented by the full kitchen. Thoughtful placement of the kitchen provides easy service to both formal and informal eating areas. A large living room enjoys two sets of double French doors that open to outdoor living areas. French doors open onto the spacious master suite and its elegant master bath. Here, a soothing whirlpool tub takes center-stage. Three other bedrooms, or two bedrooms and a study, are positioned at the opposite end of the house for privacy. Bedrooms 2 and 3 have their own walk-in closets. Please specify slab or crawlspace foundation when ordering.

Design 8076
Square Footage: 2,733

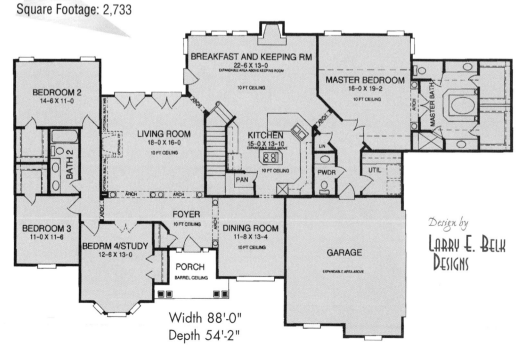

Width 88'-0"
Depth 54'-2"

Design by
LARRY E. BELK
DESIGNS

Design 3488

Square Footage: 1,944

L **D**

■ The Tudor facade of this comfortable home is just the beginning to a truly unique design. As you enter the foyer via a quaint covered porch, you are greeted by the sleeping zone on the right and the living zone on the left, beginning with the breakfast area which faces the front. A large kitchen connects to this room and includes a desk, a walk-in pantry, a spacious counter area with a snack bar that connects to the gathering room and entry to the formal dining room. The massive gathering room features a fireplace, a sloped ceiling and access to the backyard terrace. The master bedroom also accesses the terrace and revels in a master bath with a whirlpool tub, a separate shower, dual lavs and an individual vanity. A study at the front of the home could be converted into an additional bedroom.

Design by
HOME PLANNERS

Width 72'-8"
Depth 47'-4"

QUOTE ONE®
Cost to build? See page 434
to order complete cost estimate
to build this house in your area!

Design 3373
Square Footage: 1,376

L D

■ This charmingly compact plan is sure to please. The interior plan contains a large living room/dining room combination, a media room, a U-shaped kitchen with breakfast room and two bedrooms including a master bedroom with a walk-in closet. If the extra space is needed, the media room could serve as a third bedroom. Note the terrace to the rear of the plan off the dining room and the sloped ceilings throughout.

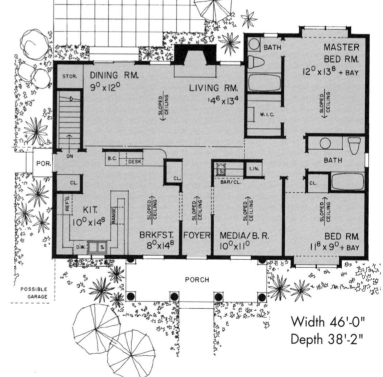

Width 46'-0"
Depth 38'-2"

Design by
Home Planners

Design by
HOMES FOR LIVING, INC.

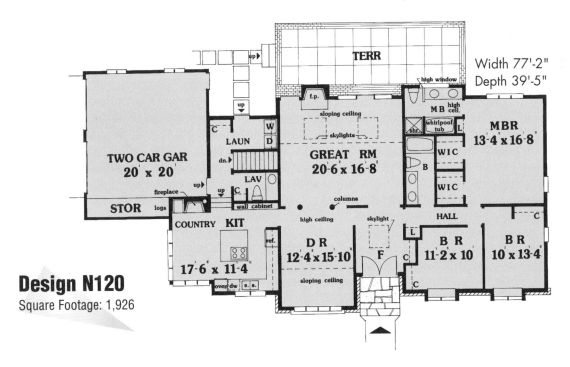

Width 77'-2"
Depth 39'-5"

TERR

f.p.

sloping ceiling

skylights

GREAT RM
20'-6 x 16'-8

MB high cell.

whirlpool tub

shr.

MBR
13'-4 x 16'-8

WIC

WIC

B

TWO CAR GAR
20 x 20

LAUN
W
D
dn.

LAV
up

C

fireplace

STOR   logs

wall cabinet

columns

high ceiling

skylight

HALL

C

COUNTRY   KIT
17'-6 x 11'-4

ref.

DR
12'-4 x 15'-10

sloping ceiling

F

L

C

C

B R
11'-2 x 10

B R
10 x 13'-4

oven dw   s. s.

Design N120
Square Footage: 1,926

■ A crisp, contemporary exterior combines with great interior elements to produce a home that accommodates today's active lifestyles. Inside, a skylit foyer opens onto a large great room that extends a hospitable welcome to all gatherings, whether cozy or lavish. The country kitchen, adjacent to the columned dining room, features an island counter, a multi-windowed eating area and its own fireplace with wood storage.

Bedrooms are contained in the right wing of the plan. Enjoying views of the backyard, the master bedroom features twin walk-in closets and a pampering bath with a whirlpool tub. Two family bedrooms—each with a bumped-out window—share a full bath. A laundry room and powder room complete this outstanding plan.

Design N104

Square Footage: 1,530

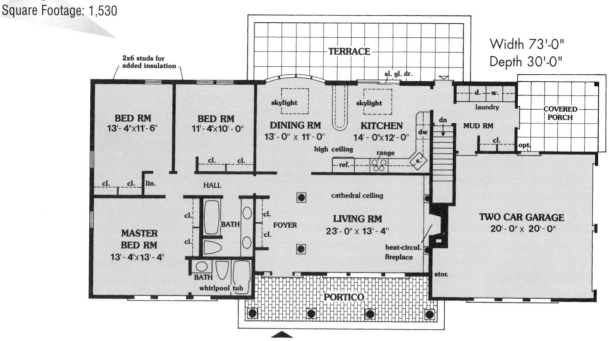

Width 73'-0"
Depth 30'-0"

2x6 studs for added insulation

BED RM
13'-4"x11'-6"

BED RM
11'-4"x10'-0"

DINING RM
13'-0" x 11'-0"

skylight

skylight

KITCHEN
14'-0"x12'-0"

sl. gl. dr.

d. w.
laundry

MUD RM

COVERED PORCH

high ceiling

range

dn

dw

cl.

opt.

ref.

s.

cl.

cl.

lin.

HALL

cl.   cl.

BATH

cl.

FOYER

cl.

cl.

cathedral ceiling

LIVING RM
23'-0" x 13'-4"

TWO CAR GARAGE
20'-0" x 20'-0"

MASTER BED RM
13'-4"x13'-4"

cl.

BATH

whirlpool tub

heat-circul. fireplace

stor.

PORTICO

TERRACE

■ Doric columns add drama to the portico and are repeated in the interior of this three-bedroom design. The cathedral living room features a heat circulating fireplace. The open dining room and kitchen have skylights, a large bow window and a sliding glass door onto the terrace. A covered porch at the back of the two-car garage leads into the house through the separate mud room and laundry.

Design by
Homes For Living, Inc.

Design F148

Square Footage: 1,732

DECK

MORNING ROOM
14'-0'' x 8'-0''
VAULTED CEILING

FP

LIVING ROOM
20'-0'' x 16'-0''
VAULTED CEILING

MASTER BATH

MASTER BEDROOM
12'-0'' x 16'-0''

KITCHEN
14'-0'' x 10'-0''

BATH

UP   DN

W D
W D

DINING ROOM
11'-0'' x 14'-0''

ENTRY FOYER

LINEN

WIC

TWO-CAR GARAGE
21'-0'' x 21'-0''

PORCH

BEDROOM
10'-0'' x 10'-0''

BEDROOM
10'-0'' x 10'-0''

Width 60'-0"
Depth 46'-4"

■ This cozy one-story plan features a volume roofline that allows vaulted ceilings in the living room, morning room and master bedroom. The dining room opens, through gracious columns, at the foyer and the living room. Special features in the living areas include a fireplace in the living room and doors leading to the rear yard from the living room and the morning room. The kitchen is designed with the gourmet cook in mind. It contains an island cooktop, over-the-sink window and loads of counter space. Family bedrooms share a hall bath and have box windows that would be perfect for window seats. The master suite is appointed with all the expected amenities including a garden whirlpool, separate shower and double sinks. A hall linen closet provides plenty of storage space, as does the two-car garage.

Design by
R.L. Pfotenhauer

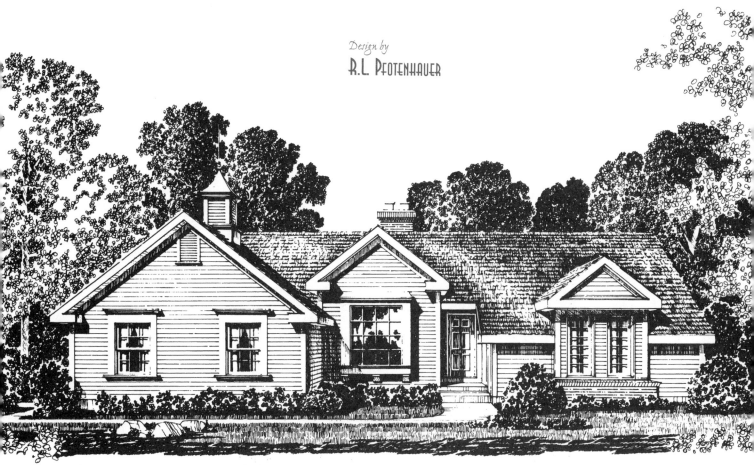

■ With clean, contemporary accents, the exterior of this home features circle and half-circle windows, sidelites at the entry and horizontal wood siding. The wide front porch is set up a few steps and leads to an entry with a small foyer opening to the great room. Here you'll enjoy a corner fireplace and access to a massive terrace with a built-in bench. The dinette also opens to this terrace and connects to the U-shaped kitchen. A more formal dining room is nearby and has its own private dining terrace. The master suite is situated on the left side of the foyer. Look for a box bay window and walk-in closet in the bedroom and separate shower and whirlpool tub in the bath. Family bedrooms are to the right of the foyer and share a full bath with double sinks. The two-car garage is to the rear of the plan and connects to the home via a convenient mud room. Please specify basement or slab foundation when ordering.

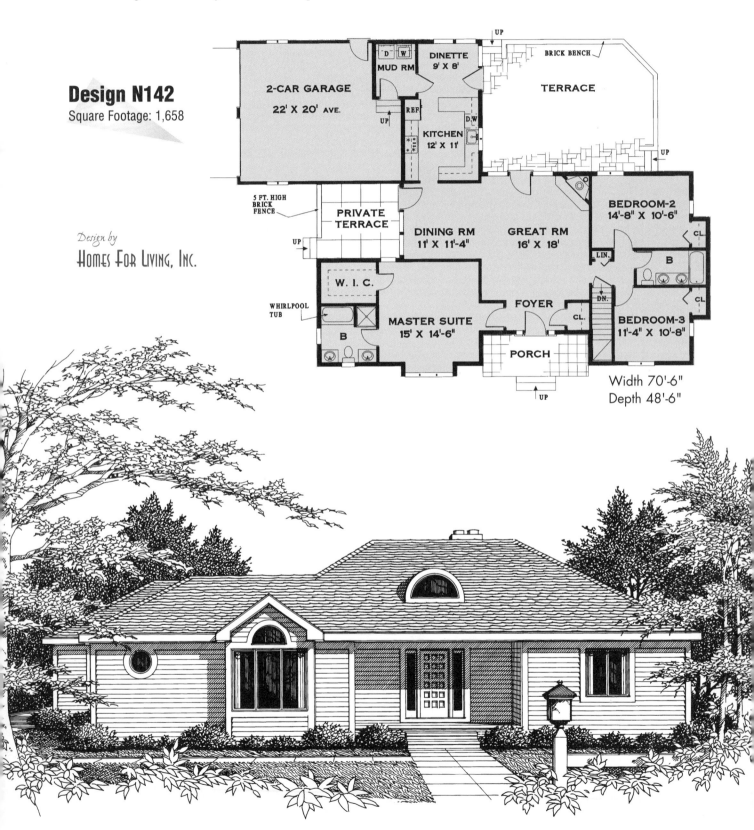

Design N142

Square Footage: 1,658

Design by
Homes For Living, Inc.

2-CAR GARAGE
22' X 20' AVE.

D W
MUD RM

DINETTE
9' X 8'

BRICK BENCH

TERRACE

UP

REF

KITCHEN
12' X 11'

D.W

5 FT. HIGH
BRICK
FENCE

PRIVATE
TERRACE

DINING RM
11' X 11'-4"

GREAT RM
16' X 18'

BEDROOM-2
14'-8" X 10'-6"

CL.

LIN.

B

CL.

UP

W. I. C.

WHIRLPOOL
TUB

B

MASTER SUITE
15' X 14'-6"

FOYER

CL.

DN.

BEDROOM-3
11'-4" X 10'-8"

PORCH

UP

Width 70'-6"
Depth 48'-6"

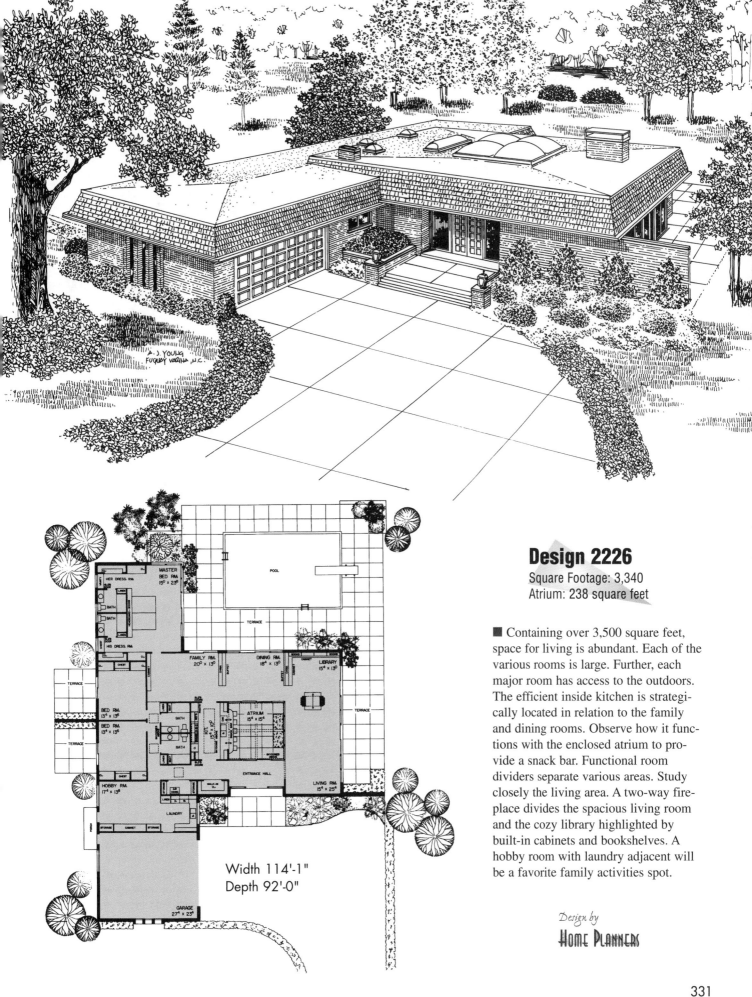

Design 2226

Square Footage: 3,340
Atrium: 238 square feet

■ Containing over 3,500 square feet, space for living is abundant. Each of the various rooms is large. Further, each major room has access to the outdoors. The efficient inside kitchen is strategically located in relation to the family and dining rooms. Observe how it functions with the enclosed atrium to provide a snack bar. Functional room dividers separate various areas. Study closely the living area. A two-way fireplace divides the spacious living room and the cozy library highlighted by built-in cabinets and bookshelves. A hobby room with laundry adjacent will be a favorite family activities spot.

Design by
HOME PLANNERS

Width 114'-1"
Depth 92'-0"

Design N108
Square Footage: 1,771

■ This ground-hugging ranch was designed for maximum use of space. The large family room with fireplace, and the kitchen and breakfast area are clustered around a covered porch with built-in barbecue. The formal living room and dining room are to the left of the large entry foyer and are separated by a partition. The fully equipped kitchen is easily accessible to the formal dining room and to the covered porch by sliding glass doors. The right wing holds a spacious master bedroom suite with plenty of closet space and separate bath. Two additional bedrooms share a hall bath with two sinks. Stairs to the full basement are located just off the combination mudroom/laundry area and rear service entrance.

Design by
Homes For Living, Inc.

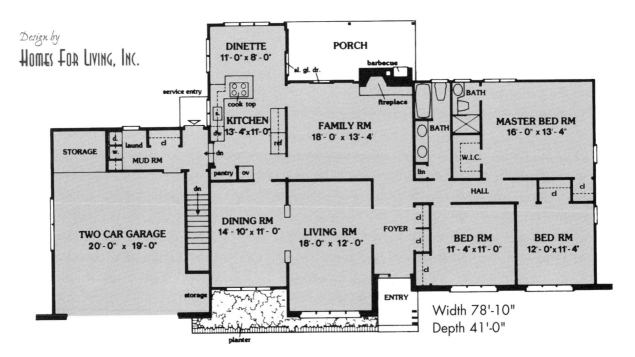

DINETTE
11'-0" x 8'-0"

PORCH

sl. gl. dr.

barbecue

service entry

cook top

fireplace

BATH

KITCHEN
13'-4" x 11'-0"

FAMILY RM
18'-0" x 13'-4"

BATH

MASTER BED RM
16'-0" x 13'-4"

STORAGE

d.
w.

laund

d

MUD RM

dw

ref

W.I.C.

dn

pantry   ov

lin

HALL

cl

cl

TWO CAR GARAGE
20'-0" x 19'-0"

dn

DINING RM
14'-10" x 11'-0"

LIVING RM
18'-0" x 12'-0"

FOYER

cl

cl

BED RM
11'-4" x 11'-0"

BED RM
12'-0" x 11'-4"

cl

storage

ENTRY

Width 78'-10"
Depth 41'-0"

planter

■ This eye-catching design with a flavor of the Spanish Southwest will be as interesting to live in as it will be to look at. The character of the exterior is set by the wide overhanging roof with its exposed beams; the massive arched pillars; the arching of the brick over the windows and the vertical siding that contrasts with the brick. The master bedroom/study suite is a focal point of the interior. However, if necessary, the study could become the fourth bedroom. The living and dining rooms are large and are separated by a massive raised-hearth fireplace. Don't miss the planter, the book niches and the china storage. The breakfast nook and the laundry flank the U-shaped kitchen. Notice the twin pantries, the built-in planning desk and the pass-through. A big lazy Susan is located to the right of the kitchen sink.

Design 2557
Square Footage: 1,955

Width 80'-8"
Depth 45'-8"

Design by
HOME PLANNERS

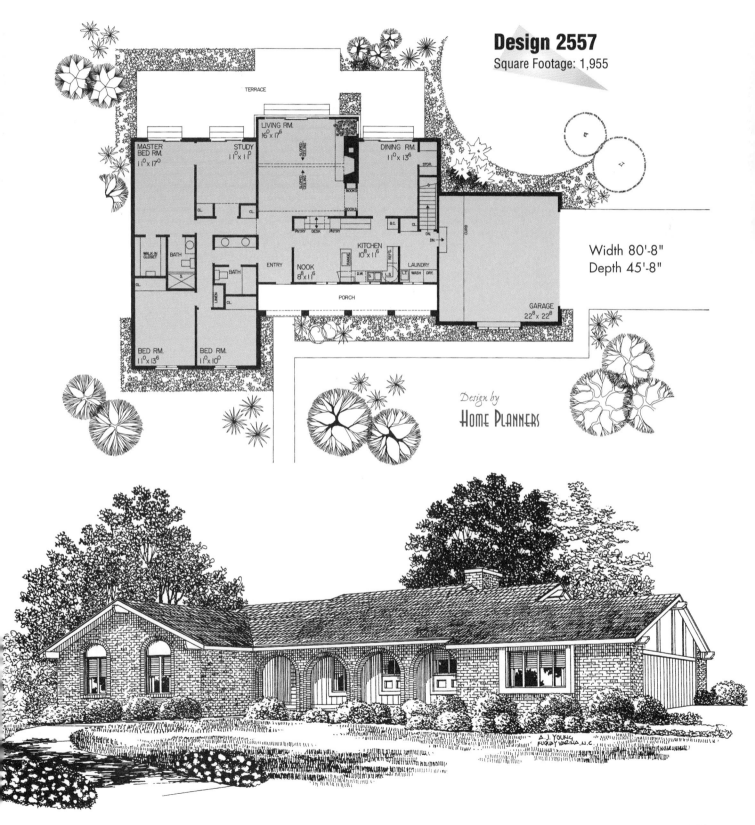

Design U151

Square Footage: 2,095

■ It's the little things that make a facade so special. In the case of this home, it's the multi-paned windows, combination of brick and siding and a columned front porch. There are more unique details on the interior. For instance, Bedroom 3 features a cathedral ceiling, the living room has a fireplace and built-ins, and the dining room has column accents and a tray ceiling. The living room, dining room and kitchen with attached nook all are placed so that casual and formal entertaining are made easy. Bedrooms are clustered to the left and include two family bedrooms and a large master suite with exquisite bath. A three-car garage holds additional space for storage or a workshop.

MBR.
11'-1 1/8" CEILING
14'0" X 16'0"

LIV.
11'-1 1/8" CEILING
17'10" X 20'0"

NK.
12'0" X 10'6"

KIT.
12'0" X 14'8"

BR.2
13'10" X 11'4"

LINEN

E.
11'-1 1/8" CEILING

SOFFIT

DIN.
11'-1 1/8" CEILING
11'7" X 13'0"

DOWN

BR.3
CATHEDRAL CEILING
12'0" X 11'4"

3 CAR GAR.
21'4" X 31'8"

CATHEDRAL CEILING

Width 67'-0"
Depth 58'-0"

Design by
Ahmann Design, Inc.

334

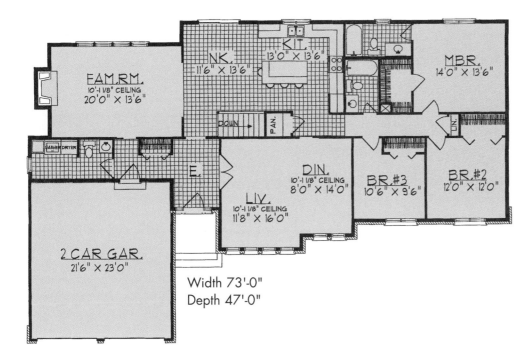

Design U224

Square Footage: 2,042

FAM. RM.
10'-1 1/8" CEILING
20'0" × 13'6"

NK.
11'6" × 13'6"

KIT.
13'0" × 13'6"

MBR.
14'0" × 13'6"

DIN.
10'-1 1/8" CEILING
8'0" × 14'0"

BR. #3
10'6" × 9'6"

BR. #2
12'0" × 12'0"

LIV.
10'-1 1/8" CEILING
11'8" × 16'0"

2 CAR GAR.
21'6" × 23'0"

Width 73'-0"
Depth 47'-0"

■ No compact ranch design, this stretched out one-story will fill your need for formal spaces, casual gathering rooms and spacious sleeping areas. The formal rooms are immediately to the right of the entry foyer and include an open living/dining room combination. Another door in the dining room takes you across a central hallway to the L-shaped island kitchen with walk-in pantry and attached nook. Sliding glass doors in the nook lead to outdoor spaces. The family room is just beyond the nook and has a fireplace and a full wall of windows overlooking the rear yard. The sleeping quarters include two family bedrooms with a shared bath and the master suite with private bath. The master bedroom is also graced by a huge walk-in closet. A two-car garage sits at the opposite end of the plan, near the laundry area and a half bath.

Design by
AHMANN DESIGN, INC.

FREILING

Design 3481B

Design 3481

Square Footage: 1,901

L

■ This pleasing one-story home bears all the livability of houses twice its size. A combined living and dining room offers elegance for entertaining; with two elevations to choose from, the living room can either support an octagonal bay or a bumped-out nook. The U-shaped kitchen finds easy access to the breakfast nook and rear family room; sliding glass doors lead from the family room to the backyard. The master bedroom has a quaint pot-shelf and a private bath with a spa tub, a double-bowl vanity, a walk-in closet and a compartmented toilet. With two additional family bedrooms—one may serve as a den if desired—and a hall bath with dual lavatories, this plan offers the best in accommodations. Both elevations come with the blueprint package.

QUOTE ONE®

Cost to build? See page 434 to order complete cost estimate to build this house in your area!

Design 3481A
Width 42'-0"
Depth 63'-6"

Design 3481B
Width 42'-4"
Depth 63'-10"

Design by
HOME PLANNERS

Design 3481A

Design 8611
Square Footage: 1,413

■ An angled side entry to this home allows for a majestic, arched window that dominates its facade. The interior, though small in square footage, holds an interesting and efficient floor plan. Because the breakfast room is placed to the front of the plan, it benefits from two large, multi-pane windows. The dining and family rooms form a single space enhanced by a volume ceiling and an optional fireplace, which is flanked by sets of optional double doors. Both the family room and master bedroom boast access to the covered patio. A volume ceiling further enhances the master bedroom, which also has a dressing area, walk-in closet and full bath. The plans include options for a family room with corner fireplace with French doors or a sliding glass door instead of a fireplace. The package includes plans for three different elevations.

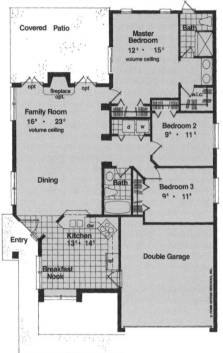

Width 38'-0"
Depth 58'-0"

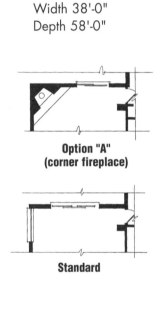

Option "A"
(corner fireplace)

Standard

Alternate Elevation

Design by
HOME DESIGN SERVICES

337

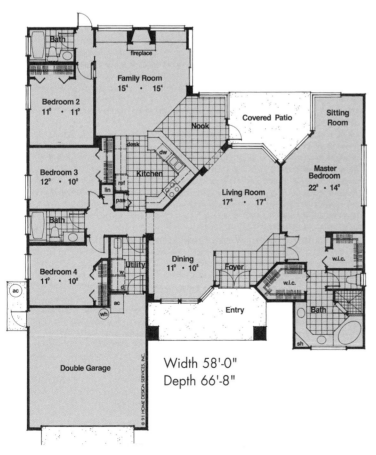

Width 58'-0"
Depth 66'-8"

Design 8641
Square Footage: 2,253

■ The functional use of angles in this house make for a plan which is exciting and full of large spaces. A formal living/dining area greets guests as they enter. The mitered glass throughout the rear of the home creates unlimited views to the outdoor living space and pool. Double doors lead to the master suite. A grand bath here boasts His and Hers walk-in closets, a wraparound vanity, a corner tub and a shower. The best feature of this home is the split-bedroom design. It contains a bedroom that has a private bath, perfect for guest or family member visits. The remaining two bedrooms share their own bath off the hall.

Design by
HOME DESIGN SERVICES

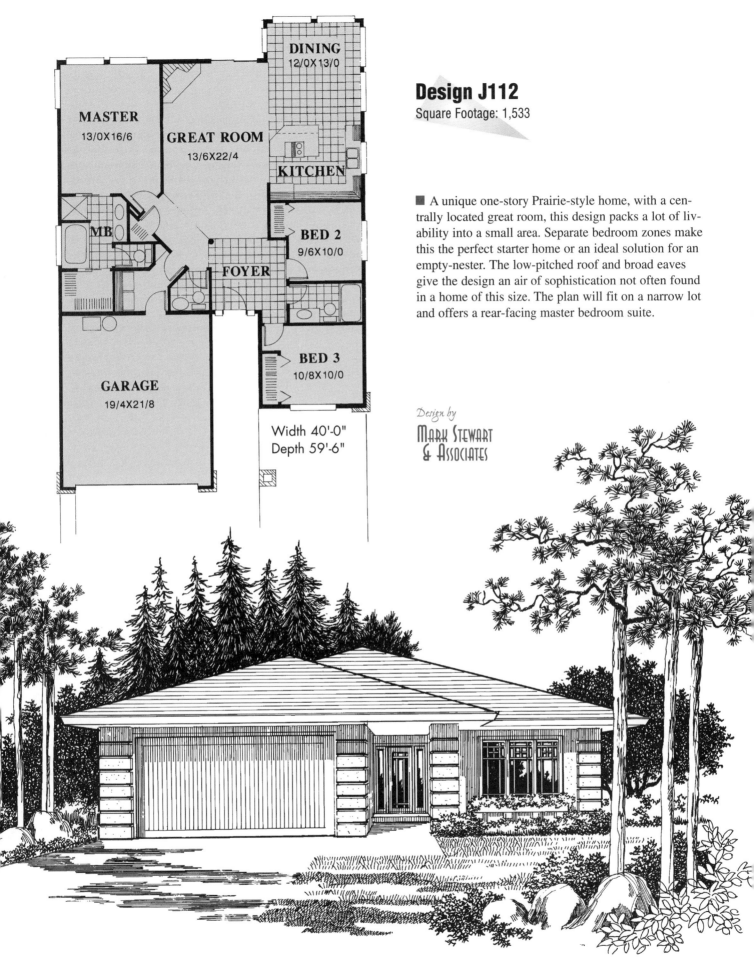

DINING
12/0X13/0

MASTER
13/0X16/6

GREAT ROOM
13/6X22/4

KITCHEN

MB

BED 2
9/6X10/0

FOYER

BED 3
10/8X10/0

GARAGE
19/4X21/8

Width 40'-0"
Depth 59'-6"

Design J112
Square Footage: 1,533

■ A unique one-story Prairie-style home, with a centrally located great room, this design packs a lot of livability into a small area. Separate bedroom zones make this the perfect starter home or an ideal solution for an empty-nester. The low-pitched roof and broad eaves give the design an air of sophistication not often found in a home of this size. The plan will fit on a narrow lot and offers a rear-facing master bedroom suite.

Design by
Mark Stewart
& Associates

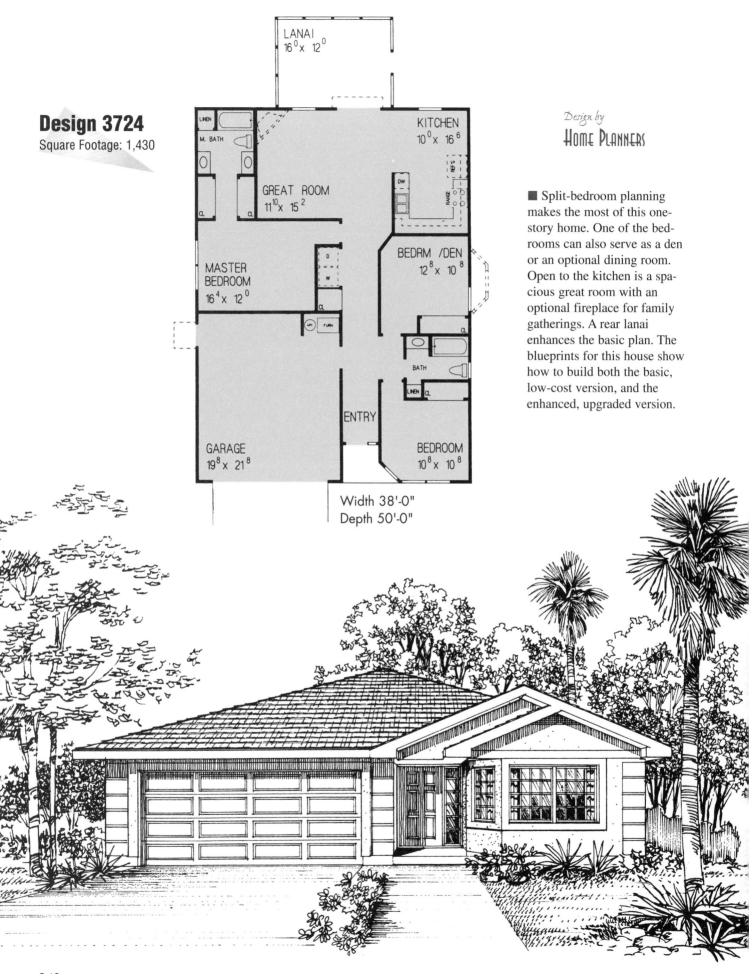

Design 3724
Square Footage: 1,430

LANAI
16⁰ x 12⁰

LINEN
M. BATH

KITCHEN
10⁰ x 16⁶

GREAT ROOM
11¹⁰ x 15²

CL
CL

DW
REF'G
RANGE

MASTER BEDROOM
16⁴ x 12⁰

D
W
CL

BEDRM /DEN
12⁸ x 10⁸

W.H.
FURN

BATH

LINEN
CL

ENTRY

GARAGE
19⁸ x 21⁸

BEDROOM
10⁸ x 10⁸

Width 38'-0"
Depth 50'-0"

Design by
HOME PLANNERS

■ Split-bedroom planning makes the most of this one-story home. One of the bedrooms can also serve as a den or an optional dining room. Open to the kitchen is a spacious great room with an optional fireplace for family gatherings. A rear lanai enhances the basic plan. The blueprints for this house show how to build both the basic, low-cost version, and the enhanced, upgraded version.

Design 3453

Square Footage: 1,442

L

■ This volume home impresses with its stately rooflines and stucco exterior. The front porch opens to an eleven-foot ceiling in the foyer. Straight ahead, an elegant living room serves as a prelude to the dramatic circular dining bay. Here, family and guests alike will revel in the fine views out the back of the house. The kitchen with a built-in snack bar offers an abundance of counter and cabinet space. The front bedroom, with its closet space and access to a full hall bath, could easily convert to a media room. In the master bedroom you'll find a lengthy closet in addition to a stunning bath. Glass block provides privacy to the toilet and shower while the spa tub delights in its well-illuminated nook. Dual lavatories complete the amenities in this room.

Design by
HOME PLANNERS

MASTER BEDRM 13°×14°

LIVING RM. 14°×15°

DINING RM. 11⁴×13°

KITCHEN 9⁴×14⁴

MASTER BATH

FOYER

BEDRM 11⁶×11²

GARAGE 18⁴×18⁸

Width 40'-0"
Depth 57'-4"

QUOTE ONE®
Cost to build? See page 434
to order complete cost estimate
to build this house in your area!

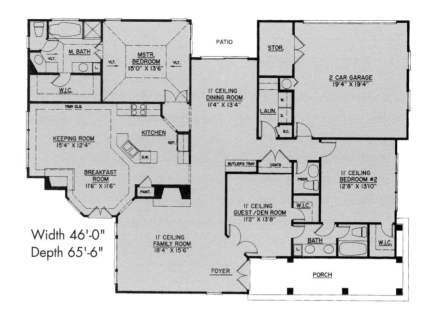

Design S124

Square Footage: 2,006

Design by
ARCHIVAL DESIGNS

Width 46'-0"
Depth 65'-6"

■ This home has elegant European styling and a most contemporary floor plan. Stuccoed walls and corner quoins accent the exterior, as does the narrow, columned porch leading to an offset entry. The entry opens directly into the huge family room, or go to the right through double doors to the guest room or den. The dining room is at the center of the plan and has sliding glass doors that open to a private patio. Casual dining takes place in the breakfast room—octagonal in shape and opening to the side yard. The keeping room is attached and both are joined by a lovely tray ceiling. The kitchen has an island sink that separates it from these two casual spaces. A private foyer introduces the master suite. The bedroom has a tray ceiling and patio access. The bath features a walk-in closet, double sinks and separate shower and tub. One additional bedroom is located on the opposite side of the plan and shares a bath with the guest room/den.

Design P146

Square Footage: 2,051

Width 56'-0"
Depth 60'-6"

■ A blend of contemporary layout with traditional themes places a formal dining room and living room to either side of the foyer, while still allowing an open view to the family room. The efficient kitchen has a welcome walk-in pantry and a serving bar facing both the vaulted breakfast room and the family room. The master suite is located on the opposite side of the plan from the family bedrooms and features twin walk-in closets and a lush bath. Two family bedrooms, both with ample closet space, and a hall bath complete this plan. A two-car garage offers more storage space. Please specify basement, crawlspace or slab foundation when ordering.

Design by

Frank Betz
Associates, Inc.

Design U129
Square Footage: 1,947

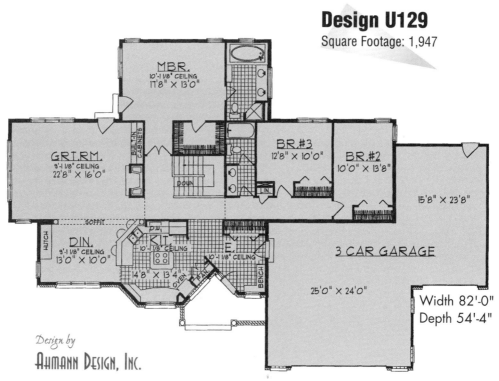

MBR.
10'-1 1/8" CEILING
17'8" × 13'0"

GRT.RM.
9'-1 1/8" CEILING
22'8" × 16'0"

BUILT-IN CABINETS

DOWN

BR.#3
12'8" × 10'0"

BR.#2
10'0" × 13'8"

15'8" × 23'8"

GOFFIT

HUTCH

DIN.
9'-1 1/8" CEILING
13'0" × 10'0"

KIT.
10'-1 1/8" CEILING

14'8" × 13'4"

OVEN

E.
10'-1 1/8" CEILING

BENCH

3 CAR GARAGE

25'0" × 24'0"

Width 82'-0"
Depth 54'-4"

Design by
Ahmann Design, Inc.

■ This contemporary home is not the standard one-story plan—it is filled with unusual features that make it a real standout. For instance, the columned entry is angled for interest and opens to a tiled foyer with built-in bench, coat closet and garage access. The kitchen is octagonal in shape and has an island cooktop and snack-bar counter to the dining room. Hutch space here makes this room convenient and attractive.

The great room also has built-ins and a warming hearth for chilly evenings. The master bedroom opens through double doors in the central hall. A walk-in closet and bath with corner shower, spa tub and double sinks grace this suite. Two family bedrooms are found at the other end of the hall and share a full bath. A three-car garage includes space for recreational vehicles.

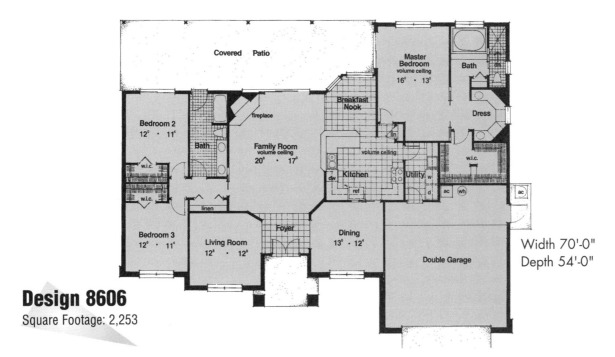

Covered Patio

Master Bedroom
volume ceiling
16⁸ · 13⁰

Bath

Breakfast Nook

Dress

Bedroom 2
12⁰ · 11⁴

Bath

fireplace

Family Room
volume ceiling
20⁸ · 17⁰

volume ceiling

w.i.c.

w.i.c.

Kitchen

Utility

w.i.c.

w.i.c.

dw

ref

ac

w

wh

ac

d

linen

Bedroom 3
12⁰ · 11⁴

Living Room
12⁸ · 12⁰

Foyer

Dining
13⁰ · 12⁴

Double Garage

Width 70'-0"
Depth 54'-0"

Design 8606
Square Footage: 2,253

■ Brick detailing makes an elegant statement in this one-story contemporary; large multi-pane windows add a touch of distinction. Past the front-facing living room and tiled foyer, the large family room is provided extra dimension by its high volume ceiling and corner fireplace. A tiled breakfast nook and kitchen are separated by a convenient eating bar; nearby is the formal dining room. The master bedroom features a walk-in closet, a U-shaped dressing area with double vanity and a full bath. Two additional large bedrooms, each with a walk-in closet, share a full bath with double vanity.

Design by
HOME DESIGN SERVICES

© HOME DESIGN SERVICES, INC.

Design 8646

Square Footage: 2,352

■ An array of varied, arched windows sets off this
striking Italianate home. Double doors reveal the foyer,
which announces the living room accented by a wet bar,
niche and patio access. The coffered dining room combines with the living room to create a perfect space for
formal entertaining. An arched entry to the informal living area presents a bayed breakfast nook and adjoining
family room warmed by a fireplace. A pass-through
kitchen comes with a deep pantry and informal eating
bar. Double doors open to the coffered master bedroom.
Its sumptuous bath has two walk-in closets, a dual vanity and spa tub. Arched entries lead to three additional
bedrooms: two share a full bath and the third boasts a
private bath with yard access. Blueprints include an
alternate elevation at no extra charge.

Width 61'-8"
Depth 64'-8"

Design by
HOME DESIGN SERVICES

Alternate Elevation

346

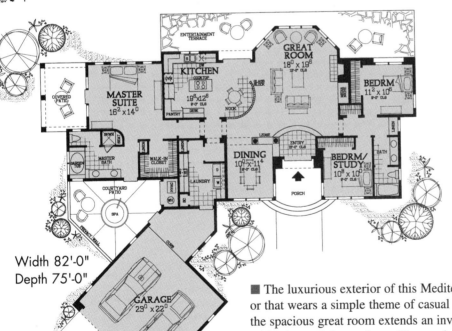

Design 3667
Square Footage: 2,085

Design by

HOME PLANNERS

Quote One®

Cost to build? See page 434
to order complete cost estimate
to build this house in your area!

Width 82'-0"
Depth 75'-0"

■ The luxurious exterior of this Mediterranean dream home conceals an interior that wears a simple theme of casual comfort. From the stylish tiled entry, the spacious great room extends an invitation to relax with a fireplace and wide views of the outdoors. The nearby gourmet kitchen serves all occasions, grand and cozy, and leads through an eating nook outdoors to the entertainment terrace. A rambling master suite enjoys its own wing, with a private covered porch and a courtyard patio. On the opposite side of the plan, two family bedrooms—or one could be a study—share a full bath with two vanities. Service access from the two-car garage is available through the utility room and the courtyard patio.

Design 8663
Square Footage: 2,597

Width 96'-6"
Depth 50'-0"

■ The angles in this home create unlimited views and spaces that appear larger. Majestic columns of brick add warmth to a striking elevation. Inside, the foyer commands special perspective on living areas including the living room, dining room and the den. The island kitchen services the breakfast nook and the family room. A large pantry provides ample space for food storage. In the master bedroom suite, mitered glass and a private bath set the tone for simple luxury. Two secondary bedrooms share privacy and quiet at the front of the house. The den may also convert to a fourth bedroom, if desired.

Design by
HOME DESIGN SERVICES

Design 8604

Square Footage: 2,153

Bedroom 3
volume ceiling
10⁴ · 10⁴

Bedroom 4
volume ceiling
11⁴ · 10⁴

Bath

Bedroom 2
volume ceiling
12⁴ · 10⁴

w d
Utility

lin

Breakfast
volume ceiling

Porch

fireplace

Family Room
volume ceiling
21⁰ · 14⁰

dw

Kitchen

ref

Living Room
volume ceiling
17⁴ · 13⁰

Master
Bedroom
volume ceiling
17⁰ · 13⁴

lin

ac wh l.t.

w.i.c.

Double Garage

Dining
16⁶ · 12⁰

Foyer

Bath

Entry

Width 61'-0"
Depth 67'-8"

Design by
HOME DESIGN SERVICES

■ Sophistication and elegance are the bywords of this four-bedroom, two bath home. Among the many special features are a dramatic foyer, column encircled dining room and twelve-foot ceilings. The kitchen is a true gourmet's delight and opens to a light-filled breakfast nook. The family room is enhanced by a barrel ceiling and a fireplace. Secondary bedrooms are separated from the master suite. Each contains a spacious closet; two contain corner windows. The master suite is luxurious with a walk-in closet, sliding glass doors to the rear porch, and bath with double sink and step-up tub.

Design K121
Square Footage: 1,452

■ A decorative low wall extends from the covered entry porch of this three-bedroom, two-bath Western contemporary design with attached garage. A second low wall extends horizontally from the corner of the living room which is to the left of the entry and features a large bay window. The family room with fireplace flows into the dining room and kitchen. Two bedrooms along the back of the house share a hall bath and the master bedroom has a separate bath and walk-in closet. Note the skylights in the hall and two baths.

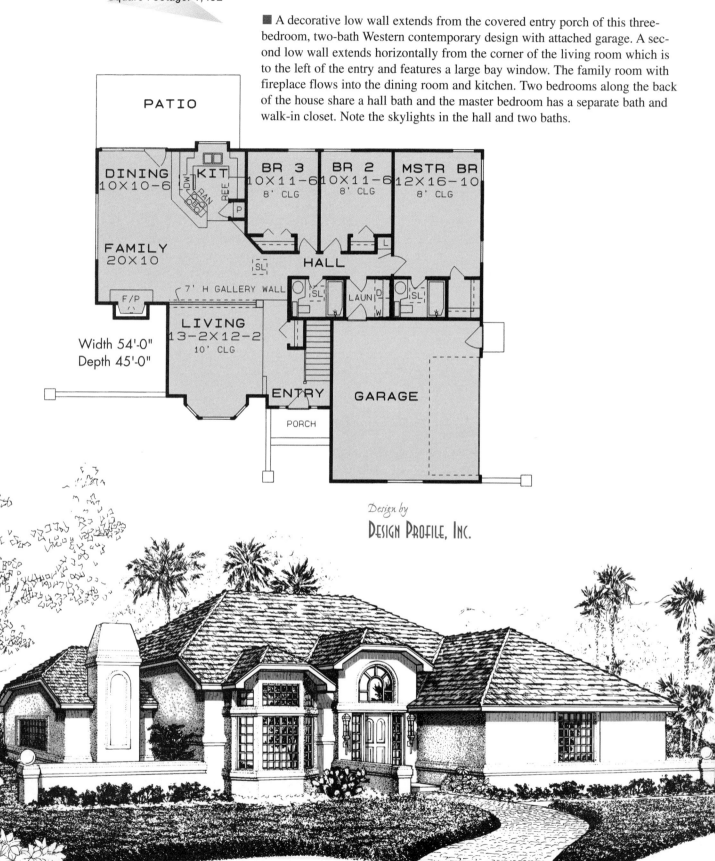

PATIO

DINING
10X10-6

KIT

BR 3
10X11-6
8' CLG

BR 2
10X11-6
8' CLG

MSTR BR
12X16-10
8' CLG

REF

DW
RAN

P

FAMILY
20X10

HALL

SL

7' H GALLERY WALL

SL

LAUN

SL

L

F/P

LIVING
13-2X12-2
10' CLG

Width 54'-0"
Depth 45'-0"

ENTRY

GARAGE

PORCH

Design by
DESIGN PROFILE, INC.

Design 8664

Square Footage: 2,660

■ This charming one-story home will accommodate families of all sizes. The entry opens onto the living room and glass doors leading to the covered patio. The kitchen leads to a family room with a fireplace and shelves that create a relaxed setting. A massive master suite provides a sitting room and an expansive master bath featuring a walk-in closet and His and Hers vanities. Two secondary bedrooms share a full bath.

Width 66'-4"
Depth 74'-4"

Design by
HOME DESIGN SERVICES

Design 8609

Square Footage: 2,359

Bedroom 2 11⁶ · 10⁶

Bedroom 3 12⁴ · 11⁶

Bath

shelf   fireplace   shelf

Utility   w.i.c.

d   w

Nook 10⁶ · 9⁸

Porch

Master Bedroom 15⁷ · 14⁶

Dining 12⁸ · 11⁶

dw

Kitchen

ref   pan

Family Room 18⁴ · 15⁰

Bedroom 4 14⁴ · 11⁶

ac   wh

w.i.c.   w.i.c.

Bath

Living Room 17⁴ · 13⁰

Foyer

Double Garage

Width 64'-8"
Depth 60'-8"

■ Abundant room for family gatherings—as well as privacy—makes this sizable one-story home especially attractive. A tall, half-circle window provides drama in the tiled foyer. Beyond the front-facing living room, the oversized family room creates a welcoming environment with a fireplace and built-in bookshelves. A vaulted master bedroom includes two walk-in closets and an adjoining garden patio. Three additional bedrooms share a tiled bath with double vanity. The bath opens to the rear patio. The plans include details for a choice of two elevations.

Design by
Home Design Services

R.BRADSHAW

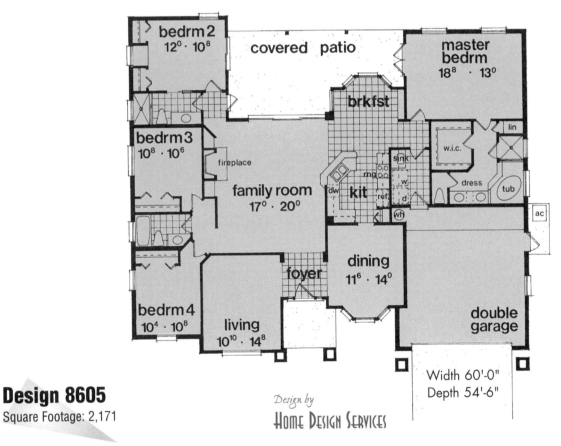

Design 8605
Square Footage: 2,171

Design by
HOME DESIGN SERVICES

■ This four-bedroom, three-bath home is designed to minimize wasted space, such as hallways. There are loads of living options, especially in the placement of the secondary bedrooms. Bedroom 2 can be a much needed mother-in-law room, with semi-private bath that doubles as a pool bath for outdoor living. The classic family room/nook area and kitchen work well together for convenient living. The secluded living room and bay windowed dining room are a special bonus for formal entertaining. The master suite provides the best of everything from twin vanities to handy linen storage. There's also a huge walk-in closet and private commode. The interior architecture of this home boasts soaring vaulted ceilings throughout.

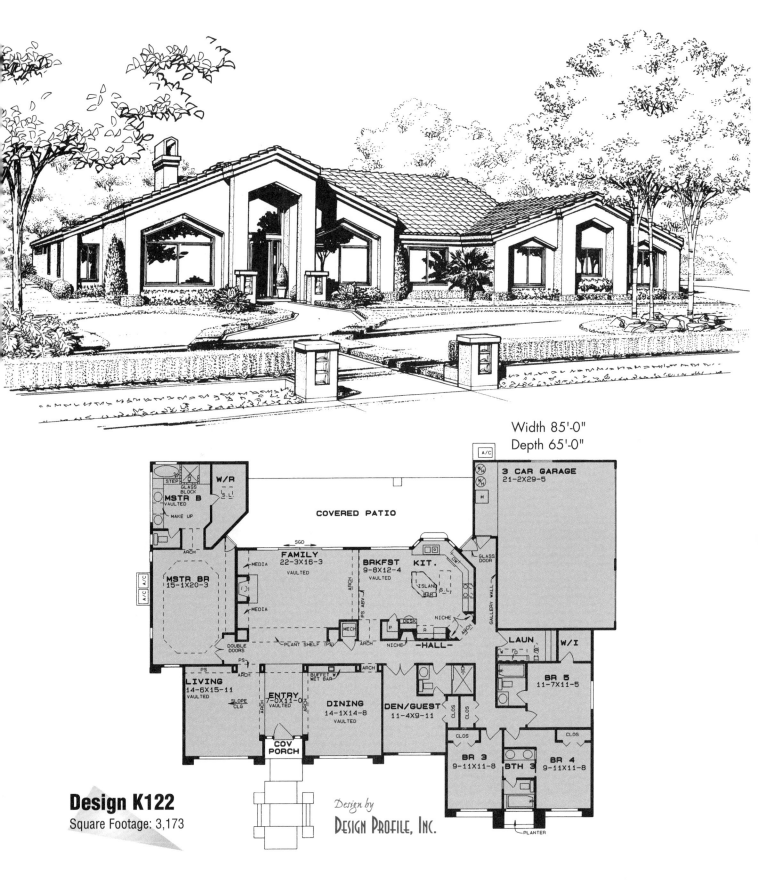

Width 85'-0"
Depth 65'-0"

Design K122
Square Footage: 3,173

Design by
DESIGN PROFILE, INC.

■ An expansive modern exterior provides all the amenities and a four- or five-bedroom floor plan. The drama continues beyond the soaring entry with columned, open living areas. The master suite has access to the covered patio. Four additional bedrooms or three-plus-den, and three baths serve family and guests. Arched passageways, vaulted ceilings, plant shelves and helpful built-ins are found throughout this fine home. A three-car garage sits to the right of the plan.

Design K124

Square Footage: 4,177

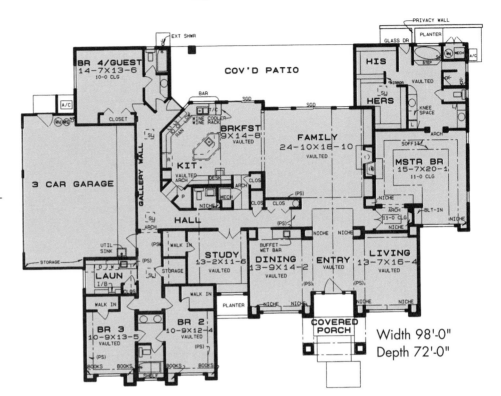

■ Walls of windows and lots of built-ins in every area enhance this expansive floor plan with as many as five bedrooms (or four, plus study) and 3½ baths. An L-shaped gallery connects the beautifully designed living areas. The master suite is luxuriously appointed and is secluded from the rest of the house and reached through a graceful arch. Note the four skylights and plant shelves, along with the vaulted ceilings in many rooms.

Design by
DESIGN PROFILE, INC.

Width 98'-0"
Depth 72'-0"

355

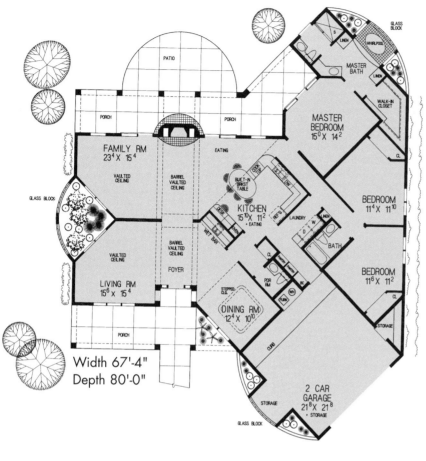

Design 3408

Square Footage: 2,388

L

■ Interesting angles make for interesting rooms. The sleeping zone features two large bedrooms with unique shapes and a master suite with spectacular bath. A laundry placed nearby is both convenient and economical, located adjacent to a full bath. The central kitchen offers a desk and built-in breakfast table. Meals can also be enjoyed in the adjacent eating area, formal dining room with stepped ceiling, or outside on the rear patio. A planter and glass block wall separate the living room and family room, which is warmed by a fireplace.

Width 67'-4"
Depth 80'-0"

Design by
HOME PLANNERS

QUOTE ONE®

Cost to build? See page 434
to order complete cost estimate
to build this house in your area!

Design 8636

Square Footage: 2,010

Bedroom 2
14⁰ · 10⁰

Covered Patio

Bath

shelf

Bedroom 3
11⁰ · 10⁴

Family Room
16⁶ · 14¹⁰

fireplace

shelf

Breakfast

Kitchen

dw

ref

Master Bedroom
15⁶ · 13⁴

w.i.c.

Bath

Utility

ac

ac

w/h

Bedroom 4
11⁰ · 10⁴

Living Room
11⁰ · 10²

Foyer

Dining
11⁰ · 10²

Double Garage

Entry

Width 62'-8"
Depth 56'-0"

■ Not only does this house look exciting from the outside with its contemporary use of glass, but upon entering this home, the excitement continues. The classic split living room and dining room sets this house apart from the rest. The family room, breakfast nook and kitchen all share the views to the rear yard. The efficient placement of the bedrooms creates privacy for family members. The master suite is ample, with a wonderful bath featuring a lounging tub, shower, private toilet room, double vanities and generous walk-in closet. Plans for this home include a choice of two exterior elevations.

Design by
Home Design Services

Alternate Elevation

357

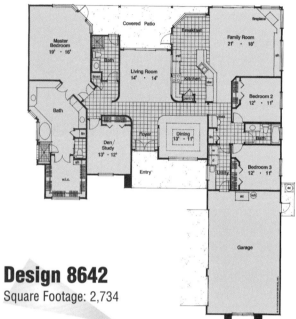

Design 8642
Square Footage: 2,734

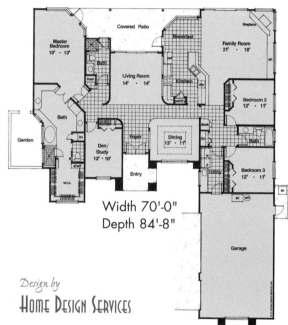

Width 70'-0"
Depth 84'-8"

Design by
HOME DESIGN SERVICES

■ This home has an award-winning, sophisticated design. From the moment you enter, you know you are in a well-planned home. Besides a formal living area with covered patio nearby and formal dining area to the front, there is a family room with a corner fireplace. It connects directly to the breakfast room and kitchen. The bedrooms are split, with family bedrooms to the right of the plan and the master suite to the left. The master bath has an angled entry, walk-in closet and spa tub. Blueprints for this home come with two different elevations and a large and small floor plan.

Alternate Elevation

Design 8613

Square Footage: 1,872

Alternate Elevation

Master Bed Rm.
13⁰·17⁰
vault or 10' flat

Covered Patio

Breakfast
11⁸·8⁴

Kitchen

Bath

Family Rm.
14⁸·23⁰
vault or 10' flat

Dining Rm.
vault or 10' flat

Bed Rm. 2
13¹⁰·9⁶
vault or 10' flat

36" Pre-Fab Fireplace

Living
vault or 10' flat

Plant Shelf Abv.

Ba.

Foyer

wh | A/C | W | D

Bed Rm. 3
13¹⁰·11⁰
vault or 10' flat

Entry

Double Garage

Width 40'-0"
Depth 66'-8"

■ Vaulted ceilings throughout this home suggest the innovative touches that add interest in a one-story plan. Sidelight and overhead windows brighten a foyer that opens to the family room and living room. A plant shelf spans the entry into the living room, which is united with the dining room under a high ceiling. A vaulted ceiling also augments the family room. Notice the two-way fireplace and access to a covered patio here. The kitchen is convenient to the dining room and to a bayed breakfast nook. The master bedroom also has a bay window plus a full bath with oversized shower. Two additional bedrooms share a full bath. Plans include two different elevation choices!

Design by
HOME DESIGN SERVICES

© HOME DESIGN SERVICES, INC.

Design 8631

Square Footage: 1,697

■ Great great-room design! This exciting plan features a main gathering area bordered on the left by the formal dining area with a decorative built-in wall for a custom touch. The unobstructed view of the rear outdoor space is maximized from the gathering space as well as the kitchen and breakfast room. The placement of secondary bedrooms toward the front of the home gives a sense of privacy. The master suite compares favorably to much larger homes, boasting a huge walk-in shower, private toilet and oversized vanity and closet. Space for a media center and fireplace are also allowed for in the design. The blueprints for this design include options for two different exteriors.

Design by
Home Design Services

Width 45'-0"
Depth 68'-4"

Alternate Elevation

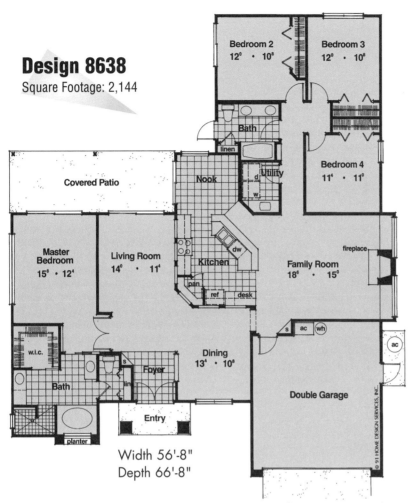

Design 8638
Square Footage: 2,144

Covered Patio

Bedroom 2
12⁰ • 10⁸

Bedroom 3
12⁰ • 10⁸

Bath

linen

Nook

Utility

Bedroom 4
11⁴ • 11⁰

Master Bedroom
15⁸ • 12⁴

Living Room
14⁰ • 11⁴

Kitchen

dw

fireplace

Family Room
18⁸ • 15⁰

pan

ref   desk

w.i.c.

Bath

s   ac   wh

ac

Foyer

lin

Dining
13⁴ • 10⁸

Double Garage

Entry

planter

Width 56'-8"
Depth 66'-8"

■ This is the ultimate family house—a unique arrangement of rooms creates spaces which are functional and individual. The entry opens to the formal living and dining room areas with a magnificent view of the outdoor living space and yard. Double doors lead to the master suite located in its very own private wing of the home for perfect privacy and quiet. The His and Hers sinks, soaking tub and step-down shower add luxury. The private toilet room and huge walk-in closet add practicality. Beyond the formal and master wing is the family space with the kitchen at its hub. The bedroom wing has great amenities for the kids—outdoor access in the shared bath and a nearby laundry room.

Design by
HOME DESIGN SERVICES

Design 8607

Square Footage: 2,271

■ The family room, with volume ceiling, serves as a hub in this spacious home. It blends with a large covered patio to form an expansive, informal space. Special amenities here include a fireplace and sliding glass doors. The high ceiling extends to the kitchen and beyond to the bayed breakfast nook. A pass-through counter permits easy access between the kitchen and family room. The master bedroom is highlighted by a volume ceiling and patio access. A tiled shower and step-up tub in the master bath overlook the solarium. Three additional bedrooms, two flanking a tiled bath, are found beyond the living room. A third bedroom is located off the family room and features its own private bath.

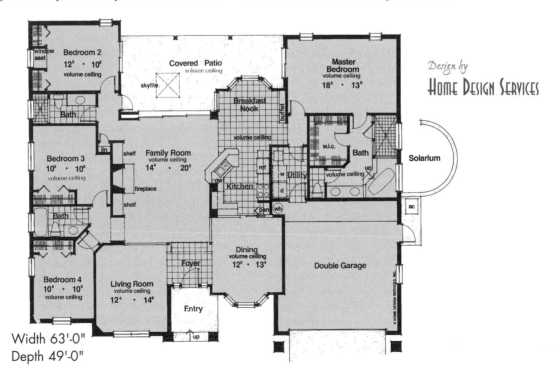

Width 63'-0"
Depth 49'-0"

Design 8627
Square Footage: 3,743

Width 86'-8"
Depth 95'-0"

■ A central foyer gives way to an expansive design. Straight ahead, the living room features French doors set in a bay area. To the left, columns and a coffered ceiling off-set the exquisite formal dining room. A fireplace warms the large family room, which adjoins the breakfast nook. Traffic flows easily through the ample kitchen with cook-top island and pass-through to the patio. The master bedroom features a tray ceiling, walk-in closet and sumptuous bath with shower and step-up tub overlooking a private garden. Two bedrooms are joined by an optional media room and optional study, which could bring the count up to five bedrooms if necessary.

Design by
Home Design Services

© 91 HOME DESIGN SERVICES, INC.

Design 7404

Square Footage: 2,564

■ The dramatic floor design of this contemporary home will make you the envy of the neighborhood. The angled entry directs you to a quiet corner den or to a uniquely designed dining room. The massive central great room features interesting ceiling detail, as well as a corner fireplace. The island kitchen includes a breakfast nook with French doors leading to the rear yard. The family bedrooms are separated by a full bath with dual basins, while the master bedroom pampers its host with a large walk-in closet, a corner whirlpool tub and a separate shower.

Design by

**ALAN MASCORD
DESIGN ASSOCIATES, INC.**

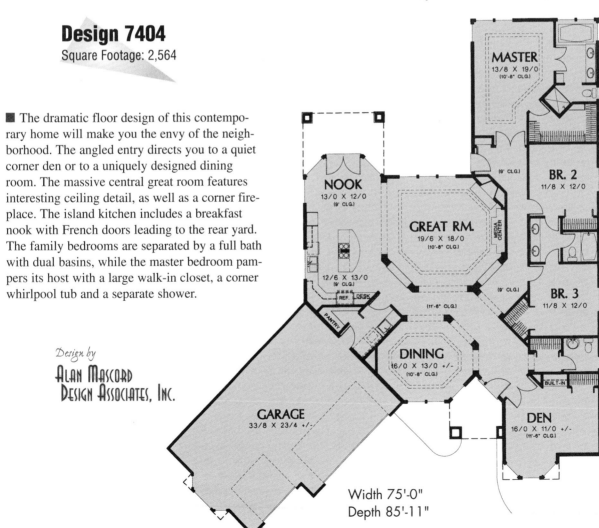

MASTER
13/8 X 19/0
(10'-8" CLG.)

BR. 2
11/8 X 12/0

NOOK
13/0 X 12/0
(9' CLG.)

GREAT RM.
19/6 X 18/0
(10'-8" CLG.)

MEDIA CENTER

12/6 X 13/0
(9' CLG.)

BR. 3
11/8 X 12/0

REF. DESK

PANTRY

DINING
16/0 X 13/0 +/-
(10'-8" CLG.)

BUILT-IN

GARAGE
33/8 X 23/4 +/-

DEN
16/0 X 11/0 +/-
(11'-6" CLG.)

Width 75'-0"
Depth 85'-11"

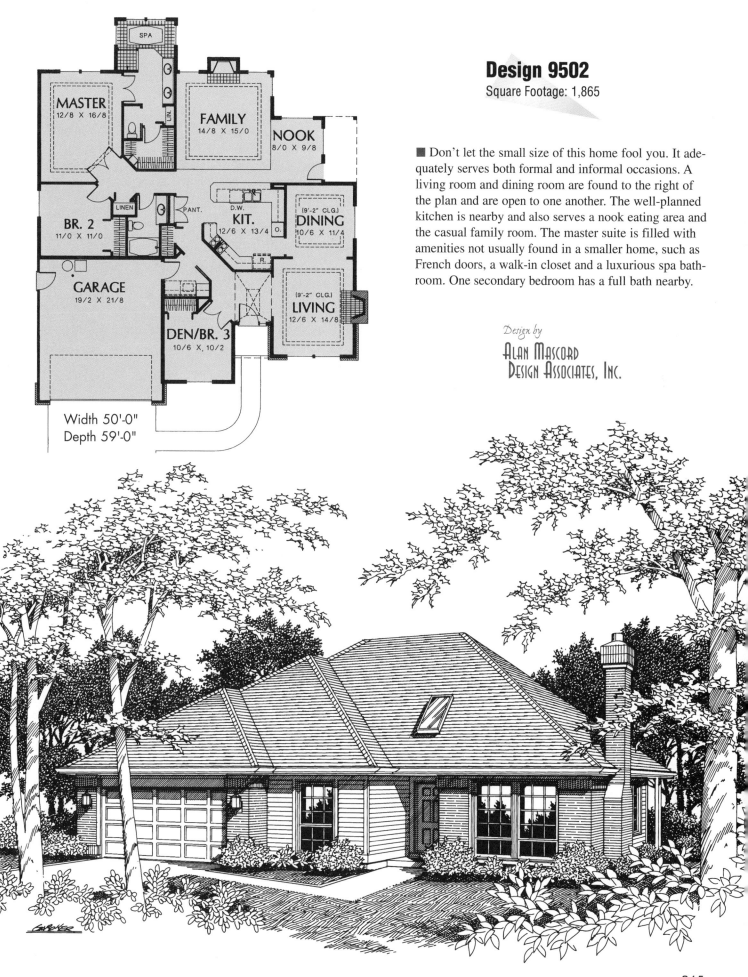

Design 9502

Square Footage: 1,865

MASTER
12/8 X 16/8

SPA

FAMILY
14/8 X 15/0

NOOK
8/0 X 9/8

BR. 2
11/0 X 11/0

LINEN

PANT.

D.W.

KIT.
12/6 X 13/4

O.

DINING
10/6 X 11/4
(9'-2" CLG.)

R.

GARAGE
19/2 X 21/8

LIVING
12/6 X 14/8
(9'-2" CLG.)

DEN/BR. 3
10/6 X 10/2

Width 50'-0"
Depth 59'-0"

■ Don't let the small size of this home fool you. It adequately serves both formal and informal occasions. A living room and dining room are found to the right of the plan and are open to one another. The well-planned kitchen is nearby and also serves a nook eating area and the casual family room. The master suite is filled with amenities not usually found in a smaller home, such as French doors, a walk-in closet and a luxurious spa bathroom. One secondary bedroom has a full bath nearby.

Design by
ALAN MASCORD
DESIGN ASSOCIATES, INC.

365

Design U257

Square Footage: 1,868

■ A large living area dominates the center of this contemporary-flavored traditional one-story. It opens off of a vaulted foyer through a doorway with soffit. At one end is a warming hearth; at the other, another soffitted opening to the dining area and island kitchen. The dining area is enhanced by a bay window with sliding glass doors to the outdoors. There is a large laundry room with a closet and space for a washer and dryer and a freezer. It connects to the two-car garage with storage space. The bedrooms are at the opposite end of the plan and include two family bedrooms and a master suite. Accents in the master suite: a sliding glass door to the rear yard, corner shower, whirlpool tub, double sinks and a large walk-in closet.

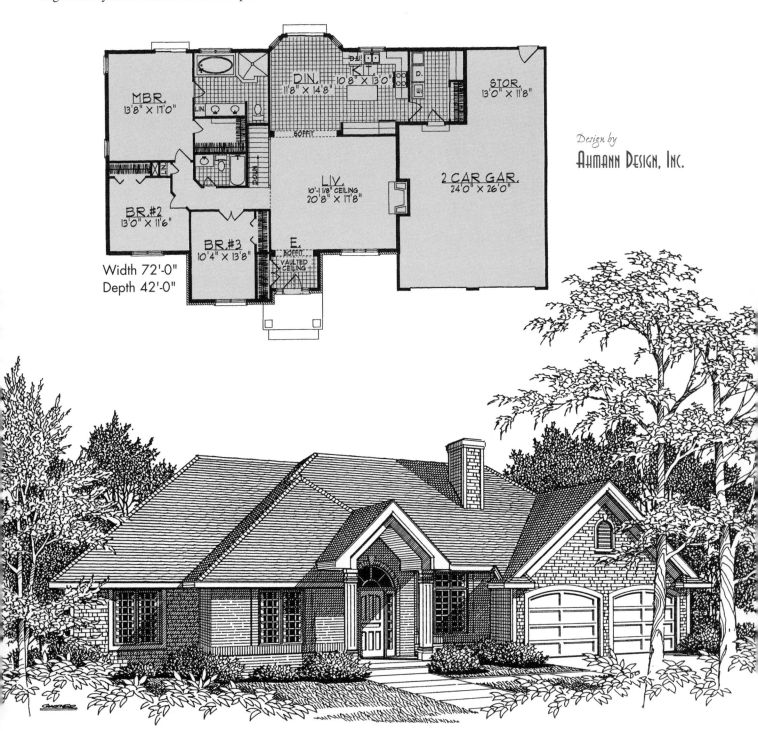

■ In this plan, a large tiled area extends from the entry foyer through to the breakfast nook and island kitchen. It unites the areas and helps to separate them from the massive great room. Look for a warming fireplace and abundant windows in this grand living area. The dining room is distinguished by soffits and columns, but is near to the kitchen for convenience. The master bedroom is exquisite with a tray-ceiling accent, walk-in closet and bath with double sinks, spa tub and separate shower. Two family bedrooms share the use of a full bath with double sinks. One of these bedrooms has a walk-in closet. A two-car garage sits to the front of the plan, but offers a side entry that does not detract from the beauty of the facade.

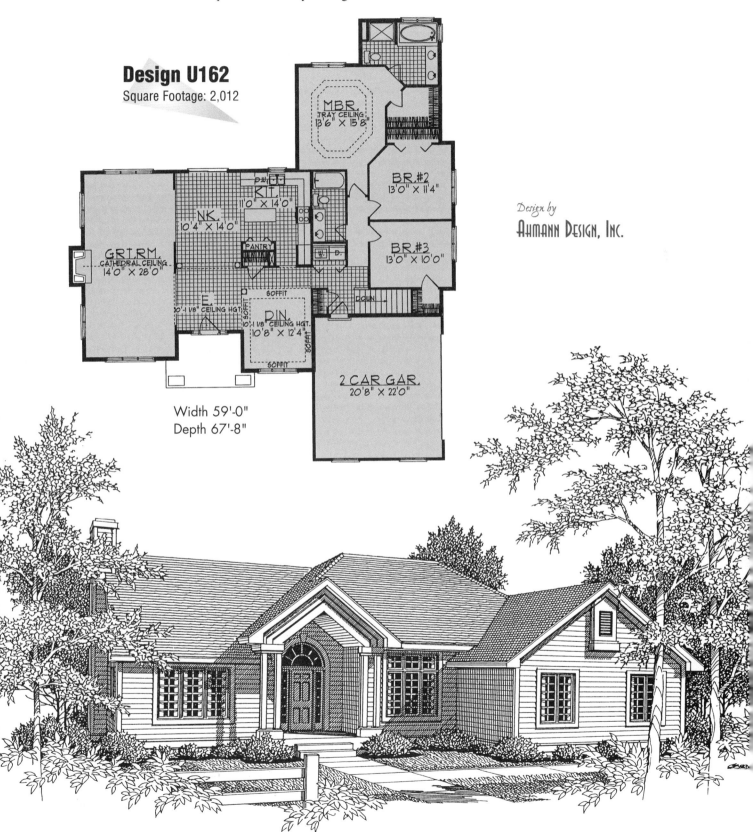

Design U162

Square Footage: 2,012

Design by
Ahmann Design, Inc.

MBR.
TRAY CEILING
13'6" X 15'8"

BR.#2
13'0" X 11'4"

BR.#3
13'0" X 10'0"

KIT.
11'0" X 14'0"

NK.
10'4" X 14'0"

GRT.RM.
CATHEDRAL CEILING
14'0" X 28'0"

PANTRY

DIN.
10'8" X 12'4"

2 CAR GAR.
20'8" X 22'0"

Width 59'-0"
Depth 67'-8"

Design 1404
Square Footage: 1,336

Width 69'-2"
Depth 39'-11"

■ Here is an exciting design, unusual in character, yet fun to live in. This design, with its frame exterior and large glass areas, has as its dramatic focal point a hexagonal living area that gives way to interesting angles. The spacious living area features sliding glass doors through which traffic may pass to the terrace stretching across the entire length of the house. The wide overhanging roofs project over the terraces, thus providing partial protection from the weather. The sloping ceilings converge above the unique, open fireplace. The sleeping areas are located in each wing from the hexagonal center.

Design by
Home Planners

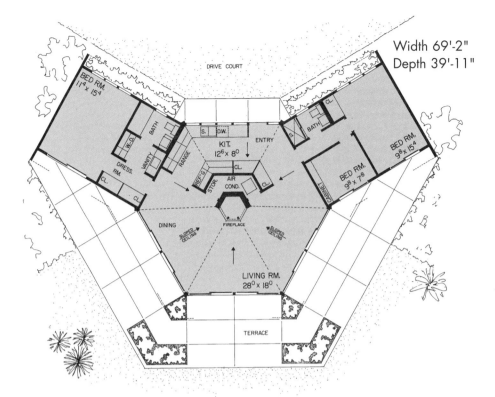

368

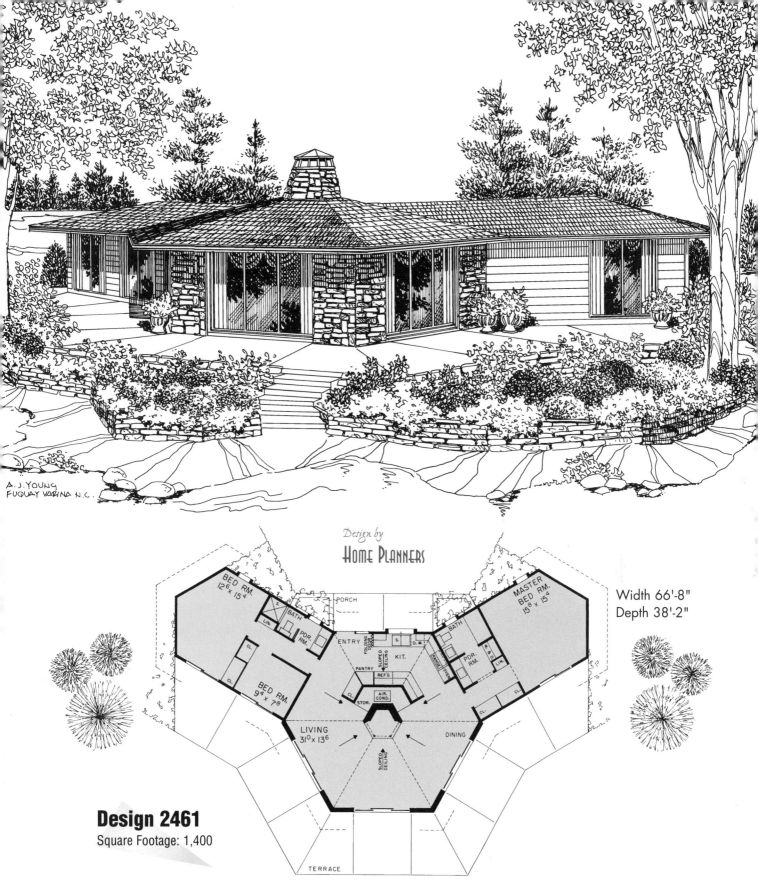

A. J. YOUNG
FUQUAY VARINA N.C.

Design by
Home Planners

Width 66'-8"
Depth 38'-2"

BED RM.
12⁶ x 15⁴

PORCH

MASTER
BED RM.
15⁸ x 15⁴

BATH

LIN.

BATH

PDR.
RM.

PDR.
RM.

ENTRY

FOLDING DOOR

S.

CL.

KIT.

LIN.

PANTRY

SLOPED
CEILING

REF'G

CL.

CL.

BED RM.
9⁴ x 7⁸

STOR.

AIR
COND.

CL.

LIVING
31⁰ x 13⁶

DINING

SLOPED
CEILING

Design 2461
Square Footage: 1,400

TERRACE

■ If you have the urge to make your vacation home one that has a distinctive flair of individuality, definite consideration should be given to the design illustrated here. Not only does this plan present a unique exterior, but it also offers an exceptional living pattern. The basic living area is a hexagon. To this space, conscious geometric shape is incorporated with the sleeping wings and baths. The center of the living area enjoys a warming fireplace as its focal point.

Design 1491

Square Footage: 576
Loft: 234 square feet

■ Wherever situated—in the northern woods, or on the southern coast—this enchanting A-frame will function as a perfect retreat. Whether called upon to serve as a ski lodge or a summer haven, it will perform admirably. The large living/dining room area offers direct access to a huge outdoor deck and an efficient kitchen fulfills all family meal needs. A bedroom and full bath complete this floor. Upstairs is a large loft perfect for bunks or use as a game room.

Design by
HOME PLANNERS

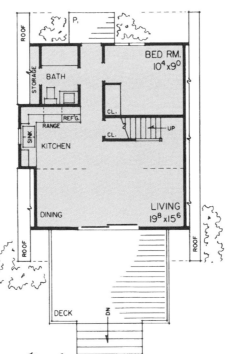

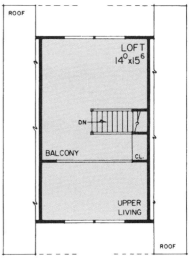

Width 24'-0"
Depth 36'-0"

Design 2439
Square Footage: 1,312

■ Here is a wonderfully organized plan with an exterior that will command the attention of each and every passerby. The rooflines and the pointed glass gable-end wall will be noticed immediately—the delightful deck will be quickly noticed, too. Inside, visitors will be thrilled by the spaciousness of the huge living room. The ceilings slope upward to the exposed ridge beam. A free-standing fireplace will make its contribution to a cheerful atmosphere. The sleeping zone has two bedrooms, two bunk rooms, two full baths, two built-in chests and fine closet space.

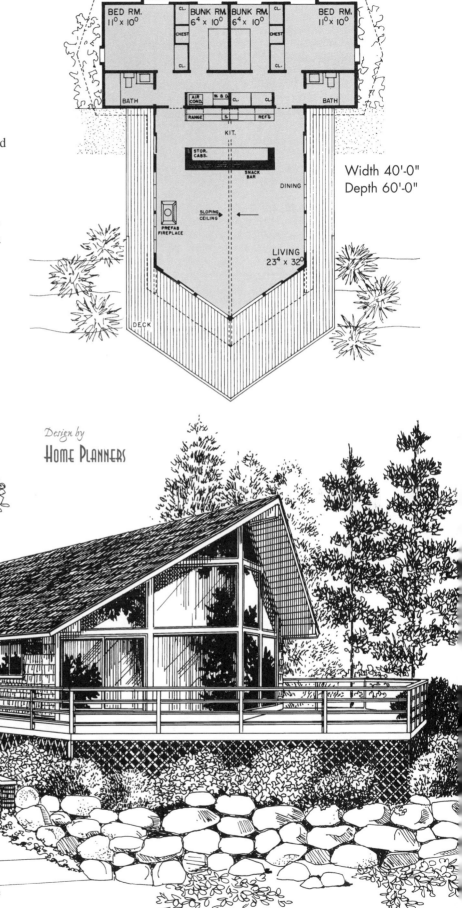

Width 40'-0"
Depth 60'-0"

Design by
HOME PLANNERS

Design 9609

Square Footage: 1,426

Design by

Donald A. Gardner Architects, Inc.

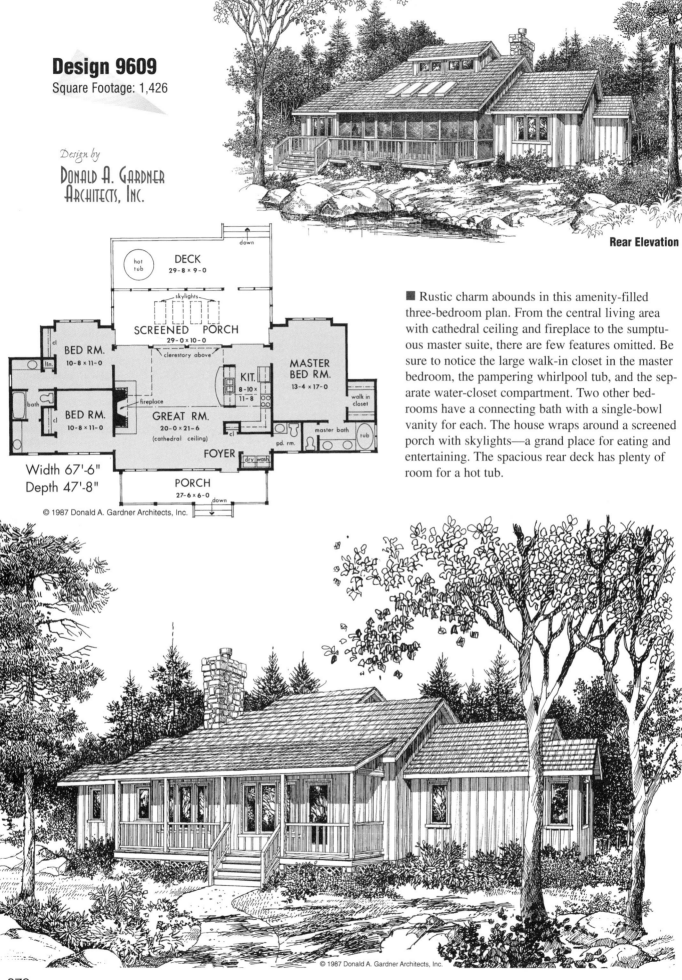

Rear Elevation

DECK
29-8 × 9-0

hot tub

down

skylights

SCREENED PORCH
29-0 × 10-0

clerestory above

BED RM.
10-8 × 11-0

cl

lin.

bath

cl

BED RM.
10-8 × 11-0

fireplace

GREAT RM.
20-0 × 21-6
(cathedral ceiling)

KIT.
8-10 ×
11-8

cl

FOYER

MASTER BED RM.
13-4 × 17-0

walk in closet

master bath

tub

pd. rm.

dry wash

Width 67'-6"
Depth 47'-8"

PORCH
27-6 × 6-0

down

© 1987 Donald A. Gardner Architects, Inc.

■ Rustic charm abounds in this amenity-filled three-bedroom plan. From the central living area with cathedral ceiling and fireplace to the sumptuous master suite, there are few features omitted. Be sure to notice the large walk-in closet in the master bedroom, the pampering whirlpool tub, and the separate water-closet compartment. Two other bedrooms have a connecting bath with a single-bowl vanity for each. The house wraps around a screened porch with skylights—a grand place for eating and entertaining. The spacious rear deck has plenty of room for a hot tub.

© 1987 Donald A. Gardner Architects, Inc.

© 1987 Donald A. Gardner Architects, Inc.

Design 9607
Square Footage: 1,299

Design by

DONALD A. GARDNER
ARCHITECTS, INC.

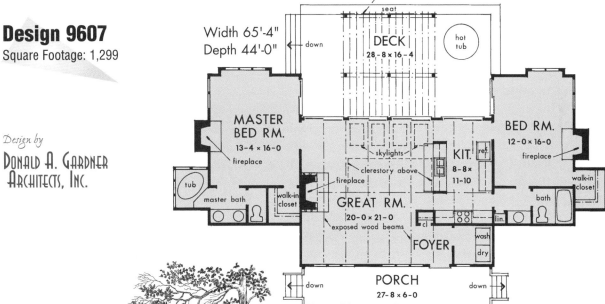

Width 65'-4"
Depth 44'-0"

wood lattice above

seat

DECK
28-8 × 16-4

hot tub

down

MASTER BED RM.
13-4 × 16-0
fireplace

skylights

clerestory above

KIT.
8-8 × 11-10

ref.

BED RM.
12-0 × 16-0
fireplace

tub

master bath

walk-in closet

fireplace

GREAT RM.
20-0 × 21-0
exposed wood beams

cl

lin.

walk-in closet

bath

FOYER

wash
dry

down

PORCH
27-8 × 6-0

down

© 1987 Donald A. Gardner Architects, Inc.

■ Though rustic in appearance, this two-bedroom plan provides all the features sought after in today's well-planned home. A large central area includes a great room, entrance foyer and kitchen with serving and eating counter. Note the use of cathedral ceilings with exposed wood beams, skylights, clerestory windows and a fireplace in this area. The master suite has an optional fireplace, a walk-in closet and a whirlpool tub. The second bedroom also has an optional fireplace and a full bath. All rooms open to the rear deck, which supplies space for a hot tub.

Rear Elevation

Design B143
Square Footage: 1,714

Garage
22 x 24

Walk

Patio

Pantry

Breakfast
12 x 10

Rear Porch
13/4 x 5/6

Br. # 2
10 x 12

Kitchen
12 x 11

Family Room
14 x 18

12' Ceiling

Master
13 x 16

9' Ceiling

Br. #3
10 x 12

9' Ceiling

Dining
10 x 12

9' Ceiling

Foyer
6 x 13

12' Ceiling

W D

Width 62'-4"
Depth 77'-0"

Porch
41 x 5/2

■ An interesting roofline accented by three shed dormers sets this home apart from the usual country design. Inside, high ceilings and thoughtful planning create uncommon livability. The formal dining room looks through a tall multi-pane window onto the covered front porch. The family room to the rear features a sloped ceiling, fireplace and a triple set of windows. The adjacent breakfast nook offers views of the rear patio, and the kitchen is equipped with an angled bar. At the left of the plan are the two family bedrooms, each of which has its own walk-in closet. The master suite includes amenities such as a separate coat closet and a walk-in closet, toilet and shower compartment and double doors to a private rear porch.

Design by
Greg Marquis & Associates

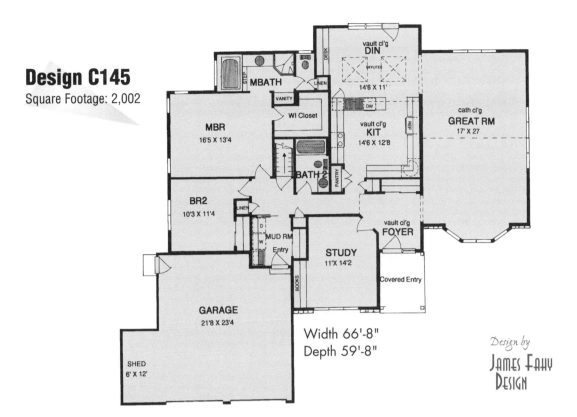

Design C145

Square Footage: 2,002

MBATH

MBR
16'5 X 13'4

WI Closet

VANITY

DESK

vault cl'g
DIN
14'6 X 11'

SKYLITES

DW

vault cl'g
KIT
14'6 X 12'8

REF

cath cl'g
GREAT RM
17' X 27

LINEN

STEP

BATH 2

PANTRY

BR2
10'3 X 11'4

LINEN

MUD RM
Entry

D
W

BOOKS

vault cl'g
FOYER

STUDY
11'X 14'2

Covered Entry

GARAGE
21'8 X 23'4

SHED
6' X 12'

Width 66'-8"
Depth 59'-8"

Design by
James Fahy
Design

■ Quaint and cozy on the exterior with a touch of contemporary virve, this home features great living spaces and vaulted ceilings on the inside. Beyond the covered entry is a vaulted foyer with access to a study with built-ins and to the great room with a cathedral ceiling and bay window. The L-shaped kitchen has an attached dining area with skylights, vaulted ceiling and built-ins. For great luxury, look no further than the master suite. You'll find a huge walk-in closet and master bath with corner shower, step-up whirlpool, compartmented toilet and make-up vanity. An additional bedroom is nearby and has the use of a full bath across the hall. The two-car garage offers a large storage area—or make it a workshop for the handyman!

Design 9611

Square Footage: 1,817

■ This inviting ranch offers many special features uncommon to a typical house this size. A large entrance foyer leads to the spacious great room with cathedral ceiling, fireplace and operable skylights that allow for natural ventilation. A bedroom just off the foyer doubles nicely as a study. The large master suite contains a walk-in closet and a pampering master bath with double-bowl vanity, shower and whirlpool tub. For outdoor living, look to the open deck with spa at the great room and kitchen, as well as the covered deck at the master suite.

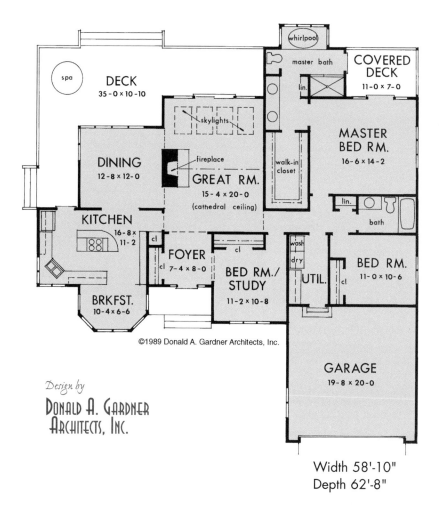

Design by
**Donald A. Gardner
Architects, Inc.**

Width 58'-10"
Depth 62'-8"

Sun-Country Vistas:

One-story homes designed for sunny climes

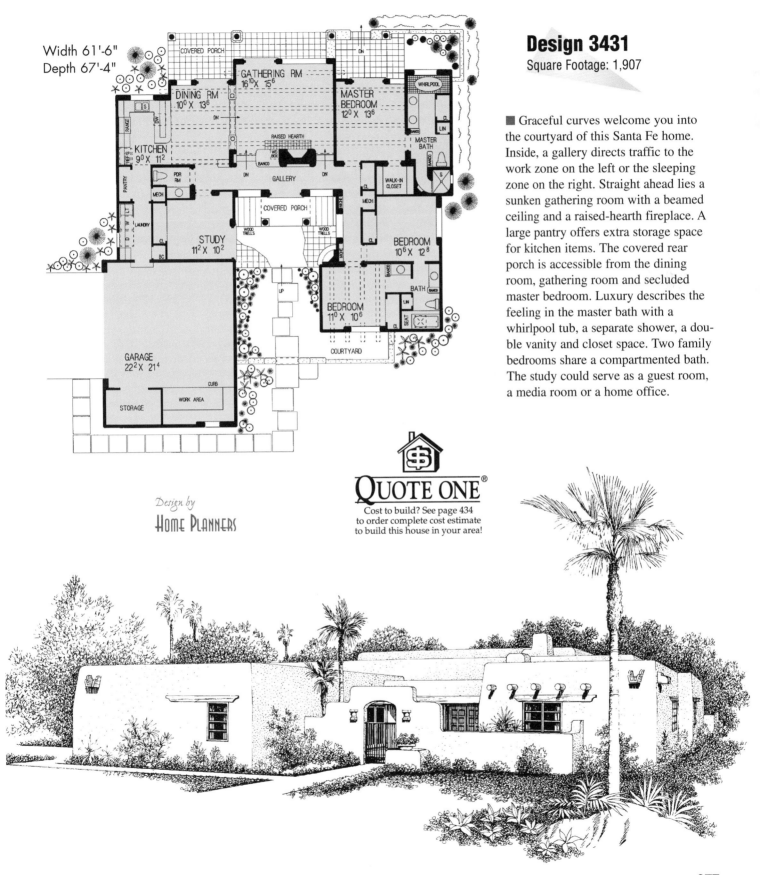

Width 61'-6"
Depth 67'-4"

Design 3431
Square Footage: 1,907

COVERED PORCH

GATHERING RM
16⁶ X 15⁶

DINING RM
10⁰ X 13⁶

MASTER
BEDROOM
12⁰ X 13⁶

WHIRLPOOL

RAISED HEARTH

KITCHEN
9⁰ X 11²

MASTER
BATH

WALK-IN
CLOSET

GALLERY

PDR
RM

MECH

PANTRY

LAUNDRY

COVERED PORCH

BEDROOM
10⁶ X 12⁸

STUDY
11² X 10²

WOOD
TRELLIS

WOOD
TRELLIS

UP

BATH

BEDROOM
11⁰ X 10⁶

GARAGE
22² X 21⁴

COURTYARD

STORAGE

WORK AREA

CURB

■ Graceful curves welcome you into the courtyard of this Santa Fe home. Inside, a gallery directs traffic to the work zone on the left or the sleeping zone on the right. Straight ahead lies a sunken gathering room with a beamed ceiling and a raised-hearth fireplace. A large pantry offers extra storage space for kitchen items. The covered rear porch is accessible from the dining room, gathering room and secluded master bedroom. Luxury describes the feeling in the master bath with a whirlpool tub, a separate shower, a double vanity and closet space. Two family bedrooms share a compartmented bath. The study could serve as a guest room, a media room or a home office.

Design by
HOME PLANNERS

QUOTE ONE®
Cost to build? See page 434
to order complete cost estimate
to build this house in your area!

377

Design 3803

Square Footage: 2,741

■ Pueblo-style architecture creates this delightful one-story home and enhances it with outdoor areas galore. The front entry leads to a central foyer with the dining room to the left and the sunken great room just beyond. A family room features a morning room dining area and raised hearth corner fireplace. Two family bedrooms offer walk-in closets and window seats. They share a full bath. The master suite has a private courtyard and a bath with a garden tub, separate shower and walk-in closet. Note the two-tier patio to the rear of the plan.

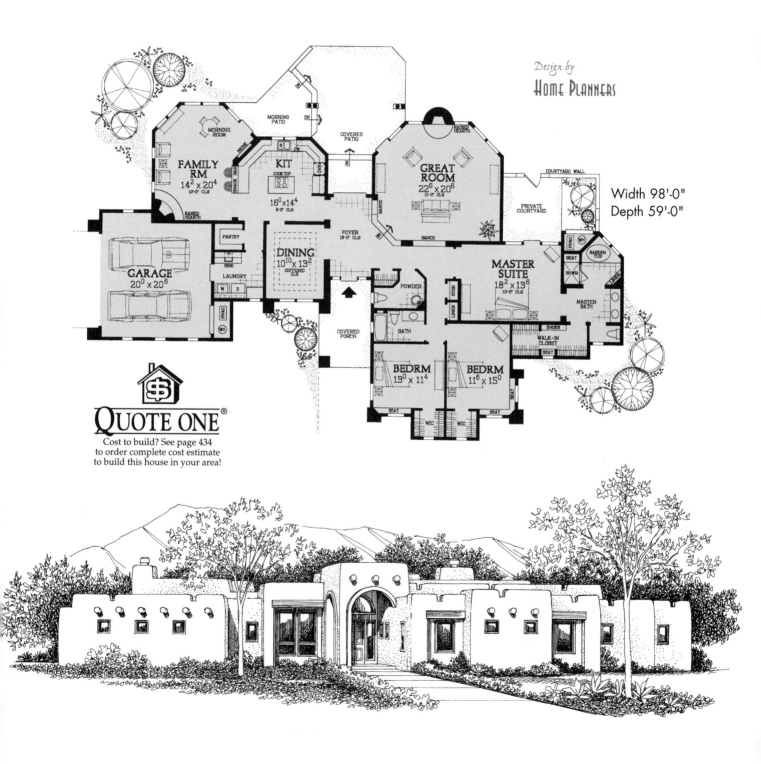

Design by
Home Planners

Width 98'-0"
Depth 59'-0"

QUOTE ONE®

Cost to build? See page 434 to order complete cost estimate to build this house in your area!

Design 3802
Square Footage: 2,982

■ Timeless architectural details mark this home as one-of-a-kind. And its unique floor plan will serve the family well for years. Enter at the covered porch to a hub foyer, around which radiates the main living spaces. Two bedrooms and a study are to the left and a third bedroom for guests is to the right. The kitchen and breakfast nook overlook the large living area and dining space. The living room has a corner fireplace and access to the patio beyond. The master suite is to the rear of the plan. It holds another corner fireplace, two walk-in closets and patio access.

Design by
Home Planners

Width 88'-6"
Depth 104'-0"

QUOTE ONE®
Cost to build? See page 434
to order complete cost estimate
to build this house in your area!

379

Design K115

■ Frontal views are no problem with this Southwest pueblo-style home. A large front courtyard with easy access to the main bath easily accommodates pool parties. The entry opens onto the great room with a twelve-foot ceiling and a kiva fireplace, and, further back to the formal dining room through a thick arch and radius wall. An open kitchen, a breakfast room and living room space are ideal for gatherings and also work well with formal areas for entertaining. The kitchen includes an eleven-foot bar and looks out the rear to the covered patio. The master suite is close to the study or home office right off the great room. Bedrooms 2 and 3 share the main bath which can also serve the pool. A three-car garage offers additional storage space. The covered patio covers the entire front of the home, offering a cool shady place to watch desert sunsets.

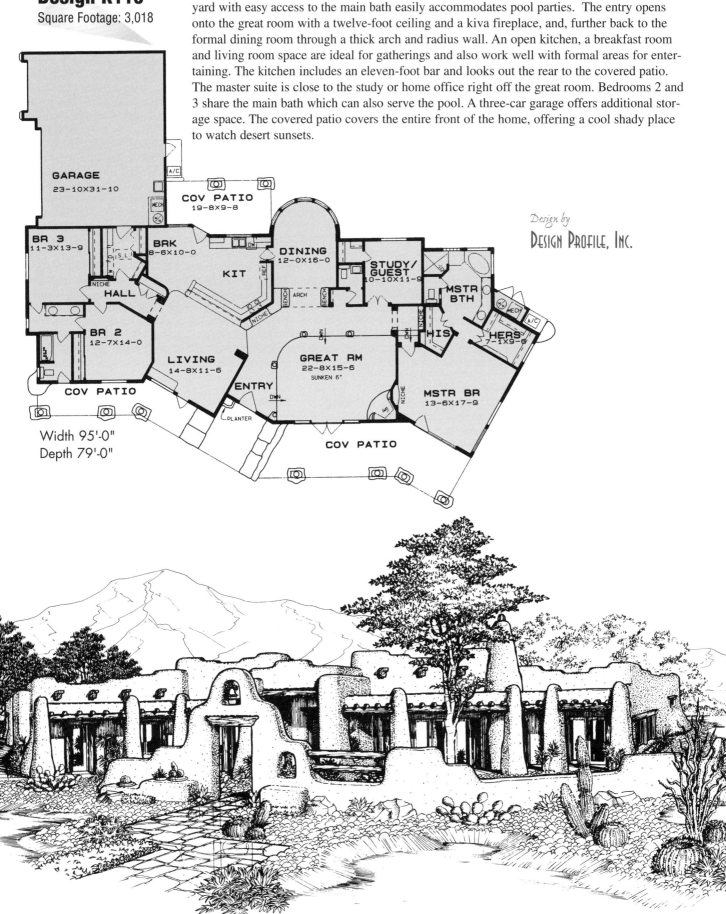

Design by
Design Profile, Inc.

Width 95'-0"
Depth 79'-0"

Design 3695
Square Footage: 2,276

Design by
HOME PLANNERS

■ Pueblo design never looked better—and its authentic styling is a tribute to architectural integrity. As in most historic homes of this type, there is an entry court with gate and stuccoed walls with viga detailing. The interior rooms are clustered around a central gallery which offers passage to a sunken great room with fireplace and patio access. The dining room and island kitchen are nearby and also access the patio. The master bedroom has a private patio area and bath with garden whirlpool, open shower and double sinks. The family bedrooms share a full bath but retain private vanity areas. For quiet pursuits, look to the study at the opposite side of the gallery. Storage space in the two-car garage makes this area even more handy.

QUOTE ONE®

Cost to build? See page 434
to order complete cost estimate
to build this house in your area!

Width 61'-6"
Depth 73'-4"

Design 3402

Square Footage: 3,212

L

■ This one-story home pairs the customary tile and stucco of Spanish design with an extremely livable floor plan. The sunken living room with its open-hearth fireplace promises to be a cozy gathering place. For more casual occasions, there's a welcoming family room with a fireplace off the entry foyer. The large galley kitchen easily serves the breakfast room and the formal dining room that has a stylish built-in buffet and shares a fireplace with the living room. The master suite has its own fireplace, a dressing area and lush bath. Two secondary bedrooms share a dual-vanity hall bath.

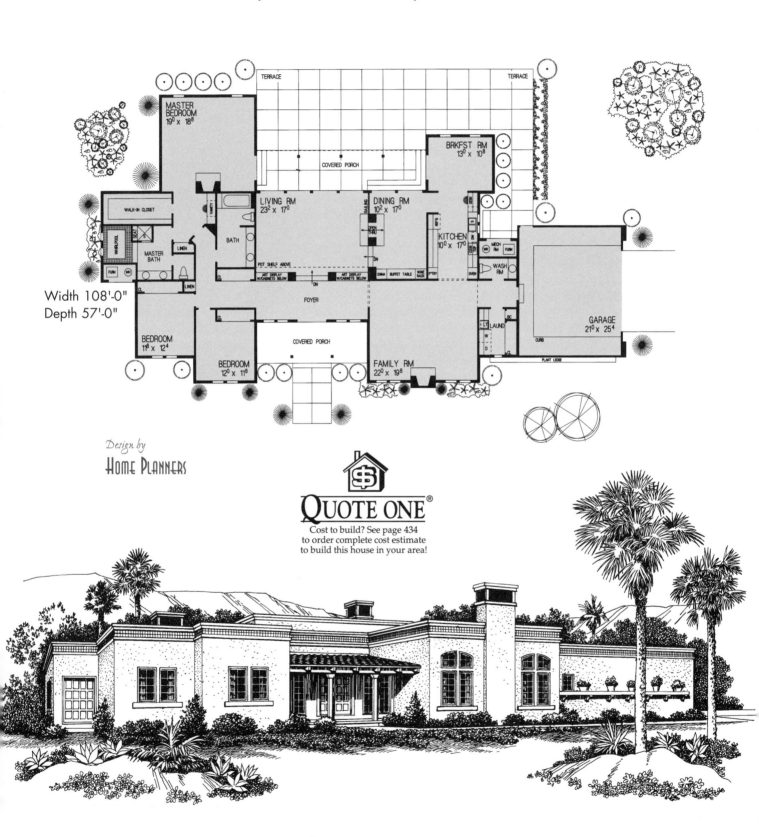

Width 108'-0"
Depth 57'-0"

Design by
HOME PLANNERS

QUOTE ONE®

Cost to build? See page 434
to order complete cost estimate
to build this house in your area!

Design 3401

Square Footage: 2,850

L

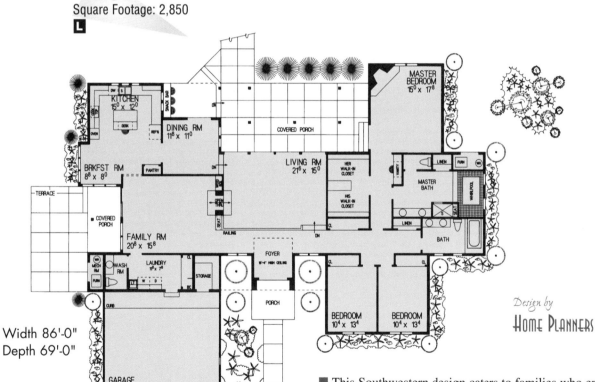

Width 86'-0"
Depth 69'-0"

QUOTE ONE®

Cost to build? See page 434
to order complete cost estimate
to build this house in your area!

Design by
Home Planners

■ This Southwestern design caters to families who enjoy out-door living and entertaining. Doors open onto a shaded terrace from the master bedroom and living room, while a sliding glass door in the family room accesses a smaller terrace. Outdoor entertaining is a breeze with the outdoor bar with pass-through window to the kitchen. In the sleeping wing, two secondary bed-rooms share a hall bath with a dual-bowl vanity, while the master suite is designed to pamper the fortunate homeowner with such amenities as a corner fireplace, His and Hers walk-in closets, a whirlpool tub, a separate shower and a separate vanity.

Design 8634

Square Footage: 1,869

Design by
HOME DESIGN SERVICES

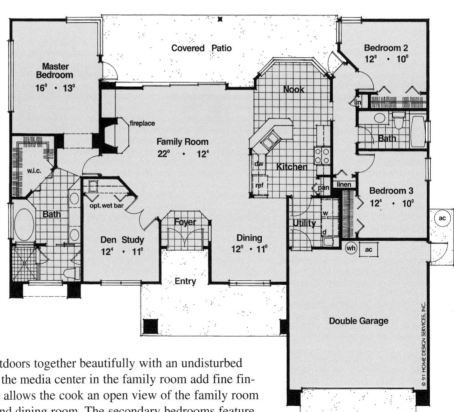

Master Bedroom
16⁰ · 13⁰

Covered Patio

Bedroom 2
12⁸ · 10⁰

fireplace

Nook

Bath

w.i.c.

Family Room
22⁰ · 12⁴

Kitchen

dw

ref

linen

pan

Bedroom 3
12⁴ · 10⁰

ac

Bath

opt. wet bar

Foyer

Utility

w

d

wh

ac

Den Study
12⁴ · 11⁰

Dining
12⁰ · 11⁰

Entry

Double Garage

■ This open plan brings indoors and outdoors together beautifully with an undisturbed view of the rear yard. The fireplace and the media center in the family room add fine finishing touches. The open kitchen design allows the cook an open view of the family room and easy service to the breakfast nook and dining room. The secondary bedrooms feature a "kids" door off the hall ideal for bathroom access from the patio area. The super master suite features mitered glass for a great view of the patio area as well as a bath with a walk-in closet, dual lavatories and spa tub. There is even a courtesy door off the toilet area accessing the den/study.

Width 61'-8"
Depth 55'-0"

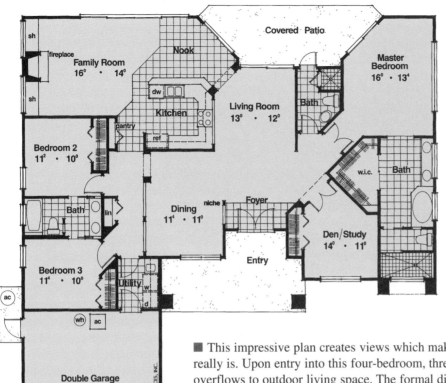

Family Room
16⁰ · 14⁰

sh

fireplace

Nook

Covered Patio

Master
Bedroom
16⁰ · 13⁴

Bath

Kitchen

dw

Living Room
13⁰ · 12⁰

pantry

ref

w.i.c.

Bath

Bedroom 2
11² · 10⁰

Bath

lin

Dining
11⁴ · 11⁰

niche

Foyer

Den/Study
14⁰ · 11⁰

Bedroom 3
11⁴ · 10⁰

Utility

w

Entry

© 91 HOME DESIGN SERVICES, INC.

Double Garage

wh

ac

ac

ac

d

Design 8639
Square Footage: 2,149

Design by
HOME DESIGN SERVICES

Width 60'-8"
Depth 62'-8"

■ This impressive plan creates views which make this house look much larger than it really is. Upon entry into this four-bedroom, three-bath home, the formal living room overflows to outdoor living space. The formal dining room is designed with open wall areas for an air of spaciousness. A decorative arch leads to the family spaces of the home. The two bedrooms share a "pullman" bath, accessible only from the rooms themselves for total privacy. The kitchen/family room/nook area is large and inviting, all with beautiful views of the outdoor living spaces. The master wing of the home is off the den/study and the pool bath. Double doors welcome you into the master suite with a glass bedwall and angled sliding glass doors to the patio. The efficient use of space makes the bath as functional as it is beautiful.

J.N.HANSEN P.T.L

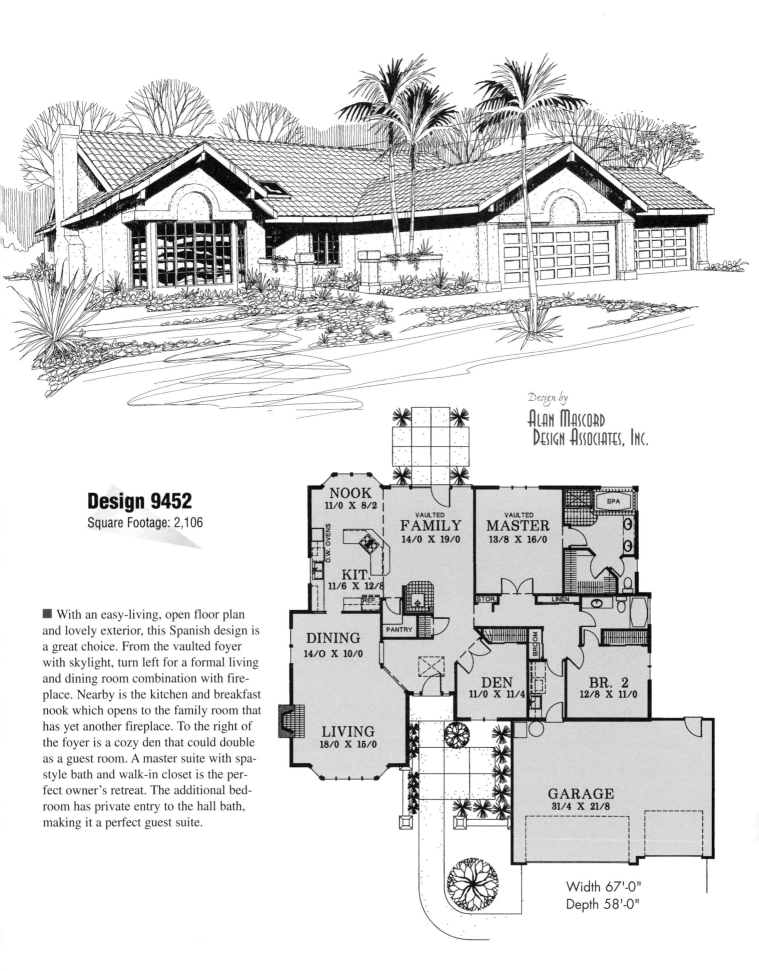

Design by
Alan Mascord
Design Associates, Inc.

Design 9452

Square Footage: 2,106

■ With an easy-living, open floor plan and lovely exterior, this Spanish design is a great choice. From the vaulted foyer with skylight, turn left for a formal living and dining room combination with fireplace. Nearby is the kitchen and breakfast nook which opens to the family room that has yet another fireplace. To the right of the foyer is a cozy den that could double as a guest room. A master suite with spa-style bath and walk-in closet is the perfect owner's retreat. The additional bedroom has private entry to the hall bath, making it a perfect guest suite.

NOOK
11/0 X 8/2

VAULTED
FAMILY
14/0 X 19/0

VAULTED
MASTER
13/8 X 16/0

SPA

D.W. OVENS

KIT.
11/6 X 12/8

REF.

STOR.

LINEN

DINING
14/0 X 10/0

PANTRY

DEN
11/0 X 11/4

BR. 2
12/8 X 11/0

BRDM

LIVING
18/0 X 15/0

GARAGE
31/4 X 21/8

Width 67'-0"
Depth 58'-0"

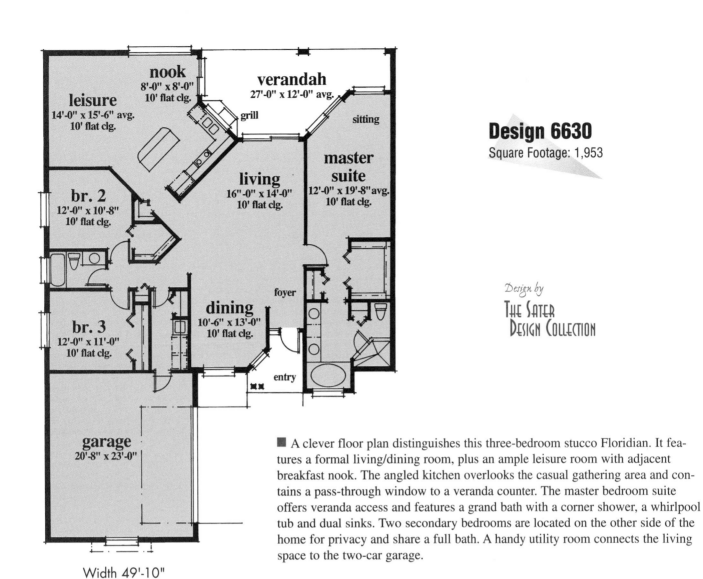

leisure
14'-0" x 15'-6" avg.
10' flat clg.

nook
8'-0" x 8'-0"
10' flat clg.

verandah
27'-0" x 12'-0" avg.

grill

sitting

br. 2
12'-0" x 10'-8"
10' flat clg.

living
16"-0" x 14'-0"
10' flat clg.

master suite
12'-0" x 19'-8" avg.
10' flat clg.

br. 3
12'-0" x 11'-0"
10' flat clg.

foyer

dining
10'-6" x 13'-0"
10' flat clg.

entry

garage
20'-8" x 23'-0"

Width 49'-10"
Depth 68'-0"

Design 6630

Square Footage: 1,953

Design by
The Sater
Design Collection

■ A clever floor plan distinguishes this three-bedroom stucco Floridian. It features a formal living/dining room, plus an ample leisure room with adjacent breakfast nook. The angled kitchen overlooks the casual gathering area and contains a pass-through window to a veranda counter. The master bedroom suite offers veranda access and features a grand bath with a corner shower, a whirlpool tub and dual sinks. Two secondary bedrooms are located on the other side of the home for privacy and share a full bath. A handy utility room connects the living space to the two-car garage.

© The Sater Group, Inc.

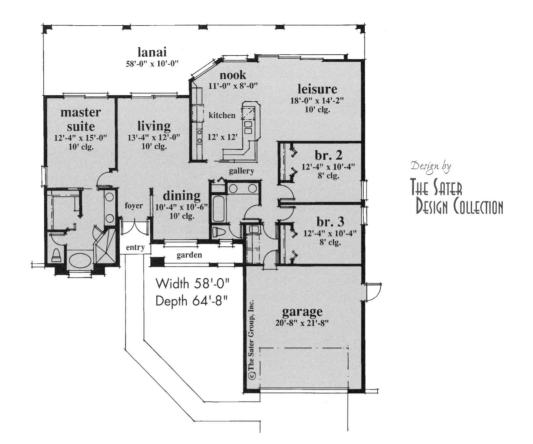

Design 6603

Square Footage: 1,784

Design by
The Sater Design Collection

■ This one-story home is filled with amenities. A raised entry features double doors that lead to the grand foyer. From the formal living room, large sliding glass doors open to the lanai, providing natural light and outdoor views. The dining room is separated from the foyer and living area by a half-wall and a column. The large kitchen, breakfast nook and leisure room round out the informal gathering areas. The secondary bedrooms are split from the master wing. The cozy master suite sports a large walk-in closet, a walk-in shower, a whirlpool tub and a private water closet.

© The Sater Group, Inc.

Design 6629

Square Footage: 2,214

■ Make yourself at home in this delightful one-story home. The dramatic entry—with an arched opening—leads to a comfortable interior. Volume ceilings highlight the main living areas which include a formal dining room and a great room with access to one of the lanais. In the turreted study, quiet time is assured with double doors closing off the rest of the house. Nearby, the master bedroom suite features a luxury bath with a double-bowl vanity, a bumped-out whirlpool tub and a separate shower. The secondary bedrooms reside on the other side of the house and utilize a full bath that also accommodates outdoor living areas.

Design by
The Sater
Design Collection

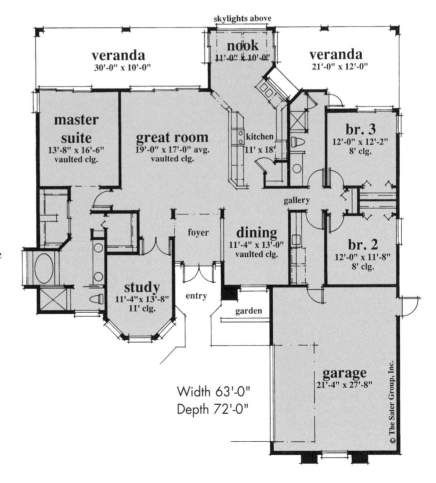

This Florida classic has been an award winner, as well as a family favorite. Just looking at the flow of this plan will tell you why it's a best seller. The formal living/dining area provides impact as you enter this home. Tiered ceiling treatments add crisp contemporary flair to the ceilings. The double-door entry to the master's retreat leads you to a portico-style space, which adds privacy when the doors are opened. The mitered glass treatment in the large sleeping area provides unobstructed views of the outdoor living areas. The master bath is second to none in terms of amenities and intelligent use of space, right down to His and Hers walk-in closets. The secondary bedroom wing has everything for the large family. Note the "kids' door" which accesses the rear patio area from the hallway to the bedrooms and bath. A summer kitchen for outdoor entertaining is icing on the cake!

Width 68'-8"
Depth 72'-8"

Design by
HOME DESIGN SERVICES

Design 8619
Square Footage: 2,385

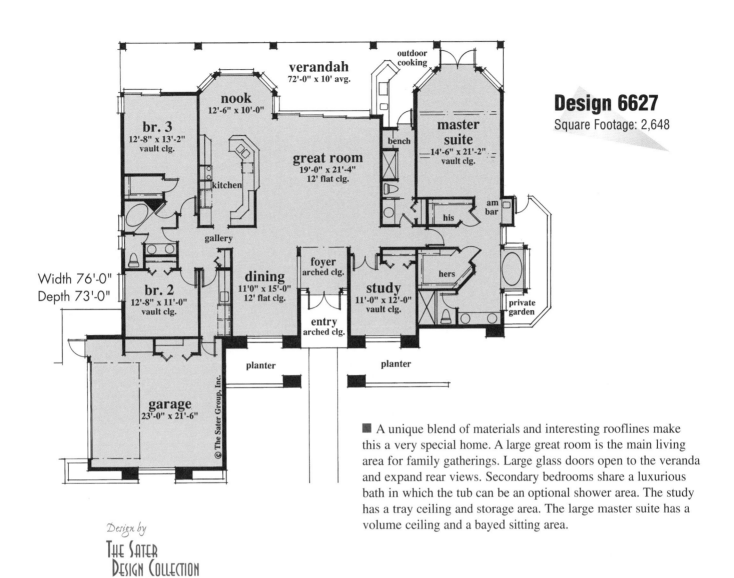

verandah
72'-0" x 10' avg.

outdoor cooking

nook
12'-6" x 10'-0"

br. 3
12'-8" x 13'-2"
vault clg.

great room
19'-0" x 21'-4"
12' flat clg.

bench

master suite
14'-6" x 21'-2"
vault clg.

Design 6627
Square Footage: 2,648

kitchen

am bar

gallery

his

hers

Width 76'-0"
Depth 73'-0"

br. 2
12'-8" x 11'-0"
vault clg.

dining
11'0" x 15'-0"
12' flat clg.

foyer
arched clg.

study
11'-0" x 12'-0"
vault clg.

private garden

entry
arched clg.

© The Sater Group, Inc.

planter

planter

garage
23'-0" x 21'-6"

Design by
THE SATER
DESIGN COLLECTION

■ A unique blend of materials and interesting rooflines make this a very special home. A large great room is the main living area for family gatherings. Large glass doors open to the veranda and expand rear views. Secondary bedrooms share a luxurious bath in which the tub can be an optional shower area. The study has a tray ceiling and storage area. The large master suite has a volume ceiling and a bayed sitting area.

Design K103

Square Footage: 2,708

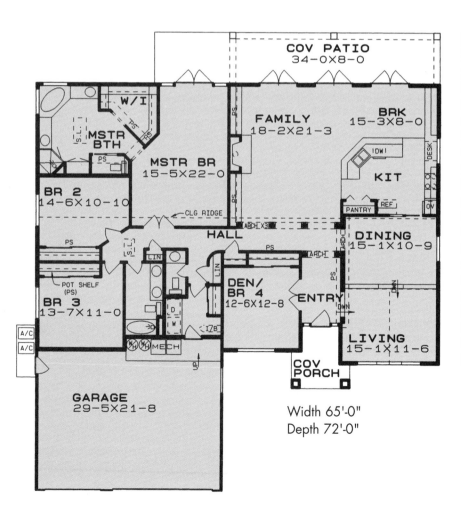

COV PATIO
34-0X8-0

FAMILY
18-2X21-3

BRK
15-3X8-0

KIT

DW

PANTRY REF OV

W/I

MSTR BTH

MSTR BR
15-5X22-0

CLG RIDGE

BR 2
14-6X10-10

PS

POT SHELF (PS)

BR 3
13-7X11-0

A/C
A/C

HALL

ARCH X3

DINING
15-1X10-9

DEN/ BR 4
12-6X12-8

ENTRY

DN

LIVING
15-1X11-6

GARAGE
29-5X21-8

COV PORCH

Width 65'-0"
Depth 72'-0"

■ An elegant exterior, graced by a beautiful arch and fine detailing, is a preview for the wonderful layout within. The separation of formal and informal areas in this Southwestern design creates casually elegant spaces. From the entry hall, with its arched openings, there is a view through the family room to the wall of glass French doors at the rear. These doors overlook the covered patio and the rear yard beyond. The colonnade of arches at the family room opens it up to a gallery wall near the fourth bedroom which doubles as a study. Double doors lead to the comfortable master suite with room for a sitting area near the French doors. A skylight in the master bath helps to complete the feel of luxury. Two nearby secondary bedrooms share a full hall bath and easily accommodate family and friends.

Design by
DESIGN PROFILE, INC.

Design K125

Square Footage: 2,791

■ The arched facade of the two-story covered porch is repeated in the interior of this four-bedroom, 2½-bath plan with arches in the entryway leading to the family room and again in arches into the formal living room and dining room. The outstanding family room features a fireplace flanked by media shelves and a fourteen-foot wall of glass facing the covered patio. The island kitchen with built-in desk is open to the breakfast room and has a pass-through window to the patio. The master suite has a vaulted ceiling in the bedroom and a glass block shower in the bath, plus access to both the rear patio and a private lanai.

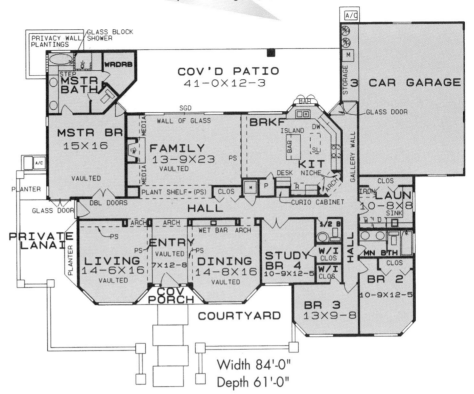

Width 84'-0"
Depth 61'-0"

Design by
DESIGN PROFILE, INC.

Design 8602

Square Footage: 2,564

■ The living areas of this Mediterranean home are enhanced by interesting angles and are designed to take advantage of sunlight. Double doors reveal a dramatic foyer that opens to the living and dining rooms. In the sunken dining room, columns add to the formality. The kitchen is centered around the breakfast nook and dining room for casual eating or formal entertaining. The master suite offers seclusion as well as a fine view of the deck area. A walk-in closet and a tiled master bath with a double vanity and spa tub complete the master suite.

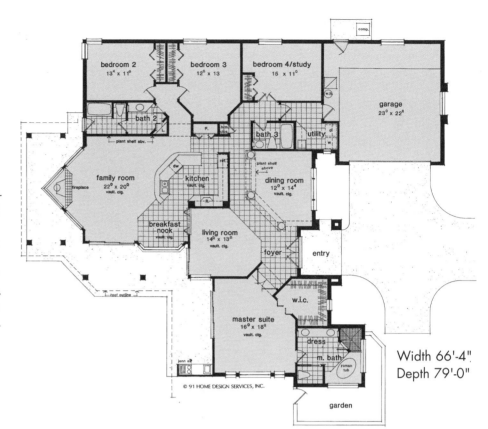

bedroom 2
13⁴ x 11⁰

bedroom 3
12⁰ x 13

bedroom 4/study
15 x 11⁰

garage
23⁰ x 22⁸

bath 2

plant shelf abv.

bath 3

utility

plant shelf above

family room
22⁰ x 20⁰
vault. clg.

fireplace

kitchen
vault. clg.

dining room
12⁰ x 14⁴
vault. clg.

breakfast nook
vault. clg.

living room
14⁹ x 13⁰
vault. clg.

foyer

entry

roof outline

w.i.c.

master suite
16⁰ x 18⁰
vault. clg.

dress

m. bath

roman tub

jenn air

garden

© 91 HOME DESIGN SERVICES, INC.

Width 66'-4"
Depth 79'-0"

Design by

Home Design Services

© HOME DESIGN SERVICES, INC.

R. BRADSHAW

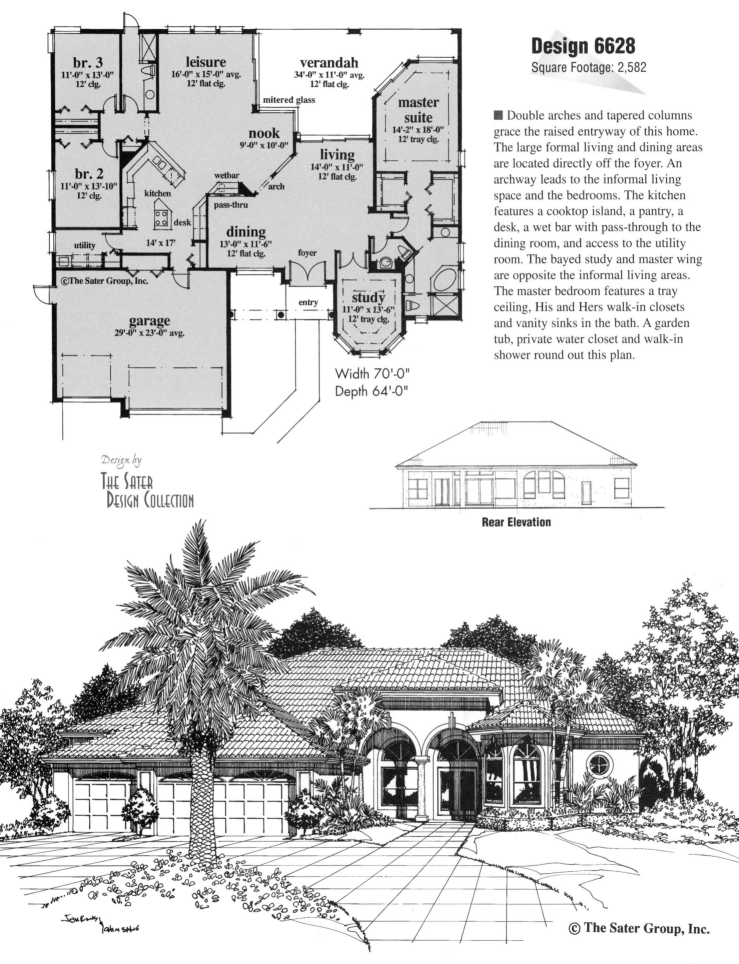

br. 3
11'-0" x 13'-0"
12' clg.

leisure
16'-0" x 15'-0" avg.
12' flat clg.

verandah
34'-0" x 11'-0" avg.
12' flat clg.

mitered glass

master suite
14'-2" x 18'-0"
12' tray clg.

nook
9'-0" x 10'-0"

living
14'-0" x 11'-0"
12' flat clg.

wetbar

arch

pass-thru

br. 2
11'-0" x 13'-10"
12' clg.

kitchen

desk

dining
13'-0" x 11'-6"
12' flat clg.

foyer

utility

14' x 17'

©The Sater Group, Inc.

garage
29'-0" x 23'-0" avg.

entry

study
11'-0" x 13'-6"
12' tray clg.

Width 70'-0"
Depth 64'-0"

Design by
THE SATER
DESIGN COLLECTION

Design 6628
Square Footage: 2,582

■ Double arches and tapered columns grace the raised entryway of this home. The large formal living and dining areas are located directly off the foyer. An archway leads to the informal living space and the bedrooms. The kitchen features a cooktop island, a pantry, a desk, a wet bar with pass-through to the dining room, and access to the utility room. The bayed study and master wing are opposite the informal living areas. The master bedroom features a tray ceiling, His and Hers walk-in closets and vanity sinks in the bath. A garden tub, private water closet and walk-in shower round out this plan.

Rear Elevation

© The Sater Group, Inc.

Design 6658

Square Footage: 1,647

Alternate Elevation

© The Sater Group, Inc.

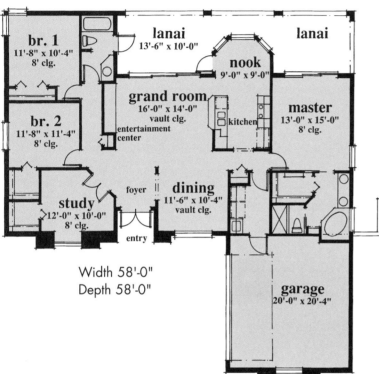

br. 1
11'-8" x 10'-4"
8' clg.

lanai
13'-6" x 10'-0"

lanai

nook
9'-0" x 9'-0"

grand room
16'-0" x 14'-0"
vault clg.

kitchen

master
13'-0" x 15'-0"
8' clg.

br. 2
11'-8" x 11'-4"
8' clg.

entertainment center

foyer

dining
11'-6" x 10'-4"
vault clg.

study
12'-0" x 10'-0"
8' clg.

entry

Width 58'-0"
Depth 58'-0"

garage
20'-0" x 20'-4"

■ This glorious sun-country cottage gives you the option of two elevations: choose from a hipped or gabled roof at the front entrance. Either way, this plan gives a new look to comfortable resort living. Designed for casual living, the foyer opens to the dining room and grand room while providing great views of the rear lanai and beyond. The grand room has a built-in entertainment center and a snack bar served from the kitchen. The galley kitchen has a gazebo dining nook with a door to the lanai. The master suite is split from the family sleeping wing and features a walk-in closet and a compartmented bath. Two secondary bedrooms, a study and full cabana bath complete this luxurious home.

Design by
THE SATER
DESIGN COLLECTION

© The Sater Group, Inc.

© The Sater Group, Inc.

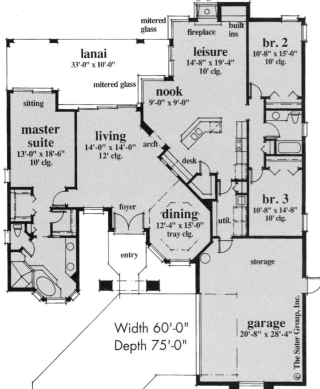

high glass

mitered glass

fireplace | built ins

lanai
33'-0" x 10'-0"

mitered glass

leisure
14'-8" x 19'-4"
10' clg.

br. 2
10'-8" x 15'-0"
10' clg.

sitting

nook
9'-0" x 9'-0"

master suite
13'-0" x 18'-6"
10' clg.

living
14'-0" x 14'-0"
12' clg.

arch

desk

foyer

dining
12'-4" x 15'-0"
tray clg.

entry

br. 3
10'-8" x 14'-8"
10' clg.

util.

storage

Width 60'-0"
Depth 75'-0"

garage
20'-8" x 28'-4"

© The Sater Group, Inc.

Design 6614
Square Footage: 2,282

■ Two elevations are yours to choose from in this stunning sun-country home. An octagonal-shaped dining room with a tray ceiling and a living room opening to the lanai make up the formal living areas. Pass through an arched doorway and enter the informal living area; comprised of an efficient kitchen, a sunlit breakfast nook and a comfortable leisure room with a fireplace and built-ins. To one side of this area is access to the lanai. The far right side of the plan contains two family bedrooms and a full bath. To the far left, a private master suite with a sitting area opens to the lanai. His and Hers walk-in closets, a compartmented toilet, a calming corner tub and separate shower and a double-bowl vanity complete this pampering suite.

Design by
THE Sater
DESIGN COLLECTION

Alternate Elevation

© The Sater Group, Inc.

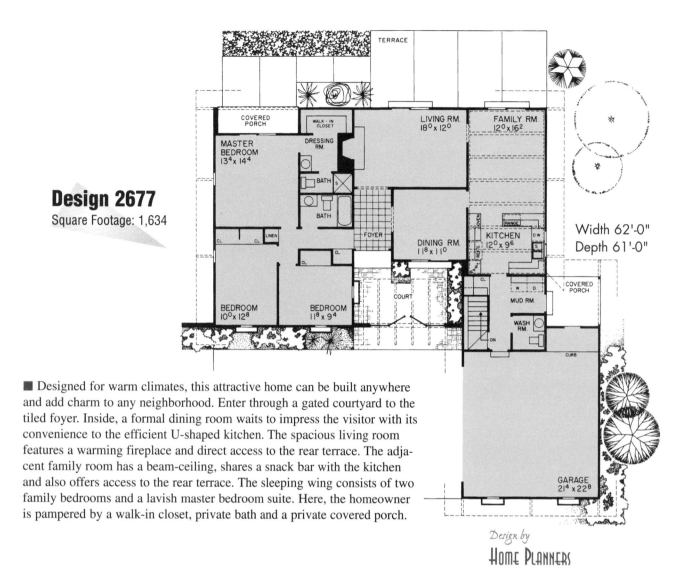

Design 2677
Square Footage: 1,634

TERRACE

COVERED PORCH

WALK-IN CLOSET

DRESSING RM.

MASTER BEDROOM
13⁴ x 14⁴

LIVING RM.
18⁰ x 12⁰

FAMILY RM.
12⁰ x 16²

BATH

BATH

Width 62'-0"
Depth 61'-0"

CL. **CL.** **LINEN**

FOYER

DINING RM.
11⁸ x 11⁰

KITCHEN
12⁰ x 9⁶

CL.

CL.

RANGE

DW

COVERED PORCH

BEDROOM
10⁰ x 12⁸

BEDROOM
11⁸ x 9⁴

COURT

MUD RM.

W **D**

WASH RM.

CURB

GARAGE
21⁴ x 22⁸

■ Designed for warm climates, this attractive home can be built anywhere and add charm to any neighborhood. Enter through a gated courtyard to the tiled foyer. Inside, a formal dining room waits to impress the visitor with its convenience to the efficient U-shaped kitchen. The spacious living room features a warming fireplace and direct access to the rear terrace. The adjacent family room has a beam-ceiling, shares a snack bar with the kitchen and also offers access to the rear terrace. The sleeping wing consists of two family bedrooms and a lavish master bedroom suite. Here, the homeowner is pampered by a walk-in closet, private bath and a private covered porch.

Design by
Home Planners

Design 2741
Square Footage: 1,842

D

Design by
Home Planners

WALK-IN CLOSET

MASTER BED RM.
12⁰ x 15⁶

DRESSING RM.

BATH

BATH

LINEN

CL. CL.

BED RM.
11⁶ x 11⁸

BED RM.
11⁶ x 11⁸

CL. CL.

STOR.

ENTRY

DN.

CAB'T BOOKS

STOR. DESK OVEN

NOOK
8² x 11⁶

KITCHEN
9⁶ x 11⁶

REFG. B.CL. PANTRY

DN.

SERV. ENT.

LAUNDRY

DRY. WASH W.H.

WASH RM.

S. D.W.

PORCH

WOOD TRELLIS ABOVE

LIVING RM.
21⁴ x 17⁶

TERRACE

TERRACE

PORCH

DINING RM.
12⁰ x 11⁶

TERRACE

CURB

GARAGE
21⁰ x 23⁴

Width 76'-0"
Depth 42'-0"

■ Here is a perfect example of what 1,800 square feet can deliver in comfort and convenience. The setting reminds one of the sun country of Arizona. However, this design would surely be an attractive and refreshing addition to any region. The covered front porch with its adjacent open trellis area shelters the center entry. From here traffic flows efficiently to the sleeping, living and kitchen zones. There is much to recommend each area. The sleeping area with its fine bath and closet facilities; the living area with its spaciousness, fireplace and adjacent dining room; the kitchen with its handy nook, excellent storage, nearby laundry and extra washroom.

E. REINKE

Design 2200
Square Footage: 1,695

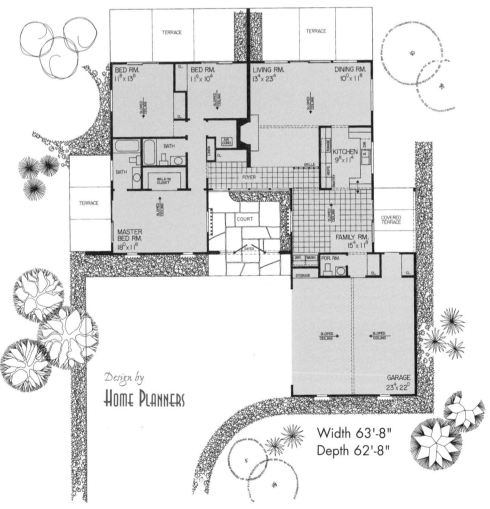

TERRACE

TERRACE

BED RM.
$11^8 \times 13^8$

BED RM.
$11^6 \times 10^4$

LIVING RM.
$13^4 \times 23^4$

DINING RM.
$10^5 \times 11^8$

SLOPED CEILING

SLOPED CEILING

SLOPED CEILING

CL.

CL.

AIR COND.

KITCHEN
$9^8 \times 11^4$

BATH

LINEN

CL.

GRILLE

REFR.

PANTRY

DW.

RANGE

BATH

FOYER

WALK-IN CLOSET

TERRACE

SLOPED CEILING

COURT

SLOPED CEILING

COVERED TERRACE

MASTER BED RM.
$18^0 \times 11^8$

GATE

FAMILY RM.
$15^4 \times 11^8$

DRY. WASH. PDR. RM.

STORAGE

CL.

CL.

Design by
HOME PLANNERS

SLOPED CEILING

SLOPED CEILING

GARAGE
$23^4 \times 22^0$

Width 63'-8"
Depth 62'-8"

■ This attractive sun-country charmer is sure to please with its many amenities, which start with the invitingly gated front court-yard. From here, the tiled foyer leads to the right, where a spacious living room, formal dining room, efficient kitchen and multi-use family room await to fulfill all of the family's needs. To the left of the foyer is the sleeping wing. Two spacious family bed-rooms, each with direct outdoor access, share a full hall bath. The master suite is designed for pampering, with its own bath, a walk-in closet and a private terrace.

BED RM.

LIVING RM.

LINEN

CL.

CL.

DN.

FOYER

**Optional
Basement Plan**

400

Design 2294
Square Footage: 3,056

Design by
HOME PLANNERS

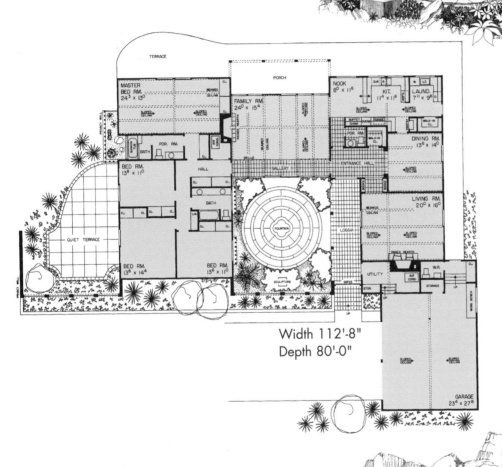

Width 112'-8"
Depth 80'-0"

■ This one-story home is spiced with authentic Spanish flavor. Striking a note of distinction, the arched privacy walls provide a fine backdrop for the long, raised planter. The low-pitched roof features tile and has a wide overhang with exposed rafter tails. The interior is thoughtfully planned. The welcoming family room is flanked by the sleeping wing and the living wing. Indoor-outdoor relationships are outstanding, further enhancing the plan. At left—the spacious interior court. The sleeping facilities include three family bedrooms and a master suite located to the rear for privacy.

Design K118

Square Footage: 1,465

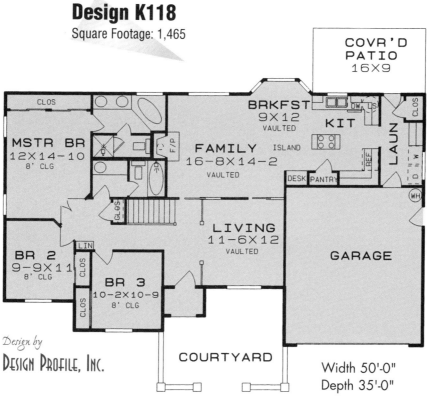

COVR'D PATIO 16X9

BRKFST 9X12 VAULTED

KIT

LAUN

CLOS

CLOS

MSTR BR 12X14-10 8' CLG

F/P

FAMILY 16-8X14-2 VAULTED

ISLAND

REF

DESK PANTRY

DW

WH

CLOS

LIN

BR 2 9-9X11 8' CLG

CLOS

LIVING 11-6X12 VAULTED

GARAGE

BR 3 10-2X10-9 8' CLG

CLOS

COURTYARD

Width 50'-0"
Depth 35'-0"

Design by
DESIGN PROFILE, INC.

■ This compact home offers lots of family living for the size. The open plan features double doors between the formal and family areas to allow flexible use or privacy as the need arises. Removing the wall between these areas opens the plan up to a 26'x17' great room. Easy access to the rear yard is gained from the breakfast and laundry rooms. The open kitchen features a center island with a range and a built-in planning desk. The unfinished basement includes room for three more bedrooms, a large game room, a bath and lots of extra storage. Please specify basement or slab foundation when ordering.

Design K119
Square Footage: 1,743

■ Attractive rooflines and an elegant column at the entryway give this design plenty of curb appeal. Though designed as a three-bedroom, it has a den/guest room that can be converted into a fourth bedroom if needed. This flexible space can also serve as a home office with its double doors facing into the formal living and dining areas. The open family-kitchen area is warmed by a fireplace and features a wall of glass leading to the large covered patio at the rear. Two secondary bedrooms share a hall bath while the deluxe master suite offers a private bath and a walk-in closet. This plan is also available with a basement which adds plenty of expansion space. Please specify basement or slab foundation when ordering.

Design by
DESIGN PROFILE, INC.

COV'D PATIO

MSTR BR
15-0X12-0

MSTR B

WALK-IN

FAMILY
13-8X15-0

NOOK
10-0X8-10

MAIN B

CLOSET

BR 1
9-8X10-0

F/P

KIT.

DINING
14-0X10-0

DW

W D

LAUN

CLOSET

BR 2
12-0X9-9

P

REF

HALL

WH

M

DEN/
GUEST
9-6X10-0

CLOSET

ENTRY

LIVING
14-1X12-5

COV'D
PORCH

GARAGE

Width 49'-0"
Depth 49'-0"

403

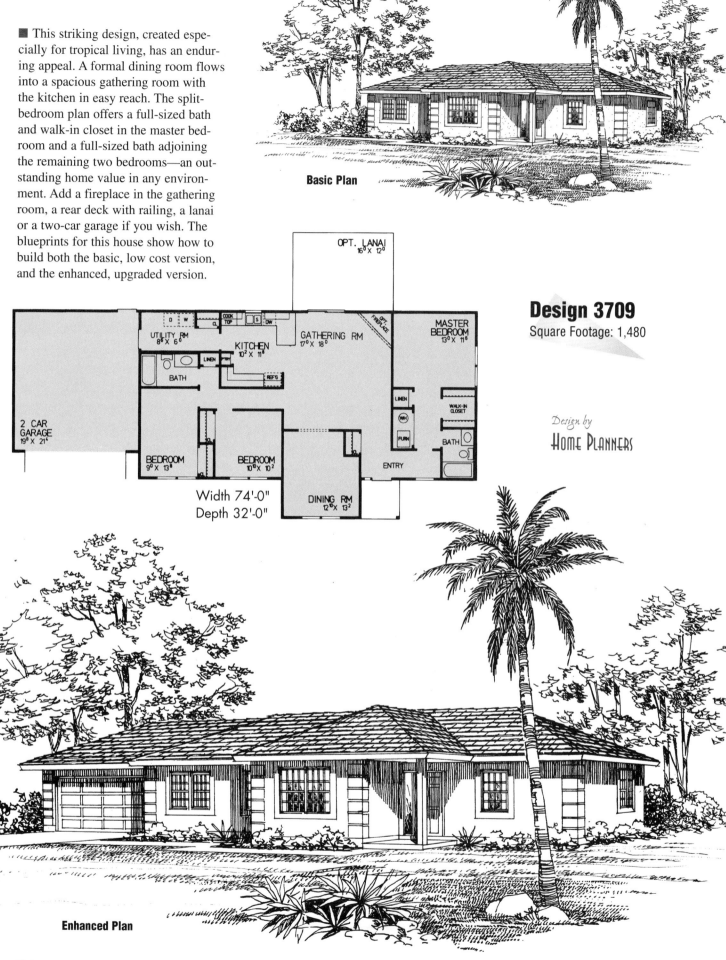

■ This striking design, created especially for tropical living, has an enduring appeal. A formal dining room flows into a spacious gathering room with the kitchen in easy reach. The split-bedroom plan offers a full-sized bath and walk-in closet in the master bedroom and a full-sized bath adjoining the remaining two bedrooms—an outstanding home value in any environment. Add a fireplace in the gathering room, a rear deck with railing, a lanai or a two-car garage if you wish. The blueprints for this house show how to build both the basic, low cost version, and the enhanced, upgraded version.

Basic Plan

OPT. LANAI
16⁰ X 12⁰

UTILITY RM
8⁶ X 6⁰

KITCHEN
10² X 11⁸

GATHERING RM
17⁰ X 18⁰

MASTER BEDROOM
13⁰ X 11⁶

OPT. FIREPLACE

BATH

LINEN

REF'G

LINEN

WALK-IN CLOSET

WH

2 CAR GARAGE
19⁸ X 21⁴

BEDROOM
9⁰ X 13⁸

BEDROOM
10⁰ X 10²

FURN

BATH

ENTRY

DINING RM
12⁰ X 13²

Width 74'-0"
Depth 32'-0"

Design 3709

Square Footage: 1,480

Design by
Home Planners

Enhanced Plan

Enhanced Plan

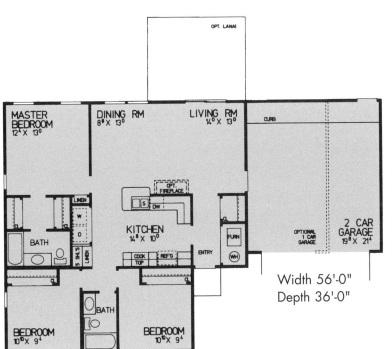

OPT. LANAI

MASTER BEDROOM 12⁴ X 13⁰

DINING RM 8⁶ X 13⁰

LIVING RM 14⁰ X 13⁰

CURB

LINEN

BATH

W

D

S SHLVS

LINEN

OPT. FIREPLACE

S DW

KITCHEN 14⁸ X 10⁰

CL

FURN

2 CAR GARAGE 19⁸ X 21⁴

OPTIONAL 1 CAR GARAGE

COOK TOP

REF'G

ENTRY

WH

BEDROOM 10¹⁰ X 9⁴

BATH

BEDROOM 10¹⁰ X 9⁴

Width 56'-0"
Depth 36'-0"

Design 3706
Square Footage: 1,200

■ Comfortable and contemporary, this one-story ranch offers versatile living space that seems much larger than its actual dimensions. Three bedrooms, two baths, a dining/living room combination and kitchen make up this home. This charming, affordable home is specially designed for warm climates. If the optional two-car garage is included, a rear lanai may be built. A rear deck with a railing and a centrally located fireplace are additional options. The blueprints for this house show how to build both the basic, low cost version, and the enhanced, upgraded version.

Design by
HOME PLANNERS

Basic Plan

Enhanced Plan

Design 3716
Square Footage: 1,419

■ Do you have a narrow lot and big dreams? Here is the perfect solution: a compact house with three bedrooms and a wonderful, open great room with space for dining. Every foot of space contributes to family livability. The master bedroom suite includes a full-sized bath and walk-in closet. A second bath is centered between the two family bedrooms. Enhanced livability options include a fireplace, front bay window, rear deck or lanai and two-car garage. The blueprints for this house show how to build both the basic, low cost version, and the enhanced, upgraded version.

Design by
HOME PLANNERS

Basic Plan

LANAI
16⁶ x 11⁸

GREAT RM
13² X 33⁴

MASTER BEDROOM
12⁶ x 13⁴

WALK-IN CLOSET

BATH

OPT. FIREPLACE

KITCHEN
9⁰ X 16²

BEDROOM
11⁴ x 9⁴

BATH

FOYER

OPT. BAY WINDOW

LAUNDRY
9⁰ x 7⁴

FURN

COVERED PORCH

BEDROOM
11⁴ x 9⁸

GARAGE
20¹⁰ X 21⁸

Width 35'-0"
Depth 78'-0"

Basic Plan

Design 3719

Square Footage: 1,634

■ This modest but handsome ranch design provides an open living environment in an excellent home for narrow lots. The master bedroom features a large walk-in closet and a full-sized bath. Three additional bedrooms are served by another full bath. A galley kitchen, with an eat-in nook, opens up to a huge great room. Indoor/outdoor livability may be expanded with the addition of a rear lanai or deck with railing. A fireplace in the great room, front bay windows and a two-car garage are wonderful options. The blueprints for this home show how to build both the basic and the expanded version.

Design by
Home Planners

Width 35'-0"
Depth 74'-0"

Enhanced Plan

Enhanced Plan

Design 3707

Square Footage: 1,345

■ Enhanced livability for warm climates is an appropriate theme for this well-laid-out ranch house. The split-bedroom plan separates the master bedroom from two family bedrooms. One of the bedrooms would make a perfect office, if needed. A large L-shaped kitchen has loads of counter space and includes an alcove for a washer and dryer. Two baths and a large great room complete the layout. Enhance livability by including the fireplace, rear deck or lanai and the two-car garage. The blueprints for this house show how to build both the basic and the enhanced version.

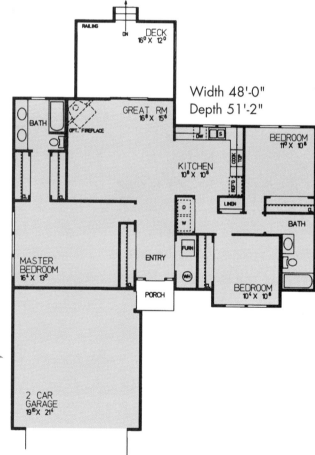

Width 48'-0"
Depth 51'-2"

DECK 16⁰ X 12⁰

RAILING

DN

BATH

GREAT RM 16⁰ X 15⁶

OPT. FIREPLACE

BEDROOM 11⁰ X 10⁶

KITCHEN 10⁸ X 10⁶

LINEN

BATH

MASTER BEDROOM 16⁴ X 13⁰

ENTRY

FURN

BEDROOM 10⁴ X 10⁸

PORCH

2 CAR GARAGE 19⁸ X 21⁴

Design by
HOME PLANNERS

Basic Plan

Enhanced Plan

■ Comfortable, contemporary and classy, this one-story plan offers versatile living space for sunny climates. The formal dining room flows into a spacious great room for all your entertaining needs. There is also a master bedroom with a full-sized bath providing utmost privacy. A second bath is situated between the remaining two bedrooms, plus a powder room is located in the entry area adjacent to the great room. The garage, lanai or rear deck and fireplace are optional. The blueprints for this house show how to build both the basic, low-cost version, and the enhanced, upgraded version.

Design by
Home Planners

Design 3711
Square Footage: 1,728

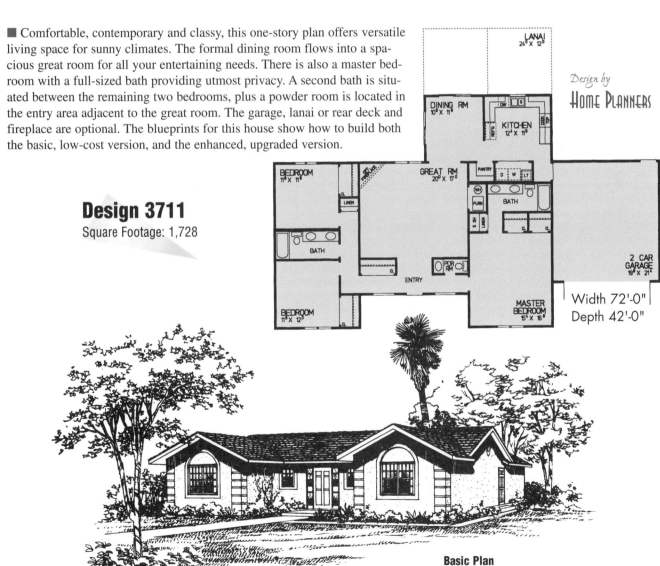

LANAI
24⁰ X 12⁰

DINING RM
10⁸ X 11⁸

KITCHEN
12⁴ X 11⁸

BEDROOM
11⁰ X 11⁰

GREAT RM
20⁰ X 17⁰

PANTRY

LINEN

BATH

FURN

BATH

2 CAR
GARAGE
19⁸ X 21⁸

PDR
RM

ENTRY

BEDROOM
11⁸ X 12⁸

MASTER
BEDROOM
15⁴ X 16⁸

Width 72'-0"
Depth 42'-0"

Basic Plan

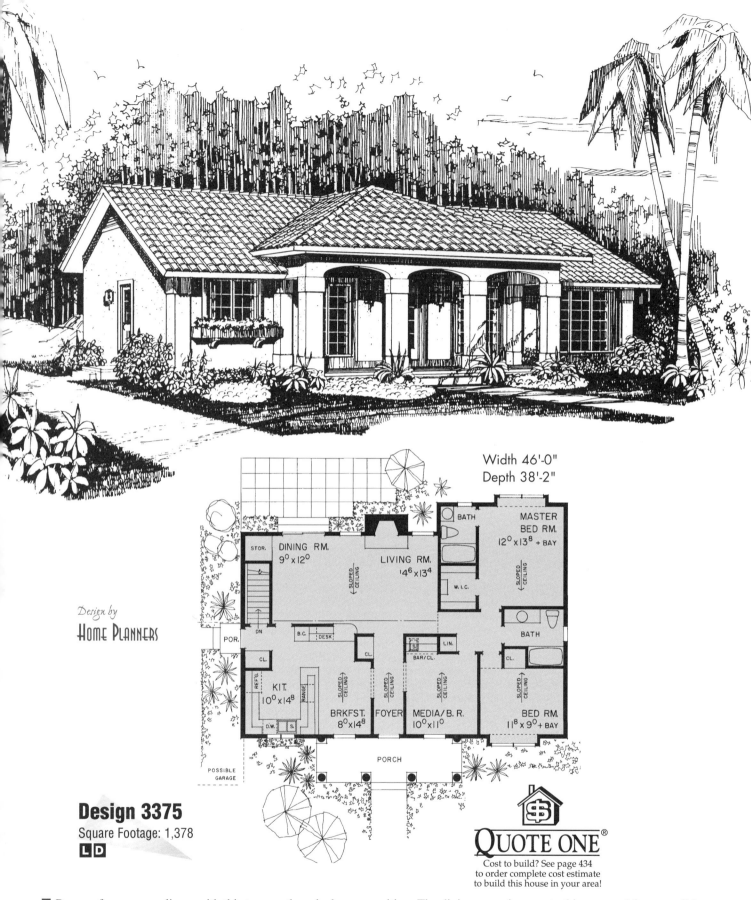

Width 46'-0"
Depth 38'-2"

Design by
HOME PLANNERS

Design 3375
Square Footage: 1,378

L D

QUOTE ONE®
Cost to build? See page 434
to order complete cost estimate
to build this house in your area!

■ Prepare for warmer climes with this two- or three-bedroom home. A covered porch with columns leads to the interior where a breakfast room sits to the left and a media room (or use this room as a bedroom) sits to the right. Directly ahead, in the living room, a fireplace and a sloped ceiling lend defin- ition. The dining room is open to this area and features slid- ing glass doors to a rear terrace. In the kitchen, a U-shape assures efficiency. Two bedrooms include a master suite with a private bath, a box-bay window and a walk-in closet.

Design 3480

Square Footage: 1,845

L D

Design by
Home Planners

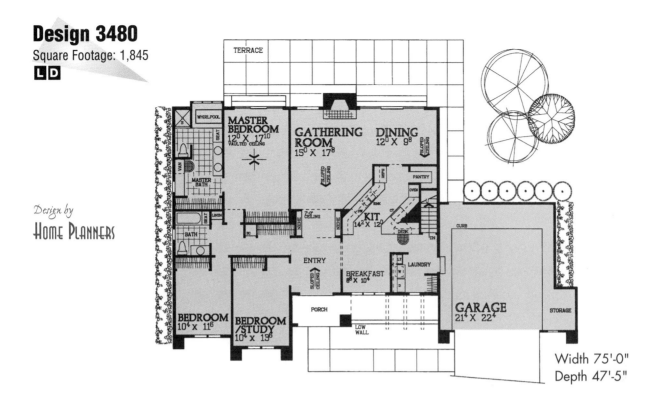

Width 75'-0"
Depth 47'-5"

■ Beyond the grand entry, a comfortable gathering room with a central fireplace shares sweeping, open spaces with the dining room. An efficiently patterned kitchen makes use of a large, walk-in pantry and a breakfast room. A snack bar offers a third mealtime eating option. Nearby, a full laundry room rounds out the modern livability of this utilitarian area. Away from the hustle and bustle of the day, three bedrooms provide ample sleeping accommodations for the whole family. Two secondary bedrooms each enjoy full proportions and the convenience of a nearby bath. In the master bedroom, look for double closets and a pampering bath with double lavs, a vanity and a whirlpool bath.

QUOTE ONE®

Cost to build? See page 434
to order complete cost estimate
to build this house in your area!

Design 6605

Square Footage: 2,762

■ A different and exciting floor plan defines this three-bedroom home. Clear and simple rooflines and a large welcoming entryway make it unique. A large archway frames the dining room entry to the gallery hall. The hall leads past the kitchen toward the informal leisure and nook area. High glass above the built-in fireplace allows for natural light and rear views. Greenhouse-style garden windows light the nook. The large master suite has a morning kitchen and sitting area. The bath features a make-up space, a walk-in shower and a private garden tub.

Design by
THE SATER
DESIGN COLLECTION

greenhouse windows
high glass
fireplace

nook
9'-8" x 11'-0"
10' clg.

leisure
16'-0" x 17'-4"
10' clg.

verandah
36'-0" x 10'-0"

kitchen

dry bar

br. 3
13'-4" x 11'-6"
10' clg.

master suite
16'-0" x 14'-2"
10' clg.

mitered glass

am kitchen

living
15'-0" x 15'-0"
10' clg.

desk

gallery

built ins

study
11' x 15'
10' clg.

arch

dining
15'-0" x 13'-0"
10' clg.

util.

br. 2
11'-4" x 12'-0"
10' clg.

foyer

entry

curved glass

private garden

garage
21'-8" x 25'-8"

Width 74'-0"
Depth 77'-0"

© The Sater Group, Inc.

Design 9083
Square Footage: 2,176

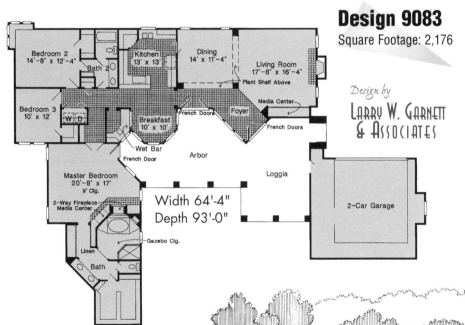

Bedroom 2
14'-8" x 12'-4"

Bath 2

Bedroom 3
10' x 12'

W D

Kitchen
13' x 13'

Dining
14' x 11'-4"

Living Room
17'-8" x 16'-4"

Plant Shelf Above

Media Center

Breakfast
10' x 10'

French Doors

Foyer

French Doors

Wet Bar

French Door

Arbor

Master Bedroom
20'-8" x 17'
9' Clg.

2-Way Fireplace
Media Center

Loggia

2-Car Garage

Linen

Gazebo Clg.

Bath

Width 64'-4"
Depth 93'-0"

Design by
Larry W. Garnett & Associates

■ This Southwestern design caters to outdoor lifestyles with ample windows, and a large arbor and covered loggia open to the front entry. The Spanish-style courtyard also includes a spa. The foyer hall runs the length of the home and leads from open living and dining areas to a convenient kitchen and breakfast nook, and then to private sleeping quarters. The master suite is especially delightful with its luxurious bath and ample closet space. There are many other extras in the plan: fireplace and media center in the living room; fireplace in the master bedroom; and an oversized pantry in the kitchen.

Quote One®

Cost to build? See page 434
to order complete cost estimate
to build this house in your area!

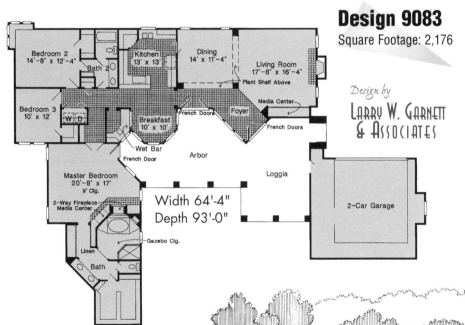

Side Elevation

413

Design 6626
Square Footage: 2,589

■ This plan has an Old World
Mediterranean look with a contemporary floor plan that's easy to
live in. The formal living areas are
just off the grand foyer. The large
living and dining rooms are easily
accessible to the wet bar. An archway leads to the family areas. An
ample kitchen has a walk-in
pantry and desk message center.
The nook and leisure room face
the rear. The owners wing features
a bayed study with bookshelves,
large sleeping quarters and a
bayed sitting area. The bath has
His and Hers walk-in closets, a
glass shower and a garden tub.

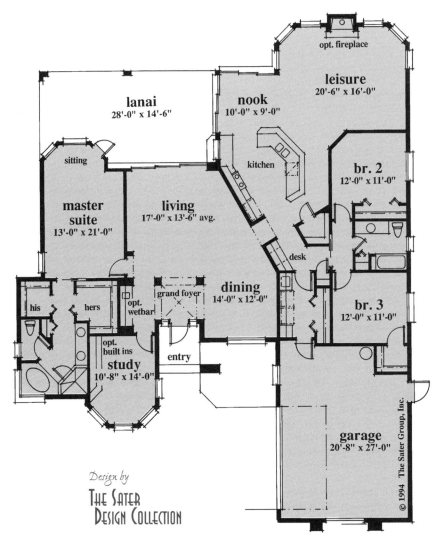

opt. fireplace

leisure
20'-6" x 16'-0"

lanai
28'-0" x 14'-6"

nook
10'-0" x 9'-0"

kitchen

sitting

br. 2
12'-0" x 11'-0"

master
suite
13'-0" x 21'-0"

living
17'-0" x 13'-6" avg.

desk

his

hers

opt.
wetbar

grand foyer

dining
14'-0" x 12'-0"

br. 3
12'-0" x 11'-0"

opt.
built ins

study
10'-8" x 14'-0"

entry

garage
20'-8" x 27'-0"

© 1994 The Sater Group, Inc.

Design by
The Sater
Design Collection

Width 64'-0"
Depth 81'-0"

© **The Sater Group, Inc.**

Arched windows and a dramatic arched entry enhance this exciting Southwestern home. The expansive great room, highlighted by a cathedral ceiling and a fireplace, offers direct access to the rear patio and the formal dining room—a winning combination for both formal and informal get-togethers. An efficient U-shaped kitchen provides plenty of counter space and easily serves both the dining room and the great room. Sunlight fills the master bedroom through a wall of windows which affords views of the rear grounds. The master bath invites relaxation with its soothing corner tub and separate shower. Two secondary bedrooms (one serves as an optional study) share an adjacent bath.

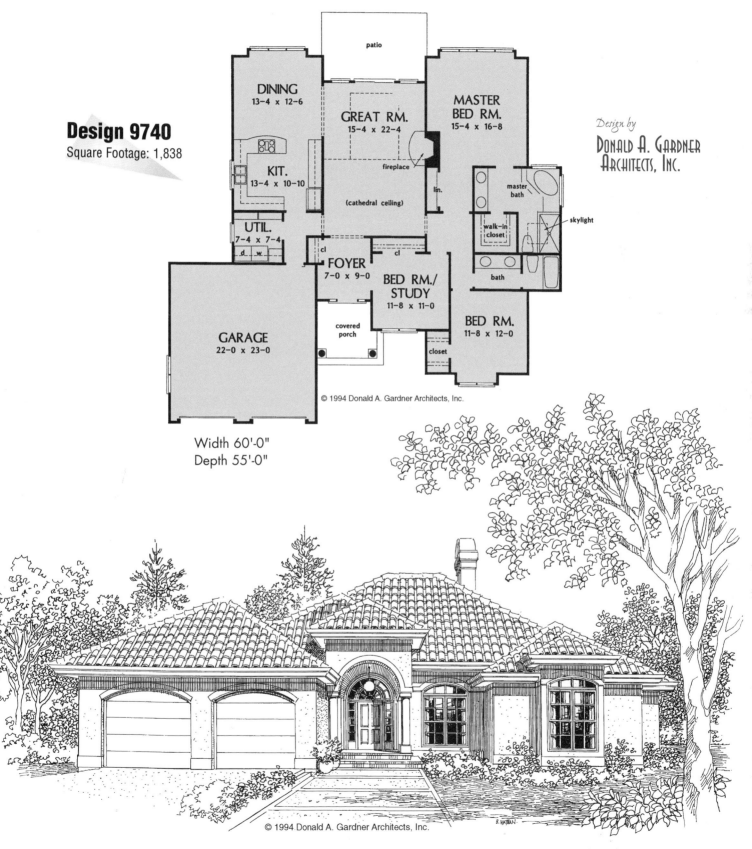

Design 9740
Square Footage: 1,838

Design by
Donald A. Gardner
Architects, Inc.

patio

DINING
13-4 x 12-6

GREAT RM.
15-4 x 22-4

MASTER
BED RM.
15-4 x 16-8

fireplace

KIT.
13-4 x 10-10

(cathedral ceiling)

lin.

master
bath

UTIL.
7-4 x 7-4

walk-in
closet

skylight

d w

cl

FOYER
7-0 x 9-0

cl

bath

BED RM./
STUDY
11-8 x 11-0

GARAGE
22-0 x 23-0

covered
porch

BED RM.
11-8 x 12-0

closet

© 1994 Donald A. Gardner Architects, Inc.

Width 60'-0"
Depth 55'-0"

© 1994 Donald A. Gardner Architects, Inc.

B. NATHAN

415

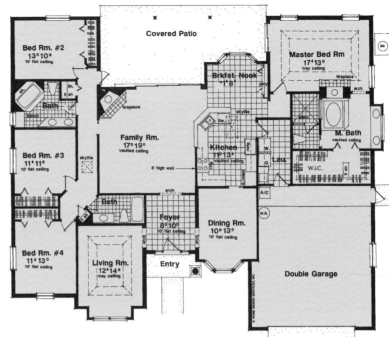

Design 8620
Square Footage: 2,454

Design by
Home Design Services

This one-story sports many well-chosen, distinctive exterior details including a cameo window and hipped rooflines. The dining and living rooms flank the foyer. A tray ceiling in the living room adds further enhancement. The bayed breakfast area admits light softened by the patio. Secluded from the main portion of the house, the master bedroom features a tray ceiling and fireplace through to the master bath. A raised tub, double vanity and immense walk-in closet highlight the bath.

Width 66'-8"
Depth 56'-8"

©1997 Donald A. Gardner Architects, Inc.

B. NATHAN

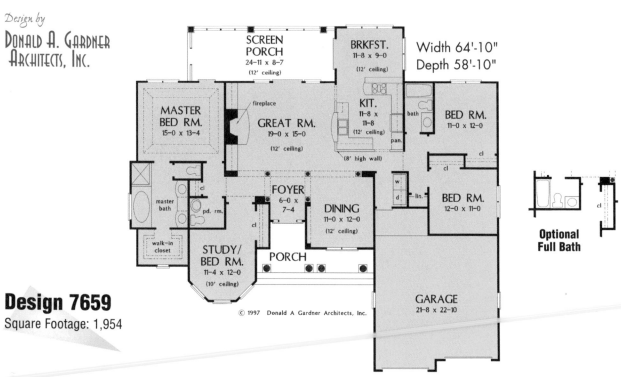

Design by
DONALD A. GARDNER ARCHITECTS, INC.

SCREEN PORCH
24-11 x 8-7
(12' ceiling)

BRKFST.
11-8 x 9-0
(12' ceiling)

Width 64'-10"
Depth 58'-10"

fireplace

KIT.
11-8 x 11-8
(12' ceiling)

bath

BED RM.
11-0 x 12-0

MASTER BED RM.
15-0 x 13-4

GREAT RM.
19-0 x 15-0
(12' ceiling)

pan.

(8' high wall)

master bath

cl

FOYER
6-0 x 7-4

DINING
11-0 x 12-0
(12' ceiling)

w
d

lin.

cl
cl

BED RM.
12-0 x 11-0

pd. rm.

walk-in closet

cl

STUDY/ BED RM.
11-4 x 12-0
(10' ceiling)

PORCH

Optional Full Bath

Design 7659

Square Footage: 1,954

© 1997 Donald A Gardner Architects, Inc.

GARAGE
21-8 x 22-10

■ Direct from the Mediterranean, this Spanish-style one-story is not only decorous, it also offers a very practical floor plan. The facade features arch-top, multi-pane windows, a columned front porch, tall chimney stack and a tiled roof. The interior has a wealth of livability. What you'll appreciate first is the juxtaposition of the great room and the formal dining room—both defined by columns. A more casual eating area is attached to the L-shaped kitchen and has access to a screen porch, as does the great room. Three bedrooms mean abundant sleeping space. The study could be a fourth bedroom—choose the full bath option in this case. A tray ceiling decorates the master bedroom, which is further enhanced by a bath with separate shower and tub, a walk-in closet and double sinks. You can also access the porch from the master bedroom. Please specify crawlspace or slab foundation when ordering.

Design 3569

Square Footage: 1,981

L D

■ An impressive arched entry graces
this Transitional one-story design.
An elegant foyer introduces an open
gathering room/dining room combination. A front-facing study with
sloped ceiling could easily be converted to a guest room with a full
bath accessible from the rear of the
room. In the kitchen, such features
as an island cooktop and a built-in
desk add style and convenience. A
corner bedroom offers front and side
views, and the nearby master suite
sports a whirlpool bath and walk-in
closet, and offers access to the rear
terrace. Other special features of the
plan include multi-pane windows, a
warming fireplace, a cozy covered
dining porch and a two-car garage.
Note the handy storage closet in the
laundry area.

Design by
HOME PLANNERS

Width 58'-0"
Depth 56'-4"

QUOTE ONE®

Cost to build? See page 434
to order complete cost estimate
to build this house in your area!

Width 64'-5"
Depth 52'-11"

BED RM.
12-0 x 11-4

walk-in closet   walk-in closet

BED RM.
12-0 x 11-4

bath

storage   up

GARAGE
21-0 x 21-0

storage

DINING
11-0 x 14-0
(11' ceiling)

SCREEN PORCH
16-8 x 12-5
(11' ceiling)

KIT.
11-0 x 15-0
(11' ceiling)

GREAT RM.
17-0 x 20-0
(11' ceiling)

fireplace

MASTER BED RM.
13-4 x 15-0

walk-in closet

UTIL.
5-6 x 6-0
d   w

cl

PORCH

lin.

master bath

© 1997 Donald A Gardner Architects, Inc.

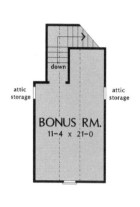

BONUS RM.
11-4 x 21-0

down

attic storage   attic storage

Design 7655

Square Footage: 1,782
Bonus Room: 229 square feet

■ Though tending toward Spanish-style, this home carries a more classic, formal look than the traditional Mediterranean of its genre. More symmetrical than most, it offers a raised porch with columns and multi-pane windows with jack-arch detailing. The interior is pure modern floor planning. The living areas are open, with eleven-foot ceilings and an easy flow from great room to dining room to kitchen. The rear screen porch supplies outdoor enchantment. The bedrooms are designed in the split style that is popular with new homes. The master suite features a tray ceiling, walk-in closet and grandly appointed master bath. Two family bedrooms have walk-in closets and share a full bath. Top it all off with a two-car garage with extra storage space and you've got one great design.

Design by
Donald A. Gardner
Architects, Inc.

©1997 Donald A. Gardner Architects, Inc.

Discreet placement of bedrooms provides for the utmost in privacy in this one-story home. The dining and living rooms flank the foyer—note the columns that add drama to the living room. A volume-ceilinged family room includes a fireplace which is flanked by sliding doors leading to a covered rear patio. The master suite includes a walk-in closet and bath with a dual vanity and step-up corner spa tub set between columns. Two bedrooms and a full bath occupy the opposite wing, which is reached via a pocket door off the family wing. Blueprints for this design include three different elevations.

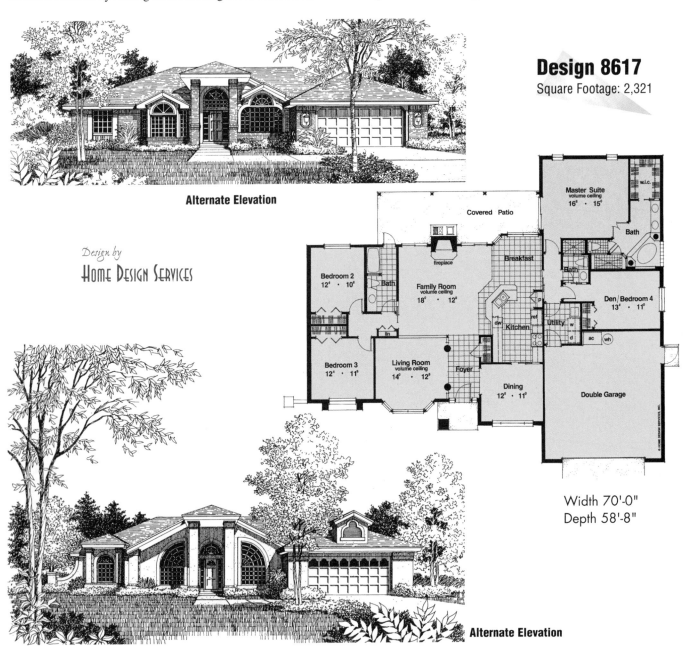

Alternate Elevation

Design by
HOME DESIGN SERVICES

Design 8617
Square Footage: 2,321

Width 70'-0"
Depth 58'-8"

Alternate Elevation

■ Make the most of warmer climes in this striking three-bedroom home. A grand entry gives way to a great room with skylights and a fireplace. A cathedral ceiling furthers the open feeling in this room. A large dining room surveys views on two sides. Adjacent, the kitchen will delight with its large island work space and abundance of counter and cabinet space.

Facing the front, the breakfast room offers ample space along with elegant ceiling detail. Three bedrooms—or two with a study—make up the sleeping quarters of this plan. In the master bedroom, large proportions include a private bath with a walk-in closet and a bumped-out garden tub. A secluded covered porch provides the opportunity for outdoor enjoyment.

Design 9737
Square Footage: 1,929

Design by
Donald A. Gardner Architects, Inc.

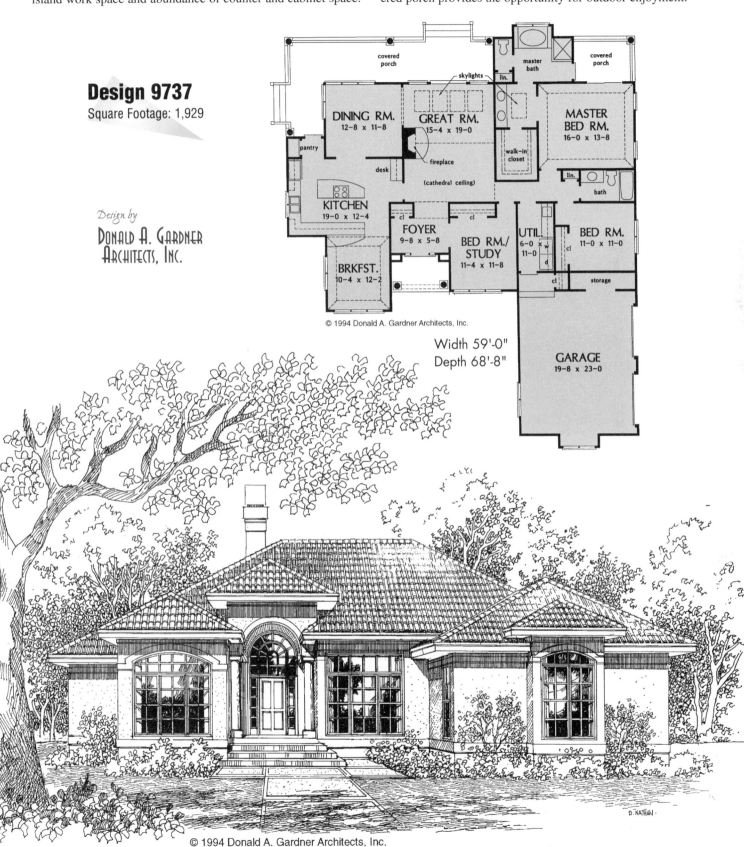

Width 59'-0"
Depth 68'-8"

© 1994 Donald A. Gardner Architects, Inc.

Design 6691

Square Footage: 1,288

■ Welcome home to casual, unstuffy living with this comfortable tidewater design. Asymmetrical lines celebrate the turn of the new century, and blend a current Gulf Coast style with vintage panache brought forward from its regional past. The heart of this home is the great room, where a put-your-feet-up atmosphere prevails, and the dusky hues of sunset can mingle with the sounds of ocean breakers. French doors open the master suite to a private area of the covered porch, where sunlight and sea breezes mingle with a spirit of bon vivant.

Design by

The Sater Design Collection

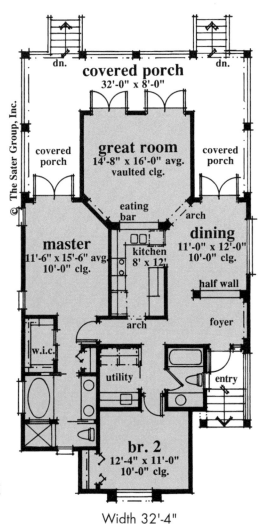

Rear Elevation

© The Sater Group, Inc.

covered porch
32'-0" x 8'-0"

dn. dn.

covered porch

great room
14'-8" x 16'-0" avg.
vaulted clg.

covered porch

eating bar

arch

master
11'-6" x 15'-6" avg.
10'-0" clg.

kitchen
8' x 12'

dining
11'-0" x 12'-0"
10'-0" clg.

half wall

w.i.c.

utility

foyer

arch

entry

br. 2
12'-4" x 11'-0"
10'-0" clg.

Width 32'-4"
Depth 60'-0"

Garages-Plus:

more than just a convenient parking space

■ The two-car garage area of this plan provides the basics, but the more than 300 square feet of optional-use area can be transformed into a game room, an exercise room, or a separate space for sewing or other hobbies. Extra convenience is provided by a full bath with a shower and both linen and storage closets. Let your imagination take over when deciding which amenities you need to create a special workspace for your projects. In the garage, you'll find more than enough room for two cars, plus plenty of storage for yard and garden equipment, garbage cans and recycling bins. Design G261 offers the same great floor plan with a farmhouse- or Victorian-style facade.

Design G261

Design G259
Square Footage: 900

Design by
HOME PLANNERS

STORAGE
CABINETS

FURN

SHWR

BATH

LINEN

STORAGE

YARD TOOL HANGING

GARAGE
22¹⁰ x 24⁴

EXERCISE/
SEWING/
HOBBY/
GAME RM
12² x 18²

WH

Width 36'-0"
Depth 25'-0"

COVERED
PORCH

Design G263

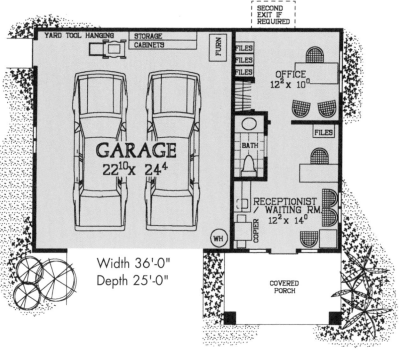

SECOND
EXIT IF
REQUIRED

YARD TOOL HANGING | STORAGE
CABINETS

FURN

FILES
FILES
FILES

OFFICE
12² x 10⁰

FILES

GARAGE
22¹⁰ x 24⁴

BATH

RECEPTIONIST /
WAITING RM.
12² x 14⁰

COPIER

WH

Width 36'-0"
Depth 25'-0"

COVERED
PORCH

Design G264

Design G265
Square Footage: 900

■ Greet your clients in the business side of this multi-use structure. There's room enough for a reception/waiting room in front with an impressive entryway through a four-column porch. Decorative recessed windows flanking the door and two more in the side wall allow for plenty of natural light.

In the back is ample space for an office with a storage closet and a bi-fold door. Add a half-bath for maximum convenience. Choose The Chevron (Design G262), The Retreat (Design G264), or The Caprice (Design G263) for a different look.

Design G262

Design G278

Design by
Home Planners

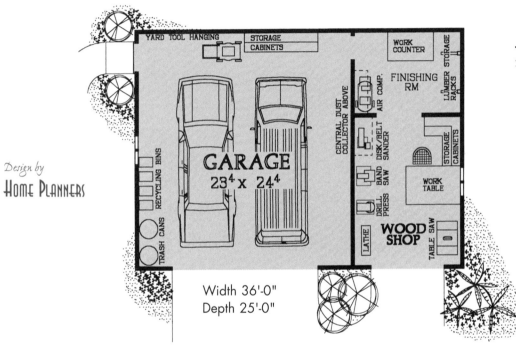

YARD TOOL HANGING

STORAGE CABINETS

WORK COUNTER

LUMBER STORAGE RACKS

CENTRAL DUST COLLECTOR ABOVE

AIR COMP.

FINISHING RM

DISK/BELT SANDER

BAND SAW

STORAGE CABINETS

RECYCLING BINS

GARAGE
23⁴ x 24⁴

DRILL PRESS

WORK TABLE

TRASH CANS

LATHE

WOOD SHOP

TABLE SAW

Width 36'-0"
Depth 25'-0"

Design G281

Design G279
Square Footage: 900

■ Behind what looks like just another garage door is just what you've always wanted—a fully equipped workshop. Accessed through an 8'x7' garage door, or from an interior door within the garage itself, is 300 square feet of workshop area. It contains plenty of room for your favorite power tools, work table, storage cabinets, counter space and overhead racks for lumber. On the garage side of this multi-use structure is a two car garage with a 16'x7' door. It allows space for yard and garden equipment, plus a convenient area for recycling bins and garbage cans. Choose The Longview (Design G280), The Traditional (Design G278), or The Elite (Design G281) for a different look.

Design G280

Design G277
Square Footage: 900

■ Locate this roomy structure near the pool and provide security for two cars, plus a spacious bathhouse with a changing room and an outdoor patio/lounge area shaded by a generous roof extension. The garage area provides plenty of space to store yard and garden equipment and other necessities like garbage cans and recycling bins. Natural light enters the interior through two skylights over the kitchen area. Built-in benches and counter tops, plus storage and linen closets, offer lots of convenience. The kitchenette is cooled by a ceiling fan and French doors leading to the patio. Choose The Echo (Design G276), The Classic (Design G274), or The Emblem (Design G275) for a different look.

Design G276

Design G274

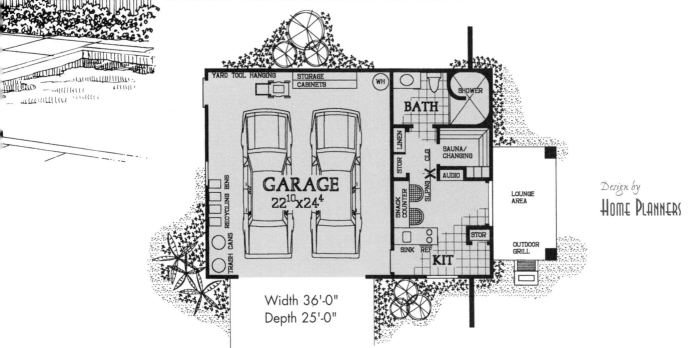

YARD TOOL HANGING

STORAGE CABINETS

WH

RECYCLING BINS

TRASH CANS

GARAGE
22¹⁰x24⁴

STOR

LINEN

SL PNG CLG

SNACK COUNTER

BATH

SHOWER

SAUNA/ CHANGING

AUDIO

STOR

LOUNGE AREA

OUTDOOR GRILL

SINK REF

KIT

Width 36'-0"
Depth 25'-0"

Design by
Home Planners

Design G275

429

Design G272

Square Footage: 900

■ Two cars and a lap pool all fit inside this 900-square-foot floor plan. If you don't happen to live where it's balmy year 'round, tuck this figure eight-style pool in the 312 square feet to the right of the garage—all under one roof. Access to the pool is through an interior door in the garage, or from outside through its own separate door. Natural light pours into the pool area through four skylights—two on each slope of the roof. The garage has space for two cars with plenty of room left over for storing yard tools, garden equipment and trash and recycling bins. Choose Northern Lights (Design G270), The Fanfare (Design G271), or The Ivy (Design G273) for a different look.

Design G270

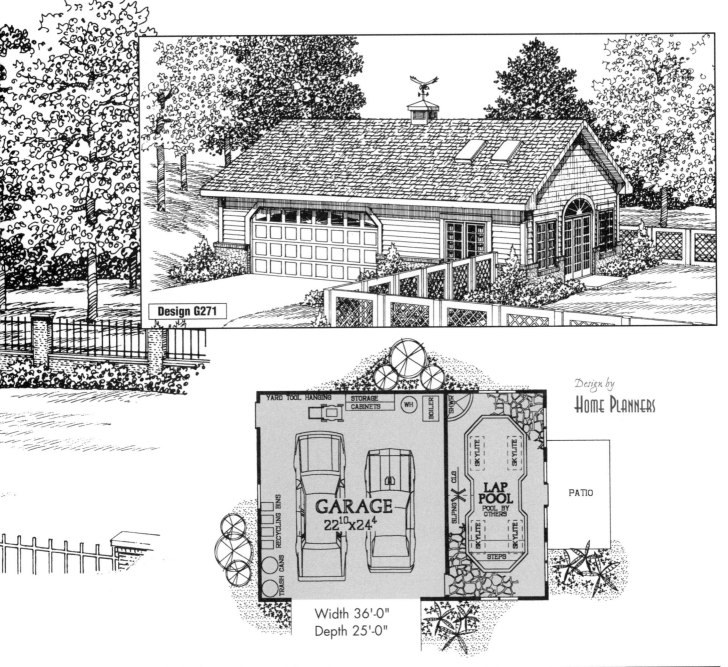

Design G271

Design by
Home Planners

YARD TOOL HANGING | STORAGE CABINETS | WH | BOILER | SHWR

RECYCLING BINS

TRASH CANS

GARAGE
22¹⁰x24⁴

SLPNG CLG

SKYLITE | SKYLITE

LAP POOL
POOL BY OTHERS

SKYLITE | SKYLITE

STEPS

PATIO

Width 36'-0"
Depth 25'-0"

Design G273

When You're Ready To Order . . .

Let Us Show You Our Home Blueprint Package.

Building a home? Planning a home? Our Blueprint Package has nearly everything you need to get the job done right, whether you're working on your own or with help from an architect, designer, builder or subcontractors. Each Blueprint Package is the result of many hours of work by licensed architects or professional designers.

QUALITY

Hundreds of hours of painstaking effort have gone into the development of your blueprint set. Each home has been quality-checked by professionals to insure accuracy and buildability.

VALUE

Because we sell in volume, you can buy professional-quality blueprints at a fraction of their development cost. With our plans, your dream home design costs only a few hundred dollars, not the thousands of dollars that custom architects charge.

SERVICE

Once you've chosen your favorite home plan, you'll receive fast, efficient service whether you choose to mail or fax your order to us or call us toll free at 1-800-521-6797. For customer service, call toll free 1-888-690-1116.

SATISFACTION

Over 50 years of service to satisfied home plan buyers provide us unparalleled experience and knowledge in producing quality blueprints. What this means to you is satisfaction with our product and performance.

ORDER TOLL FREE 1-800-521-6797

After you've looked over our Blueprint Package and Important Extras on the following pages, simply mail the order form on page 445 or call toll free on our Blueprint Hotline: 1-800-521-6797. We're ready and eager to serve you. For customer service, call toll free 1-888-690-1116.

Each set of blueprints is an interrelated collection of detail sheets which includes components such as floor plans, interior and exterior elevations, dimensions, cross-sections, diagrams and notations. These sheets show exactly how your house is to be built.

Among the sheets included may be:

Frontal Sheet
This artist's sketch of the exterior of the house gives you an idea of how the house will look when built and landscaped. Large ink-line floor plans show all levels of the house and provide an overview of your new home's livability, as well as a handy reference for deciding on furniture placement.

Foundation Plan
This sheet shows the foundation layout

SAMPLE PACKAGE

including support walls, excavated and unexcavated areas, if any, and foundation notes. If slab construction rather than basement, the plan shows footings and details for a monolithic slab. This page, or another in the set, may include a sample plot plan for locating your house on a building site.

Detailed Floor Plans

These plans show the layout of each floor of the house. Rooms and interior spaces are carefully dimensioned and keys are given for cross-section details provided later in the plans. The positions of electrical outlets and switches are shown.

House Cross-Sections

Large-scale views show sections or cut-aways of the foundation, interior walls, exterior walls, floors, stairways and roof details. Additional cross-sections may show important changes in floor, ceiling or roof heights or the relationship of one level to another. Extremely valuable for construction, these sections show exactly how the various parts of the house fit together.

Interior Elevations

Many of our drawings show the design and placement of kitchen and bathroom cabinets, laundry areas, fireplaces, bookcases and other built-ins. Little "extras," such as mantelpiece and wainscoting drawings, plus moulding sections, provide details that give your home that custom touch.

Exterior Elevations

These drawings show the front, rear and sides of your house and give necessary notes on exterior materials and finishes. Particular attention is given to cornice detail, brick and stone accents or other finish items that make your home unique.

Note: Because of the diversity of local building codes, our blueprints may not include Electrical, Plumbing or Mechanical plans or layouts.

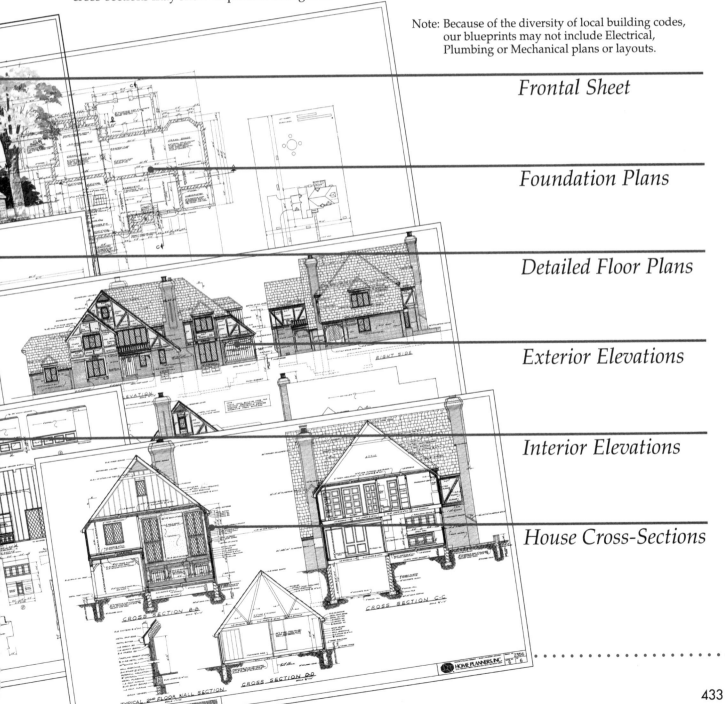

Frontal Sheet

Foundation Plans

Detailed Floor Plans

Exterior Elevations

Interior Elevations

House Cross-Sections

*I*mportant Extras To Do The Job Right!

Introducing eight important planning and construction aids developed by our professionals to help you succeed in your home-building project.

MATERIALS LIST

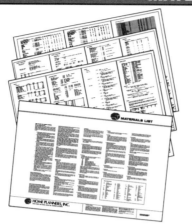

(Note: Because of the diversity of local building codes, our Materials List does not include mechanical materials.)

For many of the designs in our portfolio, we offer a customized materials take-off that is invaluable in planning and estimating the cost of your new home. This Materials List outlines the quantity, type and size of materials needed to build your house (with the exception of mechanical system items). Included are framing lumber, windows and doors, kitchen and bath cabinetry, rough and finish hardware, and much more. This handy list helps you or your builder cost out materials and serves as a reference sheet when you're compiling bids. A Materials List cannot be ordered before blueprints are ordered.

SPECIFICATION OUTLINE

This valuable 16-page document is critical to building your house correctly. Designed to be filled in by you or your builder, this book lists 166 stages or items crucial to the building process. It provides a comprehensive review of the construction process and helps in choosing materials. When combined with the blueprints, a signed contract, and a schedule, it becomes a legal document and record for the building of your home.

QUOTE ONE®

Summary Cost Report / Materials Cost Report

A new service for estimating the cost of building select designs, the Quote One® system is available in two separate stages: The Summary Cost Report and the Materials Cost Report.

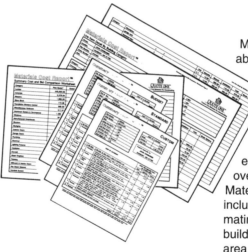

The Summary Cost report is the first stage in the package and shows the total cost per square foot for your chosen home in your zip-code area and then breaks that cost down into various categories showing the costs for building materials, labor and installation. The total cost for the report (which includes three grades: Budget, Standard and Custom) is just $29.95 for one home, and additionals are only $14.95. These reports allow you to evaluate your building budget and compare the costs of building a variety of homes in your area.

Make even more informed decisions about your home-building project with the second phase of our package, our Materials Cost Report. This tool is invaluable in planning and estimating the cost of your new home. The material and installation (labor and equipment) cost is shown for each of over 1,000 line items provided in the Materials List (Standard grade), which is included when you purchase this estimating tool. It allows you to determine building costs for your specific zip-code area and for your chosen home design. Space is allowed for additional estimates from contractors and subcontractors. This invaluable tool is available for a price of $120 ($130 for a Schedule C4–L4 plan), which includes a Materials List. A Materials Cost Report cannot be ordered before blueprints are ordered.

The Quote One® program is continually updated with new plans. If you are interested in a plan that is not indicated as Quote One®, please call and ask our sales reps. They will be happy to verify the status for you. To order these invaluable reports, use the order form on page 445 or call 1-800-521-6797.

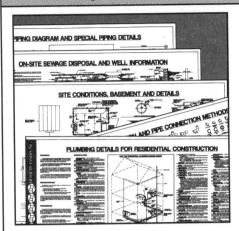

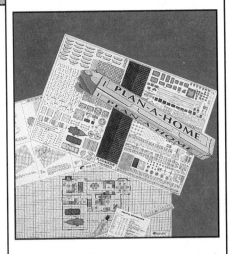

D The Deck Blueprint Package

Many of the homes in this book can be enhanced with a professionally designed Deck Plan. Those home plans highlighted with a D have a matching or corresponding deck plan available that includes a Deck Plan Frontal Sheet, Deck Framing and Floor Plans, Deck Elevations and a Deck Materials List. A Standard Deck Details Package, also available, provides all the how-to information necessary for building any deck. Our Complete Deck Building Package contains one set of Custom Deck Plans of your choice, plus one set of Standard Deck Building Details all for one low price. Our plans and details are carefully prepared in an easy-to-understand format that will guide you through every stage of your deck-building project. See these pages for 25 different deck layouts to match your favorite house. See page 440 for prices and ordering information.

SPLIT-LEVEL SUN DECK
Deck Plan D100

BI-LEVEL WITH COVERED DINING
Deck Plan D101

FRESH-AIR CORNER DECK
Deck Plan D102

BACKYARD EXTENDER DECK
Deck Plan D103

WRAPAROUND FAMILY DECK
Deck Plan D104

DRAMATIC DECK WITH BARBECUE
Deck Plan D105

SPLIT-PLAN COUNTRY DECK
Deck Plan D106

DECK FOR DINING AND VIEWS
Deck Plan D107

BOLD, ANGLED CORNER DECK
Deck Plan D108

SPECTACULAR "RESORT-STYLE" DECK
Deck Plan D109

TREND-SETTER DECK
Deck Plan D110

TURN-OF-THE-CENTURY DECK
Deck Plan D111

WEEKEND ENTERTAINER DECK
Deck Plan D112

STRIKING "DELTA" DECK
Deck Plan D113

CENTER-VIEW DECK
Deck Plan D114

KITCHEN-EXTENDER DECK
Deck Plan D115

BI-LEVEL RETREAT DECK
Deck Plan D116

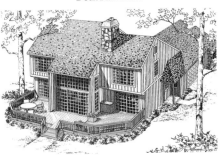

SPLIT-LEVEL ACTIVITY DECK
Deck Plan D117

OUTDOOR LIFESTYLE DECK
Deck Plan D118

TRI-LEVEL DECK WITH GRILL
Deck Plan D119

CONTEMPORARY LEISURE DECK
Deck Plan D120

ANGULAR WINGED DECK
Deck Plan D121

DECK FOR A SPLIT-LEVEL HOME
Deck Plan D122

GRACIOUS GARDEN DECK
Deck Plan D123

TERRACED DECK FOR ENTERTAINING
Deck Plan D124

For Deck Plan prices and ordering
information, see page 440.
 Or call Toll Free,
1-800-521-6797.

L The Landscape Blueprint Package

For the homes marked with an **L** in this book, Home Planners has created a front-yard landscape plan that matches or is complementary in design to the house plan. These comprehensive blueprint packages include a Frontal Sheet, Plan View, Regionalized Plant & Materials List, a sheet on Planting and Maintaining Your Landscape, Zone Maps and Plant Size and Description Guide. These plans will help you achieve professional results, adding value and enjoyment to your property for years to come. Each set of blueprints is a full 18" x 24" in size and clear, complete instructions and easy-to-read type. See the following pages for 18 different front-yard Landscape Plans to match your favorite house.

Regional Order Map

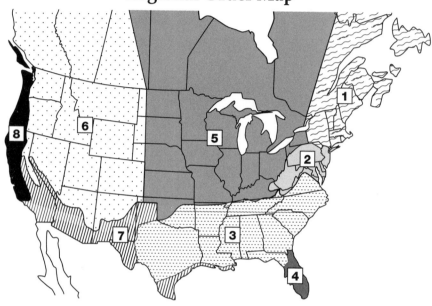

Most of the Landscape Plans shown on these pages are available with a Plant & Materials List adapted by horticultural experts to 8 different regions of the country. Please specify Geographic Region when ordering your plan. See page 440 for prices, ordering information and regional availability.

Region	1	Northeast
Region	2	Mid-Atlantic
Region	3	Deep South
Region	4	Florida & Gulf Coast
Region	5	Midwest
Region	6	Rocky Mountains
Region	7	Southern California & Desert Southwest
Region	8	Northern California & Pacific Northwest

CAPE COD TRADITIONAL
Landscape Plan L200

WILLIAMSBURG CAPE
Landscape Plan L201

CAPE COD COTTAGE
Landscape Plan L202

GAMBREL-ROOF COLONIAL
Landscape Plan L203

CENTER-HALL COLONIAL
Landscape Plan L204

CLASSIC NEW ENGLAND COLONIAL
Landscape Plan L205

SOUTHERN COLONIAL
Landscape Plan L206

COUNTRY-STYLE FARMHOUSE
Landscape Plan L207

PENNSYLVANIA STONE FARMHOUSE
Landscape Plan L208

RAISED-PORCH FARMHOUSE
Landscape Plan L209

NEW ENGLAND BARN-STYLE HOUSE
Landscape Plan L210

NEW ENGLAND COUNTRY HOUSE
Landscape Plan L211

TRADITIONAL COUNTRY ESTATE
Landscape Plan L212

FRENCH PROVINCIAL ESTATE
Landscape Plan L213

GEORGIAN MANOR
Landscape Plan L214

GRAND-PORTICO GEORGIAN
Landscape Plan L215

BRICK FEDERAL
Landscape Plan L216

COUNTRY FRENCH RAMBLER
Landscape Plan L217

Price Schedule & Plans Index

Blueprint Price Schedule
(Prices guaranteed through December 31, 2000)

Tiers	1-set Study Package	4-set Building Package	8-set Building Package	1-set Reproducible Sepias	Home Customizer® Package
P1	$20	$50	$90	N/A	N/A
P2	$40	$70	$110	N/A	N/A
P3	$60	$90	$130	N/A	N/A
P4	$80	$110	$150	N/A	N/A
P5	$100	$130	$170	N/A	N/A
P6	$120	$150	$190	N/A	N/A
A1	$400	$440	$500	$600	$650
A2	$440	$480	$540	$660	$710
A3	$480	$520	$580	$720	$770
A4	$520	$560	$620	$780	$830
C1	$560	$600	$660	$840	$890
C2	$600	$640	$700	$900	$950
C3	$650	$690	$750	$950	$1000
C4	$700	$740	$800	$1000	$1050
L1	$750	$790	$850	$1050	$1100

Options for plans in Tiers A1–A4
Additional Identical Blueprints in same order for "A1–L4" price plans......................................$50 per set
Reverse Blueprints (mirror image) with 4- or 8-set order for "A1–L4" price plans............ $50 fee per order
Specification Outlines.....................................$10 each
Materials Lists for "A1–C3" price plans..........$60 each
Materials Lists for "C4–L4" price plans...........$70 each

Options for plans in Tiers P1–P6
Additional Identical Blueprints in same order for "P1–P6" price plans..................................$10 per set
Reverse Blueprints (mirror image) for "P1–P6" price plans...$10 per set
1 Set of Deck Construction Details...............$14.95 each
Deck Construction Package...........add $10 to Building Package price
   (1 set of "P1–P6" price plans, plus 1 set Standard Deck Construction Details)
1 Set of Gazebo Construction Details.........$14.95 each
Gazebo Construction Package.......add $10 to Building Package price
   (1 set of "P1–P6" price plans, plus 1 set Standard Gazebo Construction Details)

IMPORTANT NOTES
The 1-set study package is marked "not for construction."
Prices for 4- or 8-set Building Packages honored only at time of original order.

Index

To use the Index below, refer to the design number listed in numerical order (a helpful page reference is also given). Note the price index letter and refer to the House Blueprint Price Schedule above for the cost of one, four or eight sets of blueprints or the cost of a reproducible sepia. Additional prices are shown for identical and reverse blueprint sets, as well as other very useful products for many of the plans. Also note in the Index below those plans that have matching or complementary Deck Plans or Landscape Plans. Refer to the schedules above for prices of these plans. All plans in this publication are customizable. However, only Home Planners plans can be customized with Home Planners Home Customizer® Package. These plans are indicated below with this symbol: 🐭. See page 445 for information. Some plans are also part of our Quote One® estimating service and are indicated by this symbol: 🏠. See page 434 for more information. Many plans offer Materials Lists and are indicated by this symbol: ✓. See page 434 for more information.

To Order: Fill in and send the order form on page 445—or call toll free 1-800-521-6797 or 520-297-8200. Fax: 1-800-224-6699 or 520-544-3086.

DESIGN	PRICE	PAGE	MATERIALS LIST	CUSTOMIZABLE	QUOTE ONE®	DECK	DECK PRICE	LANDSCAPE	LANDSCAPE PRICE	REGIONS
1404	A3	368	✓	🐭						
1491	A2	370	✓	🐭						
2200	C1	400	✓	🐭						
2226	C3	331	✓	🐭						
2294	C2	401	✓	🐭				L236	P4	3,4,7
2439	A3	371	✓	🐭						
2461	A3	369	✓	🐭						
2557	A3	333	✓	🐭						
2559	A4	160	✓	🐭		D112	P2			
2677	C1	398	✓	🐭						
2741	A3	399	✓	🐭		D114	P2			
3345	A3	242	✓	🐭	🏠			L220	p3	1-3,5,6,8
3350	A3	251	✓	🐭	🏠	D115	P2	L205	P3	1-3,5,6,8
3373	A4	326	✓	🐭	🏠	D110	P2	L202	P3	1-3,5,6,8
3375	A4	410	✓	🐭	🏠	D110	P2	L202	P3	1-3,5,6,8
3401	C3	383	✓	🐭	🏠			L233	P3	3,4,7
3402	C4	382	✓	🐭	🏠			L236	P4	3,4,7
3408	C2	356	✓	🐭	🏠			L230	P4	1-8
3431	A4	377	✓	🐭	🏠					
3433	C1	10	✓	🐭	🏠			L213	P4	1-8
3451	A3	36	✓	🐭	🏠			L220	P3	1-3,5,6,8
3453	A4	341	✓	🐭	🏠			L238	P3	3,4,7,8
3460	A3	180	✓	🐭	🏠			L200	P3	1-3,5,6,8
3465	A2	67	✓	🐭	🏠			L205	P3	1-3,5,6,8
3475	C2	94	✓	🐭	🏠			L236	P4	3,4,7
3480	C1	411	✓	🐭	🏠	D112	P2	L238	P3	3,4,7,8
3481	C1	336	✓	🐭	🏠			L200	P3	1-3,5,6,8
3487	A4	245	✓	🐭	🏠			L209	P3	1-6,8
3488	C1	325	✓	🐭	🏠	D112	P2	L220	P3	1-3,5,6,8
3489	A4	246	✓	🐭	🏠	D112	P2	L220	P3	1-3,5,6,8
3490	C1	248	✓	🐭	🏠	D112	P2	L220	P3	1-3,5,6,8
3491	A4	247	✓	🐭	🏠	D111	P3	L215	P4	1-6,8
3496	C2	163	✓	🐭	🏠			L202	P3	1-3,5,6,8
3498	C2	147	✓	🐭	🏠					
3569	A3	418	✓	🐭	🏠	D105	P2	L238	P3	3,4,7,8
3629	C1	106	✓	🐭	🏠			L239	P4	1-8
3667	C1	347	✓	🐭	🏠					
3676	C1	166	✓	🐭	🏠	D110	P2	L222	P3	1-3,5,6,8
3695	C2	381	✓	🐭	🏠					
3699	A4	16	✓	🐭	🏠	D115	P2	L292	P3	1-8
3706	A2	405	✓	🐭						
3707	A4	408	✓	🐭						

DESIGN	PRICE	PAGE	MATERIALS LIST	CUSTOMIZABLE	QUOTE ONE®	DECK	DECK PRICE	LANDSCAPE	LANDSCAPE PRICE	REGIONS
3709	A2	404	✓	⌂						
3710	A4	249	✓	⌂						
3711	C1	409	✓	⌂						
3716	A4	406	✓	⌂						
3719	A3	407	✓	⌂						
3724	A4	340	✓	⌂						
3725	A2	59	✓	⌂						
3728	A3	72	✓	⌂						
3802	C3	379	✓	⌂	⌂					
3803	C3	378	✓	⌂	⌂					
3804	A4	151	✓	⌂	⌂			L209	P3	1-6,8
3810	C2	270	✓	⌂	⌂					
6602	C2	5						L203	P3	1-3,5,6,8
6603	A3	388						L213	P4	1-8
6604	C2	92						L200	P3	1-3,5,6,8
6605	C1	412						L211	P3	1-8
6606	C1	99						L207	P4	1-6,8
6607	A4	278	✓		⌂			L211	P3	1-8
6609	C2	98						L211	P3	1-8
6614	A4	397						L211	P3	1-8
6624	C1	101						L200	P3	1-3,5,6,8
6626	C1	414						L211	P3	1-8
6627	C1	391						L207	P4	1-6,8
6628	C2	395						L200	P3	1-3,5,6,8
6629	C1	389						L211	P3	1-8
6630	A3	387						L213	P4	1-8
6636	C4	9						L207	P4	1-6,8
6639	C3	8						L211	P3	1-8
6641	C4	96						L216	P3	1-3,5,6,8
6642	C3	97						L213	P4	1-8
6643	C4	100						L203	P3	1-3,5,6,8
6657	C2	95								
6658	A3	396								
6659	C1	222								
6691	A2	422								
7003	A3	183	✓							
7004	C1	198	✓							
7006	A3	39	✓							
7009	A3	193	✓							
7012	A3	233	✓							
7300	A3	250	✓							
7304	A2	38	✓							
7307	A3	14	✓							
7308	A4	199	✓							
7315	A3	223	✓							
7318	A4	227	✓							
7320	A4	293	✓							
7332	A4	153	✓							
7333	A3	182	✓							
7334	A2	40	✓							
7341	C1	280	✓							
7344	A4	226	✓							
7345	C1	224	✓							
7349	A2	49	✓							
7350	A3	41	✓							
7351	A3	144	✓							
7352	A3	145	✓							
7365	A3	232	✓							
7371	A3	48	✓							
7372	A2	177	✓							
7373	A2	150	✓							
7374	A2	46	✓							
7375	A2	51	✓							
7388	C2	81	✓							
7396	A3	133	✓							
7404	C1	364								
7407	C2	103								
7411	C1	7								
7447	A3	279								
7448	A2	32								
7449	A3	241								
7601	A3	142	✓							
7603	A3	168	✓							
7616	A4	171	✓							
7619	A3	239	✓							
7623	C1	203	✓							
7624	A3	197	✓							
7625	A4	243	✓							
7632	A3	66	✓							
7634	A3	309	✓							
7635	A2	68	✓							
7636	A4	202	✓							
7637	A3	130	✓							
7639	A3	35	✓							
7641	A4	115	✓							
7645	A3	137	✓							
7655	A3	419	✓							
7657	A4	196	✓							
7658	A3	169	✓							
7659	A3	417	✓							
8056	C2	265						L207	P4	1-6,8
8064	A3	186						L203	P3	1-3,5,6,8
8076	C1	324						L204	P3	1-3,5,6,8
8087	L1	102								
8113	A4	15								
8170	A4	28								
8180	A4	204								
8181	A3	25								
8183	A4	206								
8197	A2	235								
8198	A2	212								
8199	A2	52								
8224	A4	122								
8229	A4	253								
8239	A3	23								
8241	A3	134								
8243	A4	252								
8244	A3	207								
8246	A2	17								
8247	A3	184								
8248	A2	60								
8249	A2	63								
8250	A2	62								
8253	C1	83								
8602	C1	394								
8604	A4	349								
8605	C1	353								
8606	A4	345								
8607	A4	362								
8609	A4	352								
8610	A3	65								
8611	A3	337								
8612	A4	6								
8613	A3	359								
8614	A4	165								
8617	A4	420								
8619	A4	390								
8620	C1	416								
8624	C2	93								
8627	C3	363								
8631	A4	360								
8634	A3	384								
8636	C1	357								
8638	A4	361								
8639	C1	385								
8641	A4	338								
8642	C1	358								
8646	C1	346								
8663	C2	348								
8664	C1	351								
8665	C1	104								
8997	A4	170								
8998	A3	175								
9049	A3	162	✓		⌂					
9083	A4	413	✓		⌂					
9156	C1	84								

DESIGN	PRICE	PAGE	MATERIALS LIST	CUSTOMIZABLE	QUOTE ONE®	DECK	DECK PRICE	LANDSCAPE	LANDSCAPE PRICE	REGIONS
9179	C1	80	✓							
9182	A4	205								
9184	A4	260								
9203	A4	291	✓							
9205	A4	261	✓							
9236	A2	234	✓							
9263	A3	37	✓							
9264	A4	218	✓							
9267	A4	200	✓							
9295	A4	216	✓							
9304	A3	277	✓							
9305	A4	201	✓							
9307	A3	228	✓							
9321	A3	229	✓							
9322	A3	276	✓							
9328	A2	231	✓							
9333	A4	282	✓							
9396	C1	225	✓							
9450	A4	230	✓					L204	P3	1-3,5,6,8
9451	A4	273	✓					L204	P3	1-3,5,6,8
9452	A4	386	✓					L204	P3	1-3,5,6,8
9454	C1	13	✓					L200	P3	1-3,5,6,8
9455	C1	88	✓					L207	P4	1-6,8
9502	A3	365	✓					L200	P3	1-3,5,6,8
9507	A2	69	✓							
9508	A3	19	✓					L200	P3	1-3,5,6,8
9567	C1	185	✓							
9602	A3	123	✓							
9607	A2	373	✓							
9609	A2	372	✓							
9611	A3	376	✓							
9637	A3	26	✓							
9651	A4	195	✓							
9656	A4	269	✓							
9657	A4	131	✓							
9665	A2	21	✓							
9670	A4	126	✓							
9682	A3	129	✓							
9684	A2	121	✓							
9686	A3	161	✓							
9689	A4	124	✓							
9716	A4	240	✓							
9718	A3	128	✓							
9720	C1	125	✓							
9724	A3	194	✓							
9735	C1	192	✓							
9737	A3	421	✓							
9740	A3	415	✓							
9750	A3	116	✓							
9763	A3	119	✓	⌂						
9793	A2	24	✓							
9797	A2	140	✓							
A101	A2	27								
A107	C2	85								
A131	C1	299								
A132	C1	268								
A149	A3	213								
A150	A3	220								
A157	A4	274								
A163	C1	298								
A209	C3	82								
A221	C4	91								
A245	A3	254								
A246	A3	215								
A247	A3	315								
B100	C1	172								
B105	A2	43								
B106	A3	42	✓							
B107	A2	178	✓							
B112	A4	272								
B113	A3	219								
B130	A3	158								
B132	A2	159								
B133	A2	20								
B136	A3	146								
B137	A3	322								
B143	A3	374								
C101	A4	238								
C102	A4	188								
C127	A3	61								
C145	A4	375								
C146	A4	141								
C147	A4	290								
C148	A3	54								
C149	A4	139								
C151	A3	236								
C153	A2	33								
C154	A2	58								
E103	C1	154								
E104	C3	107								
E106	A3	155								
E112	C1	262								
E116	C1	259								
E120	C1	295								
E138	C1	301								
E140	A3	303								
F117	A3	56								
F131	C1	264								
F147	A3	176								
F148	A3	329								
F149	A3	292								
F150	A4	288								
G259	P4	423	✓							
G261	P4	423	✓							
G262	P4	425	✓							
G263	P4	425	✓							
G264	P4	425	✓							
G265	P4	424	✓							
G270	P4	431	✓							
G271	P4	431	✓							
G272	P4	430	✓							
G273	P4	431	✓							
G274	P4	429	✓							
G275	P4	429	✓							
G276	P4	429	✓							
G277	P4	428	✓							
G278	P4	427	✓							
G279	P4	426	✓							
G280	P4	427	✓							
G281	P4	427	✓							
G300	A1	70	✓							
J100	C2	105								
J112	A3	339								
J123	A4	308								
J155	A3	64								
J170	A2	181								
K103	C1	392								
K115	C2	380								
K118	C1	402								
K119	C2	403								
K121	C1	350								
K122	C2	354								
K124	C4	355								
K125	C1	393								
M102	C2	271								
M103	C2	75								
M104	C2	263								
M111	C3	114								
M113	C1	164								
M117	A4	179								
M131	C2	319								
M135	A4	34								
M139	C3	111								
M150	L1	73								
M156	C2	76								
M157	C3	79								

DESIGN	PRICE	PAGE	MATERIALS LIST	CUSTOMIZABLE	QUOTE ONE®	DECK	DECK PRICE	LANDSCAPE	LANDSCAPE PRICE	REGIONS
M158	C3	77								
N101	A3	57		✓						
N104	A3	328		✓						
N107	A2	55		✓						
N108	A3	332		✓						
N119	A2	143		✓						
N120	A3	327								
N142	A3	330		✓						
N143	A2	138		✓						
N145	A2	127		✓						
P109	A3	294		✓	🏠					
P110	A2	44			🏠					
P111	A3	29								
P115	A3	136			🏠					
P122	A3	300								
P123	A3	296		✓	🏠					
P126	A4	221								
P128	A3	45			🏠					
P129	A3	297			🏠					
P146	A4	343								
P189	A3	30								
P191	A3	306								
P233	A3	237			🏠					
P235	A2	22								
P236	A3	305								
P288	A2	47								
P289	A2	31								
P290	A2	53								
P294	A2	190								
P295	A2	214								
P296	A3	132								
S119	A4	313								
S124	A4	342								
S126	A3	173								
S128	C1	307								
S129	A4	217								
S130	A3	304								
S131	A3	191								
S132	C3	90								
T038	C1	302								
T042	C2	318								
T043	C2	289		✓	🏠					
T054	C1	323								
T072	C2	152								
T091	C1	209								
T110	C1	211								
T154	C3	120								
T156	C3	110								
T157	C3	108								
T159	C3	109								
T165	C4	112								
T183	C2	157								
T187	C1	174								
T194	C2	156								
T207	C1	320								
T208	C2	255								
T209	C2	311								
T211	A4	310								
T212	C2	257								
T213	C2	208								
T214	C2	258								
T215	C1	210								
T233	C2	244								
T234	C2	314								
T235	C4	189								
T236	C3	287								
T237	C3	256								
T238	C3	86								
T239	C3	113								
T240	C3	87								
U112	C1	12								
U129	A3	344								
U135	A4	286								
U151	A4	334								
U152	A4	316								
U154	A4	148								
U162	A4	367								
U178	A4	187								
U179	A3	149								
U183	A2	50								
U207	C1	74								
U208	C1	78								
U214	A3	321								
U217	A3	312								
U224	A4	335								
U232	A3	266								
U248	A4	283								
U257	A3	366								
U258	A3	267								
U266	C2	18								
V001	A3	284		✓						
V002	A3	317		✓						
V003	A3	281		✓						
V004	C1	89		✓						
V005	C1	275		✓						
V006	A3	167		✓						
V007	A3	118		✓						
V008	A2	285		✓						
W008	A4	135								
W012	A4	117								

Before You Order . . .

Before filling out the coupon at right or calling us on our Toll-Free Blueprint Hotline, you may want to learn more about our services and products. Here's some information you will find helpful.

Quick Turnaround
We process and ship every blueprint order from our office within two business days. Because of this quick turnaround, we won't send a formal notice acknowledging receipt of your order.

Our Exchange Policy
Since blueprints are printed in response to your order, we cannot honor requests for refunds. However, we will exchange your entire first order for an equal number of blueprints at a price of $50 for the first set and $10 for each additional set; $70 total exchange fee for 4 sets; $100 total exchange fee for 8 sets . . . *plus* the difference in cost if exchanging for a design in a higher price bracket or *less* the difference in cost if exchanging for a design in lower price bracket. One exchange is allowed within a year of purchase date. **(Sepias and reproducibles are not refundable, returnable or exchangeable.)** All sets from the first order must be returned before the exchange can take place. Please add $18 for postage and handling via Regular Service; $30 via Priority Service; $40 via Express Service. Returns and cancellations are subject to a 20% restocking fee, and shipping and handling charges are not refundable.

About Reverse Blueprints
If you want to build in reverse of the plan as shown, we will include an extra set of reverse blueprints (mirror image) for an additional fee of $50. Although lettering and dimensions will appear backward, reverses will be a useful aid if you decide to flop the plan.

Revising, Modifying and Customizing Plans
The wide variety of designs available in this publication allows you to select ideas and concepts for a home to fit your building site and match your family's needs, wants and budget. Like many homeowners who buy these plans, you and your builder, architect or engineer may want to make changes to them. Some minor changes may be made by your builder, but we recommend that most changes be made by a licensed architect or engineer. If you need to make alterations to a design that is customizable, you need only order our Home Customizer® Package to get you started. As set forth below, we cannot assume any responsibility for blueprints which have been changed, whether by you, your builder or by professionals selected by you or referred to you by us, because such individuals are outside our supervision and control.

Architectural and Engineering Seals
Some cities and states are now requiring that a licensed architect or engineer review and "seal" a blueprint, or officially approve it, prior to construction due to concerns over energy costs, safety and other factors. Prior to application for a building permit or the start of actual construction, we strongly advise that you consult your local building official who can tell you if such a review is required.

About the Designers
The architects and designers whose work appears in this publication are among America's leading residential designers. Each plan was designed to meet the requirements of a nationally recognized model building code in effect at the time and place the plan was drawn. Because national building codes change from time to time, plans may not comply with any such code at the time they are sold to a customer. In addition, building officials may not accept these plans as final construction documents of record as the plans may need to be modified and additional drawings and details added to suit local conditions and requirements. We strongly advise that purchasers consult a licensed architect or engineer, and their local building official, before starting any construction related to these plans.

Local Building Codes and Zoning Requirements
At the time of creation, our plans are drawn to specifications published by the Building Officials and Code Administrators (BOCA) International, Inc.; the Southern Building Code Congress (SBCCI) International, Inc.; the International Conference of Building Officials; or the Council of American Building Officials (CABO). Our plans are designed to meet or exceed national building standards. Because of the great differences in geography and climate throughout the United States and Canada, each state, county and municipality has its own building codes, zone requirements, ordinances and building regulations. Your plan may need to be modified to comply with local requirements regarding snow loads, energy codes, soil and seismic conditions and a wide range of other matters. In addition, you may need to obtain permits or inspections from local governments before and in the course of construction. Prior to using blueprints ordered from us, we strongly advise that you consult a licensed architect or engineer—and speak with your local building official—before applying for any permit or beginning construction. We authorize the use of our blueprints on the express condition that you strictly comply with all local building codes, zoning requirements and other applicable laws, regulations, ordinances and requirements. **Notice:** Plans for homes to be built in Nevada must be redrawn by a Nevada-registered professional. Consult your building official for more information on this subject.

Foundation and Exterior Wall Changes
Most of our plans are drawn with either a full or partial basement foundation. Depending on your specific climate or regional building practices, you may wish to change this basement to a slab or crawlspace. Most professional contractors and builders can easily adapt your plans to alternate foundation types. Likewise, most can easily change 2x4 wall construction to 2x6, or vice versa.

Disclaimer
We and the designers we work with have put substantial care and effort into the creation of our blueprints. However, because we cannot provide on-site consultation, supervision and control over actual construction, and because of the great variance in local building requirements, building practices and soil, seismic, weather and other conditions, WE CANNOT MAKE ANY WARRANTY, EXPRESS OR IMPLIED, WITH RESPECT TO THE CONTENT OR USE OF OUR BLUEPRINTS, INCLUDING BUT NOT LIMITED TO ANY WARRANTY OF MERCHANTABILITY OR OF FITNESS FOR A PARTICULAR PURPOSE.

Terms and Conditions
These designs are protected under the terms of United States Copyright Law and may not be copied or reproduced in any way, by any means, unless you have purchased Sepias or Reproducibles which clearly indicate your right to copy or reproduce. We authorize the use of your chosen design as an aid in the construction of one single family home only. You may not use this design to build a second or multiple dwellings without purchasing another blueprint or blueprints or paying additional design fees.

How Many Blueprints Do You Need?
A single set of blueprints is sufficient to study a home in greater detail. However, if you are planning to obtain cost estimates from a contractor or subcontractor—or if you are planning to build immediately—you will need more sets. Because additional sets are cheaper when ordered in quantity with the original order, make sure you order enough blueprints to satisfy all requirements. The following checklist will help you determine how many you need:

___ Owner

___ Builder (generally requires at least three sets; one as a legal document, one to use during inspections, and at least one to give to subcontractors)

___ Local Building Department (often requires two sets)

___ Mortgage Lender (usually one set for a conventional loan; three sets for FHA or VA loans)

___ TOTAL NUMBER OF SETS

Have You Seen Our Newest Designs?

Home Planners is one of the country's most active home design firms, creating nearly 100 new plans each year. At least 50 of our latest creations are featured in each edition of our New Design Portfolio. You may have received a copy with your latest purchase by mail. If not, or if you purchased this book from a local retailer, just return the coupon below for your FREE copy. Make sure you consider the very latest of what Home Planners has to offer.

Yes! Please send my FREE copy of your latest New Design Portfolio.

Offer good to U.S. shipping address only.

Name _____

Address _____

City_____ State_____ Zip _____

HOME PLANNERS, LLC
Wholly owned by Hanley-Wood, LLC
3275 WEST INA ROAD, SUITE 110
TUCSON, ARIZONA 85741

Order Form Key

MOS

Toll Free 1-800-521-6797

Regular Office Hours:
8:00 a.m. to 8:00 p.m. Eastern Time, Monday through Friday
Our staff will gladly answer any questions during regular office hours. Our answering service can place orders after hours or on weekends.

If we receive your order by 4:00 p.m. Eastern Time, Monday through Friday, we'll process it and ship within two business days. When ordering by phone, please have your credit card ready. We'll also ask you for the Order Form Key Number at the bottom of the coupon.

By FAX: Copy the Order Form on the next page and send it on our FAX line: 1-800-224-6699 or 1-520-544-3086.

Canadian Customers
Order Toll-Free 1-877-223-6389

For faster service and plans that are modified for building in Canada, customers may now call in orders directly to our Canadian supplier of plans and charge the purchase to a credit card. Or, you may complete the order form at right, adding the current exchange rate to all prices, and mail in Canadian funds to:

Home Planners 301-611 Alexander Street
Canada Vancouver, B.C., Canada
c/o Select Home Designs V6A 1E1

OR: Copy the Order Form and send it via our Canadian FAX line: 1-800-224-6699

The Home Customizer®

"This house is perfect...if only the family room were two feet wider." Sound familiar? In response to the numerous requests for this type of modification, Home Planners has developed **The Home Customizer® Package**. This exclusive package offers our top-of-the-line materials to make it easy for anyone, anywhere to customize any Home Planners design to fit their needs. Check the index on pages 520-523 for those plans which are customizable.

Some of the changes you can make to any of our plans include:

- exterior elevation changes
- kitchen and bath modifications
- roof, wall and foundation changes
- room additions and more!

The Home Customizer® Package includes everything you'll need to make the necessary changes to your favorite Home Planners design. The package includes:

- instruction book with examples
- architectural scale and clear work film
- erasable red marker and removable correction tape
- ¼"-scale furniture cutouts
- 1 set reproducible, erasable Sepias
- 1 set study blueprints for communicating changes to your design professional
- a copyright release letter so you can make copies as you need them
- referral letter with the name, address and telephone number of the professional in your region who is trained in modifying Home Planners designs efficiently and inexpensively.

The price of the **Home Customizer® Package** ranges from $650 to $1350, depending on the price schedule of the design you have chosen. **The Home Customizer® Package** will not only save you 25% to 75% of the cost of drawing the plans from scratch with a custom architect or engineer, it will also give you the flexibility to have your changes and modifications made by our referral network or by the professional of your choice. Now it's even easier and more affordable to have the custom home you've always wanted.

📞 **ORDER TOLL FREE!**
For information about any of our services or to order call 1-800-521-6797 or 520-297-8200 Browse our website: www.homeplanners.com

---

BLUEPRINTS ARE NOT REFUNDABLE EXCHANGES ONLY

For Customer Service, call toll free 1-888-690-1116.

HOME PLANNERS, LLC
Wholly owned by Hanley-Wood, LLC
3275 WEST INA ROAD, SUITE 110
TUCSON, ARIZONA 85741

THE BASIC BLUEPRINT PACKAGE
Rush me the following (please refer to the Plans Index and Price Schedule in this section):

_____	Set(s) of blueprints for plan number(s) _____.	$_____
_____	Set(s) of sepias for plan number(s) _____.	$_____
_____	Home Customizer® Package for plan(s)_____.	$_____
_____	Additional identical blueprints in same order @ $50 per set.	$_____
_____	Reverse blueprints @ $50 per set.	$_____

IMPORTANT EXTRAS
Rush me the following:

_____	Materials List: $60 (Must be purchased with Blueprint set.) Add $10 for a Schedule C4–L4 plan.	$_____
_____	**Quote One®** Summary Cost Report @ $29.95 for 1, $14.95 for each additional, for plans _____ Building location: City _____ Zip Code _____	$_____
_____	**Quote One®** Materials Cost Report @ $120 Schedule P1–C3; $130 Schedules C4–L4 for plan_____ (Must be purchased with Blueprints set.) Building location: City _____ Zip Code_____	$_____
_____	Specification Outlines @ $10 each.	$_____
_____	Detail Sets @ $14.95 each; any two for $22.95; any three for $29.95; all four for $39.95 (save $19.85). ❏ Plumbing ❏ Electrical ❏ Construction ❏ Mechanical (These helpful details provide general construction advice and are not specific to any single plan.)	$_____
_____	Plan-A-Home® @ $29.95 each.	$_____

DECK BLUEPRINTS

_____	Set(s) of Deck Plan _____	$_____
_____	Additional identical blueprints in same order @ $10 per set.	$_____
_____	Reverse blueprints @ $10 per set.	$_____
_____	Set of Standard Deck Details @ $14.95 per set.	$_____
_____	Set of Complete Building Package (Best Buy!) Includes Custom Deck Plan _____. (See Index and Price Schedule) Plus Standard Deck Details	$_____

LANDSCAPE BLUEPRINTS

_____	Set(s) of Landscape Plan _____.	$_____
_____	Additional identical blueprints in same order @ $10 per set.	$_____
_____	Reverse blueprints @ $10 per set.	$_____

Please indicate the appropriate region of the country for Plant & Material List. (See Map on page 438): Region _____

POSTAGE AND HANDLING	1–3 sets	4+ sets
Signature is required for all deliveries. **DELIVERY** (No CODs) (Requires street address—No P.O. Boxes)		
•Regular Service (Allow 7–10 business days delivery)	❏ $15.00	❏ $18.00
•Priority (Allow 4–5 business days delivery)	❏ $20.00	❏ $30.00
•Express (Allow 3 business days delivery)	❏ $30.00	❏ $40.00
CERTIFIED MAIL If no street address available. (Allow 7–10 days delivery)	❏ $20.00	❏ $30.00
OVERSEAS DELIVERY Note: All delivery times are from date Blueprint Package is shipped.	fax, phone or mail for quote	

POSTAGE (From box above)	$_____
SUBTOTAL	$_____
SALES TAX (AZ, MI, & WA residents, please add appropriate state and local sales tax.)	$_____
TOTAL (Subtotal and tax)	$_____

YOUR ADDRESS (please print)
Name _____

Street _____

City _____ State _____ Zip _____

Daytime telephone number (_____) _____

FOR CREDIT CARD ORDERS ONLY
Please fill in the information below:
Credit card number _____

Exp. Date: Month/Year _____

Check one ❏ Visa ❏ MasterCard ❏ Discover Card ❏ American Express

Signature _____

Please check appropriate box: ❏ Licensed Builder-Contractor
                                          ❏ Homeowner

📞 **ORDER TOLL FREE!**
1-800-521-6797 or 520-297-8200

Order Form Key

MOS

Helpful Books & Software

Home Planners wants your building experience to be as pleasant and trouble-free as possible. That's why we've expanded our library of Do-It-Yourself titles to help you along. In addition to our beautiful plans books, we've added books to guide you through specific projects as well as the construction process. In fact, these are titles that will be as useful after your dream home is built as they are right now.

ONE-STORY

1 448 designs for all lifestyles. 860 to 5,400 square feet. 384 pages $9.95

TWO-STORY

2 460 designs for one-and-a-half and two stories. 1,245 to 7,275 square feet. 384 pages $9.95

VACATION

3 345 designs for recreation, retirement and leisure. 312 pages $8.95

MULTI-LEVEL

4 214 designs for split-levels, bi-levels, multi-levels and walkouts. 224 pages $8.95

COUNTRY

5 200 country designs from classic to contemporary by 7 winning designers. 224 pages $8.95

MOVE-UP

6 200 stylish designs for today's growing families from 9 hot designers. 224 pages $8.95

NARROW-LOT

7 200 unique homes less than 60' wide from 7 designers. Up to 3,000 square feet. 224 pages $8.95

SMALL HOUSE

8 200 beautiful designs chosen for versatility and affordability. 224 pages $8.95

BUDGET-SMART

9 200 efficient plans from 7 top designers, that you can really afford to build! 224 pages $8.95

EXPANDABLES

10 200 flexible plans that expand with your needs from 7 top designers. 240 pages $8.95

ENCYCLOPEDIA

11 500 exceptional plans for all styles and budgets—the best book of its kind! 352 pages $9.95

AFFORDABLE

12 Completely revised and updated, featuring 300 designs for modest budgets. 256 pages $9.95

ENCYCLOPEDIA 2

13 500 completely new plans. Spacious and stylish designs for every budget and taste. 352 pages $9.95

VICTORIAN

14 160 striking Victorian and Farmhouse designs from three leading designers. 192 pages $12.95

ESTATE

15 Dream big! Twenty-one designers showcase their biggest and best plans. 208 pages. $15.95

LUXURY

16 154 fine luxury plans—loaded with luscious amenities! 192 pages $14.95

COTTAGES

17 25 fresh new designs that are as warm as a tropical breeze. A blend of the best aspects of many coastal styles. 64 pages. $19.95

BEST SELLERS

18 Our 50th Anniversary book with 200 of our very best designs in full color! 224 pages $12.95

SPECIAL COLLECTION

19 70 romantic house plans that capture the classic tradition of home design. 160 pages $17.95

COUNTRY HOUSES
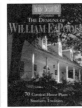
20 208 unique home plans that combine traditional style and modern livability. 224 pages $9.95

CLASSIC

21 Timeless, elegant designs that always feel like home. Gorgeous plans that are as flexible and up-to-date as their occupants. 240 pages. $9.95

CONTEMPORARY

22 The most complete and imaginative collection of contemporary designs available anywhere. 240 pages. $9.95

EASY-LIVING

23 200 efficient and sophisticated plans that are small in size, but big on livability. 224 pages $8.95

SOUTHERN

24 207 homes rich in Southern styling and comfort. 240 pages $8.95

SUNBELT

25 215 designs that capture the spirit of the Southwest. 208 pages $10.95

WESTERN

26 215 designs that capture the spirit and diversity of the Western lifestyle. 208 pages $9.95

ENERGY GUIDE

27 The most comprehensive energy efficiency and conservation guide available. 280 pages $35.00

Design Software

BOOK & CD ROM

28 Both the Home Planners Gold book and matching Windows™ CD ROM with 3D floorplans. $24.95

3D DESIGN SUITE

29 Home design made easy! View designs in 3D, take a virtual reality tour, add decorating details and more. $59.95

Outdoor Projects

OUTDOOR

30 42 unique outdoor projects. Gazebos, strombellas, bridges, sheds, playsets and more! 96 pages $7.95

GARAGES & MORE
31 101 multi-use garages and outdoor structures to enhance any home. 96 pages $7.95

DECKS
32 25 outstanding single-, double- and multi-level decks you can build. 112 pages $7.95